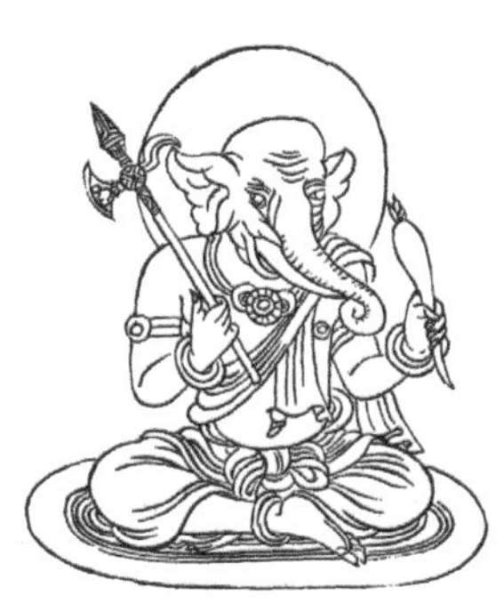

Hidden in Plain Sight

Dharma to Daruma, Homa to Goma, and More

Ganapathi Pamula

Foreword by Prof. Kishor Trivedi

For permissions requests, please contact:
ganapathi.pamula@gmail.com

First edition. Paperback edition.
Published by Kangiten Press, Cary, NC, USA
Print preparation by Parrot Communications, Hyderabad, India.

ISBN: 979-8-9948153-0-4
Library of Congress Control Number (LCCN): 2026904950

Dedicated to *San Dai Benzaiten* (the Three Great Benzaiten) in my life, my mother, my sister, and my grandmother

---

I'm grateful to my teachers who helped shape the way I think about history and culture. I'm especially grateful to Dr. Rob Policelli, my 11th-grade history teacher, who encouraged me to look into the role of this subject matter in Japanese nation-building. Thank you to Dr. Brian Fennessy, my 10th-grade history teacher, for the lively discussions and to Ms. Brown, my 7th-grade history teacher, for bringing East Asian history alive so vividly.

Thank you to Prof. Kishor Trivedi for encouraging me to write about this journey, sharing his experiences of living in Japan, and for contributing the foreword. I'm also grateful to Sruthi Valluru and Nithya Indlamuri for sharing thoughtful feedback on the draft manuscript.

I want to thank the priests, monks, pilgrims, and temple staff who welcomed questions, and the Japanese people who were gracious and patient as I tried to communicate in imperfect Japanese.

I'm especially grateful to my maternal uncle, Krishna Komaragiri, who has traveled thousands of kilometers with us across India and spent a cumulative year on the road over 17 years, visiting hundreds of temples and teaching me what devotion looks like in lived, everyday practice; my first exposure to a Buddhist *vihāra* was in his hometown (photo in Appendix), where he took me to see a 2,500-year-old monastery that stayed in my mind as I later walked through Japan's temple complexes. I also want to thank my paternal and maternal uncles, aunts, and cousins, who have enriched my understanding of Hindu practices in ways that helped me recognize parallels when I encountered Japanese ritual life.

This book would not have been possible without my father's encouragement. He handled the logistics so I could stay focused on the research and photography, and he shared the depth of Hindu philosophical knowledge, which helped me recognize connections in Japan. He was always open to my ideas, critiquing them sometimes and building on them at other times, and he was always willing to visit one more temple or take one more turn down an unknown alley.

All photos, research, and writing decisions in this book are my own. Any misinterpretations are unintentional, and I welcome corrections.

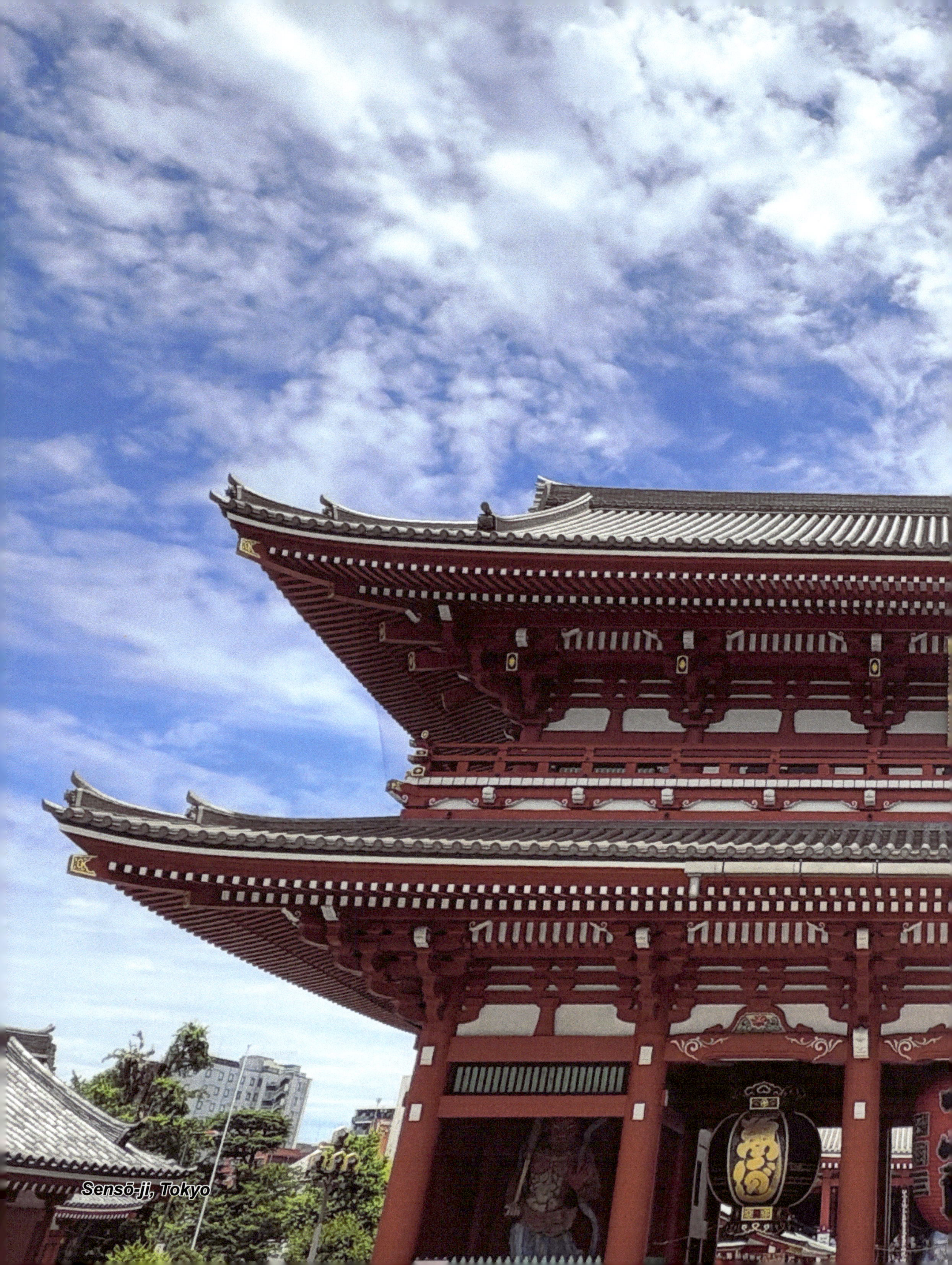

Sensō-ji, Tokyo

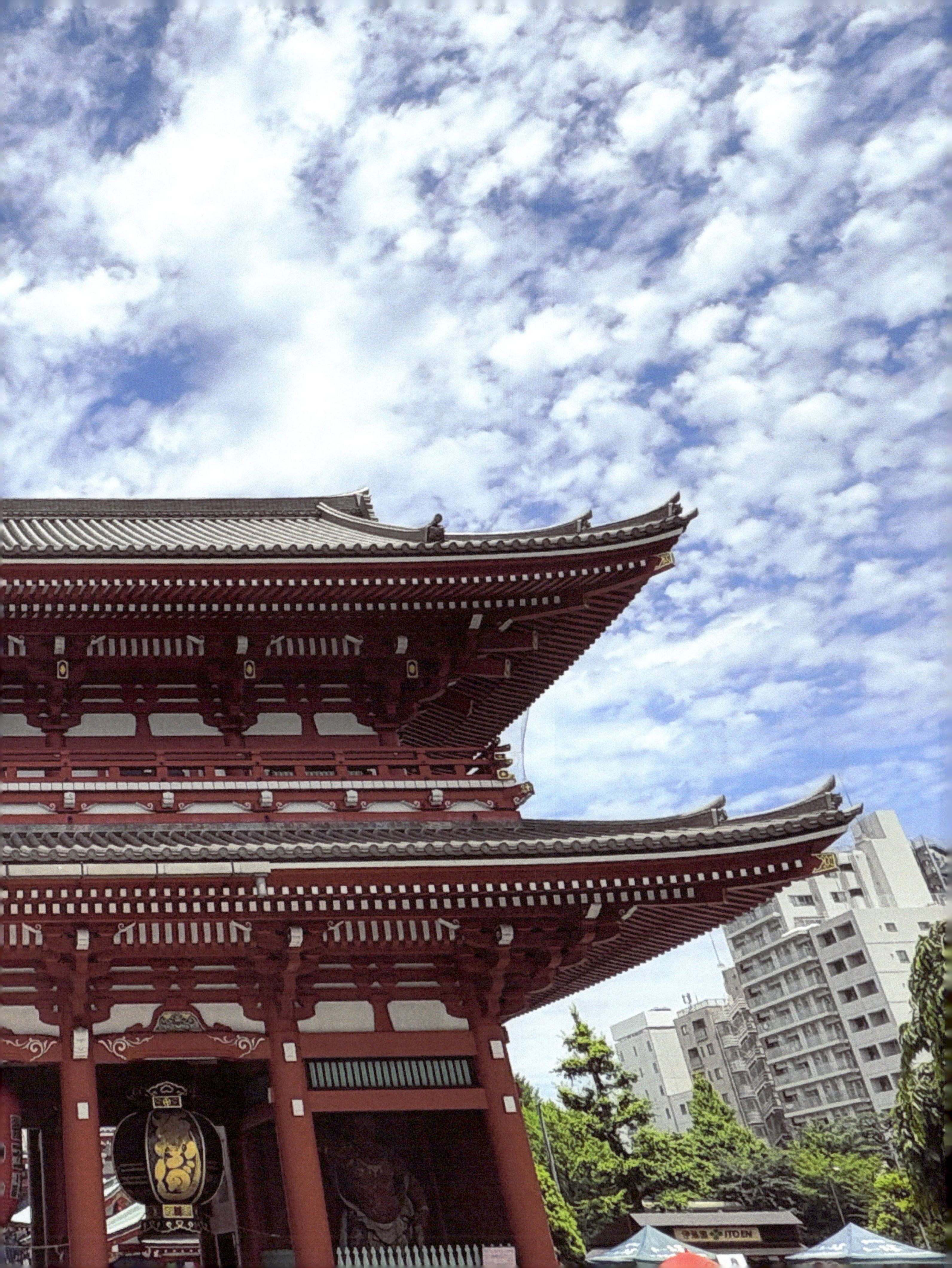
ITOEN

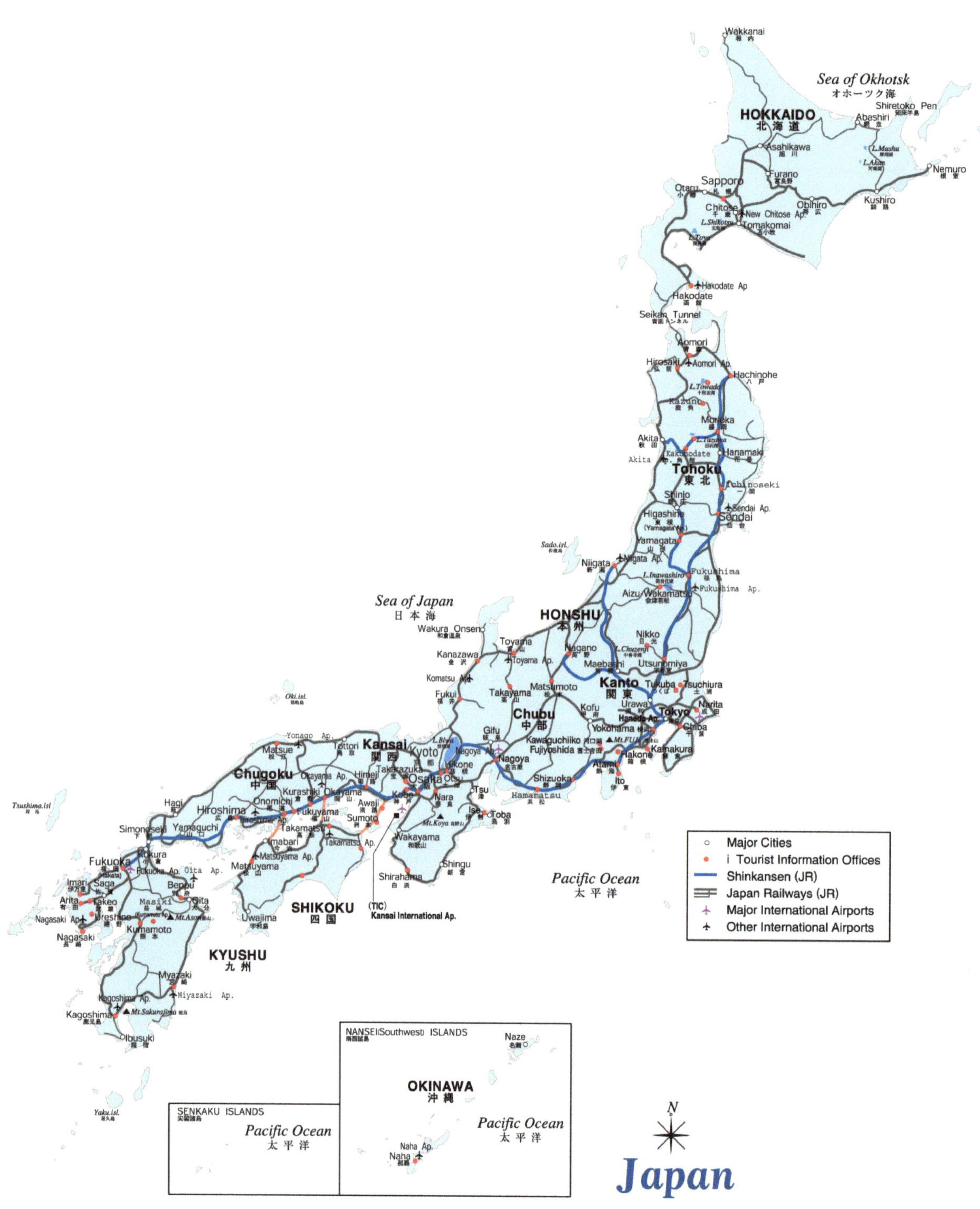
Japan
Sea of Okhotsk
オホーツク海
HOKKAIDO
北海道
Wakkanai
Shiretoko Pen
Abashiri
Asahikawa
Furano
Sapporo
Otaru
Chitose
New Chitose Ap.
Tomakomai
Obihiro
Kushiro
Nemuro
Hakodate Ap
Hakodate
Seikan Tunnel
Aomori
Hirosaki
Aomori Ap.
Hachinohe
Morioka
Akita
Kakunodate
Hanamaki
Tohoku
東北
Ichinoseki
Shinjo
Sendai Ap.
Sendai
Yamagata
Sado.isl.
Niigata
Niigata Ap.
Fukushima
Aizu Wakamatsu
Sea of Japan
日本海
HONSHU
本州
Wakura Onsen
Toyama
Toyama Ap.
Kanazawa
Komatsu
Nagano
Maebashi
Nikko
Utsunomiya
Takayama
Matsumoto
Kanto
関東
Tsukuba
Tsuchiura
Fukui
Oki.isl.
Chubu
中部
Kofu
Urawa
Tokyo
Narita
Chiba
Yokohama
Kamakura
Kawaguchiko
Fujiyoshida
Mt.FUJI
Hakone
Atami
Ito
Shizuoka
Hamamatsu
Gifu
Nagoya
Hikone
Yonago Ap.
Tottori
Kansai
関西
Kyoto
Matsue
Chugoku
中国
Okayama Ap.
Himeji
Takarazuka
Osaka
Otsu
Kurashiki
Okayama
Kobe
Nara
Tsu
Ise
Toba
Mt.Koya
Hagi
Hiroshima
Onomichi
Fukuyama
Awaji
Sumoto
Takamatsu
Takamatsu Ap.
Imabari
Matsuyama Ap.
Matsuyama
Wakayama
Shingu
Shirahama
Pacific Ocean
太平洋
Tsushima.isl.
Simonoseki
Yamaguchi
Kokura
Fukuoka
Fukuoka Ap.
Oita Ap.
Beppu
Oita
Imari
Saga
Arita
Takeo
Ureshino
Nagasaki Ap.
Nagasaki
Mt.Aso
Kumamoto
Uwajima
SHIKOKU
四国
(TIC)
Kansai International Ap.
KYUSHU
九州
Miyazaki
Miyazaki Ap.
Kagoshima Ap.
Kagoshima
Mt.Sakurajima
Ibusuki
Yaku.isl.
SENKAKU ISLANDS
Pacific Ocean
太平洋
NANSEI(Southwest) ISLANDS
Naze
OKINAWA
沖縄
Naha Ap.
Naha
Pacific Ocean
太平洋
N
Major Cities
i Tourist Information Offices
Shinkansen (JR)
Japan Railways (JR)
Major International Airports
Other International Airports

Contents

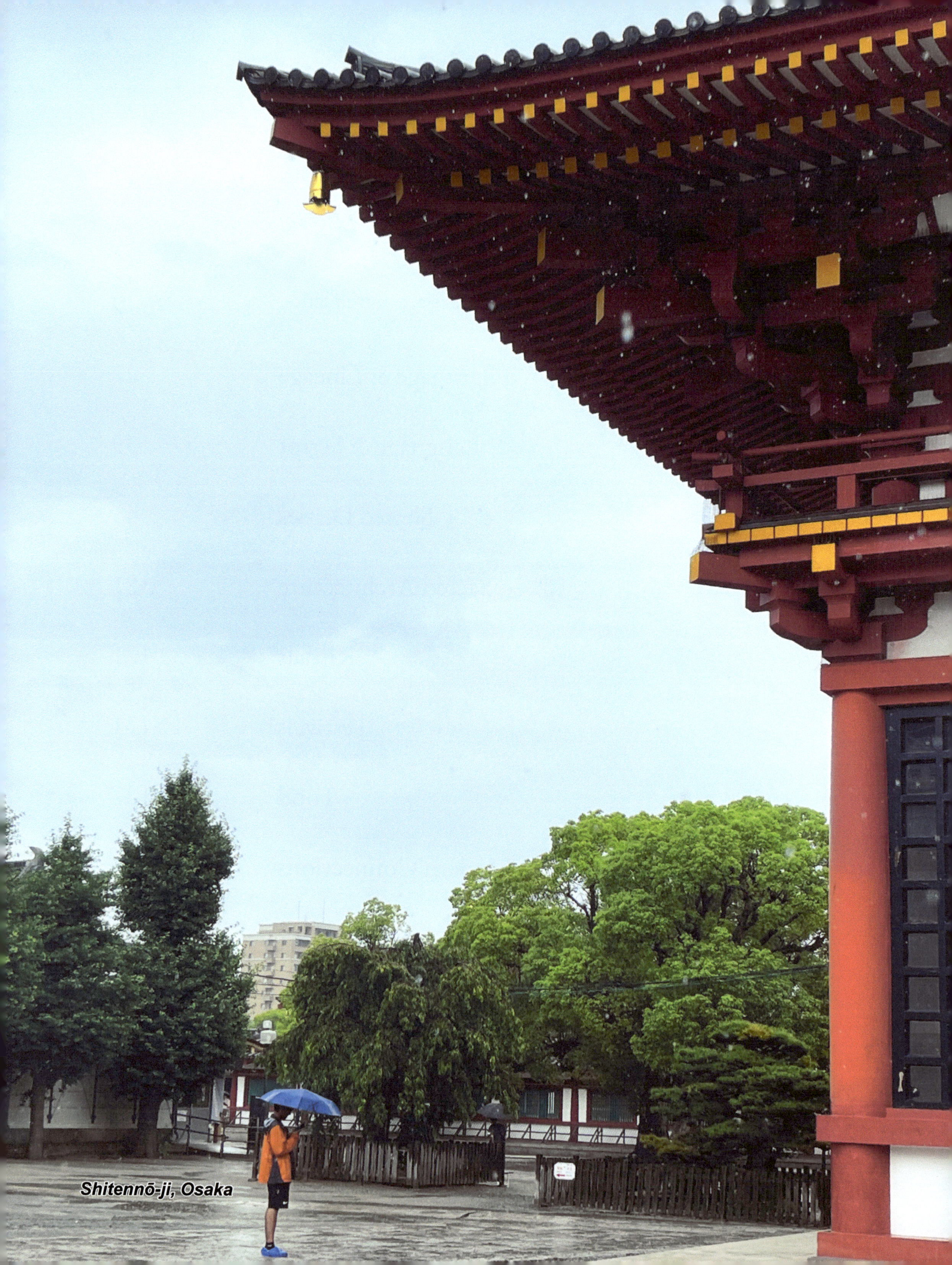

Shitennō-ji, Osaka

Foreword

Siddhartha Gautama was born a Hindu Prince in Kapilvastu, became a Buddha in Gaya and gave his first sermon in Sarnath, on the outskirts of Varanasi in India – these are all well known facts. Thus, the connection of Buddhism to India and Hinduism is evident. It is also well known that Buddhism spread from India to Japan variously via Korea and by direct travels of pioneers such as Bodhisena and Kukai. But the pervasiveness of Hindu influence on Japanese art, architecture both Temple and secular, rituals, festivals, food, language, religious iconography and deities is not as widely known. This book is thus a unique contribution that sheds light on this topic. By bringing these connections into clear view, the author helps readers notice what is often present but easily overlooked. As a practicing Hindu who has lived in Japan, I found some new insights in this book that were truly "hidden in plain sight."

The book is unique from several angles: first the topic itself and then the passion and depth with which the author has taken up the subject. What is truly remarkable is that while being a teenager, the author has so much maturity in observation, analysis and presentation. The love and passion for both the cultures, Japanese-Buddhist and Hindu permeates throughout the pages of the book. Each idea or artifact in Japan is examined carefully, followed by a deep analysis resulting in a Hindu equivalent. This deconstruction or reverse engineering is a master class in itself! What stands out to me, as an engineering Professor, is the author's method: keen observation, meticulous documentation, and a clear chain of reasoning from evidence to interpretation.

Ganapathi's interests have never been confined to one domain. He is building the future through his engineering innovations, with proven credentials such as published papers, patents, and technical talks, and yet he is equally grounded in the past through serious engagement with history, language, and living religious traditions. This ability to bridge domains that are often kept separate is rare, and I hope his example inspires other young innovators who create new technologies to remain firmly rooted in cultural understanding.

I hope that many more young and not-so-young people will follow up this line of research as presented in the book. I also hope that this book will lead to greater cooperation between two great civilizations! It is lovely to see that Ganapathi (Kangiten) found his favorite Deities: Benzaiten and Kichijoten in Japan. I have no doubt he will continue to connect ideas, cultures, and disciplines in ways that benefit both scholarship and society. I wish the remarkable young man, Ganapathi Pamula, the best that life can offer.

Kishor Trivedi
F. Hudson Professor of Electrical and Computer Engineering
Duke University, USA

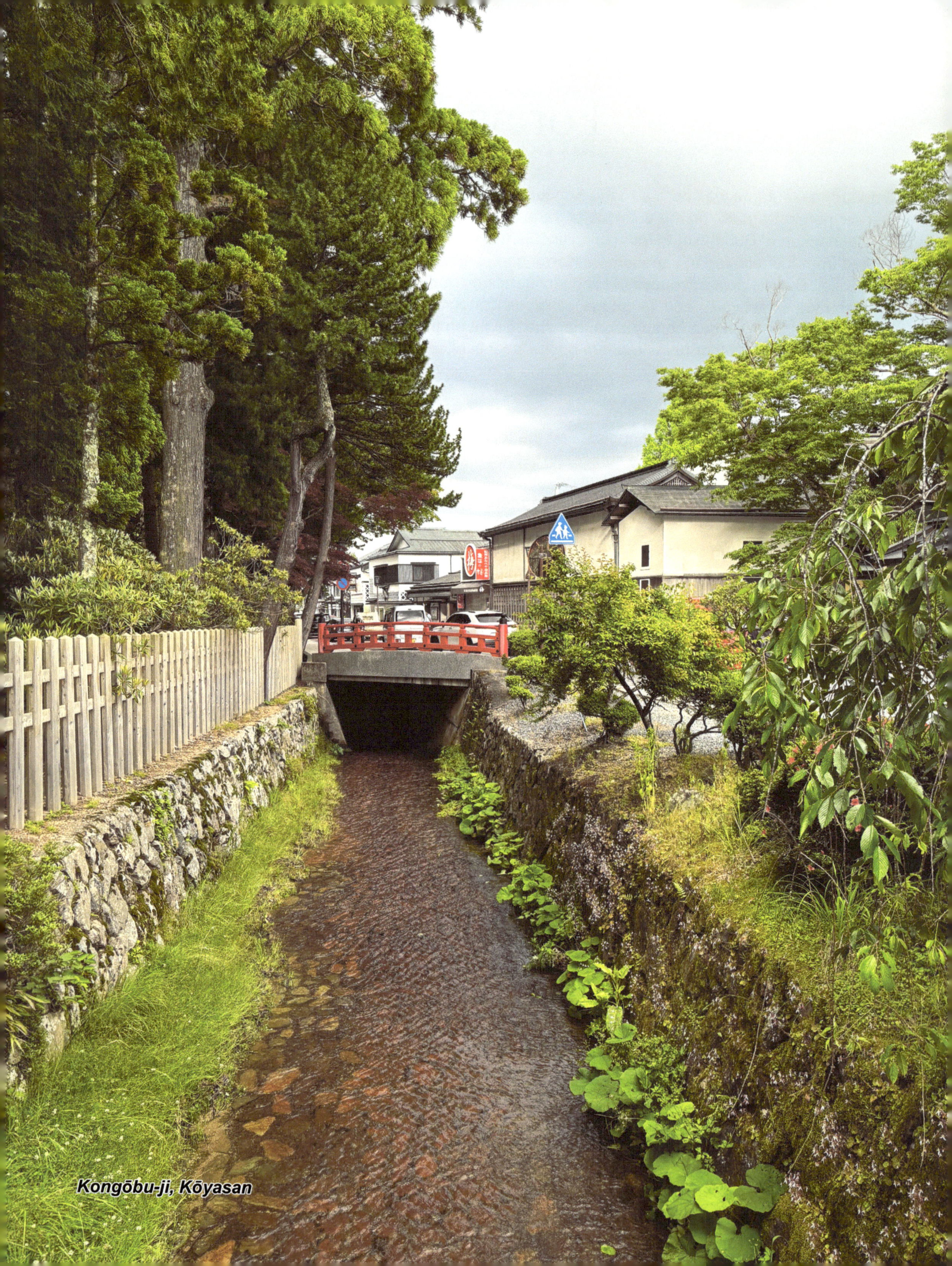

Kongōbu-ji, Kōyasan

Preface

A memory that will forever be etched in my mind is my visit, on my first day in Japan, to Matsuchiyama Shōden in Tokyo, one of the oldest Ganesha temples in the world. I was awestruck even before I entered. It sits in the middle of downtown Tokyo, in the shadow of glass towers competing to reach the sky. I walked through a stone *torii* gate to see a temple with a bell hanging at the entrance. An automated, traditional sliding Japanese door opened into a tatami room. At the center was an ornate, flower-covered altar. There was a Ganesha inside, but he was considered too powerful for ordinary people to see, so it was hidden and only the priests could see him. Nevertheless, all sorts of people, from elderly devotees quietly reciting sutras to businessmen ducking in for a quick prayer, were spread throughout the hall.

I began to talk with the priests and told one of them that my name was Ganapathi. His eyes widened in shock and he said, *"Ee, Kangiten-sama!"* (Oh, honorable Lord Ganesha!). He excitedly called over another priest, who heard the story, audibly gasped, and started bowing down to me. They asked me why I had this name, and I said my mom was a devotee of Ganesha. They told me I was a very lucky man, and that I must have done something great in my previous life to have such a noble mother who gave me such a sacred name.

That incident framed the rest of my travels through Japan. Priests at a prominent temple in one of the most developed cities on the planet did not treat my name like an unpronounceable foreign word the way it often gets treated in the U.S. They recognized its meaning and its significance. Throughout the trip, I saw more and more of these connections, which I will explain in detail in the rest of the book.

Ever since I was a toddler, I've been interested in Japanese culture. As a child, my dream job was engineering cars like Toyotas. My favorite movie was *Cars*, and my favorite scene was the race in Tokyo. I was mesmerized by my favorite characters speeding through the neon lights.

As I got into elementary school, I got a Nintendo console and loved playing games with my sister and grandma. My parents would also tell me about their honeymoon in Kyoto and how they saw beautiful temples and shrines. It was my mom's first time out of India, and she'd tell us how everything surprised her, from the cold to the cleanliness, the safety, and everyday technology.

Then, early in middle school, I wrote and published a storybook about an odyssey through Japan. To research for it, I traced the entirety of my protagonist's journey by virtually roaming the streets of Japan, spending countless hours on Google Earth.

For a high school research paper on cultural diffusion, I took the opportunity to explore the spread of Hindu deities into Japanese Buddhism, because I vaguely knew there were connections. Then, in 2025, when our trip to visit temples and family in India got disrupted by terrorist attacks, I proposed we go to Japan to experience the culture. When we finally went, I had the privilege of seeing some of these places with my own eyes. A week before we left, I shared my experience finding these cultural parallels with Prof. Kishor Trivedi, who suggested I write a magazine article about it. Then I thought: why not write a book?

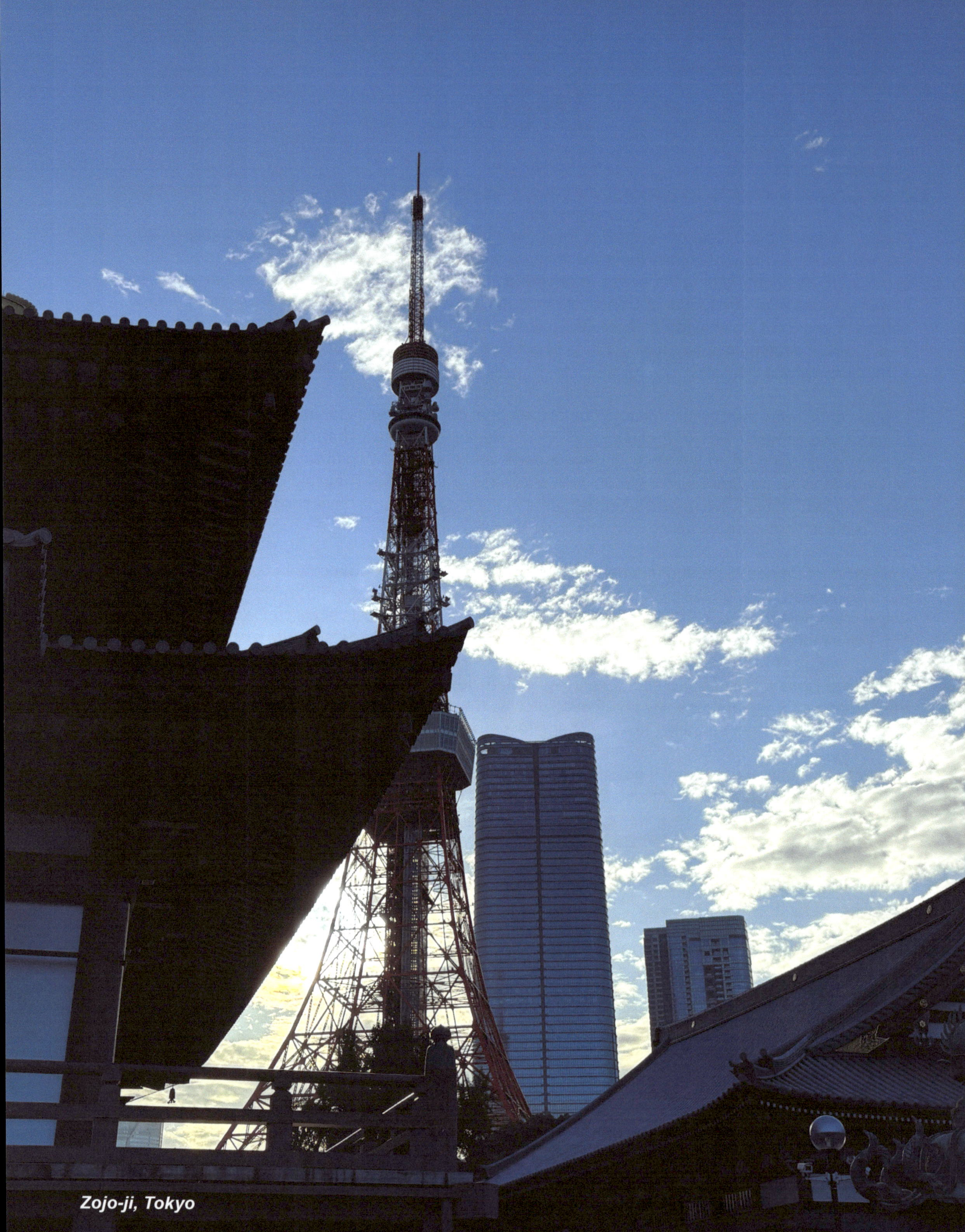

Zojo-ji, Tokyo

I wanted to write something informative, but also packed with visuals so the reader could truly see what they were reading. I felt like this would also show the prevalence and context of these practices in Japanese life, while explaining the stories behind them. I also enjoy learning languages and have studied Sanskrit (for eight years) and Japanese, among others. Over the years, I've also visited hundreds of temples in India, which shaped what I noticed in Japan.

Reading about the culture was one thing, but experiencing it in person and living it was life-changing. Growing up as a devoted Hindu-American, I lived in two different worlds. In the United States, I saw plenty of material wealth and development, along with great attention to history, with artifacts less than 100 years old placed in museums with detailed explanations and analysis. In India, I saw an extremely rich spiritual tradition, but also material poverty. Tragically, children my age and orphaned elders would beg for their livelihood outside ancient temples with storied histories. Some of the finest sculptures made by man, dating back thousands of years, would be left outside to the elements with no explanation, and with gaudy ads plastered over them. I also knew about colonialism and looting by the British that reduced India to this squalor, and I vaguely knew of the material and cultural wealth and reach of ancient India.

I had read about how Japan preserved its traditions, many of which have parallels to my own, while becoming a highly developed society, and in some ways even more advanced than the U.S. In Japan, I saw temples with museums, documentaries, exhibits, and galleries just like in the U.S., but with massive ancient wooden statues of Kichijōten (Lakshmi) and Benzaiten (Saraswati) meticulously preserved for over a thousand years. Passersby would remove their shoes and bow when they saw these statues that were behind glass walls.

It is important to note that Japan is its own distinct civilization, even as it adopted, internalized, and built upon ancient Indian cultural elements as it sought to syncretize and advance its own.

I hope this book can show Hindu and Buddhist readers how their traditions are kept alive, flourishing, and interpreted in a technologically advanced and ordered society. A visit to Japan is often said to be life-changing for anyone because of its blend of tradition and modernity, but it is especially so for Hindu and Buddhist people, because so many of these traditions feel familiar. It can be even more transformative for Hindus and Buddhists living in the West to see those traditions thriving in a country that is orderly, technologically advanced, and economically developed, and that has still chosen to preserve its distinct age-old customs and traditions.

This book is written for a general audience. Widely known historical facts (such as basic dates and temple founders) are presented without citation. More surprising or specific connections between India and Japan are supported by the books and articles listed in the References section. In a few places, I describe visual or symbolic parallels drawn from my own observations. These are intended as invitations to look more closely, not as definitive historical claims.

Ganapathi Pamula

Introduction

The book starts with Pilgrimage because that is where Buddhism entered Japan, and that is also where the connections to India and Hindu ideas begin, even if not always directly. Much like Japanese society, or any society for that matter, it is hard to understand Japanese Buddhism without understanding the language, its evolution, and its connections to Sanskrit. Once that foundation is in place, it becomes easier to recognize how many Japanese Buddhist deities trace back to Hindu forms. From there, the next step is the sacred spaces themselves, where these ideas show up in architecture and design. Rituals follow naturally, because they are what people do inside those spaces. Festivals come next as they take ritual out into public life, not only inside temples and shrines. Food follows because it is closely tied to festivals and devotional practice. After that, the book steps outward from religious settings into everyday and secular spaces, but with the same cultural underpinnings still visible. Finally, I close with Reflection, where I offer my own interpretation based on lived experience. Now let's start with Pilgrimage. *Ja, hajimeyō*!

Pilgrimage

Before Buddhism was officially introduced to Japan, it had already arrived through wandering practice. One of the best examples is the story of Seigantō-ji. Temple tradition said that an Indian ascetic named Ragyō Shōnin, washed upon the Kumano coast in 313 CE, followed the river inland to a place for meditation, and found a waterfall pouring out of the forest. After long austerities, Kannon was believed to have appeared, and he built a small hermitage to enshrine that presence. The formal introduction of Buddhism is traditionally dated to 538 CE, when the kingdom of Baekje presented the Japanese court with Buddhist images and scriptures. Prince Shōtoku is often considered the "father of Japanese Buddhism" for backing the new religion at court, overcoming resistance from skeptical courtiers, and placing the prestige and resources of the imperial system behind its spread. Under his patronage, temples were built across the Keihanshin region, and he made it his mission to spread the religion through monks to all corners of the archipelago. In his Seventeen-Article Constitution

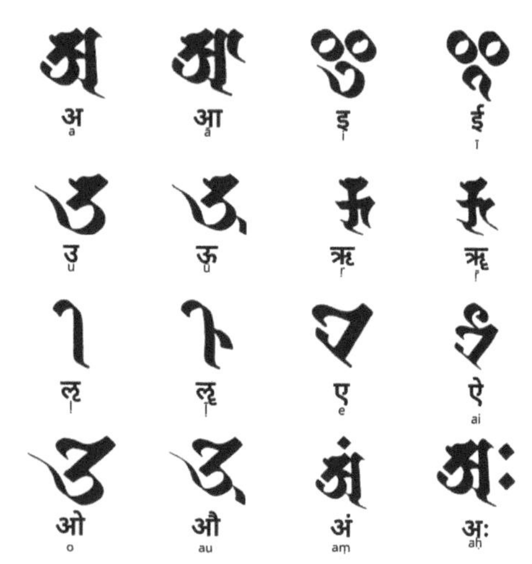

Siddham/Bonji, Sanskrit Devanagari and IAST

Spelling & Pronunciation Key
Sanskrit (Skt. saṃskṛtam, anglicized as Sanskrit) words are romanized using IAST (International Alphabet of Sanskrit Transliteration), which uses dots and lines to preserve the original sounds precisely; Japanese words are given in romaji (modified Hepburn), the standard way to write Japanese in the Latin alphabet. Abbreviations: **Skt.** = Sanskrit (IAST); **Jp.** = Japanese (romaji).

Diacritics in this book (quick guide)
Macrons mark long vowels: ā ī ū ē ō; vocalic vowels: ṛ ṝ ḷ ḹ; nasal ending: ṃ; breathy ending: ḥ; a dot below marks retroflex consonants: ṭ ḍ ṇ ṣ ḷ; Sanskrit "sh" sounds appear as ś and ṣ; nasal consonants include ṅ ("ng" as in *sing*) and ñ ("ny" as in *canyon*).

written in 604 CE, often described as the world's first constitution, he wove Buddhist ideals into governance by urging harmony, humility, and reverence for the Three Treasures (Buddha, Dharma, Sangha) as the moral foundation for officials.

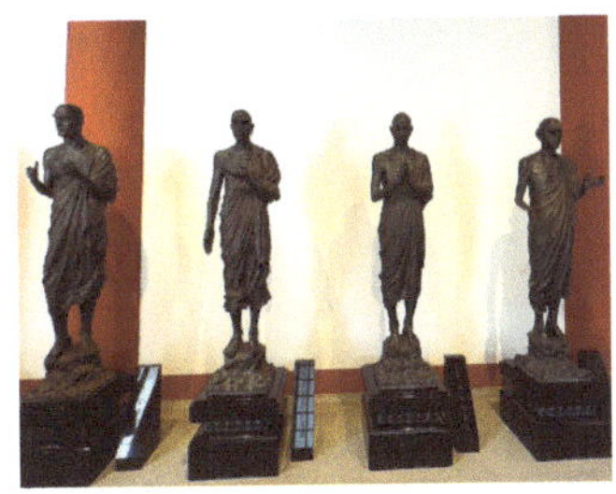

Shitei (Buddha's four disciples: Skt. Śāriputra, Maudgalyāyana, Mahākāśyapa, Subhūti), Yakushi-ji

If Shōtoku introduced Buddhism, Kōbō Daishi (literally, "the great master who propagated the Dharma"), more popularly known as Kūkai, introduced and popularized many esoteric practices. With direct travel to India effectively out of reach due to Islamic caliphates, he went to Tang China (9th century CE) to study esoteric Buddhism and Sanskrit with Chinese, Indian, and Tibetan monks. After returning to Japan, he helped establish Shingon as a distinct esoteric tradition, centered at Tō-ji in Kyoto. Later, to escape the bustle of the capital and focus on his penance, he created the monastic sanctuary of Kōyasan with imperial support, which became one of Japan's most enduring pilgrimage sites. But his reputation spread far beyond ritual. He was celebrated as a master of language and writing, and later tradition even credited him with shaping a Sanskrit-influenced syllabary optimized for Japanese. He became Kōbō Daishi in the public imagination: a teacher, a miracle-worker, and a protector. In modern Japan, he is remembered so widely that proverbs like *Kūkai ni mo fude no ayamari* ("Even Kūkai slips with his brush") are used to mean that even experts make mistakes. He is honored with the mantra *Namu Daishi Henjō Kongō* ("salutations to the great master vajra shining in all directions"). He is also closely associated with the 1,200-km, 88-temple Shikoku pilgrimage on his home island, where tradition holds that he achieved enlightenment at Mikurodo Cave. Today, it is Japan's most famous pilgrimage route, with more than 300,000 people completing it annually. This mirrors similar practices in the Hindu-Buddhist world, such as *tīrtha yātrā* in India or *kora* in Tibet.

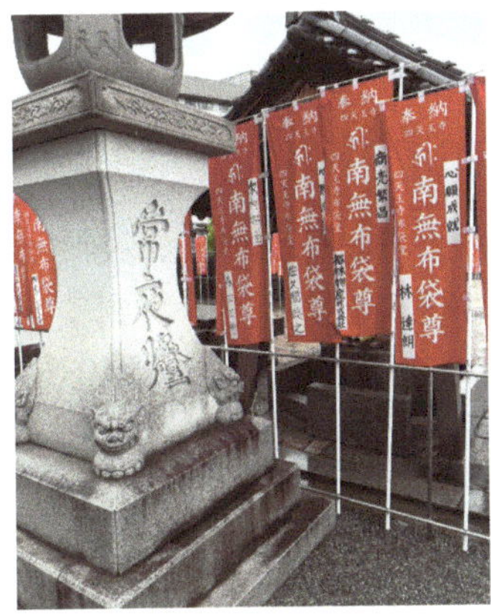

Nobori prayer banners with bonji seed syllable (Skt. bījākṣara) hrīḥ (ह्रीः), Shitennō-ji

While Shingon emphasized esoteric practice through mantra, mudrā, and maṇḍala (more in Rituals section), Tendai was another major esoteric tradition that wove those same ritual principles into a broader framework centered on Lotus Sūtra doctrine, meditation, and mountain monastic training on Mt. Hiei. Other major sects include Pure Land (*Jōdo-shū*), now Japan's largest tradition, and similar to Hinduism's *bhakti* movement in how it emphasizes simple devotion, especially the recitation of Amida's name, as a path open to people from all walks of life. Zen, created by the Indian monk Bodhidharma, placed its weight on disciplined meditation. Although it does not dominate in numbers like Pure Land or Shingon has, it has been extremely influential in Japanese spiritual and secular life. Zen shaped *bushidō*, the ethics of the samurai, and also shaped Japanese aesthetic ideals of simplicity and elegance. It even influenced global design aesthetic, including Apple's products. Nichiren centered the Lotus Sūtra and the chanting of its title as a single-minded path of faith. Modern lay movements also emerged such as *Sōka Gakkai,* which carried Buddhist identity into public life in new ways.

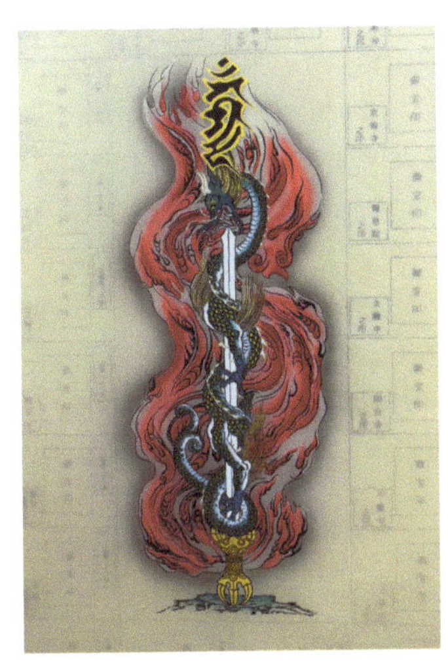

Kurikara-ken (Kurikara "dragon-sword" motif), Shitennō-ji

Language & Script

With the advent of Buddhism the Japanese written language advanced, leading to the three main scripts used in modern Japan for secular purposes.

In the 4th century CE came kanji, the logographic Chinese characters that were imported along with sutras coming from China. Monks learned this script to read sutras, most of which came from the continent. However, each Chinese character does not represent a sound but an object or an idea. For example, 大 means "big" in both Chinese and Japanese, but the pronunciation can be completely different. This meant that kanji could be used to write Japanese without adopting Chinese pronunciations. It is also important to remember that kanji in Japan have largely been preserved for over a thousand years, whereas they have changed quite a lot in China, making Japanese kanji unintelligible to a modern Chinese reader, and vice versa. It is also interesting to note that Japan coined many logographic kanji for modern concepts like trains, cars, phones, or electricity due to its status as the first industrialized East Asian nation. China then borrowed these heavily, with some estimates calculating that around 20% of characters in use in China were invented in Japan, and that the number jumps to 80% in technology and humanities fields.

After studying Sanskrit under Indian masters on the continent, Kūkai (9th century CE), founder of Shingon sect, brought back Siddhaṃ (a Sanskrit script related to Devanagari) to write mantras. In his view, Sanskrit was the supreme language, superior to Chinese or Japanese, and the divine source of truth. For that reason, Siddhaṃ in Japan came to be called bonji, with *bon* meaning Brahma and *ji* meaning script. Interestingly, emoji, which were invented in Japan, can be glossed as "picture characters," with *emo* meaning picture and *ji* meaning character. He particularly valued the *shūji,* Sanskrit *bījākṣaras* (seed syllables), as having inherent power in the way they were written and pronounced. He wanted a Sanskrit-based script that could convey the subtleties of Japanese more precisely and also make literacy more accessible to the average person. However, he did not want to use bonji directly, because he thought it was far too sacred for mundane, everyday writing. That is why he is credited with inventing hiragana. Hiragana uses Sanskrit as a visual and sound base, but it is adapted for Japanese, including sounds such as *za* and *fu*, which are common in Japanese but not in Sanskrit. He is also credited with inventing katakana from man'yōgana, which were Chinese characters used to represent Sanskrit words in sutras because of their similar sound to a given Sanskrit character. This is why hiragana visually feels more flowy, like Sanskrit, while katakana feels more blocky, like Chinese. Together these are called kana, and they are used to write almost everything in Japanese, except for many nouns and verb stems, which still benefit from a visual representation of kanji.

Kūkai's aim of increasing literacy also led to temple-based *terakoya* education, which is often credited with spreading kana literacy beyond elites. One estimate puts terakoya (lit. "temple child house") attendance in Japan at ~70% by the late 18th to early 19th century, while literacy in Europe at that time was estimated to be around ~30%.

Bonji (Siddhaṃ) never became an everyday script in Japan because it was reserved for the highest register of religious life. In Vajrayana Buddhism, like in Hinduism, a written syllable is not just a unit of sound. It is a sacred form that can stand in for an entire deity or principle, which is why bonji appears as *shūji* (seed syllables) that function almost like icons. *Ajikan* is the clearest expression of this idea: practitioners meditate on the Siddhaṃ letter *a* (pronounced as *u* in tusk) placed inside a moon disk, often resting on a lotus, using one letter as a complete spiritual tool, something you see and internalize through breath and attention. *a* is the first letter in both Sanskrit and Japanese, and it is treated as the primal, "unborn" syllable from which all sounds unfold, so it is associated with Dainichi Nyorai, the cosmic Buddha at the center of Shingon.

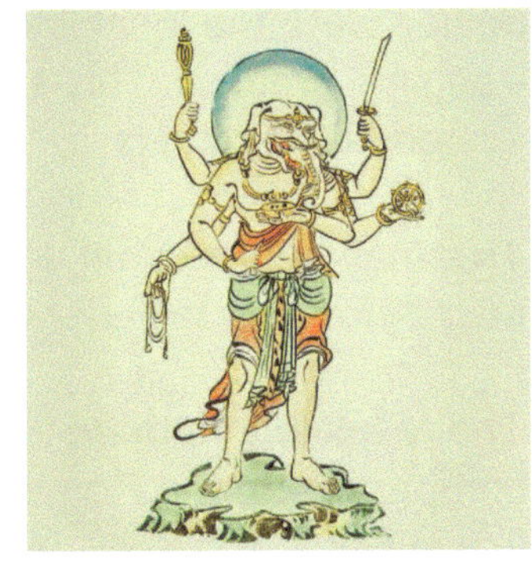

Six-armed Kangiten (Skt. Gaṇapati), holding a wheel (cakra), bowl (modaka), sword (khaḍga), noose (pāśa), and broken tusk (danta)

This is also why bonji became the most prestigious form of calligraphy. Calligraphy was already a mark of refinement and status in elite culture, but bonji sat at the summit because it demanded two kinds of mastery at once: artistic control and ritual correctness. To be a master in bonji calligraphy was one of the highest marks of a Japanese scholar.

Bonji also belongs to the world of endurance practice, not only still meditation. Mt. Hiei's *kaihōgyō* is an extreme, multi-year discipline, spread over 1,000 days across seven years, and described as totaling up to about 27,000 miles on foot. Only 46 practitioners have completed it since 1885, making it one of the rarest ascetic paths in Japan. In the *kaihōgyō*, the practitioner circambulates Mt. Hiei, stopping at halls and sacred sites for prayer and contemplation. As he circles the mountain, he holds the Ajikan "a" in mind, turning the entire pilgrimage into meditation: the letter is the inner focus, and the mountain becomes the mandala that surrounds it.

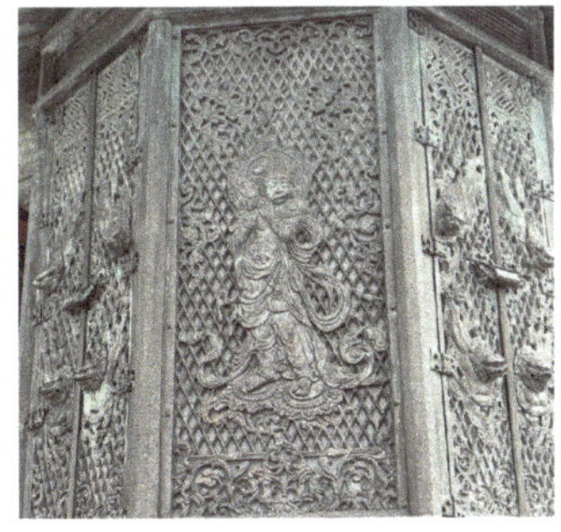

Vaṃśī Kṛṣṇa on a lamp post, Tōdai-ji (Nara)

Japan also has the largest number of people studying Sanskrit outside India, but the context is very different from learning it as a spoken language. In Japan it is most often studied for the sound and precision of mantras, and many monks learn it to grasp the linguistic subtleties of sutras they believe can only be fully understood through Sanskrit. In addition to spiritual vocabulary, everyday Japanese still preserves a few Sanskrit-derived words that feel more "lay" in nature, such as *setsuna*, "a fleeting instant" (from Skt. *kṣaṇa*); *rasetsu*, "a demon" (from Skt. *rākṣasa*); *aun*, "being in sync" (from Skt. *a-hūṃ*); *maka*, a prefix meaning "great" (from Skt. *mahā*); *danna*, "patron; boss" (from Skt. *dānapati*); *ringo*, "apple" (from Skt. *bimba*); *hannya*, "wisdom" (from Skt. *prajñā*); and *garan*, "temple compound/buildings" (from Skt. *saṃghārāma*).

Shared Deities

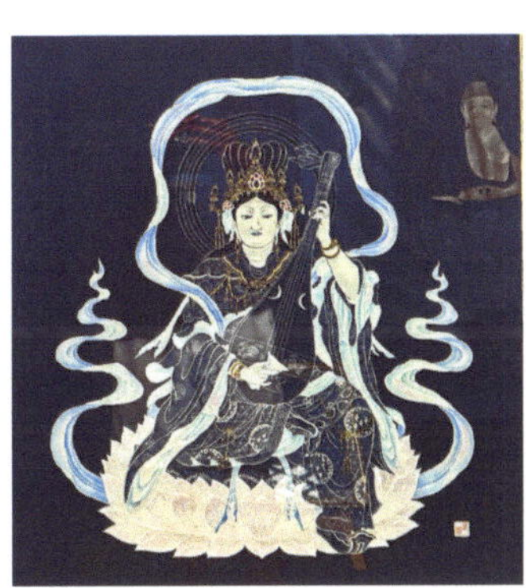

Benzaiten (Skt. Sarasvatī), holding a biwa (Skt. vīṇā), goddess of all that flows: water and knowledge

When one thinks of Japanese Buddhism, one will invariably picture tranquil statues of the Buddha seated in meditation. While this is indubitably part of Japan's spiritual landscape, the assimilation of Hindu deities is also a huge part of Japanese Buddhism. It is important to note that these deities did not arrive directly from India, but through a long chain of countries, such as China and Korea. One reason they were so readily and deeply assimilated in Japan is that indigenous Shinto beliefs were already comfortable with a large pantheon of deities. Additionally, the *Honji Suijaku* came about in Japan and it posited that many Shinto deities were the local Japanese manifestations (*Suijaku* - traces) of Indian Buddhist deities (*Honji* - original ground). This syncretic framework allowed both religions to coexist as a single, indivisible system for centuries.

This may help explain why the worship of these deities quickly fell out of practice in China and Korea long before the broader decline of Buddhism in those countries.

The result is that there is a parallel for nearly every Hindu deity in Japanese Buddhism. It is comparable to the Roman adoption of Greek gods, except that they are not confined to museums like in Europe, but still alive and active in temples across Japan. For example, Gaṇapati becomes Kangiten, Lakṣmī becomes Kichijōten, and Sarasvatī becomes Benzaiten. However, it is not only the major deities: almost every deity has a parallel, including Indra, Agni, Vāyu, and Varuṇa.

Taishakuten (Skt. *Indra*) is the Japanese form of *Śakra* (Jp. *shaku*), the historic epithet for him in Sanskrit, paired with the characters for emperor (Jp. *tai*) and deity (Jp. *ten*). Other name translations are more literal, such as Katen (Skt. *agni*), the Vedic deity of fire, whose name is rendered directly from the Japanese characters for fire (Jp. *ka*) and deity (Jp. *ten*).

The roles and forms of these deities fall on a spectrum of similarity when compared with their Hindu counterparts. For example, Skt. *Brahmā*, known in Japan as *Bonten*, is nearly identical to his Indian form, with four heads and the familiar meditation posture, seated on a swan. Other deities are more distinctly Japanized versions of major Vedic deities. For example, Benzaiten, as explained in several Japanese temple museums, is not only the goddess of knowledge and eloquence, but also the deity of all that flows, reflecting Benzaiten's older Vedic identity as a river and as the divine presence behind all that flows. Yet her form is uniquely Japanized: she wears a kimono and holds a *biwa*, the Japanese lute derived from the Skt. *vīṇā*. This widespread "flow" role made her blend into Shinto as well, alongside Shinto ideas of the sacredness of rivers, water, and the arts. Her broad appeal has made her one of the most popular deities in Japan. There are thousands of Benzaiten shrines across Japan, with nearly every city, town, or village having one, and dedicated pilgrimage routes for her, including a prominent temple on the campus of the University of Tokyo. I felt she was more popular in Japan than in India!

Interestingly, Japan's largest lake, Biwa-ko, which is also one of the oldest lakes in the world, resembles the shape of a *biwa* and was named Lake Biwa. According to Hōgon-ji temple tradition, Emperor Shōmu of the 8th century had a dream in which Benzaiten told him to build a temple for her on Chikubu-shima, since she had done penance there for thousands of years. He authorized the monk Gyōki, a friend of Bodhisena (an esteemed Indian monk invited to Japan by Emperor Shōmu) to build the temple for national peace on the island. From then on, Lake Biwa has been regarded as a holy place for Benzaiten.

An example of a Hindu deity who is worshipped slightly differently in Japan, while the core remains the same, is Gaṇapati, who became Kangiten in Japan, also called Shōten, and is often treated as a *hibutsu*, a "hidden deity." This is because he is believed to be too powerful to be seen by laypeople and is usually viewed only by monks, and only on special festival days. He is perceived as a very generous deity who grants any wish that devotees ask. He is also seen as a deity who values purity, and as such priests at Kangiten temples do not perform funerals. His talismans are not meant to be placed casually around the home, and especially not on household altars where ancestors are also revered. He also has special rituals such as the sesame oil bath, in which highly qualified monks bathe his icon in sesame oil 108 times on festival days, symbolizing the washing away of the 108 traits said to bring human suffering. Popular belief holds that one cannot worship Kangiten unless one has a karmic connection with him, which itself is considered a blessing. A famous 11th century Shingon monk, Kakuban, said, "Birth as a human being is hard to attain and yet I have unexpectedly attained it; Shōten's dharma is difficult to encounter and yet I am fortunate to have encountered it. Having arrived at this opportune moment to worship him, I cannot hold back my tears."

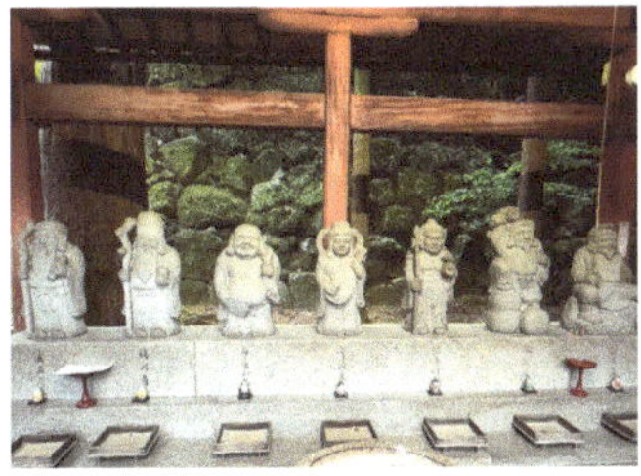

Shichi Fukujin (Seven Lucky Gods), including Daikokuten (Skt. Mahākāla) and Benzaiten (Skt. Sarasvatī)

Famous devotees of Kangiten include Tenjin (the 9th-century courtier later deified as a Shinto deity of learning), Emperor Go-Daigo, and the shōguns Toyotomi Hideyoshi and Tokugawa Ieyasu. Kangiten was also popular with merchants, artists, Noh and Kabuki actors, and the geisha. Although he is revered throughout Japan, with hundreds of temples dedicated to him across the country, he is especially popular in the Kansai region, particularly around Osaka, historically the city of merchants. Indeed, Hōzan-ji, located in the mountains east of Osaka, has long been a favored spot for merchants from the city. It became customary for any merchant in Osaka to visit the temple before starting a business. This patronage even led to the mountain receiving Japan's first cable car in 1918, indigenously designed through the initiative of Osaka's merchants.

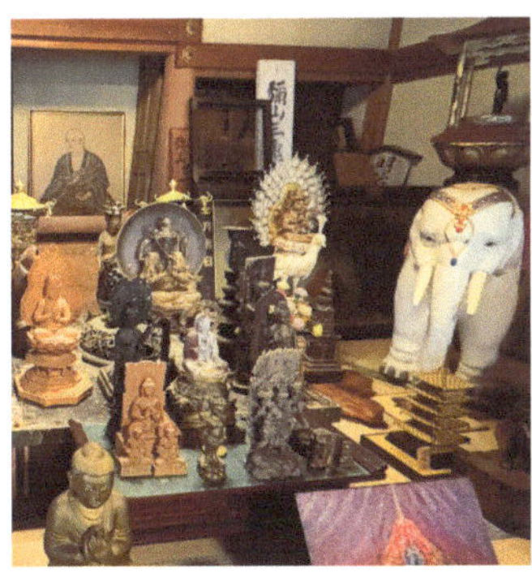

Kujaku Myōō (Skt. Mahāmāyūrī), Dainichi Nyorai (Skt. Mahāvairocana), Kūkai, and a tanjō-butsu (Birth Buddha) on a white elephant, Daishō-in (Miyajima)

For this reason, Kangiten's motifs in Japan are the money bag and the *daikon* (Japanese radish). The money bag signifies his status as a deity who bestows wealth and plenty on his devotees. The daikon represents two things: first, its pure white color symbolizes the ritual purity associated with Kangiten worship, and the "clean removal" of obstacles. Second, daikon is traditionally valued for aiding digestion and relieving stomach troubles due to its high fiber content, mirroring Kangiten's role in helping devotees "digest" and clear away problems in life. When he is shown in drawings or statues, he may be depicted holding daikon in one hand and a trident in the other. Another common depiction is Sōshin Kangiten, the dual Kangiten form featuring a male and female Kangiten in an embrace.

Skt. *Kārttikeya* also enters the Japanese pantheon as *Idaten*, where he is depicted as a Japanese general. Skt. *Garuḍa* appears in Japan as *Karura*, and is revered as a protective figure. He appears frequently in *Bugaku*, the traditional Japanese court dance style, and is honored as a protector of ordinary people, Buddhism, and the Japanese nation itself. In modern times, many anime characters who are skilled fighters are often named Karura.

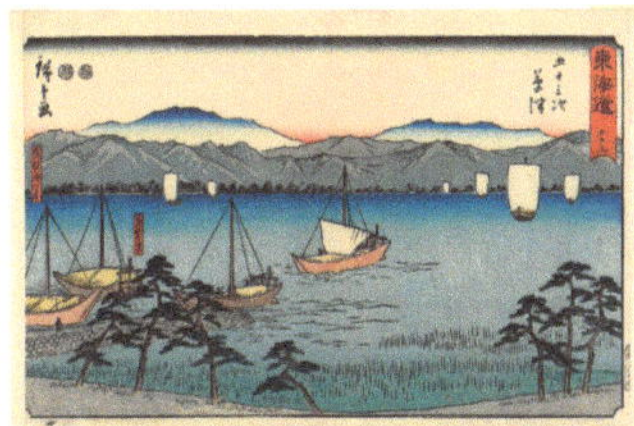

Biwa-ko (Lake Biwa), waters of Benzaiten (Skt. Sarasvatī)

Kichijōten (Skt. *Lakṣmī*) appears in Japan as a deity of wealth and prosperity, and also as a protector of women and children. Skt. *Yama*, the Hindu deity of death and the afterlife, is prominent as *Enmaten* in Japan, with multiple temples and festivals in his honor. Japanese legend even ties him to the courtier Ono no Takamura (802–853), who is said to have served as Enmaten's secretary every night by secretly climbing down a well to the underworld at Rokudō Chinno-ji Temple in Kyoto. In my personal experience, I saw some of the highest numbers of ceremonial offerings, like convenience store snacks and juices, placed in front of Enmaten! Interestingly, *enma-chō* is commonly used to refer to a teacher's gradebook, based on the idea of Enmaten's ledger of deeds. Enma is also popular in Japanese pop culture, e.g., the character Great King Enma (*Enma Daiō*) in the manga series *Yū Yū Hakusho*.

Although rare, Skt. *Śiva-liṅga* icons are also present and worshipped. They are understood not only as symbols of Śiva, but also as pointing to the Zen idea of primordial energy as Skt. *Dharmakāya*, the cosmic body of the Buddha. The practice around this worship is quite similar to Hindu temples, with *kanjō* (Skt. *abhiṣeka*) performed in its honor. A more popular form of Śiva is Skt. *Acala*, known in Japan as *Fudō Myōō*, a wrathful protector revered as a deity of persistence and grit. He stands before flames, gripping a rope to bind wayward desires and a sword to cut through illusion. Due to his martial qualities, he was a favored deity of the samurai, who often had his Sanskrit character embossed on their *katana* (sword) as they went off to war. The *goma* (Skt. *homa*) fire ceremony is also performed in his honor. In modern times, he continues to be a patron deity of the *Yamabushi*, ascetics who live in seclusion in the mountains of Japan and practice *Shugendō*, a combination of tantric Buddhist practices and Shinto nature veneration. These Yamabushi meditate on Fudō Myōō in isolation, hoping to achieve Skt. *nirvāṇa* in this body.

Another form of Śiva is Skt. *Mahākāla*, known in Japan as *Daikokuten*, and he is one of the most widespread and beloved "everyday" deities in Japan. Unlike the more wrathful Hindu Mahākāla, Daikokuten is often depicted as a very jolly god, holding a bag of endless treasures. He is especially popular for home altars, and is sometimes conflated with *Ebisu*, a Shinto deity of wealth. His cheerful form has made him one of Japan's most recognizable deities, and he appears in modern Japan everywhere from supermarket logos to the Daikoku parking area on the Daikoku expressway, a hub for Japanese Domestic Market (JDM) exhibits and an inspiration for the movie, *Fast and Furious: Tokyo Drift*.

Skt. *Vaiśravaṇa* (also known *Kubera*), the Hindu deity of wealth, takes a major role in Japanese Buddhism as *Bishamonten*, a deity of wealth and the protector of the northern direction among the *Shitennō* (Skt. *Lokapāla*) who guard the four directions. He is often shown as a protector of temples, holding a miniature Skt. *stūpa* in one hand and a weapon in the other, dressed in the garb of a Japanese general.

Skt. *Piṇḍola Bhāradvāja*, known in Japan as *Binzuru*, was a disciple of the Buddha who gained extraordinary yogic Skt. *siddhi* abilities and loved to show them off. The Buddha rebukes him and makes him remain on earth helping those with ailments until the coming of the next Buddha. He is extremely popular in Japan and is found in nearly every temple. People often offer satsuma oranges to him, then rub the part of his statue corresponding to the pain they feel, and finally touch the same place on their own bodies as they pray for relief.

Other Vedic deities such as Skt. *Dhruva*, the North Star deity, and Skt. *Dhanvantari*, the deity of medicine, appear as *Myōken Bosatsu* and *Yakushi Nyorai* respectively. At this point, in the interest of space, instead of listing each Vedic deity and its Japanese counterpart, one can assume that nearly every Vedic deity is not only present in Japanese Buddhism, but most likely also has dedicated temples somewhere in Japan.

Although there are a few key philosophical differences between Hinduism and Buddhism, the vast majority of the traditions, including daily practice, are strikingly similar. Skt. *Mahāvairocana*, known in Japan as *Dainichi Nyorai*, is the supreme deity of esoteric Buddhism and is quite similar to Skt. *brahman* in Hinduism. He represents the beginning and end of everything and is believed to be all-pervasive.

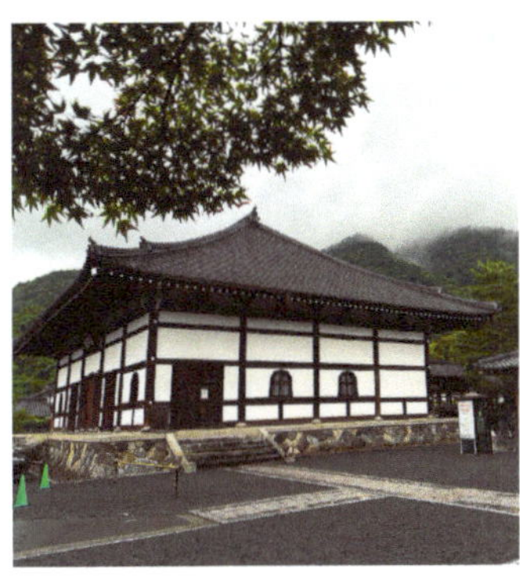

Daruma-dō (Skt. Bodhidharma) Hall, Tenryū-ji

But by far the most ubiquitous Buddhist deity in Japan is Skt. *Kṣitigarbha Bodhisattva*, known in Japan as *Jizō Bosatsu*. Jizō figures are easy to recognize by their monk's robes, shaven heads, calm expressions, and, interestingly, with red bibs or caps. Many hold a ring-topped staff (*shakujō*, from Skt. *khakkhara*) or a wish-granting jewel (Skt. *cintāmaṇi*), while others carry a scroll, a begging bowl, or other simple objects that identify them as wandering protectors and compassionate guides. They are Skt. *bodhisattvas*, beings who have delayed their own final Skt. *nirvāṇa* until the problems of all sentient beings are solved.

Sacred Architecture

When I looked out from my room in Tokyo, I saw glass skyscrapers rising toward the heavens in every direction with toriis and pagodas breaking the skyline. This shows how prevalent these architectural styles still are in Japan.

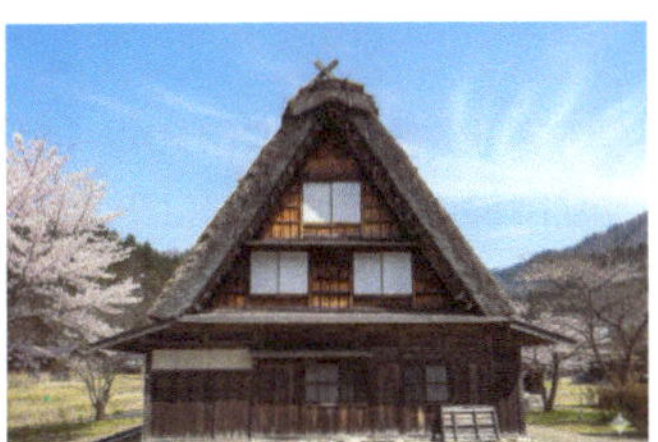

Gasshō-zukuri traditional house, named for its "praying-hands" roof (Skt. añjali mudrā)

I always wondered why so many pieces of architecture, from the ubiquitous pagodas to the Tokyo Skytree, seemed to have five levels. After some research, I learned that the reason for this was the Japanese concept of *godai*, directly derived from the ancient Indian philosophy of the Skt. *pañca mahābhūta*, or the five great elements, which describes the material world as comprised of earth, water, fire, wind, and space. Pagodas are meant to express this architecturally, beginning with earth at the base and rising upward toward space.

Sotoba are seen everywhere in Japan: small wooden "mini-stūpas" (hence the name), often topped with the Sanskrit characters for the five elements, with sutras or blessings written below. Other temple elements, such as ponds, bells, and painted patterns on temples, are also shared. The tama, a parallel to the Skt. *cintāmaṇi*, is a wish-granting jewel that is prominent in both Buddhist and Shinto lore. In fact, it is so common that there is a major river called the Tama River in Tokyo. Interestingly, there is a Benzaiten shrine at the point where it merges into the Pacific near Haneda Airport. It is interesting to note that there is an ancient *Śiva* temple at the confluence of the *Sarasvatī* river and the sea near Somnāth in India.

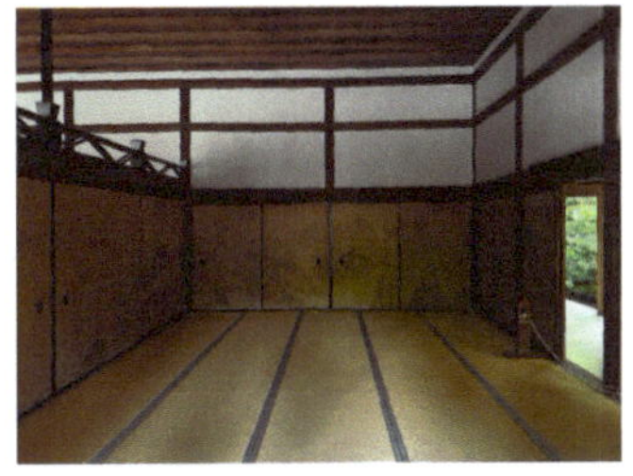

Shōin with tatami mats for sutra copying, Ryōan-ji

The torii, which are ubiquitous throughout the country and a national cultural icon, are said to derive from ancient Buddhist Skt. *toraṇa*, standing outside early Buddhist monasteries. Guardian deities, seen across the Hindu–Buddhist world, are also found in Japan; however, Japan's guardian figures often feel more martial, and are often sculpted in ways that suggest they are reciting Skt. *aum*. Ritual purity has also carried over, with purification of body and mind serving as an important preface to entering temples and shrines.

The same ideas carried into secular life. The traditional Japanese thatched-roof house style is called *gasshō-zukuri* because of its similarity in appearance to *gasshō* (Skt. *añjali mudrā*): its triangular rooflines meet like palms pressed together. The traditional *shoin* room, with tatami mats and sliding doors, was originally associated with spaces for sutra copying, but it became part of Japanese secular life as well. In fact, even though Japanese and American suburban homes are similar in purpose, Japanese are often built using temple-like tiled rooflines, tatami rooms, and a built-in *butsudan* (home altar) area. One of the things that surprised me most was how prominently traditional architectural styles were used in very modern homes across Japan.

Lastly, Buddhist deity names and temple names show up throughout the country. Examples include the neighborhood of Kichijōji in Tokyo, named after *Kichijōten*, and the city of Kan'onji-shi in Shikoku, named after Kannon.

Rituals

Japanese are deeply ritualistic, with ancient Shinto–Buddhist practices embedded in everyday life and with nearly every Japanese person participating in them in some form. One of the most ordinary, and also most revealing, rituals is the *butsudan*, the home altar, found in the vast majority of Japanese households, with the main exception being some families living in cramped downtown apartments. Other daily acts of devotion include *kanjō* (Skt. *abhiṣeka*), in which devotees bathe Buddhist images, a practice seen at temples and, in some Nichiren households, even at the home altar. Incense is ubiquitous, with many people lighting it at temples or before the *butsudan* as part of routine reverence for deities and ancestors.

Japan is widely regarded as one of the cleanest countries in the world, which is especially striking given its high population density. A common cultural explanation points to Shinto–Buddhist ideas of cleanliness and ritual purity, where "clean" is not just hygienic but moral and spiritual, too. You can see this at temples and shrines, which often provide places to wash hands, rinse the mouth, and sometimes even clean the feet before entering a sacred space.

Temples and shrines have also historically served as the social center of towns, shaping how people moved, traded, and gathered. That pattern carries into the present: many *shōtengai*, the covered pedestrian shopping streets that function as an everyday "third place" across cities, suburbs, and small towns, trace their origins to the market streets and vendor clusters that grew around major temples and shrines.

Goma, the Shingon fire ceremony (Skt. *homa*), makes the rituals strikingly vivid: the priest offers wooden prayer sticks and oil into a blazing altar, believing the fire to carry human wishes toward the deity. In Shingon, practice is often described as the union of *mantra*, *mudrā*, and *maṇḍala*: mantra is sacred sound recited as chant, mudrā is the expression with the hands and ritual tools, and the mandala is the cosmic map that the rite is meant to activate. In a goma hall, these three meet in one place, where sound, gesture, and the fire altar itself turn devotion into something physical, seen, and felt.

Shingon's mantra–mudrā–maṇḍala triad parallels *trikaraṇa-śuddhi in* Hinduism - purifying speech (*vāk*), action (*karmaṇa*), and thought (*manas*) - since mantra disciplines speech, mudrā disciplines the body's actions, and the mandala trains the mind through focused visualization.

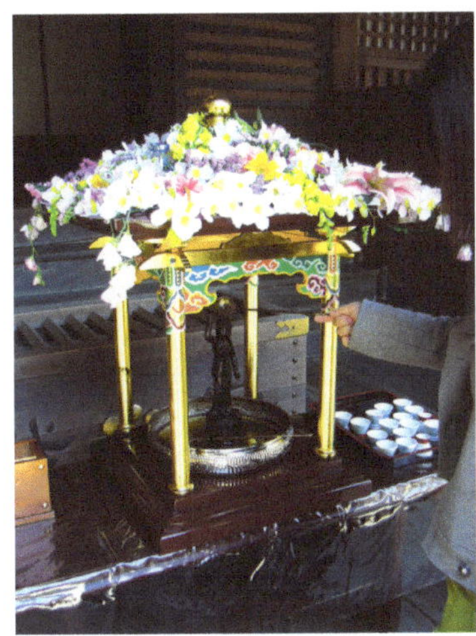

Hanamatsuri (Buddha's Birthday flower festival)

Festivals

Japan is the land of 300,000 festivals. Nearly every one of Japan's 160,000 temples and shrines has a special festival held on a day sacred to the deity enshrined in that place. We were fortunate enough to see the San Dai Benzaiten Matsuri (Festival of the Three Great Benzaiten). This festival happens on Chikubushima, which is Japan's oldest Benzaiten shrine and the first of the Three Great Benzaiten. In this festival, you can see many of the elements of a typical Japanese festival.

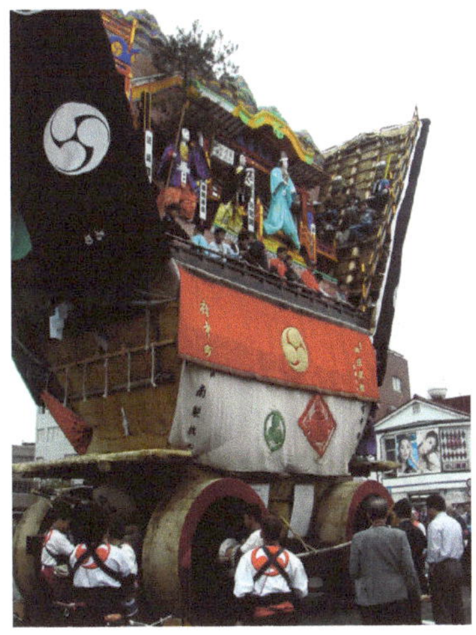

Dekayama giant float, Seihakusai Festival, a Japan-style Skt. ratha yātrā

At the front of the procession, priests play *gagaku* music as the procession climbs up the hill to the main hall of Benzaiten. Gagaku is the traditional court music of Japan. It is over 1,300 years old, and it blends indigenous Japanese music with Indian, Korean, and Chinese influences. It is still played today at festivals and imperial ceremonies. Even Japan's anthem, the oldest in the world dating to 905 CE, uses a gagaku arrangement. *Bugaku* is the dance component of gagaku, and it is ceremoniously offered to the deities of temples and shrines. Just like gagaku, it is based on the dance forms of India, China, and Korea. At Hie Jinja, we were fortunate enough to see a bugaku performance offered to the deity of the shrine as part of their preparation for the shrine's festival, Sannō Matsuri. Bodhisena, an Indian monk, is credited with introducing the eight pieces of the *Tenjikugaku* repertoire within bugaku. *Karyōbin* is the most revered and best-known piece from this repertoire. It is said to have first been witnessed by *Ānanda*, a disciple of the Buddha, in the *Jetavana* grove. There, he is said to have seen the *karyōbinga* (Skt. *kalaviṅka*), a half-human, half-bird celestial being, dancing in the grove as Benzaiten played music from the heavens.

Beyond these pieces, several instruments used across repertoires are also traced to Indian origins. These include the *taiko*, based on Indian drums; the *ryūteki*, connected to Indian flutes; the *biwa*, linked to the *vīṇā*; and the *tsuzumi*, derived from the *ḍamaru*.

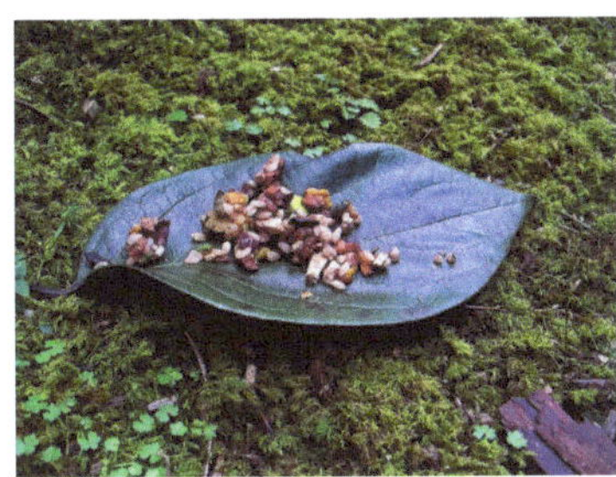

Obon (Skt. Ullambana) offering at Okunoin Cemetery (Kōyasan), honoring the departed spirits of one's ancestors

Another important part of Japanese festivals is the *mikoshi*. The mikoshi is traditionally a covered palanquin containing a small

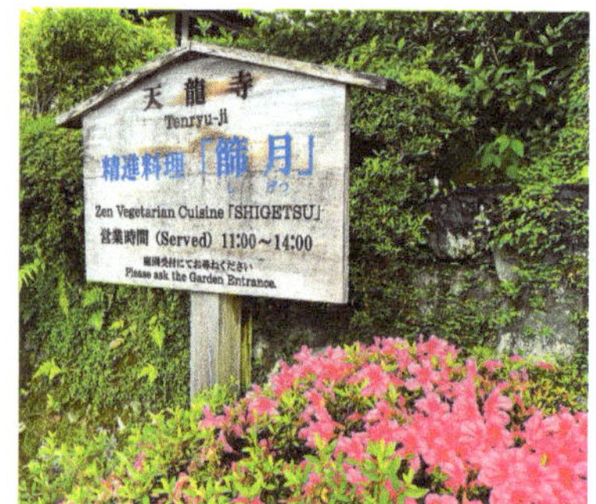

Shōjin ryōri (temple vegetarian cuisine), Tenryū-ji

version of the main deity, and it is used for taking it to other shrines or throughout the town. For example, during the festival at Chikubushima, the small versions of the main deities of Miyajima and Enoshima were brought to Chikubushima. During the *Sannō Matsuri*, the deity of that shrine is taken around the Nagatachō neighborhood to bless the government buildings in that neighborhood.

Tenjin Matsuri, one of Japan's biggest festivals, is held in honor of the 9th-century courtier Sugawara no Michizane, who was later deified as Tenjin. Buddhist temples take a prominent role during New Year's time. On New Year's Eve, many temples perform *jōya no kan*e, where a great bell is rung 108 times to mark the passing year and symbolically clear the mind for the year ahead. Then, on New Year's Day, almost every Japanese person visits a temple or shrine to pray for good luck for the new year and buy *omamori* (blessed amulet). New Year's Day is so significant that it is credited with playing a large role in making Tokyo's Sensō-ji, the world's most visited religious site, with New Year's Day accounting for 2 million of the temple's 30 million annual visitors.

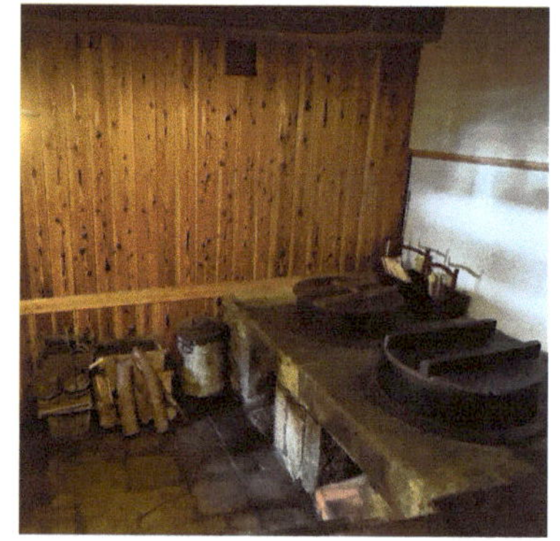

Shōjin ryōri vegetarian kitchen, Shōjoshin-in (Kōyasan)

Other prominent festivals include *Hana Matsuri*, the festival of flowers, which is held on April 8, celebrated as the birthday of the Buddha. On this day, people visit temples and bathe statues of baby Buddhas with a hydrangea tea before enjoying the cherry blossoms, which are in full bloom at this point in time.

But Japan's biggest festival is undoubtedly *Obon*. Obon, which originates from the Sanskrit word *Ullambana*, is the Japanese festival of the ancestors. On this day, Japanese people return to their ancestral villages and meet family. It is Japan's largest travel season, and the Shinkansen network's ability to run with minimal delays during this extremely busy period is often described as a logistical marvel. They visit the temples where the ashes of their ancestors are, clean graves, and offer *shōjin ryōri* food to them before enjoying a vegetarian meal at home with family. Then they light lanterns, take part in community dances, and end the evenings with fireworks.

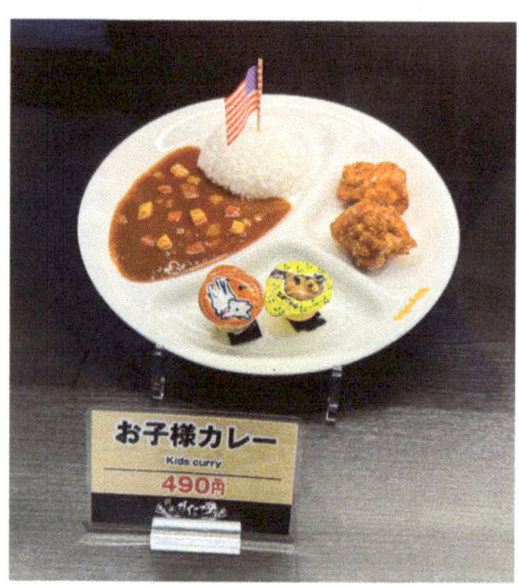

Kodomo karē (kids' curry), a Tokyo restaurant

Food

There's a perception that Japan is a decidedly non-vegetarian country. That isn't quite true. For over a thousand years, from the advent of Buddhism, meat, and beef in particular, carried a strong taboo, shaped by compassion ethics and ideas of ritual purity. Even before Buddhism's arrival, Shinto practices of purification already leaned toward simple, vegetarian eating, and this helped vegetarianism, along with norms around the five pungent roots, gain wider acceptance in Japan than in many other Buddhist countries. That older baseline still leaves traces today. Japan's per capita meat consumption is less than a third that of the United States and many other developed nations. Additionally, its per capita consumption of meat is less than half that of its East Asian neighbors, even though Japan is wealthier than them.

Historically, the *Sendara* (Skt. *caṇḍāla*), also known as *Burakumin*, were relegated to the bottom of the feudal hierarchy as "outcasts" who existed outside the four-tier class system, performing stigmatized tasks like animal slaughter, leatherworking, and cremation. Their social exclusion was reinforced by Shinto and Buddhist doctrines that labeled their contact with death and blood as *kegare* (spiritual impurity), a stigma that persists to this day in some places through private background checks during the *omiai* (arranged marriage) process to ensure prospective spouses do not have *Buraku* ancestry.

Vegetarianism in Japan was profoundly influenced by Buddhism, and you can see it most clearly inside temple food rules. Japan adopted the concept of the five pungent roots (*gokun*), where ingredients like garlic and onions are avoided in *shōjin ryōri* because they are believed to agitate the body and disturb a meditative mind. The same logic is applied to meat, which is often framed as disruptive to compassion, and therefore disruptive to one's spiritual center. For this reason, most of Japan's ~360,000 Buddhist monks and priests avoid meat and the five pungent roots in temple settings, and abstain from meat even in secular settings. Meat, or anything containing the five pungent roots, is also strictly forbidden as an offering to deities in Buddhist temples or home altars. It is also interesting to note that, because of Buddhist–Shinto syncretism, Shinto shrines often frown upon offerings of meat as well.

Norms around food were not the only thing that traveled with Buddhism; foods themselves traveled too. For example, with Buddhism came *wagashi*, traditional Japanese confections, originally brought home by monks returning to Japan from across Asia. The first wagashi to arrive was the *kangidan*. Kangidan arrived with the worship of Kangiten, and it is derived from the Indian *modaka*, traditionally offered to his Hindu equivalent, Ganesha. It is the oldest surviving wagashi in Japanese history. Over time, it adapted to Japan's climate and pantry, using curds, honey, and red bean paste instead of the coconut filling typical in India. Traditionally, wagashi are also shaped by Buddhist food norms, so they tend to be naturally lacto-vegetarian in their classic forms.

Tea, Japan's preferred beverage, also arrived with Buddhism. The tea ceremony is a Zen practice that emphasizes austere and mindful attention. Monks developed matcha as a drink to stay awake during long sessions of meditation, and its powdered form allows for quicker caffeine diffusion. Tea, along with *shōjin ryōri*, has traditionally been served to pilgrims in Japanese temples. It is prepared with such ceremony that it has earned international acclaim, with the eateries of a number of temples in Kyoto being Michelin-starred. Indeed, Kyoto has the third-highest number of Michelin-starred restaurants after Tokyo and Paris.

Curry was a more recent arrival, since the spices needed to make it do not grow in Japan. It was adopted en masse by the Japanese navy and schools, and then permeated every sector of society. The Indian revolutionary Rash Behari Bose is credited with popularizing curry in Japan by introducing an easy-to-make, "pure" Indian curry. He also ran a newspaper on Indian culture and philosophy. His culinary abilities, academic knowledge, and revolutionary activities earned him the nickname *Tenrai*, "the heavenly being." Today, curry is Japan's national dish and is consumed more widely than ramen or sushi. It is analogous to pizza in the United States in terms of its comfort-food status, ubiquitous consumption, and regional variations.

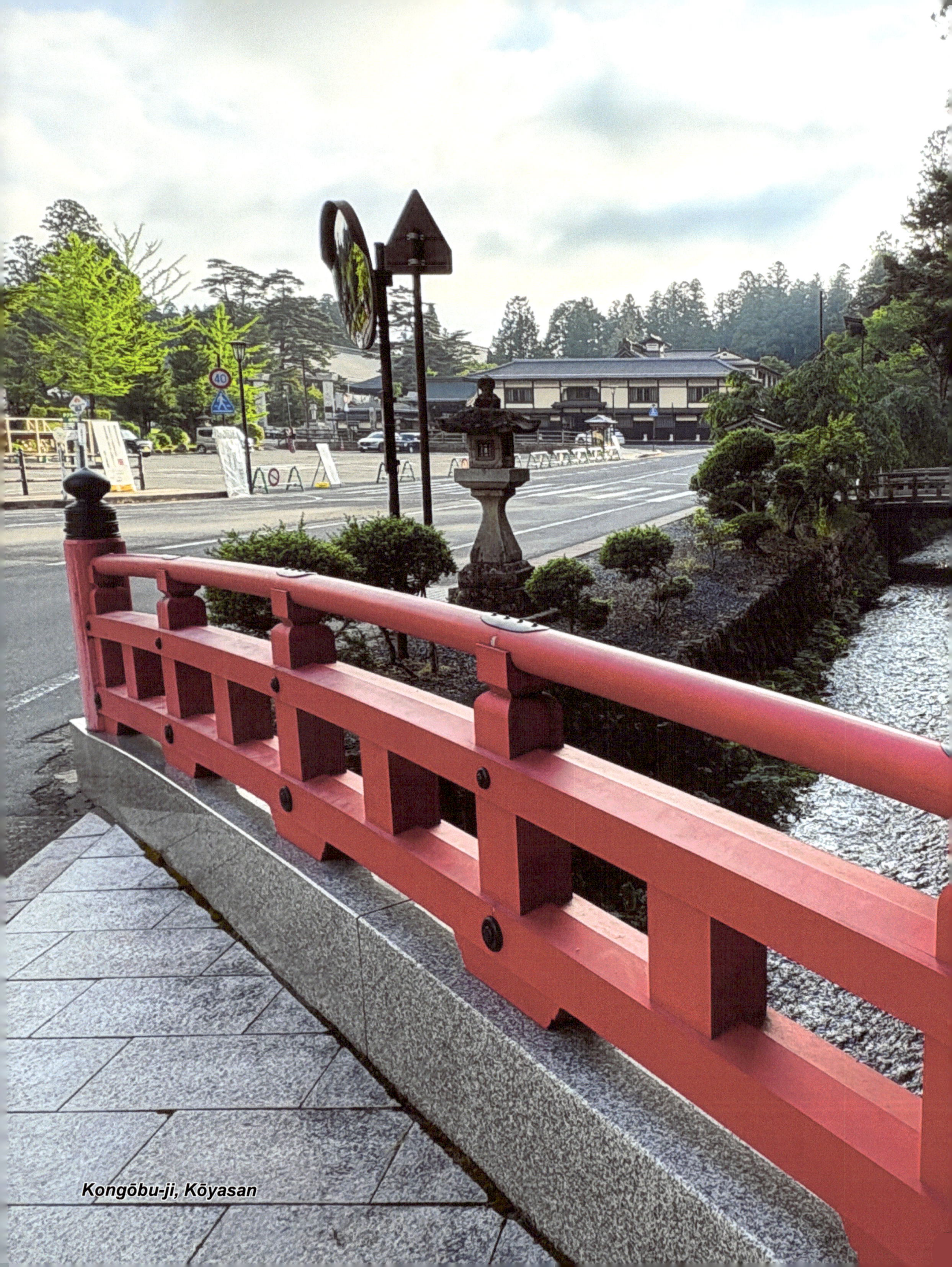

Kongōbu-ji, Kōyasan

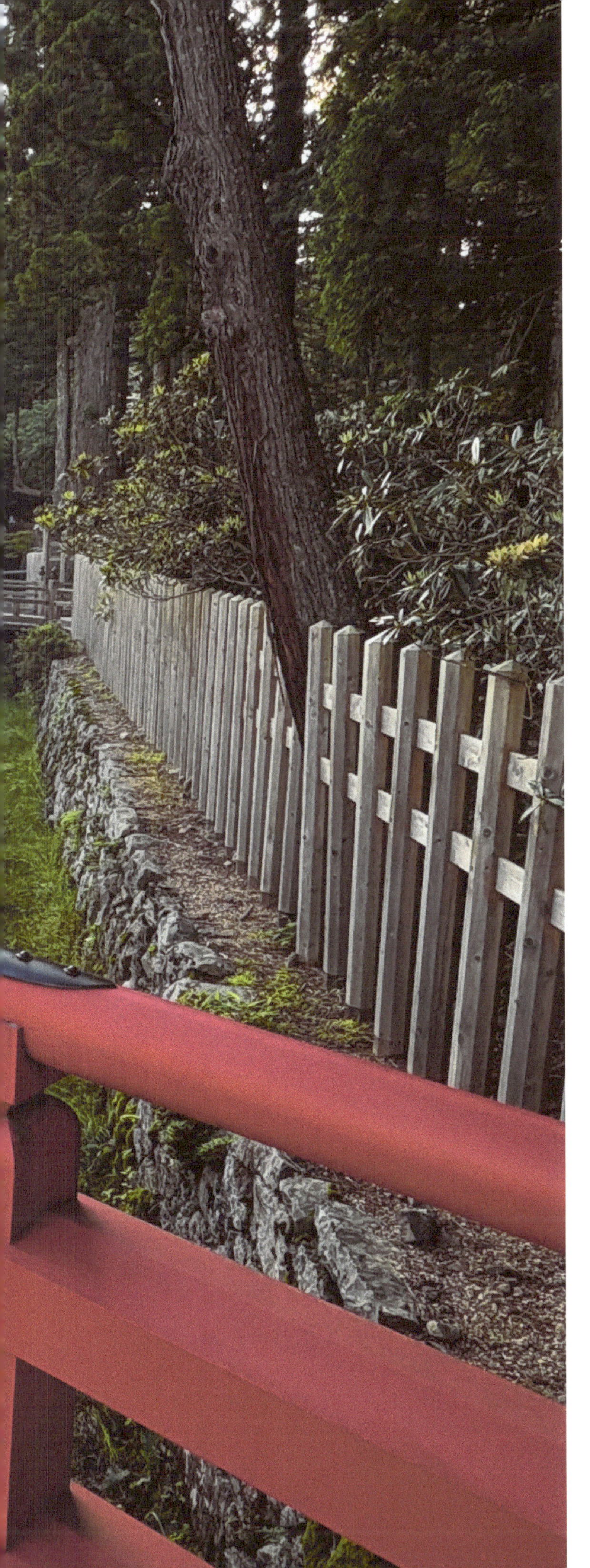

Pilgrimage & Lineage

ONE

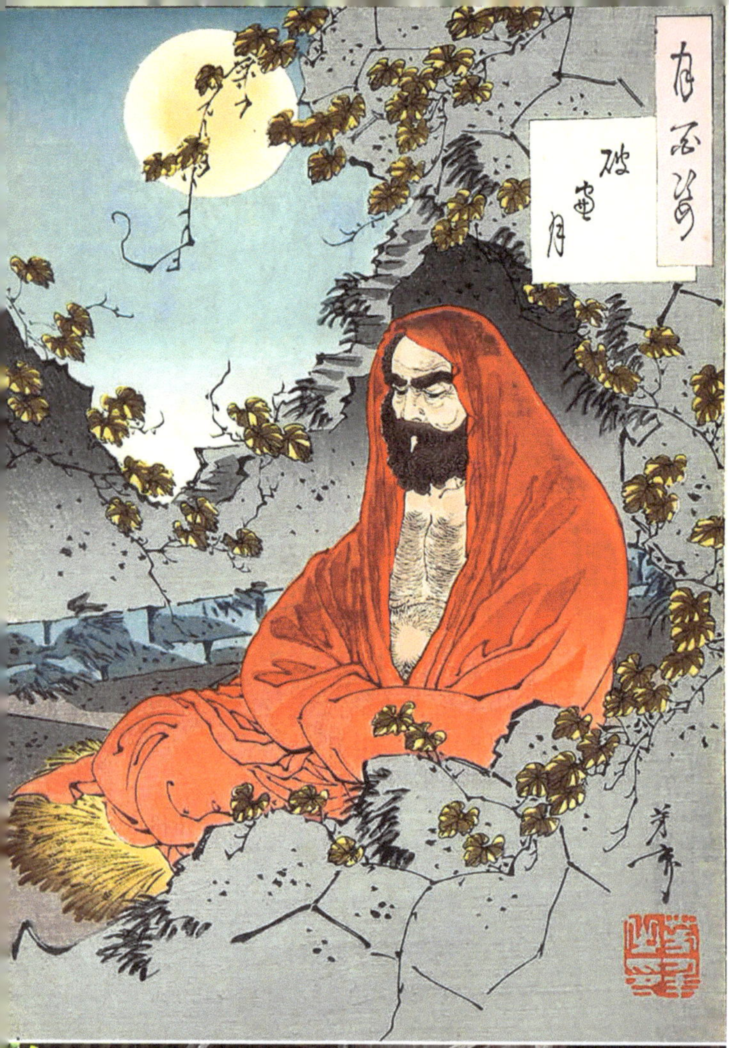

Bodhidharma's Zen – *Tsukioka Yoshitoshi, "The Moon Through a Crumbling Window" (1887). Image via Wikimedia Commons*

Bodhidharma, the South Indian monk from Kanchipuram, is traditionally placed around 440 CE and remembered as the founder of *Chan* (Zen) Buddhism in China. Legends describe his journey across the sea, his solitary meditation, and his teaching of disciplined practice at Shaolin, including elements of South Indian martial arts he carried with him, which later evolved into Shaolin kung fu.

Zen reaches Japan in the 12th century through monks who study mature Chan lineages in China. Through them, Bodhidharma's teachings take root in Japan and become central to its monastic and cultural life. Daruma, as he is known in Japanese tradition, is remembered not only as the father of Zen but also as a source martial discipline, with some lineages tracing the roots of karate back to him.

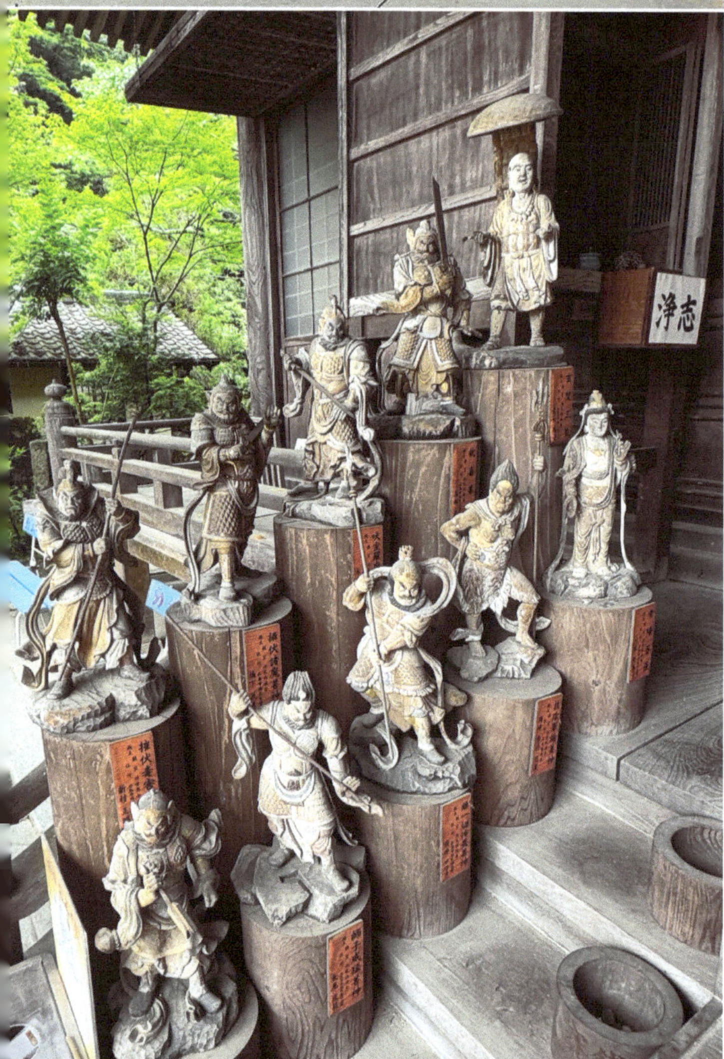

Xuanzang's Legacy – *Daishō-in, Miyajima*

Xuanzang, known in Japan as Genjō Sanzō, shown here as a traveling monk, stands at the top of this arrangement overlooking the guardian figures below. In 629 CE he sets out from Chang'an for India, studies at Nālandā under renowned gurus, and eventually returns to China with hundreds of Sanskrit manuscripts. There he helps systematize *Yogācāra* ("consciousness-only") philosophy and leads major translation projects that reshape Buddhist scholarship across East Asia. His Japanese disciple Dōshō studies with him, then returns to Japan in 661 CE and starts the Hossō school in Nara.

Beneath Xuanzang are the Twelve Heavenly Generals (Jp. *Jūni Shinshō*), traditional protectors of Yakushi Nyorai, the Medicine Buddha, whose healing role is similar to that of the Vedic deity of medicine, Skt. *Dhanvantari.* Each general guards a direction and defends devotees from illness and misfortune. Together they suggest a lineage where Sanskrit learning and divine medicine travel from India to China and onward to Japan.

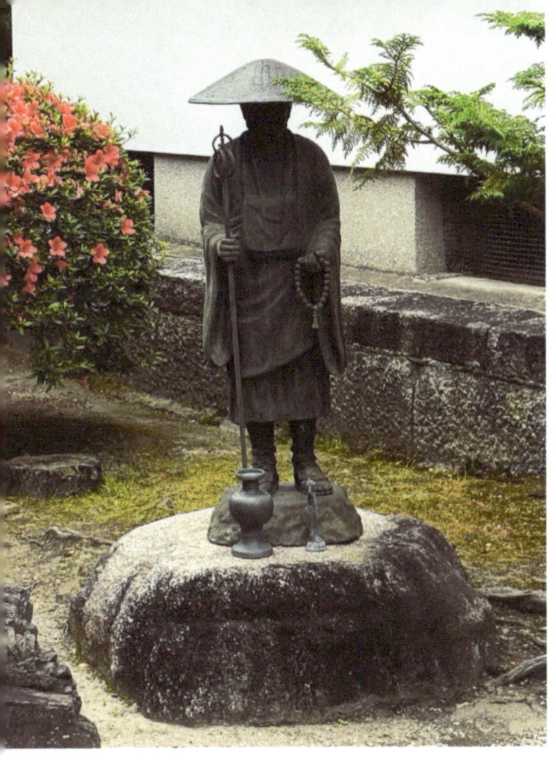

Kūkai – *Kanchi-in, Kyoto (left), and Kōyasan*

Kūkai (Kōbō Daishi), founder of Shingon Buddhism, travels to China in 804 CE to study the *Vajrayāna* tradition, whose roots lie in Hinduism's *tantra* with the lineage tracing back to Indian teachers. Like Hindu philosopher-saint Ādi Śaṅkara, Kūkai transforms religious practice, ritual, language, and lineage in enduring ways.

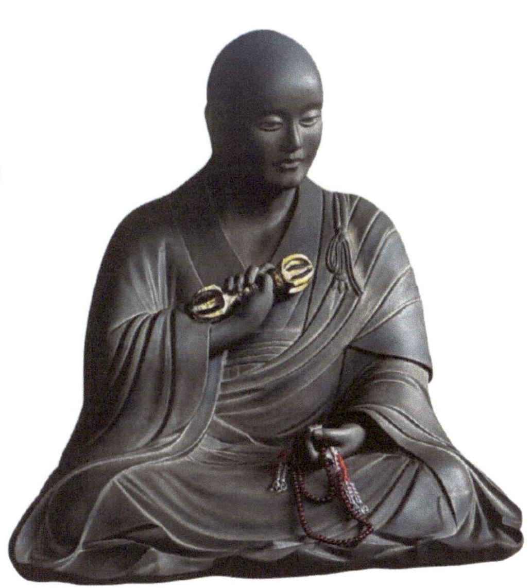

Gobyobashi and the Path to Okunoin – *Kōyasan*

The bridge at Gobyobashi ("Bridge to Mausoleum") is at the entrance to Okunoin in Kōyasan. The bridge has 37 planks, and each is carved with a Sanskrit letter representing the 37 Buddhist deities of the Diamond World Mandala. Kūkai is believed to be in eternal meditation here. This tradition echoes the Hindu idea of the ever-living guru, similar to Rāghavendra Swami's *jīva samādhi* ("conscious entombed meditation") in 1595 in Mantrālayam, India. Pilgrims cross this bridge quietly before entering the forest of memorials and walking toward Kūkai's hall. The rituals, mantras, and meditative disciplines that animate this mountain all reflect the deeper Indian sources of Shingon Buddhism, carried through China and planted firmly in Japan by Kūkai's journey.

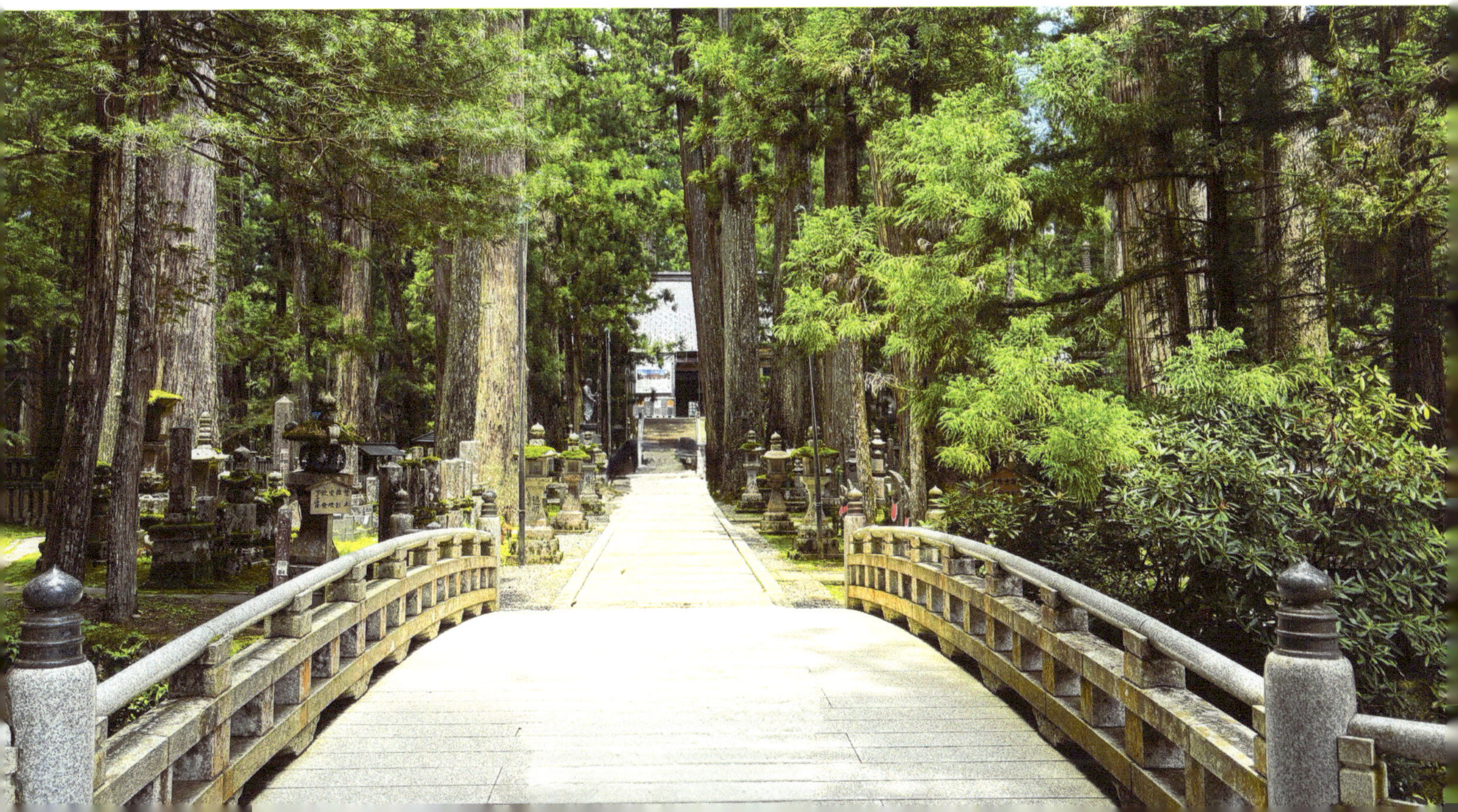

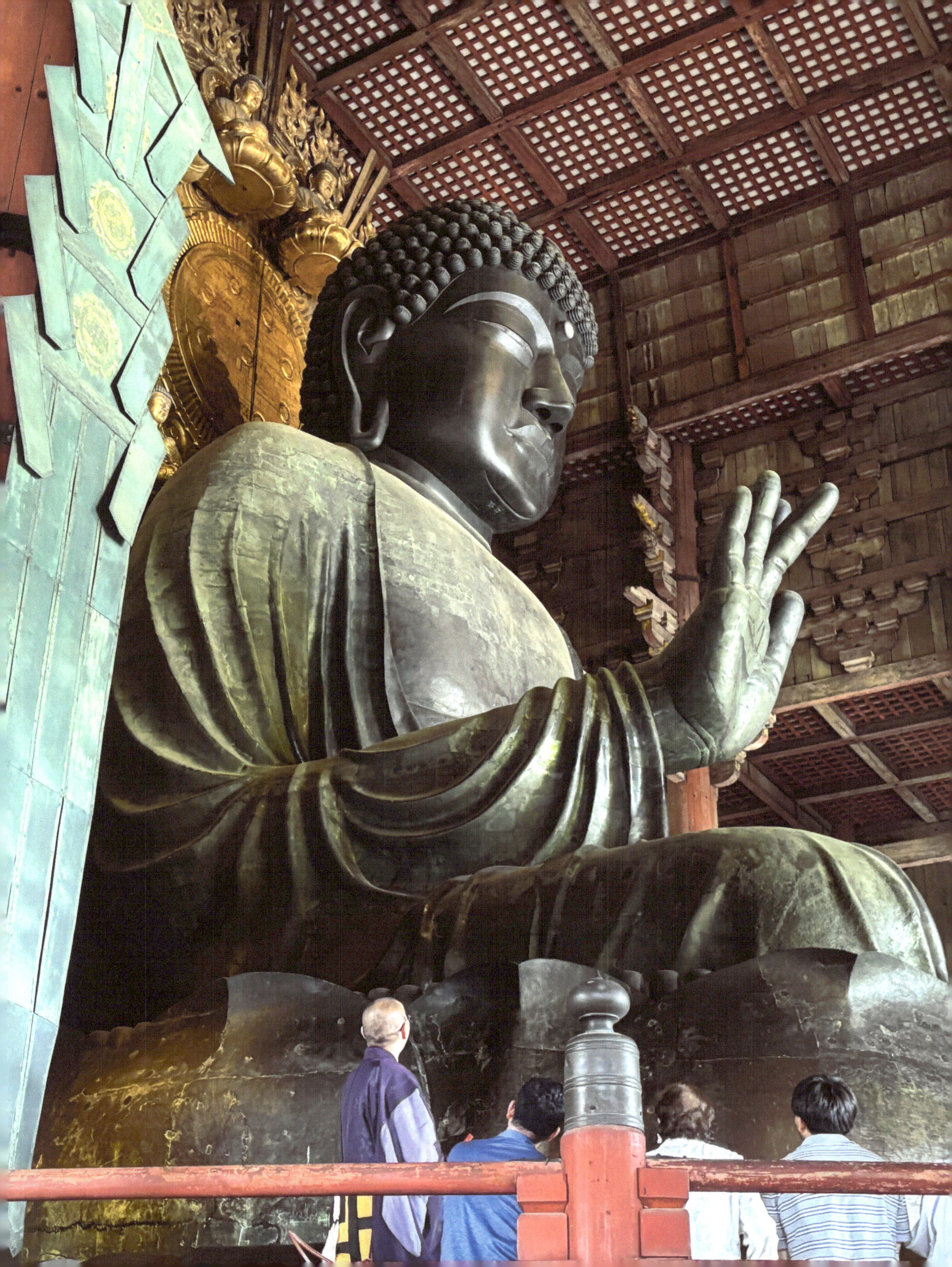

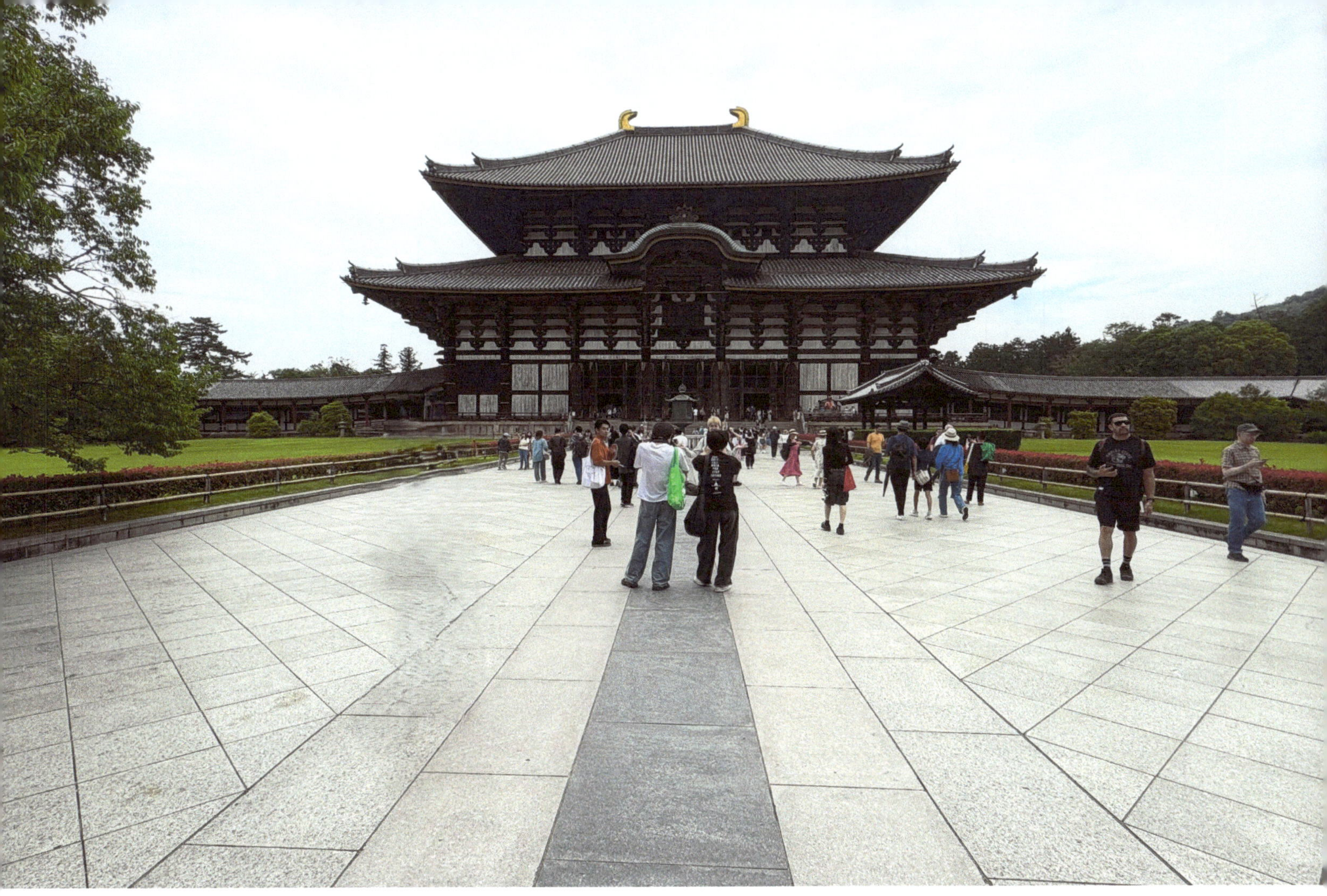

Sangoku Denshō Stones – *Tōdai-ji, Nara*

The outermost stones on either side represent India, the next rows represent China and Korea, and the gray stones in the center stand for Japan, reflecting the *Sangoku Denshō* ("Transmission through the Three Kingdoms"), with the stones sourced from those respective countries. Together they symbolize the route by which Buddhism travels from its birthplace in India, through the great cultural centers of East Asia, before finally flourishing in Japan.

Opposite page.
Great Buddha (Daibutsu) – *Tōdai-ji, Nara*

The Daibutsu is consecrated in 752 CE in a ceremony led by the South Indian monk Bodhisena, known in Japan as Baramon Sōjō ("the Brahmin priest"), who travels from India to China and then on to Japan at Emperor Shōmu's invitation. Gyōki, a celebrated Nara-period priest who helps organize the building of Tōdai-ji and later serves as general administrator of priests, greets him as a friend from a previous life and as the reincarnation of one of the Buddha's disciples. Bodhisena's eye-opening of the statue gives the temple a direct ritual link back to India and anchors it as a center of Kegon (Huayan) Buddhism. In Nara, Bodhisena teaches Sanskrit and Buddhist doctrine at Daian-ji, and later Japanese tradition recognizes his influence in early experiments with phonetic writing alongside Sanskrit *Siddham* letters. He spends the rest of his life at a temple on Mt. Tomi, just outside Nara, whose ridgeline reminds him of Vulture Peak in Bihar, India, where the Buddha is said to have preached, and he is buried there according to his wishes. Some later folklore even credits him with introducing chess to Japan.

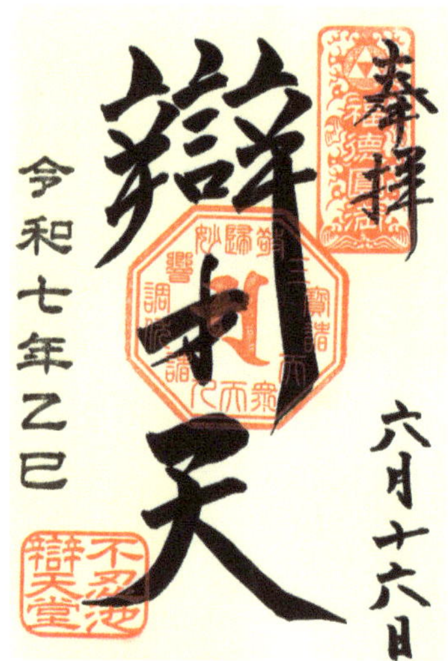

Bentendō – *Tokyo*

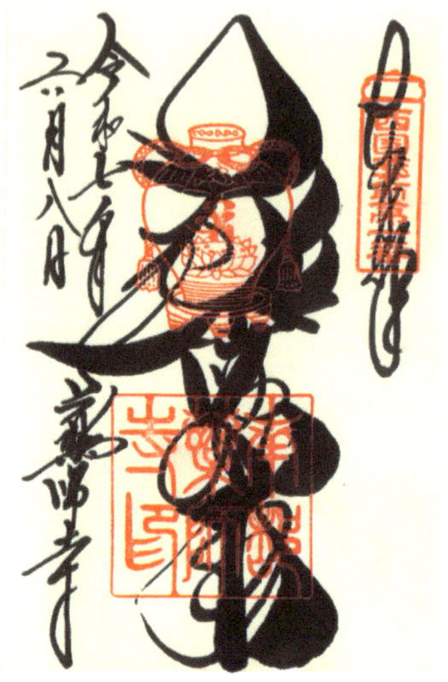

Yakushi-ji – *Nara*

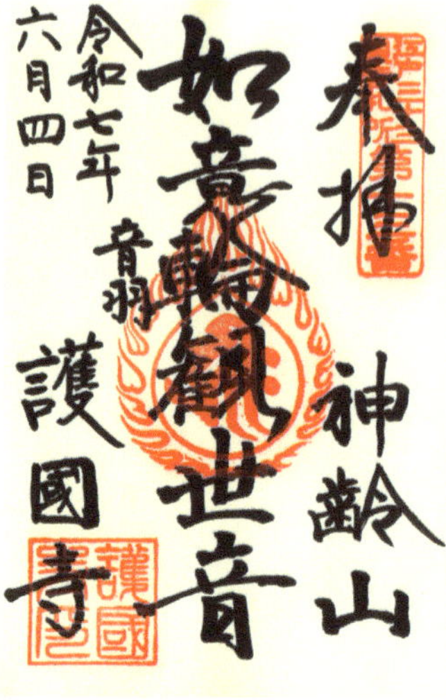

Gokoku-ji – *Tokyo*

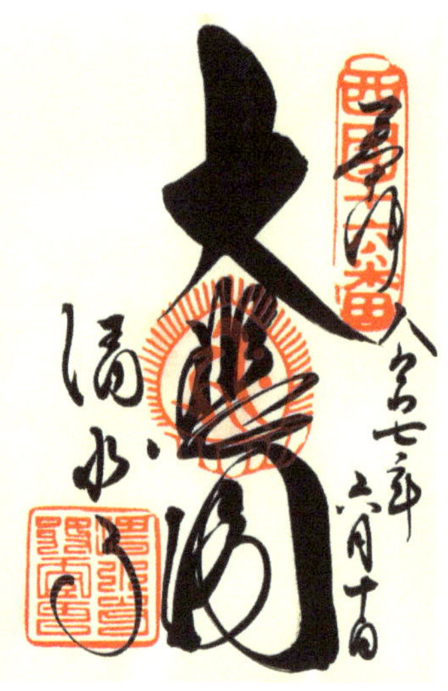

Daigan-ji – *Miyajima*

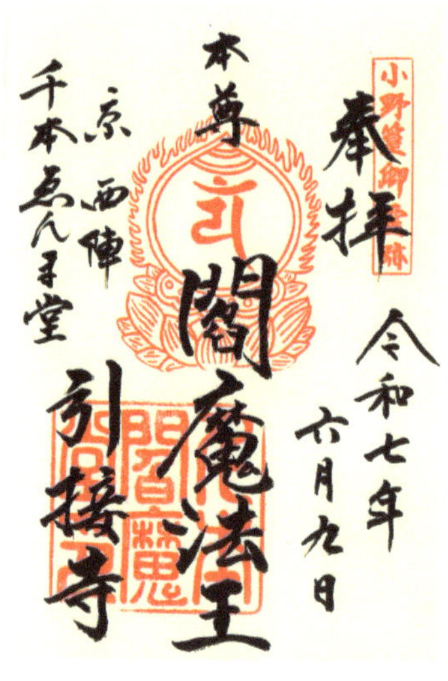

Injō-ji – *Kyoto*

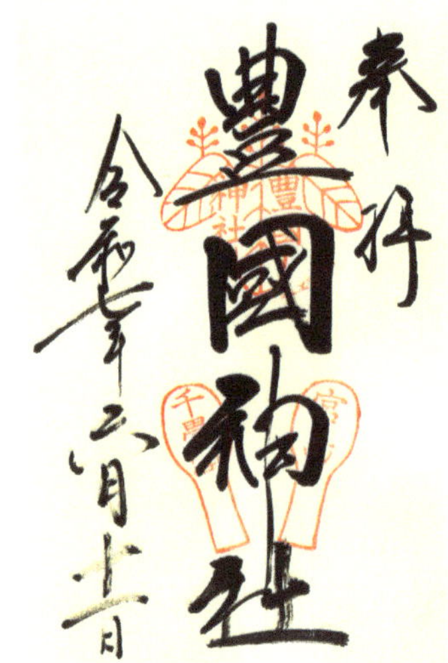

Hōkoku Jinja – *Miyajima*

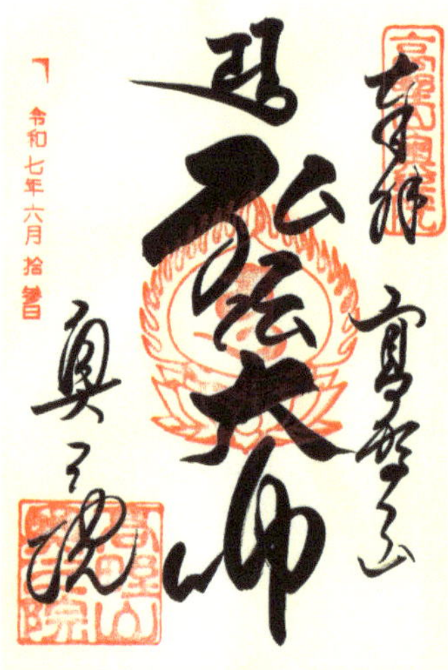

Okunoin (Kōbō Daishi) – *Kōyasan*

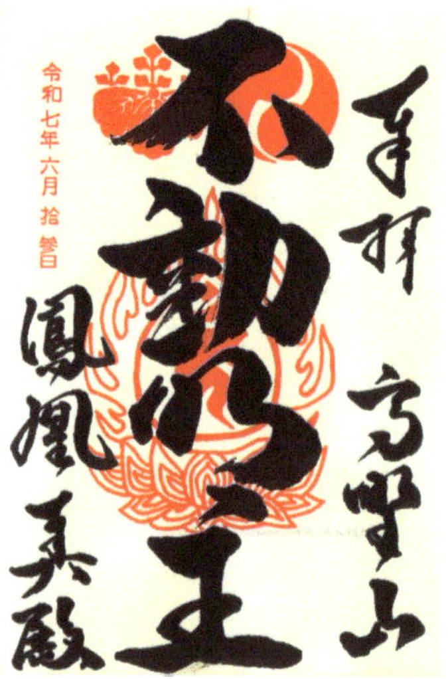

Shōjōshin-in – *Kōyasan*

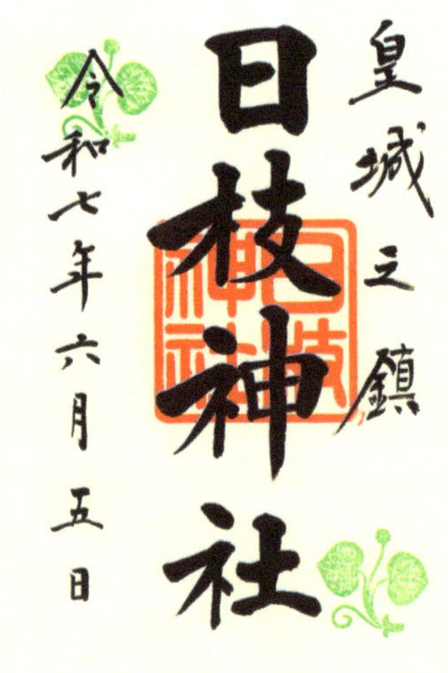

Hie Jinja – *Tokyo*

Opposite page.
Goshuin with Bonji Seed Syllables – *Sample of My Own Goshuin from Temples Across Japan*

Goshuin begin in the 8th century CE as proof of sutra-copying by pilgrims and later become the record of a visit. Temple staff calligraph the name of the temple, the principal deity, the date, and add vermilion seals. Many stamps include *bonji* (Siddhaṃ) seed syllables for deities such as Fudō Myōō (Skt. *acala*). In the 88-temple Shikoku (one of the main islands) *henro* established by Kūkai, modern pilgrims still walk, pray, and collect goshuin-style stamps at each stop of the 1,200 km beginning and ending with Kōyasan.

This page (bottom).
Gokoku-ji – *Tokyo*

Gokoku-ji is founded in 1681 CE as a Shingon temple dedicated to Nyoirin Kannon and later becomes one of the Edo 33 Kannon (for Kannon's 33 forms) pilgrimage sites in the Tokyo area. Its main hall is a rare wooden structure in Tokyo that survives major earthquakes and the World War II air raids, including the firebombing raids that devastated much of the city.

Next page.
Kiyomizu-dera – *Kyoto*

Kiyomizu-dera ("Pure Water Temple") stands above a spring on Mount Otowa and has welcomed pilgrims for over a thousand years as one of Japan's great Kannon temples. It is Temple 16 on the Saigoku Kannon pilgrimage, an earlier 33-temple circuit that takes shape around the 11th–12th centuries CE and links sites devoted to Kannon (Skt. *Avalokiteśvara*) in Kansai area. The suffix -dera, meaning temple in Japanese, is derived from Skt. *vihāra* and still used in many Indian languages today as *ḍerā* or *dera*, meaning a sacred space or monastic dwelling. Medieval works such as *Sangoku denki* (14th–15th centuries CE, "Stories of the Three Countries"), a renowned classic of Japanese medieval literature which takes place at Kiyomizu-dera, describe India (*Tenjiku*), China (*Daimin*), and Japan (*Wa*) as a connected Buddhist world.

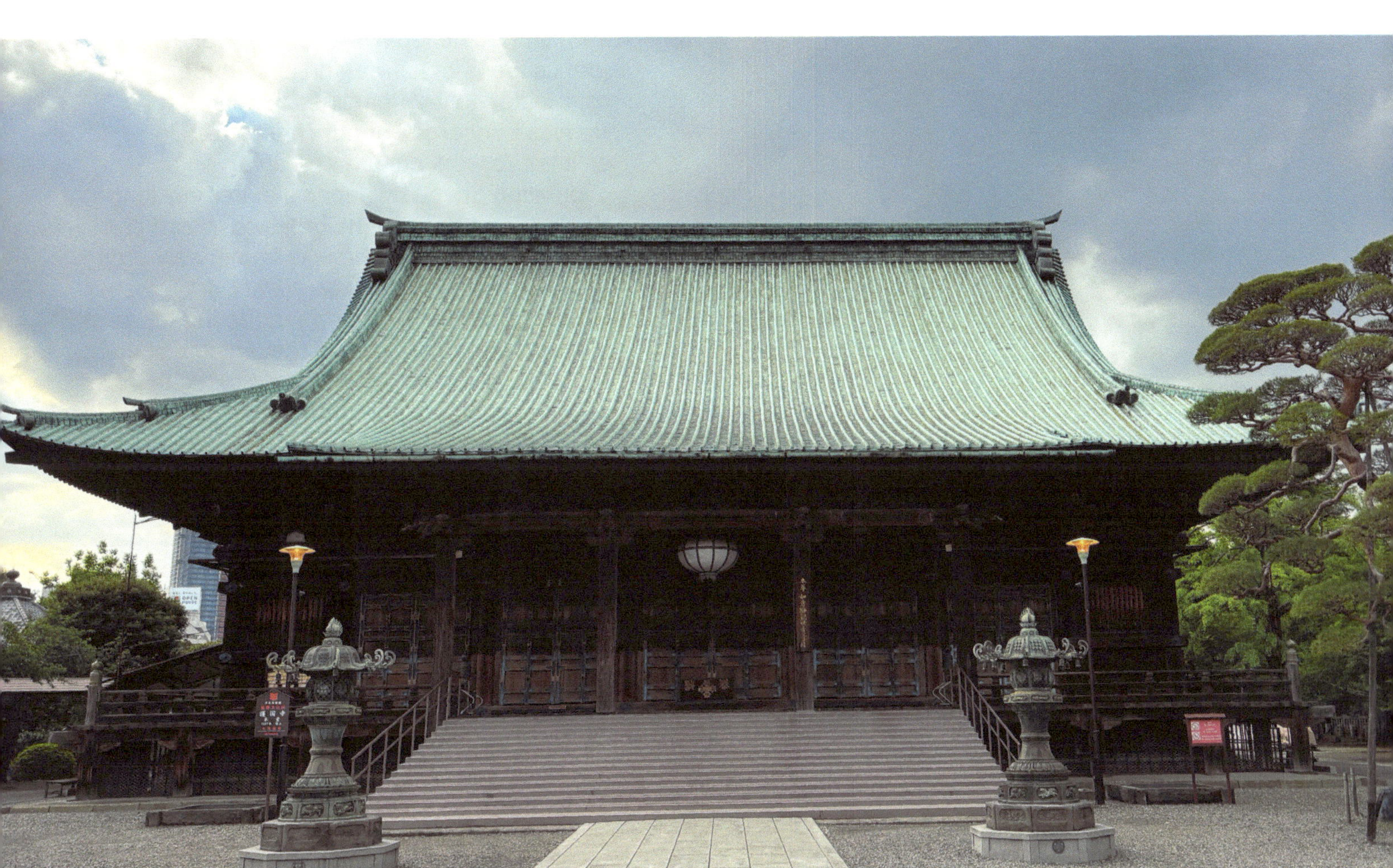

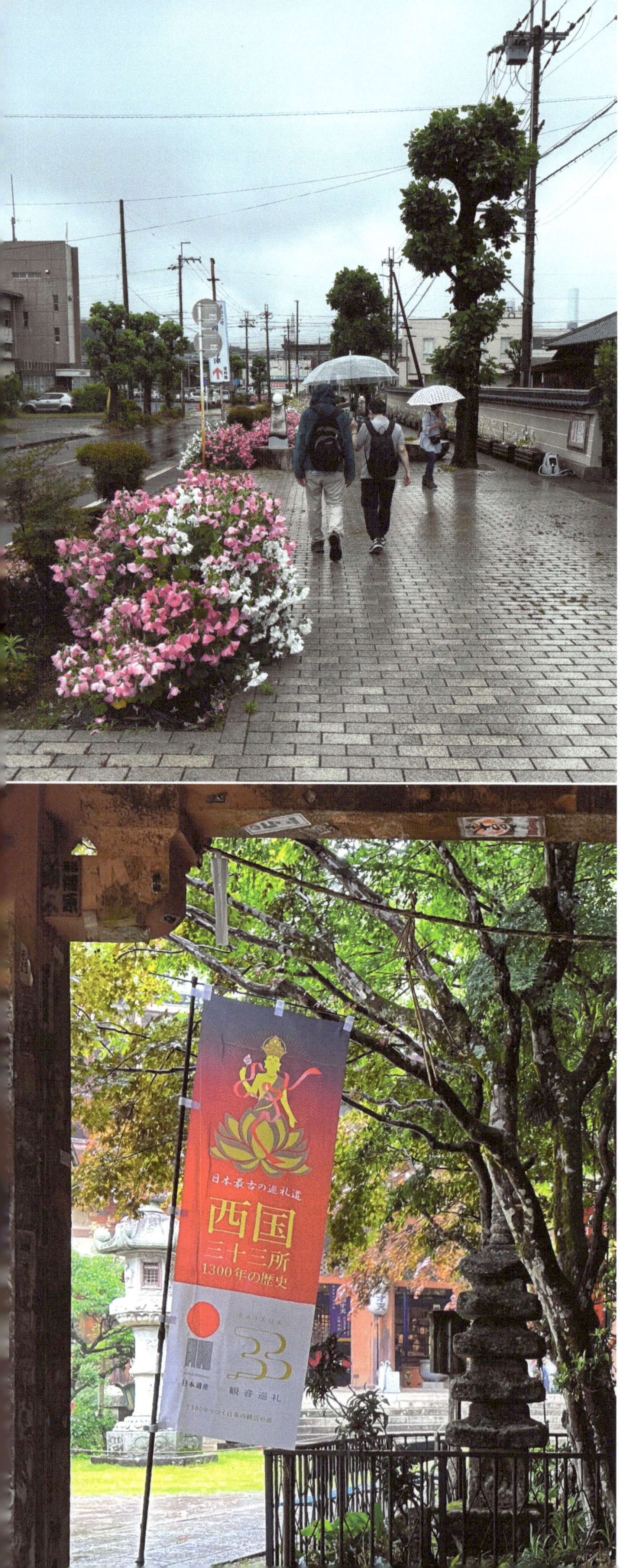

This page (top and bottom).
Walking with a Saigoku Pilgrim – *Takashima*
Saigoku Kannon Prayer Flag – *Hōgon-ji, Chikubushima*

During my travels in Japan, I had the privilege of meeting many pilgrims. On my return journey from Chikubushima, I had a memorable meeting with Mr. Ueda from Osaka, who was completing the Saigoku Kannon pilgrimage: 33 temples dedicated to Kannon, plus 3 *bangai* (additional temples for prominent deities), across the Kansai region. He told me that even though he grew up Buddhist, as he put it, "like the vast majority of people in Japan," he never had the time to visit all the temples on this route. In his youth, he visited a few near Osaka and felt a real sense of spiritual tranquility. Now, with more time as he's gotten older, he has made it his mission to complete the full pilgrimage.

He also shared insights into Buddhism in modern Japan, saying that Buddhism and the Buddhist worldview has long been, and still is, deeply intertwined with almost every aspect of Japanese life. Having lived in the U.S. for a while, he felt Japan's Buddhist worldview, with its ideas of karma and accountability, contributes to it's cleanliness and safety. He was concerned about challenges like an intense work culture and an aging population driven by Japan's extremely long life expectancies, but he believed Japan can overcome them, and he was immensely proud of Japan's ethos of *wakon yōsai* ("Japanese spirit, Western techniques"): adopting the best of global technology while remaining distinctly Japanese, to make one of the most developed societies on the planet and a major global economic and cultural superpower. He was also proud of the fact that Japan is the 3rd most popolous dharmic country and, in his opinion, the only one to have preserved that worldview throughout all aspects of society as a result of not being colonized. He also said that he is looking forward to visiting the original Buddhist sites in India once he retires.

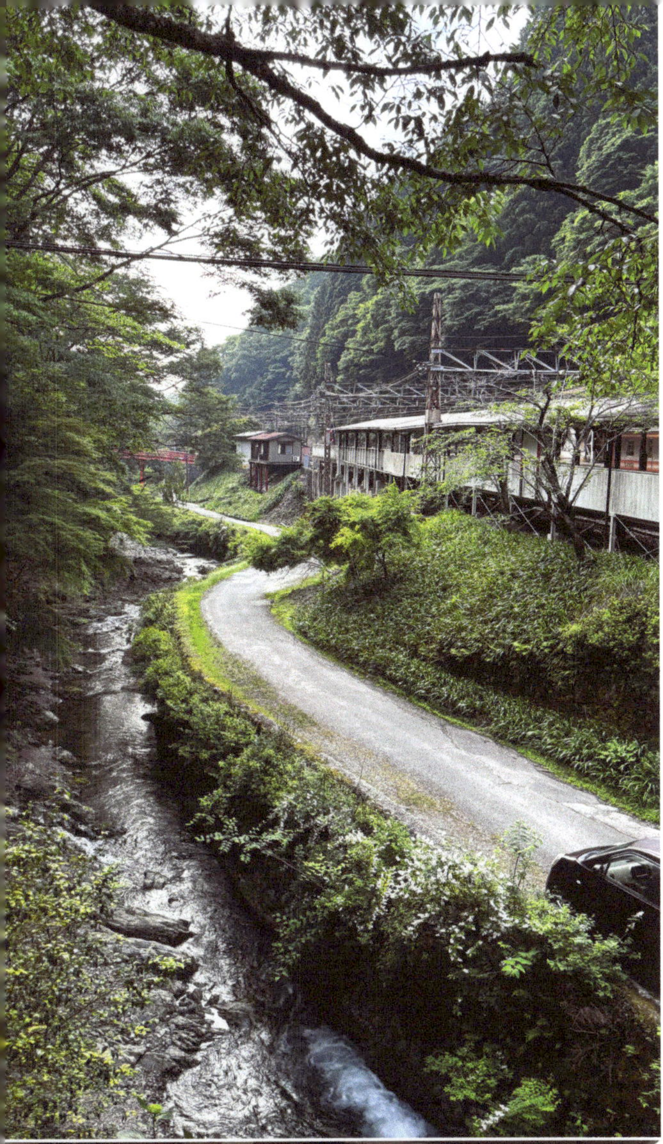

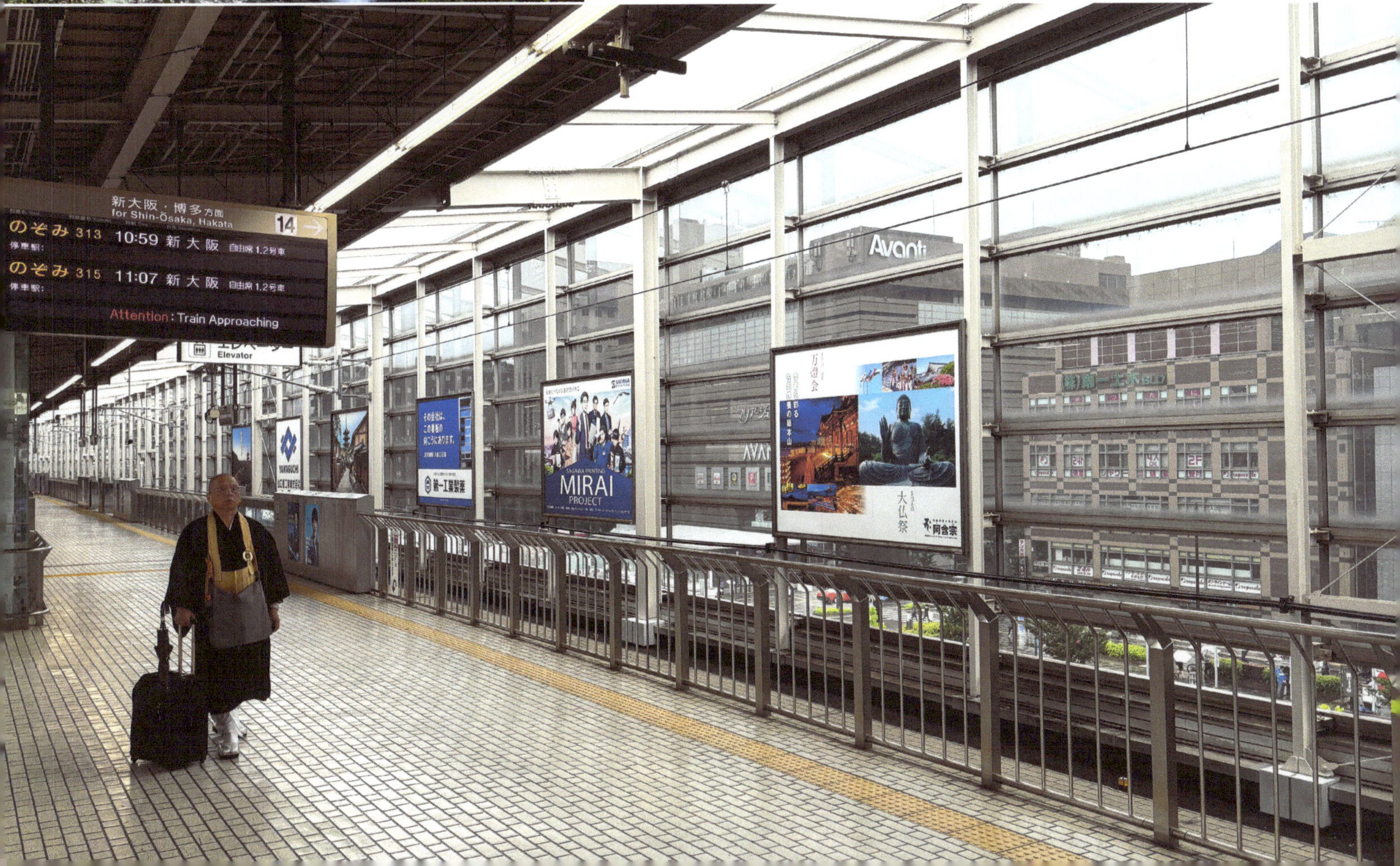

This page (top and bottom).
Fudōtani River – *Near the entrance to Kōyasan*
Monk Waiting for the Shinkansen – *Kyoto Station*

I met a father and daughter from Tokyo on the funicular railcar climbing into the mountains of Kōyasan. As the car inched upward, he told me that, in his youth, he had walked the entire 1,200 km Shikoku 88-temple pilgrimage on foot. Now he had come back to do the full circuit again, this time with his daughter, starting their journey at Kōyasan. As I rode the bus from the Kōyasan rail station at the mountain's edge to the main temple complex, I spotted them waving from the roadside in the traditional clothing of Shikoku pilgrims featuring the following on their clothing: *dōgyō ninin* ("two traveling together"), signifying the belief that Kūkai is traveling with them, along with *Namu Daishi Henjō Kongō* mantras for Kūkai, some of their favorite sutras, the Sanskrit character for Kūkai and their favorite deity. They chose to approach the main temple in the traditional way, bowing at the *chōishi* stone markers along the way, each one linked to the five elements, with bonji seed syllables *a*, *va*, *ra*, *ha*, *kha* carved into the stone.

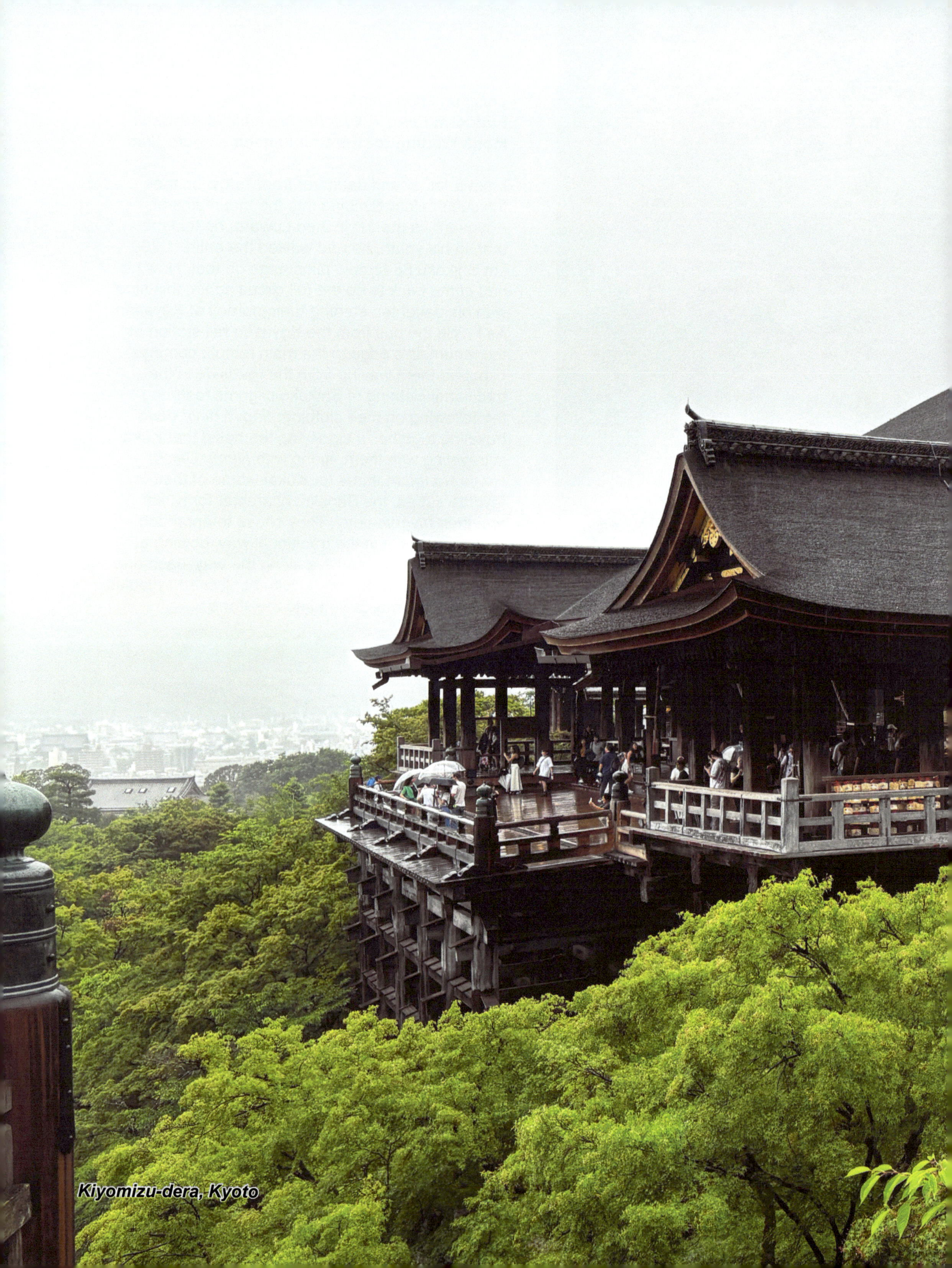

Kiyomizu-dera, Kyoto

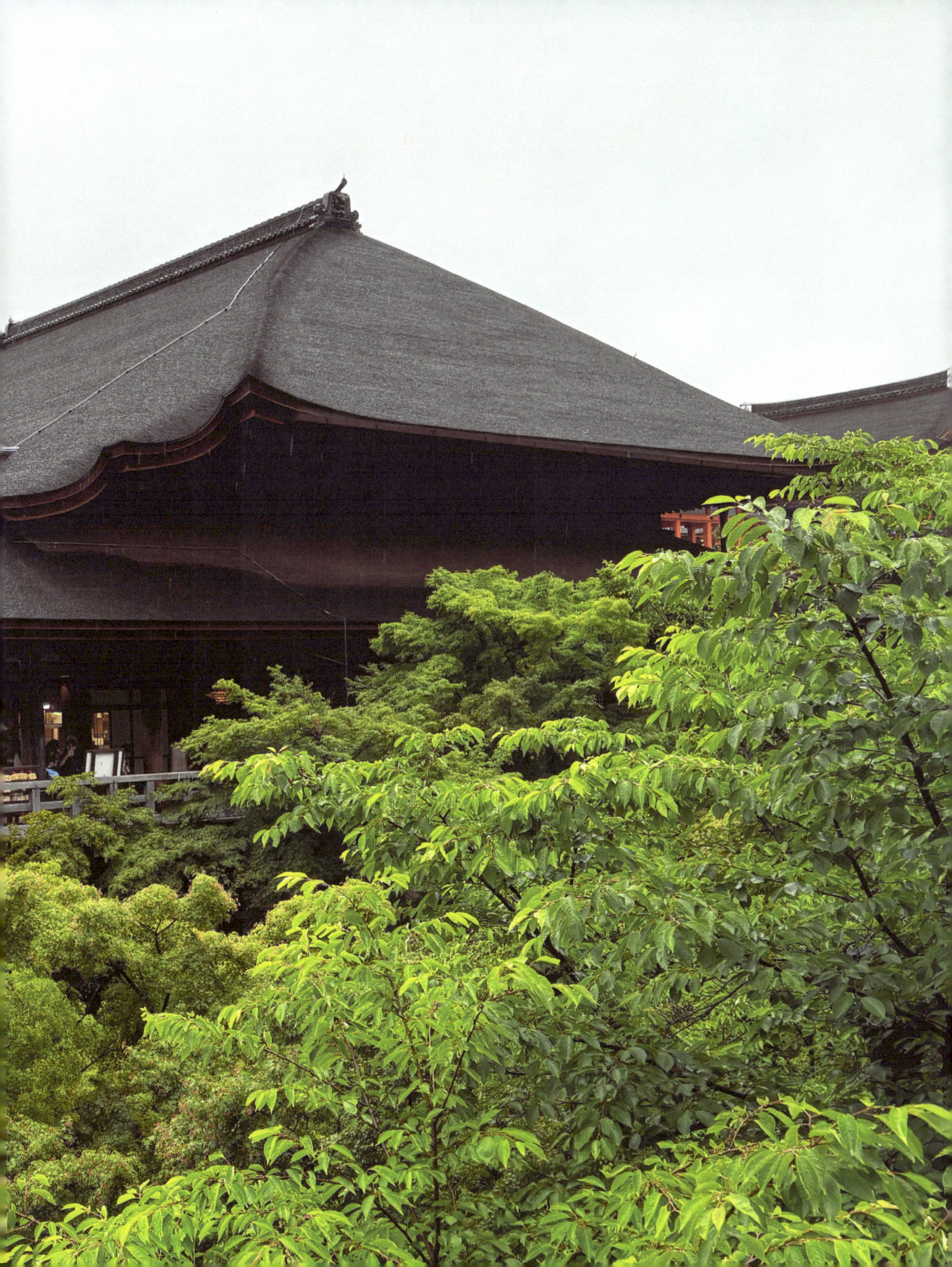

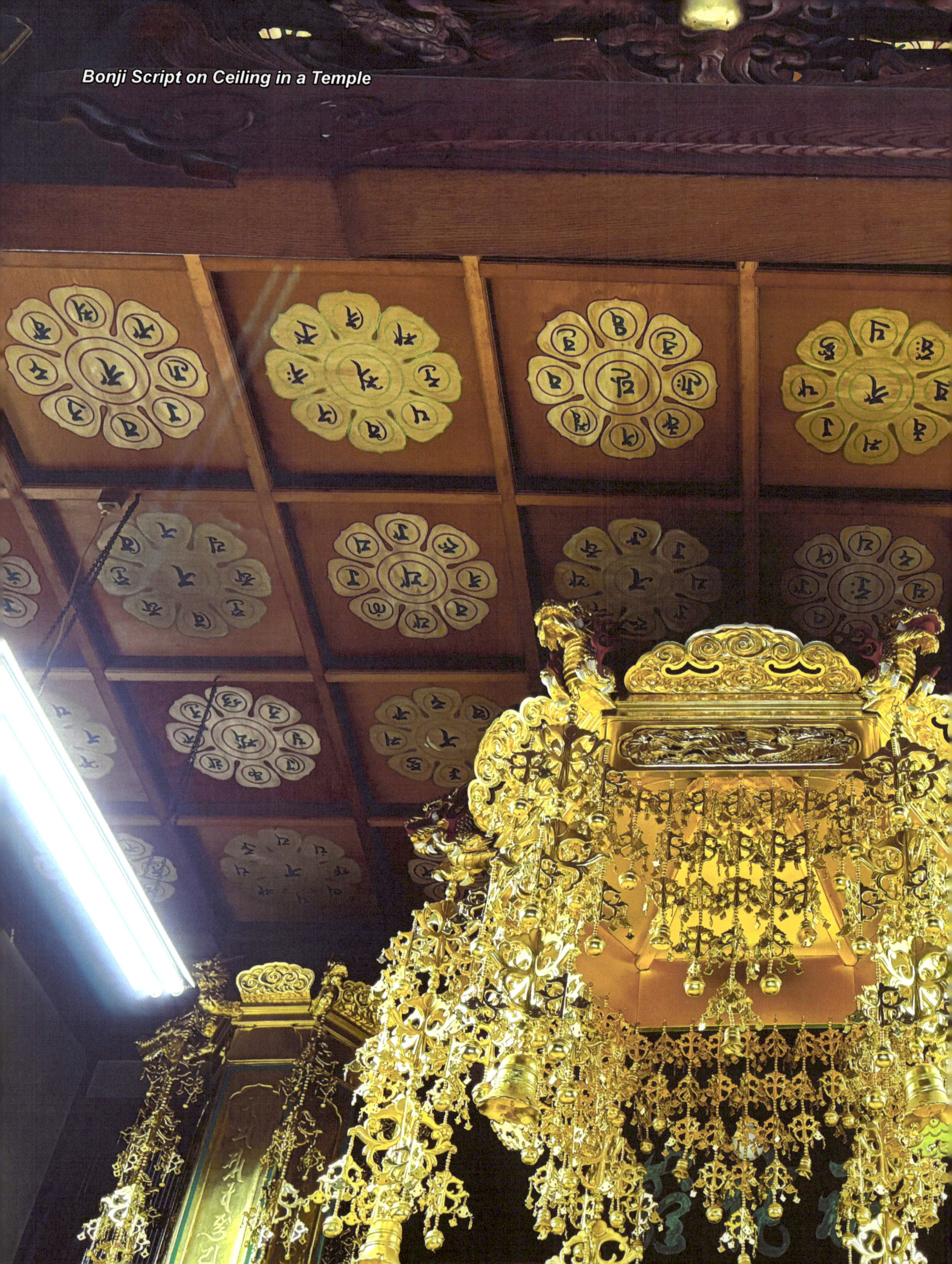

Bonji Script on Ceiling in a Temple

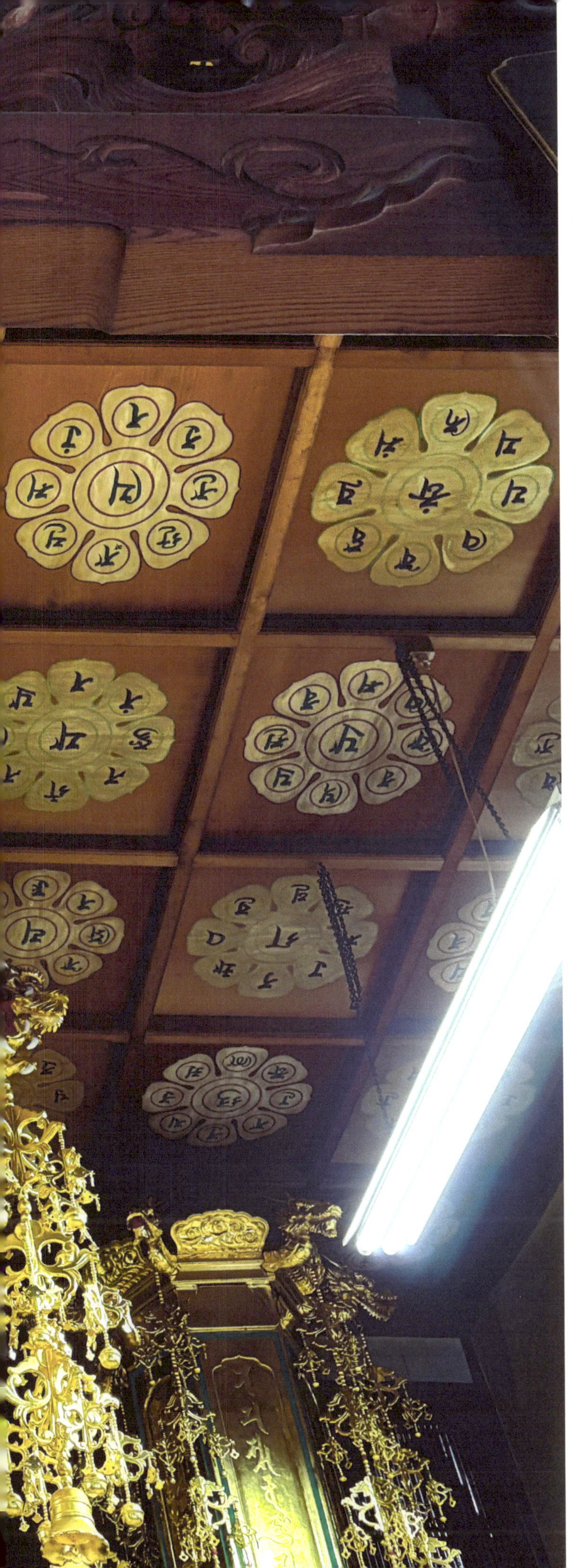

Language & Script

TWO

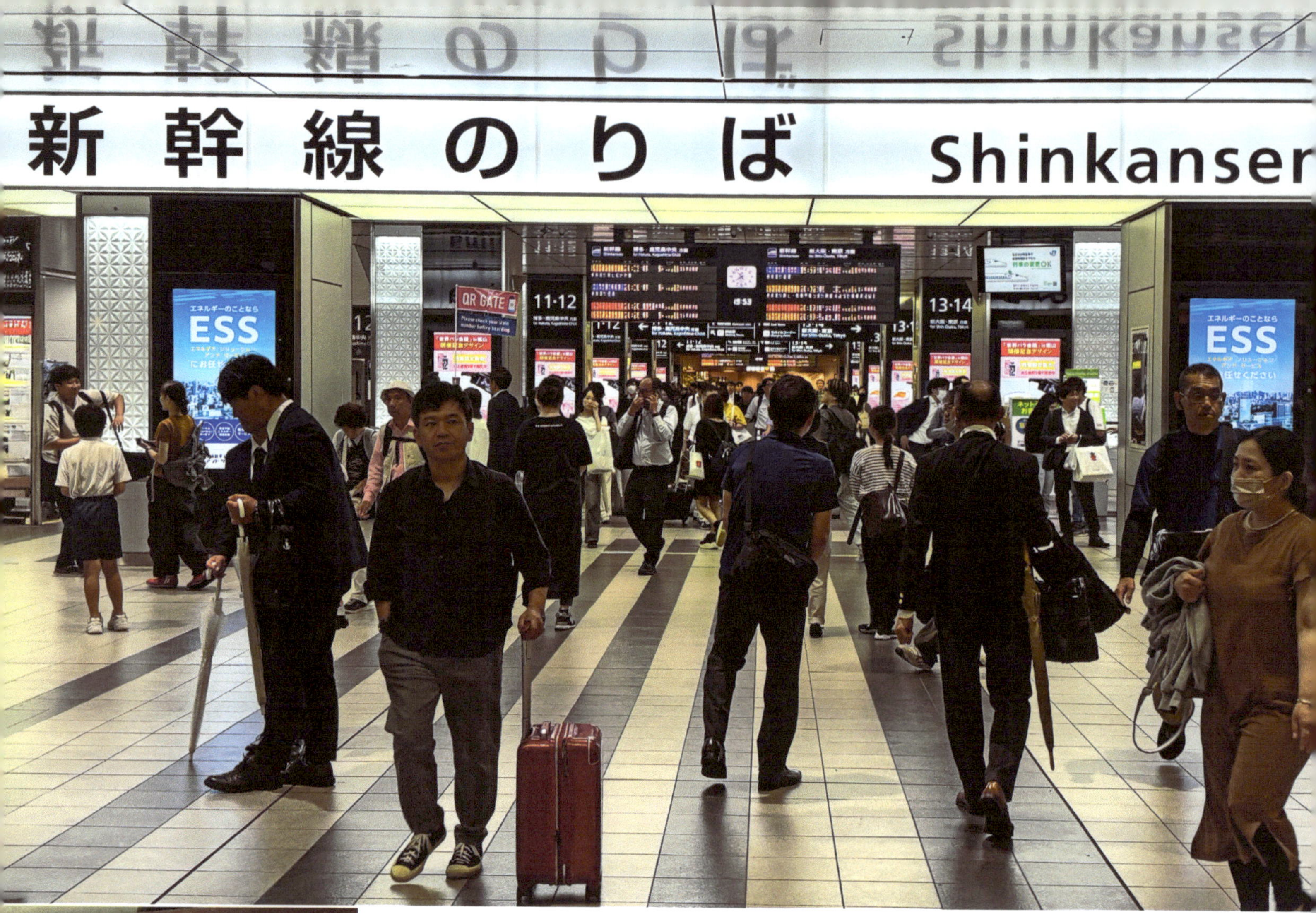

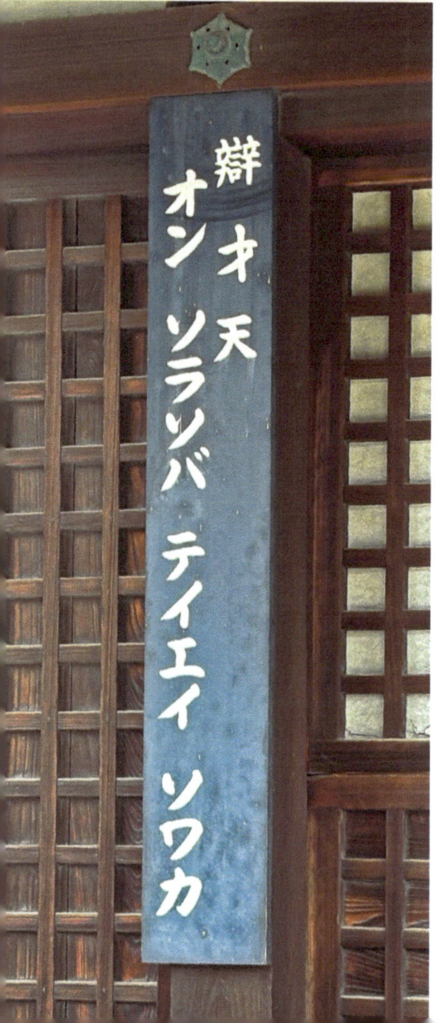

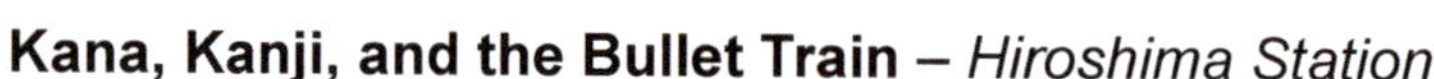

Kana, Kanji, and the Bullet Train – *Hiroshima Station*

Japanese writing uses four parallel scripts: kanji for meaning, hiragana and katakana as phonetic syllabaries, and bonji (Siddham) for sacred mantras preserved in temples. Above the Shinkansen concourse, three bold kanji spell 新幹線, literally "new main line," the formal name of the bullet train. Beside them, のりば (no-ri-ba) is written in hiragana to show how to read *noriba* in a simple sound-only script. Sanskrit sound and writing patterns helped shape Japan's kana, as seen in the rounded shapes of の and り (ri), whose curves resemble Devanagari न and रि.

Sarasvati Mantra in Katakana – *Tō-ji, Kyoto*

At Kūkai's Tō-ji temple in Kyoto, the Benzaiten hall doorway carries Sarasvati's mantra written vertically in katakana: オン ソラソバ ティエイ ソワカ (*on sorasobateiei sowaka*). This spells out the Sanskrit oṃ sarasvatyai svāhā in Japanese phonetic script, with "Benzaiten" written in kanji beside it. Katakana began as monks' simplified marks in the margins of sutras, a way to spell out difficult Chinese and Sanskrit sounds more clearly. Together with hiragana, kanji, and bonji, Japan's writing system still carries the visual and sound imprint of Sanskrit.

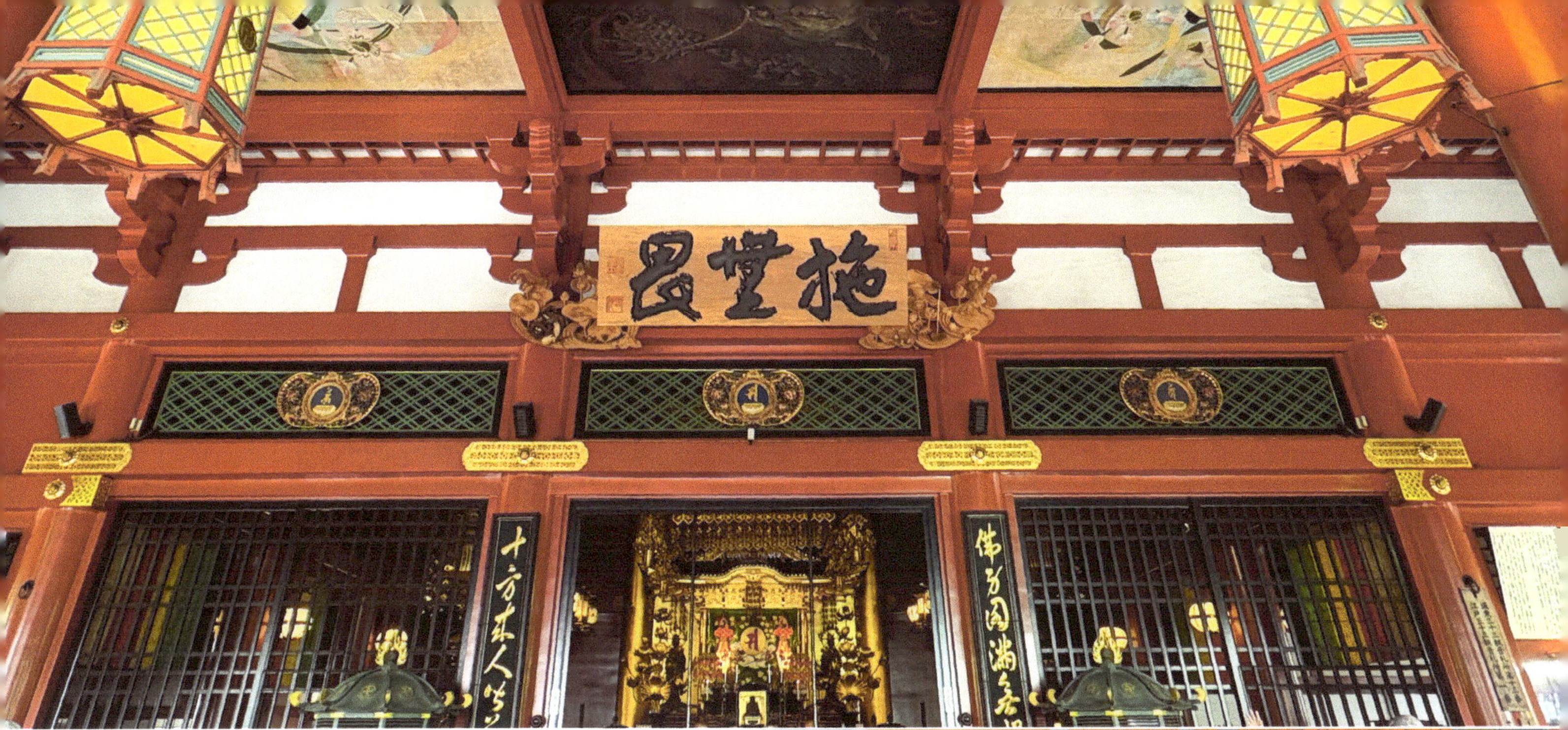

Clockwise from above.
Bonji Seed Syllables Across Japan – *Sensō-ji, Tokyo; Injō-ji, Kyoto; Hōgon-ji, Chikubushima; Shitennō-ji, Osaka*

At Sensō-ji, the bonji *sa* for Kannon is flanked by *hūṃ* and *hāṃ*, seed syllables of Aizen Myōō (Skt. *Manmatha*, a Hindu deity of love) and Fudō Myōō (Skt. *Acala*, related to Śiva). At Injō-ji, protective prayer books pair the Japanese zodiac animals with Sanskrit *bījākṣaras* (seed syllables). In Hōgon-ji, the *sa* of Sarasvatī/Benzaiten in bonji sits at the center of a dense field of mantras. The hanging lamps at Shitennō-ji are inscribed with bonji syllables. Anyone who can read Sanskrit will find plenty to read in Japanese temples.

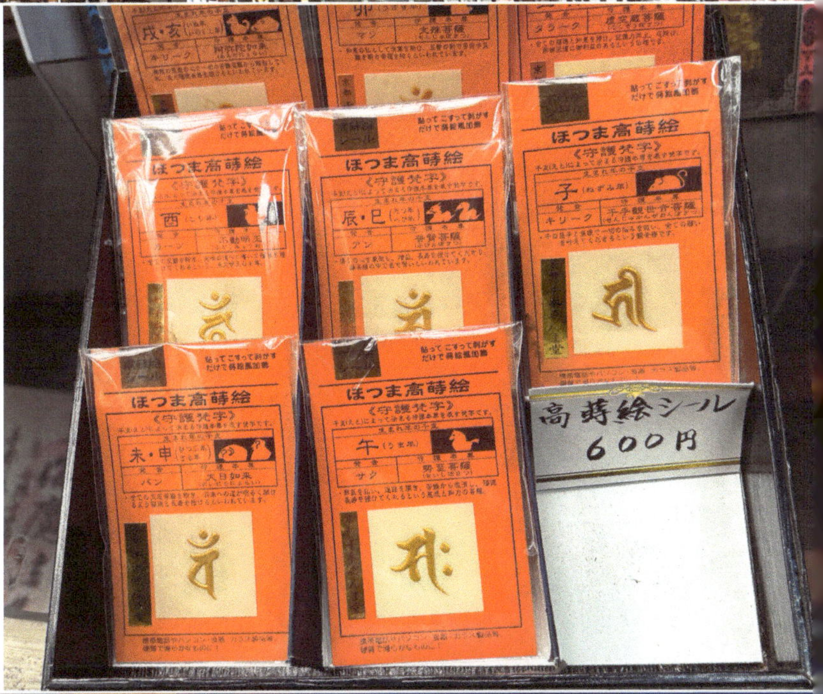

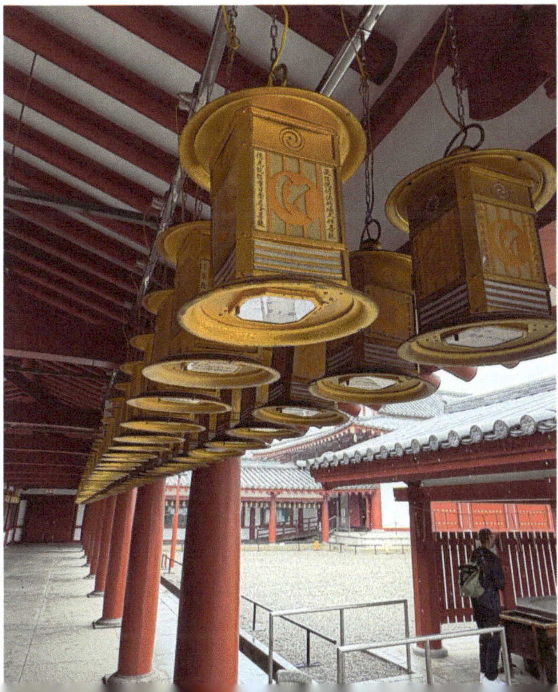

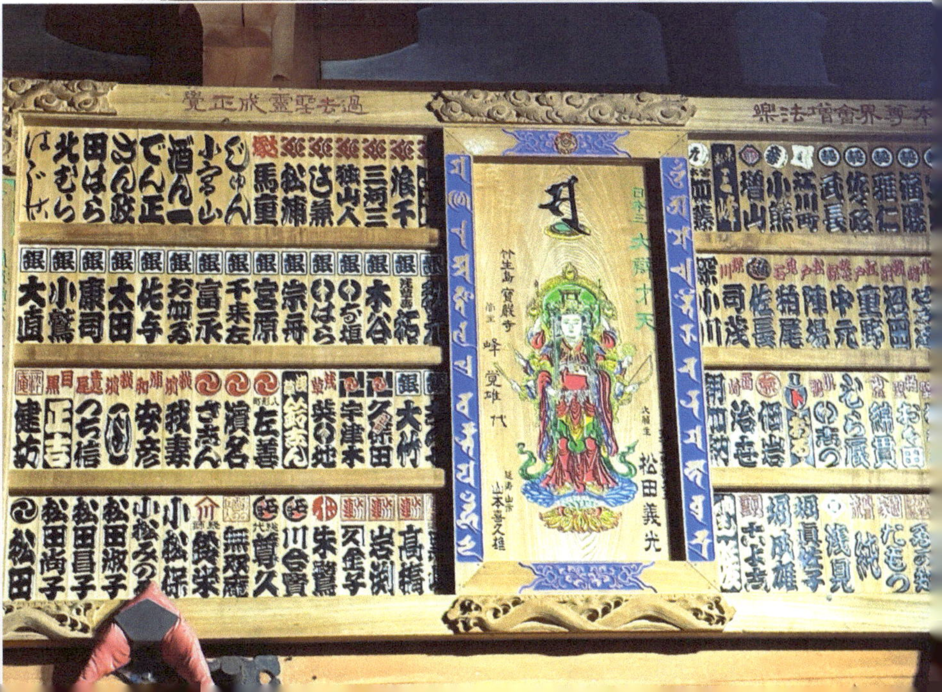

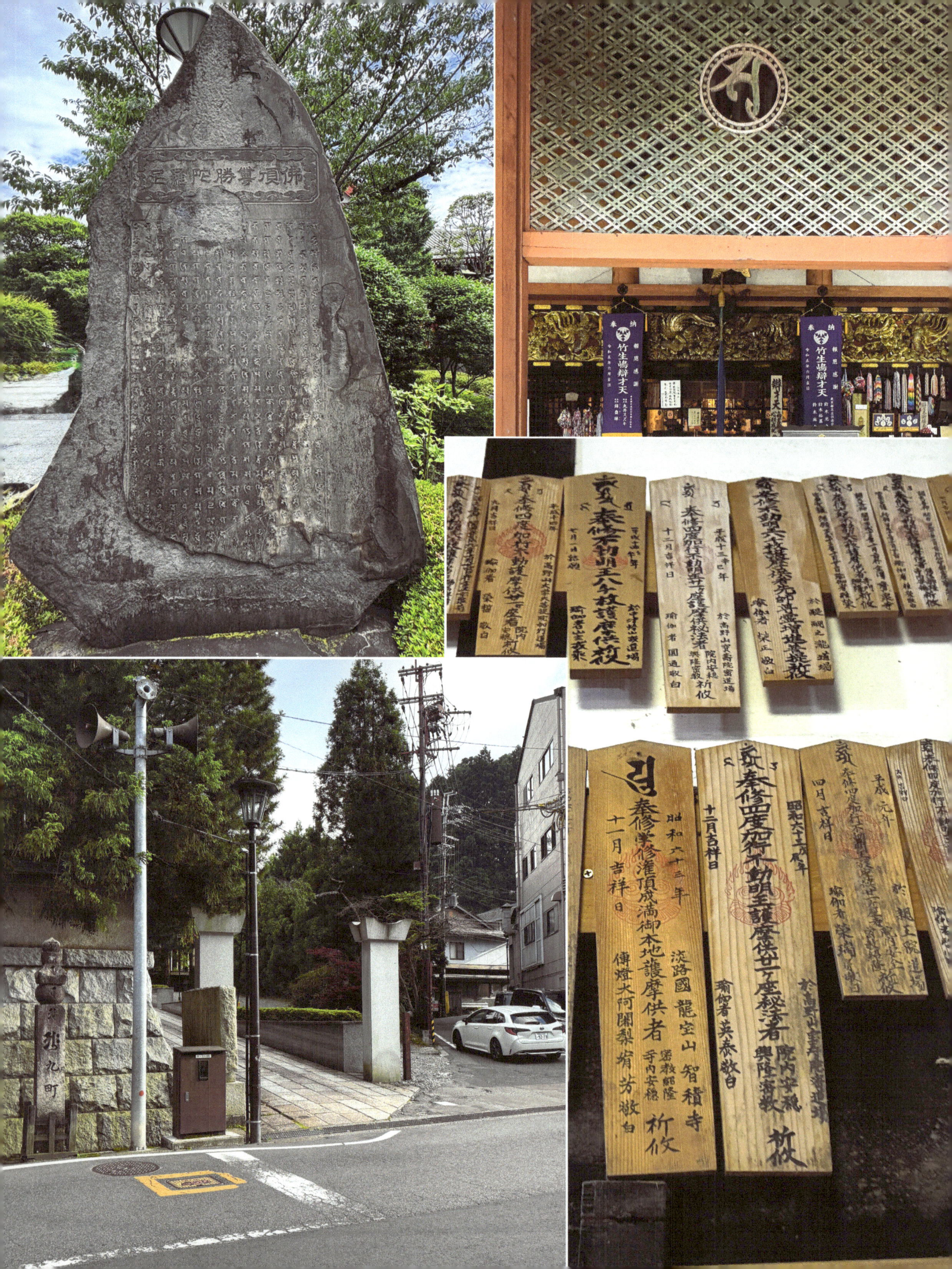

佛頂尊勝陀羅尼
竹生島辯才天
竹生島辯才天
奉修学修灌頂成満御本地護摩供者
昭和六十三年
十一月吉祥日
淡路國 龍宝山 智積寺
傳燈大阿闍梨宥芳敬白
祈攸
奉修四度加行不動明王護摩供廿一ケ座秘法者
十二月吉祥日
瑜伽者 英泰敬白
祈攸

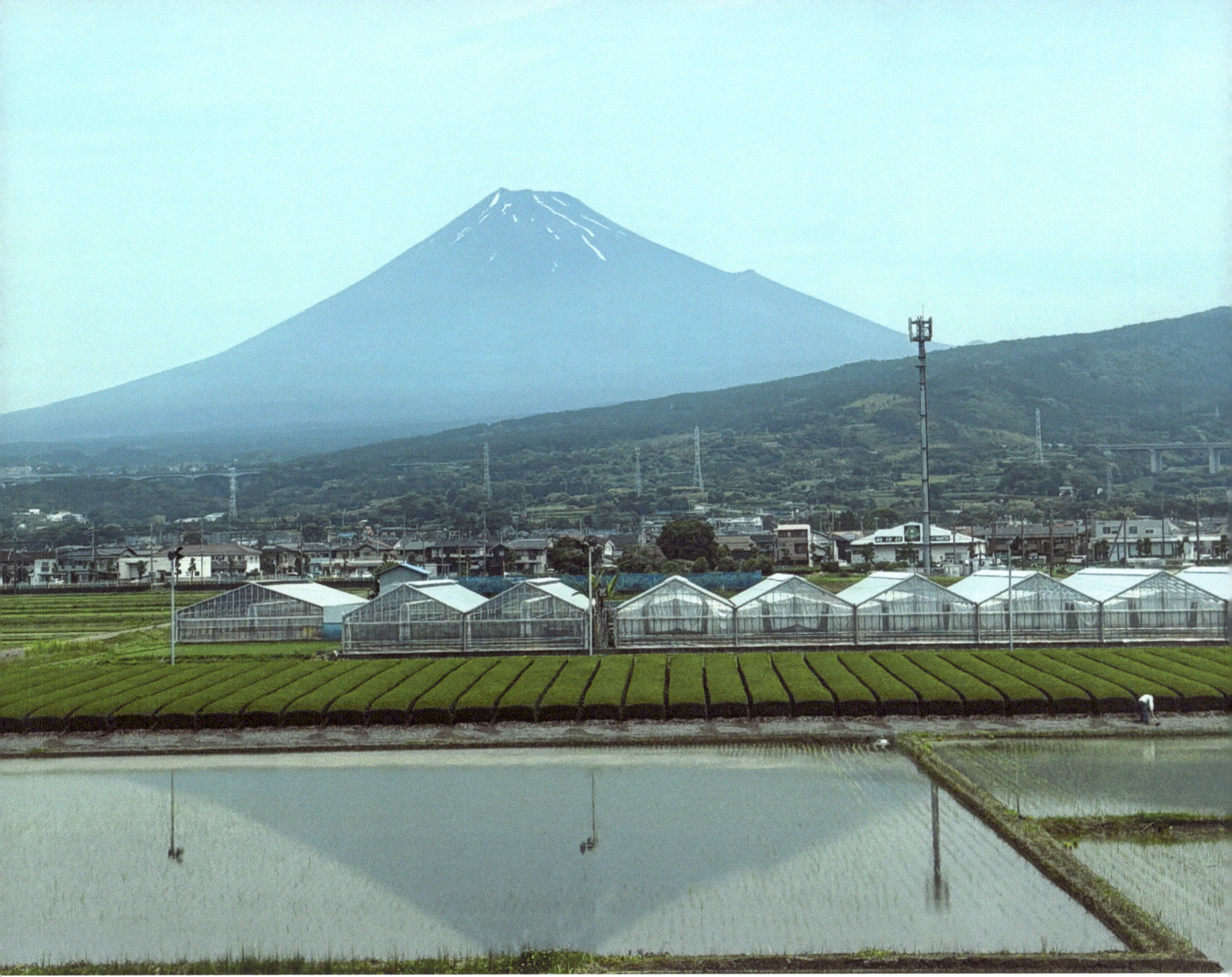

Opposite page (clockwise from top left).

At Sensō-ji, this stone tablet has Skt. *uṣṇīṣa-vijayā dhāraṇī* in *bonji*, and you will find Sanskrit words from Hindu prayers, such as *oṃ*, *svāhā*, and *namo*. Vajrayāna adopted the Hindu belief in the power of sacred sound, where the force of a mantra lies not only in meaning but in the vibration of the syllables themselves. At a Benzaiten (Skt. *Sarasvatī*) temple, the *bonji* syllable *sa* is placed prominently at the entrance. A monk at Shōjōshin-in in Kōyasan shared that the wooden plaques with *bonji* denote the graduation of their students. And in Kōyasan, even a roadside stone pillar carries *bonji*; you can clearly see *a*, *va*, *ra*, *ha*, and *kha* on the upper layers, with shapes strikingly close to present-day Sanskrit Devanāgarī script.

This page above.
Fujisan and Rice Fields – *Fuji*

Japanese and Telugu share a few striking parallels. Both come from rice-based cultures, where food and rice blur into the same everyday word: *gohan* in Japanese can mean rice and "a meal," much like *annam* in Telugu (my mother tongue). There is also a theory linking the kanji character for "rice" to *manji* (Skt. *svastika*), a symbol of fortune and abundance in a rice-centered world. Structurally, both languages follow a subject–object–verb order, are agglutinative, and it is postulated that Japonic and Dravidian languages may be distantly related.

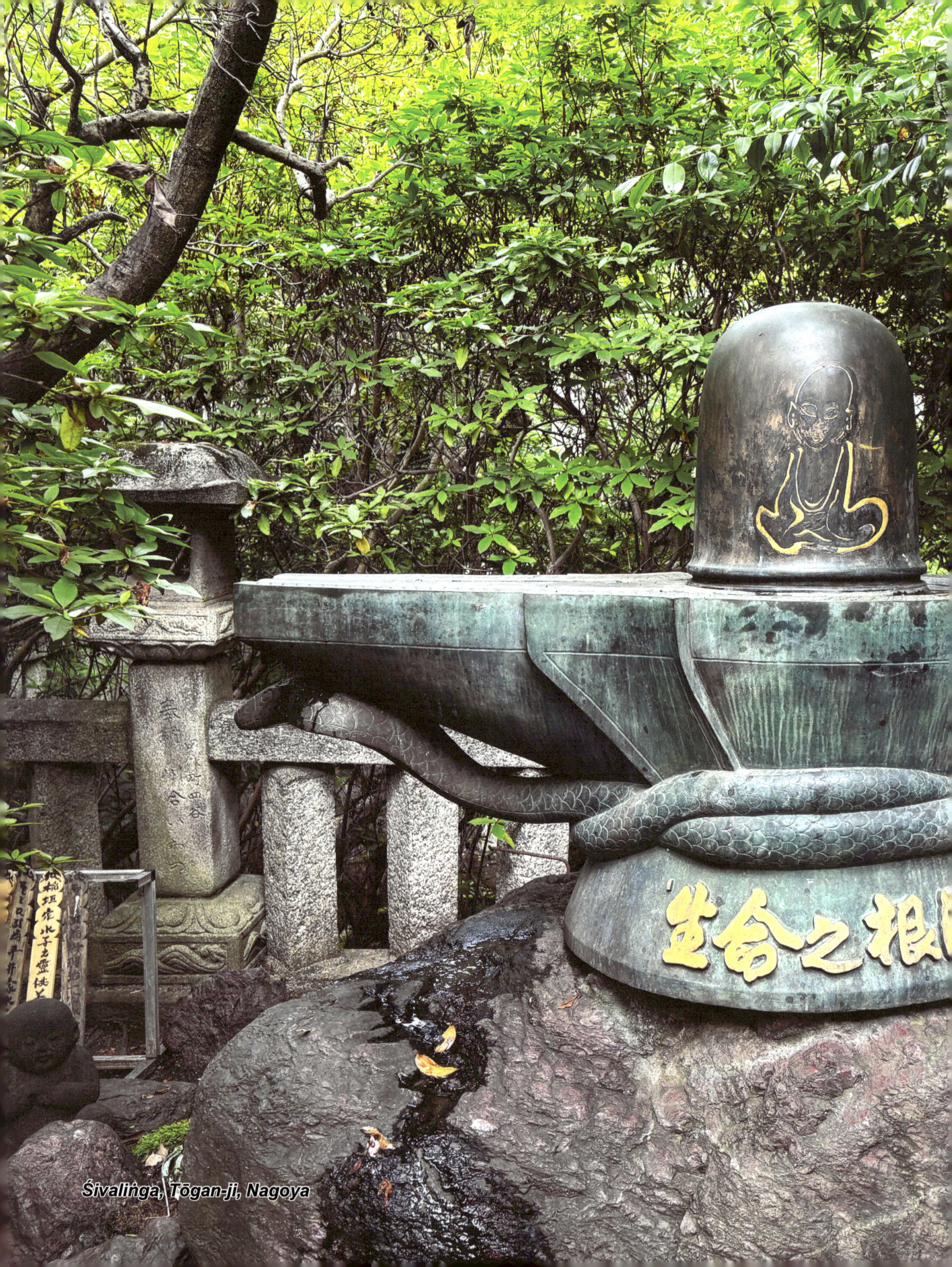

Śivaliṅga, Tōgan-ji, Nagoya

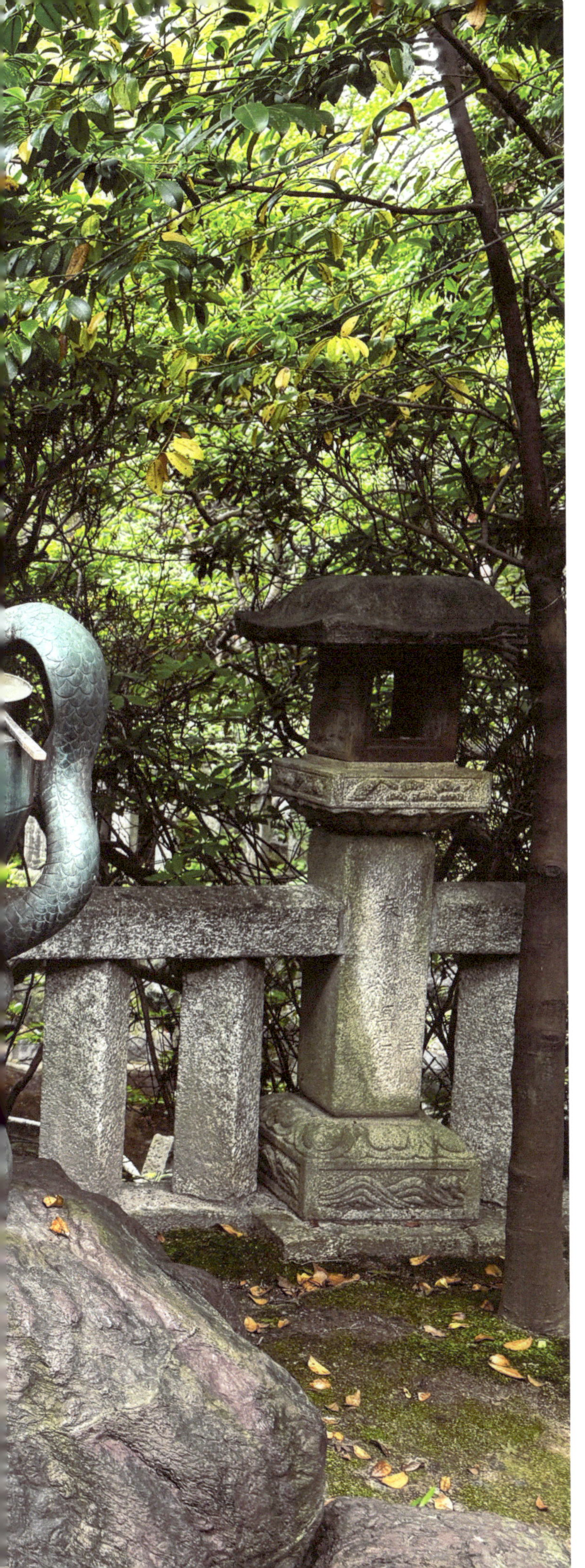

Shared Deities

THREE

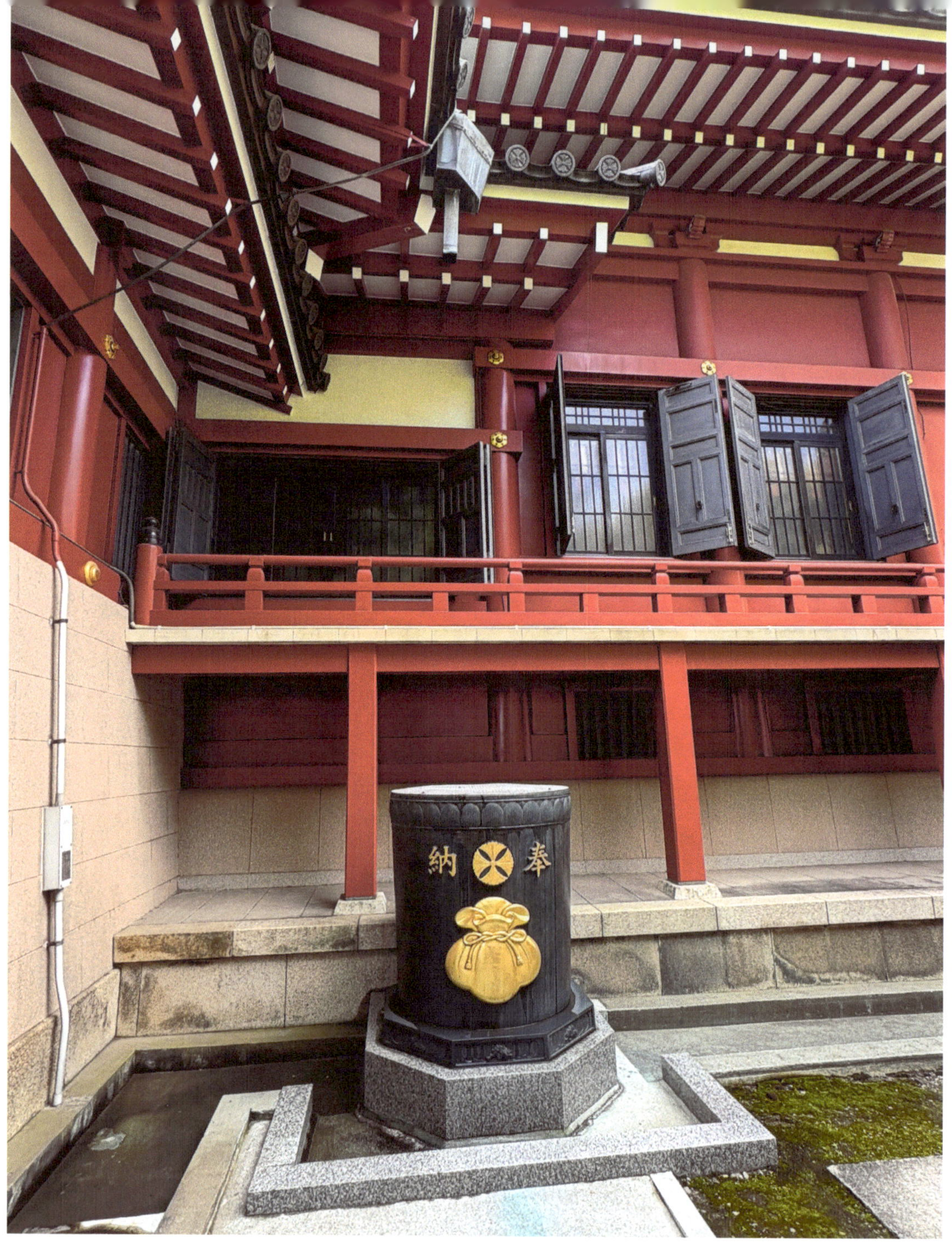

This page and opposite page (clockwise from above).
Hibutsu temples – *Matsuchiyama Shōden, Tokyo; Tōgan-ji, Nagoya; Matsuchiyama Shōden, Tokyo*

Hibutsu is "hidden Buddha," a practice of treating certain Buddhist icons as so potent that they're kept out of sight and only revealed on special occasions. This reflects restricted access and ritual secrecy, and it treats icons as living presences rather than just images. The formal custom of unveiling them to worshippers for a limited time is *kaichō* (display).

Varaha Narasimha in Simhachalam near Visakhapatnam (my maternal uncle's city) in India has parallels, where the deity is kept covered in sandalwood paste and revealed once a year (Skt. *nijarūpa darśanam*). Hibutsu and Varaha Narasimha may have evolved independently, but a shared fundamental philosophical outlook underlies both traditions.

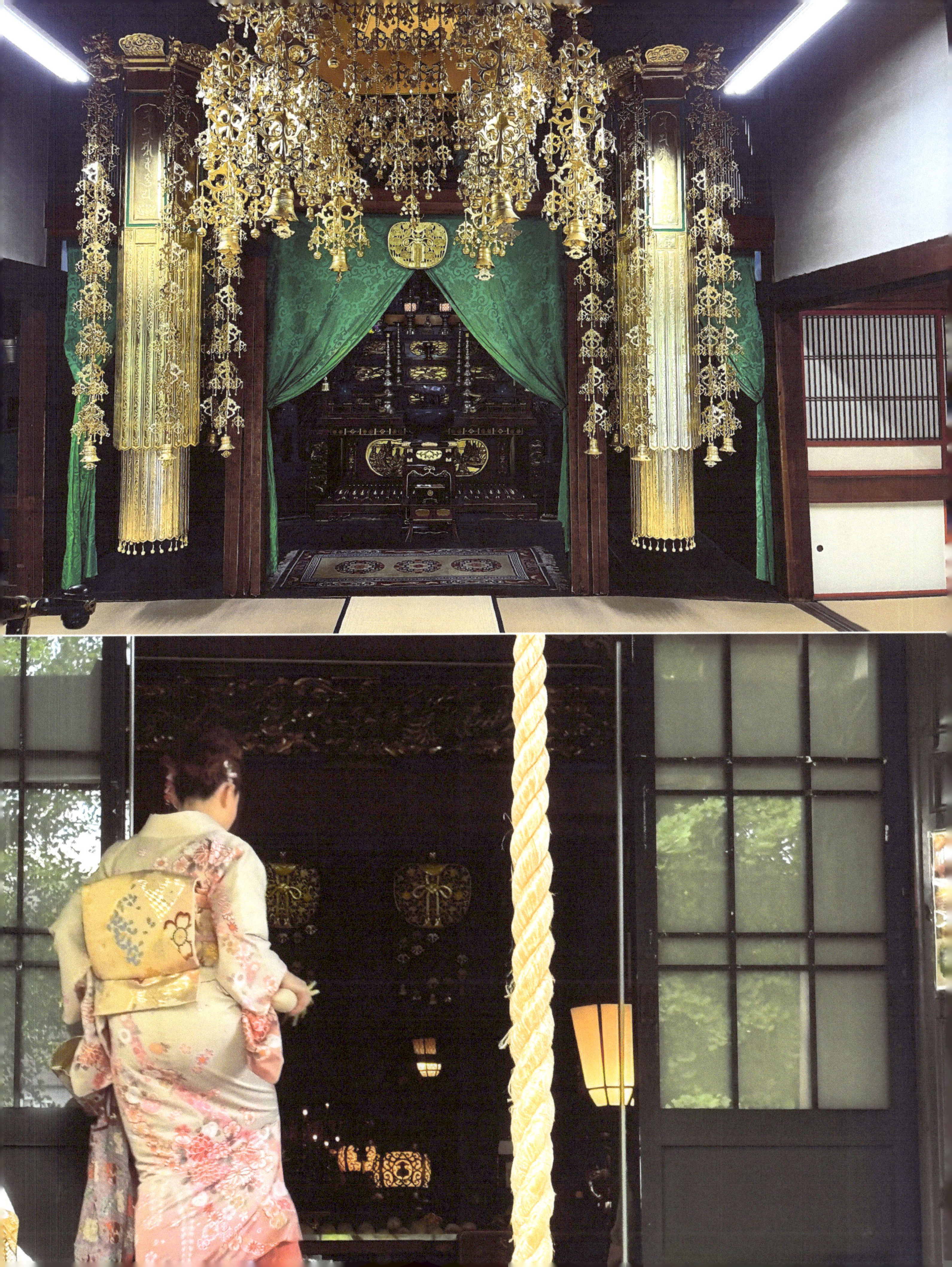

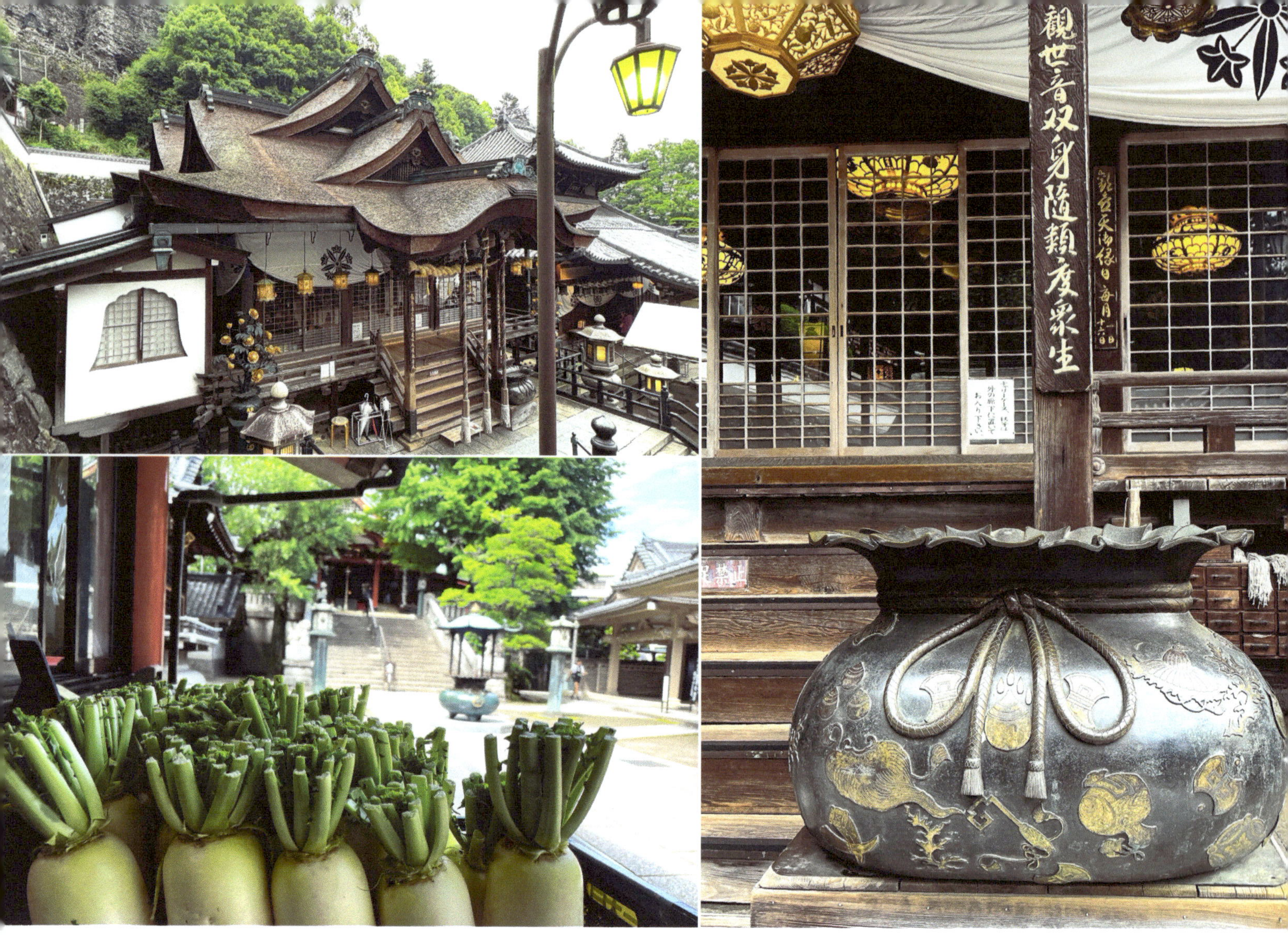

This page (clockwise from above).
Kangiten (Skt. *Gaṇapati*): Daikon Offering, Kangiten Hall, and Money Bag Votive –
Matsuchiyama Shōden, Tokyo; Hōzan-ji, Ikoma

Kangiten (歓喜天), literally "Deva of Bliss," is the Japanese esoteric form of Gaṇapati whose tantric role as a bliss-bestowing, obstacle-removing deity was translated in Japan as Kangiten, combining *kangi* "delight" (歓喜) with *ten* "heavenly deity" (天). The familiar form of two embracing elephant-headed deities, Sōshin Kangiten, develops in Chinese esoteric Buddhist texts on Gaṇapati/Vināyaka, where a once-unruly obstacle-causing deity is pacified by his consort in an embrace that symbolizes bliss and the transformation of passion into beneficent power. Gaṇapati worship reaches Japan through Kūkai and Ennin, representing the Shingon and Tendai traditions respectively, who traveled in Tang China (7th–9th centuries CE) and brought back a broad corpus of esoteric texts and practices from Indian, Tibetan, and Chinese gurus.

In the top left photo, the principal Kangiten icon at Hōzan-ji is treated as a *hibutsu* ("hidden deity") and kept in inner halls, in contrast to the open, ubiquitous worship of Gaṇapati in Hinduism. This is due to the belief that Kangiten is too powerful to be viewed casually. The *daikon* (white radish) offering at Matsuchiyama Shōden symbolizes purification, vitality, and fertility in Japanese folk belief; its "cooling" nature is said to balance Kangiten's passionate energy. The money bag votive at Hōzan-ji emphasizes prosperity and good fortune and reflects Kangiten's role in smoothing personal, commercial, and social relationships. Kangiten and Gaṇapati are revered in both cultures for prosperity, removal of obstacles, and auspicious beginnings.

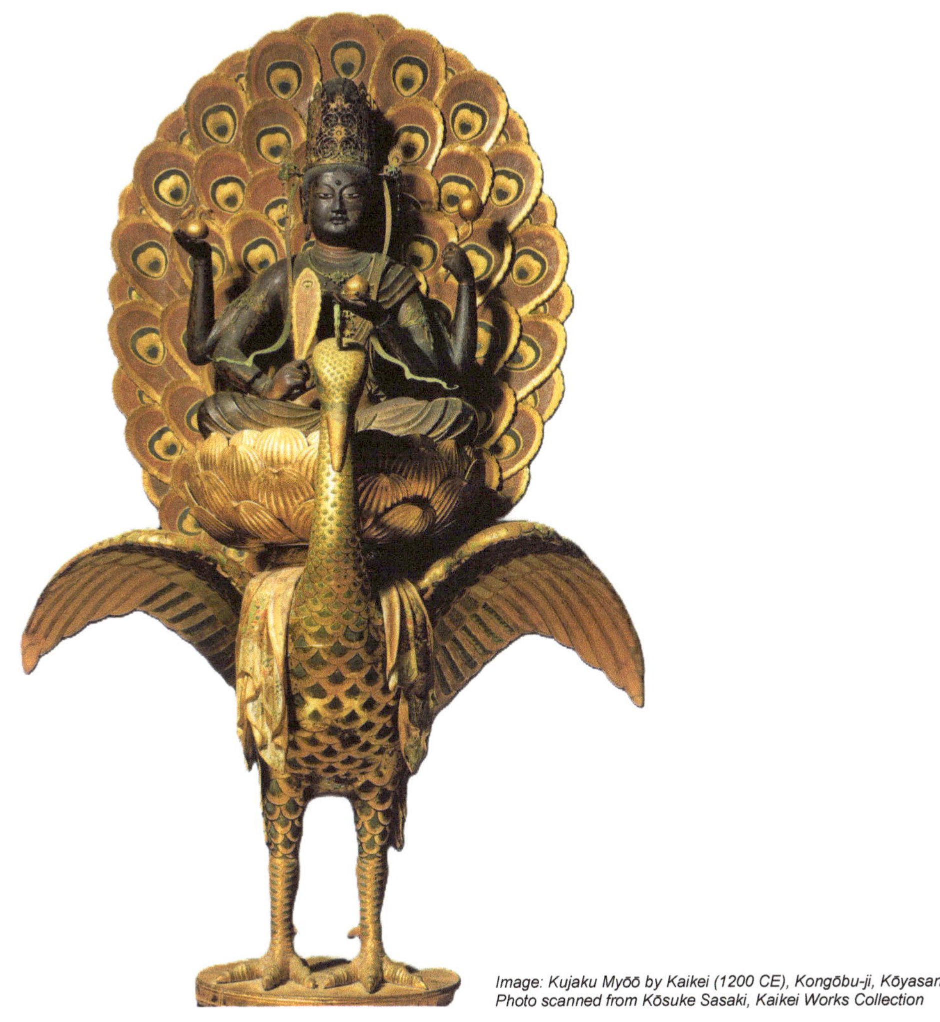

Image: Kujaku Myōō by Kaikei (1200 CE), Kongōbu-ji, Kōyasan. Photo scanned from Kōsuke Sasaki, Kaikei Works Collection

Kujaku Myōō (Skt. *Mahāmāyūrī*) – *Kōyasan Reihōkan Museum, Kōyasan*

Mahāmāyūrī Vidyārājñī's Sanskrit name means "Great Peacock," tying this Buddhist goddess to the sacred peacock of Hindus that devours snakes and survives their venom. In one early story, a monk is bitten by a poisonous snake and collapses; when Ānanda begs Śākyamuni Buddha for help, the Buddha teaches the Great Peacock mantra. Chanted over the monk, it forces the poison out, and the Buddha explains that invoking this peacock goddess protects all beings from snakebite and poison.

In the early 9th century, Kūkai adopts Mahāmāyūrī into Shingon esoteric practice at court and on Kōyasan, using her in rituals for national safety, rain-making, and averting calamities. The gilded wooden sculpture on this page is carved in 1200 CE by the master sculptor Kaikei as the principal image of the Kujaku-dō at Kongōbu-ji on Kōyasan.

Kujaku's posture and attributes draw on shared Hindu–Buddhist peacock symbolism: she holds a lotus (rising pure from the mud), a citrus "karma-fruit" often identified with Skt. *bilva* fruit (used to worship *Śiva*) standing for the ripening of causes, and a peacock feather that sweeps away poison and misfortune. The Hindu god *Subrahmaṇya* (also *Skanda*) also rides a peacock as a youthful war-god, and at first glance his peacock mount can look uncannily like Mahāmāyūrī's. Subrahmaṇya channels the peacock's energy into martial courage and victory over evil; Mahāmāyūrī turns it toward healing, rain, and protection of the good. In Japan, *Skanda* is separately worshipped as *Idaten*, a swift, young guardian of monasteries and the Dharma.

Bonten (Skt. *Brahmā*) – *Tō-ji Kodo, Kyoto*

In Hinduism, *Brahmā* is the four-headed creator whose faces stand for the four *Vedas*. His four hands often carry a Skt. *kamandalu* (water pot filled with the primordial waters of creation), an Skt. *akṣamālā* (rosary that denotes the continuous process of creation), the Vedas, and the Skt. *sruk*, a long wooden ladle used to place offerings into the sacred fire during Skt. *homa* (Jp. *goma*), the Vedic fire ritual.

In Japan's Shingon Buddhism, *Brahmā* is adapted as Bonten, who retains his four heads, a boon-granting open palm, and a lotus posture on a pedestal supported by swans (Skt. *haṃsa*). In this Tō-ji sculpture, his remaining hands carry a lotus bud, a fly whisk (Jp. *hossu*), and a spear-like Jp. *hoko* staff. The *sruk* that was used to feed the sacrificial fire is, in a sense, reborn as the *hoko*: as *Brahmā* crosses into Buddhism, the god of knowledge and creation becomes Bonten the guardian, now wielding a weapon to defend the Dharma. Kūkai envisioned Bonten as part of a three-dimensional mandala for the Tō-ji Lecture Hall, which was completed in 839 CE.

Taishakuten (Skt. *Śakra* or *Indraḥ*) – *Tō-ji Kodo, Kyoto*

Praised in the *Vedas* by the epithet *Śakra*, "the mighty one," *Indra* is the thunderbolt-wielding king of the gods and guardian of the eastern quarter. In the *Ṛg Veda*'s *Puruṣa Sūkta*, he is extolled as "Śakra, having fully understood *Puruṣa* (Cosmic Being), made Him known in all four directions" - *śakraḥ pravidvān pradiśaś catasraḥ*, RV 10.90.17.

As Buddhism spreads, this Vedic deity is adopted almost intact: he rules the *Trāyastriṃśa* (33 Vedic deities = 8 *Vasus* + 11 *Rudras* + 12 *Ādityas* + 2 *Aśvins*) heaven atop Mount Sumeru, commands the Four Heavenly Kings, and protects monasteries and ritual mandalas. *Śakra* becomes Japanese Taishakuten, *tai* meaning "emperor" and *shaku* from *Śakra*. In this Tō-ji sculpture, Taishakuten sits on his white elephant, gripping the diamond-thunderbolt Skt. *vajra* (Jp. *kongōsho*) as a weapon of clarity and protection. Kūkai envisioned Taishakuten along with Bonten in his three-dimensional mandala for the Tō-ji Lecture Hall.

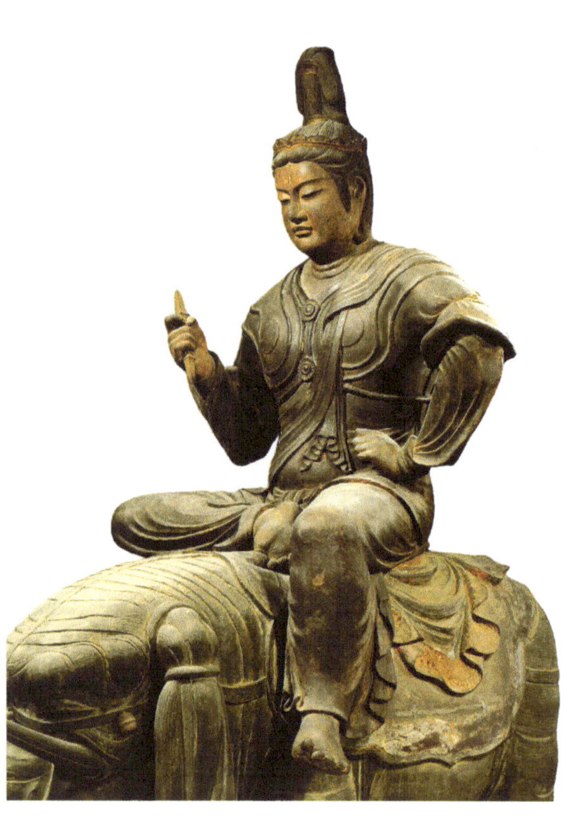

Images: Bonten and Taishakuten, Tō-ji, Kyoto. Photo scanned from Tō-ji Temple's Heavenly Being Statues

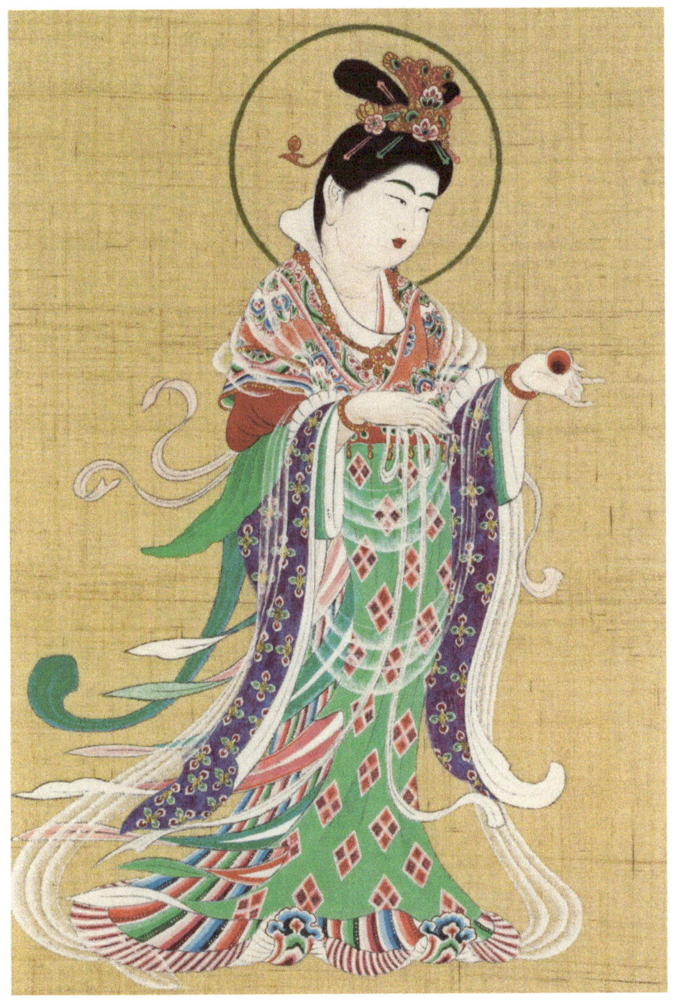

Image: Post card replica of Kichijoten Image, Yakushi-ji, Nara

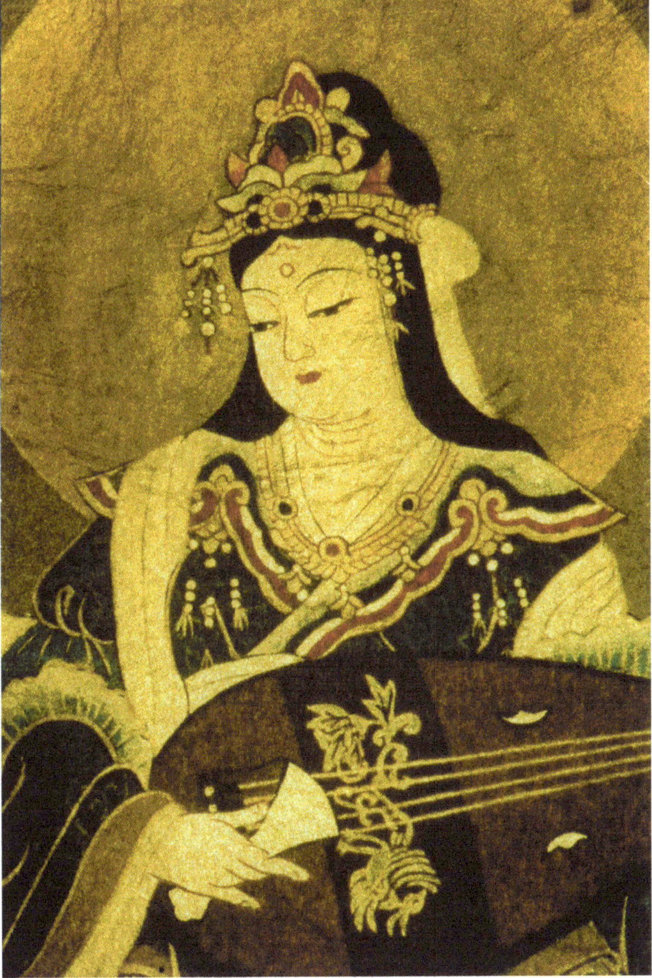

Image: Temple information pamphlet at Daiganj-i

Kichijōten (Skt. *Lakṣmī*) – *Yakushi-ji, Nara*

Kichijōten is the Japanese Buddhist form of the Hindu goddess of wealth, *Lakṣmī*. Her name *Kichijō-ten* means "auspicious heavenly deity," from *kichi* "good fortune" and *jō* "omen." She is worshipped at temples such as Yakushi-ji from 8th century, where she stands beside Bishamonten (Skt. *Vaiśravaṇa*), as his sister. Like *Lakṣmī*, she grants prosperity, fertility, and beauty, holding Skt. *cintāmaṇi (*a wish-granting jewel) and making the Skt. *varada-mudrā* (boon-giving hand gesture), yet in Japan she appears in a Kimono and is especially invoked for charm, happiness, and the well-being of women and children. In India *Lakṣmī* is best known as *Viṣṇu*'s consort, but Japanese Buddhism keeps her linked to wealth and auspiciousness, often in parallel with Benzaiten.

Benzaiten (Skt. *Sarasvatī*) – *Daigan-ji, Miyajima*

Benzaiten is a literal rendering of Sarasvatī as a goddess of eloquence, where *ben* means "eloquent speech," *zai* "treasure," and *ten* "heavenly deity." In Hindu tradition, Sarasvatī is the goddess of learning, arts, speech, and the river that bears her name. Through Buddhism she travels from India to Japan, where she is revered as a Buddhist protector of the Dharma and the state. Over time she was adopted as a Shinto *kami* (a local deity) at shrines, often on islands. She guards harbors while granting learning, eloquence, artistic skill, and good fortune. Her *biwa* lute is derived from Sarasvatī's *vīṇā*, and esoteric images sometimes show her with many arms holding weapons and wish-granting jewels.

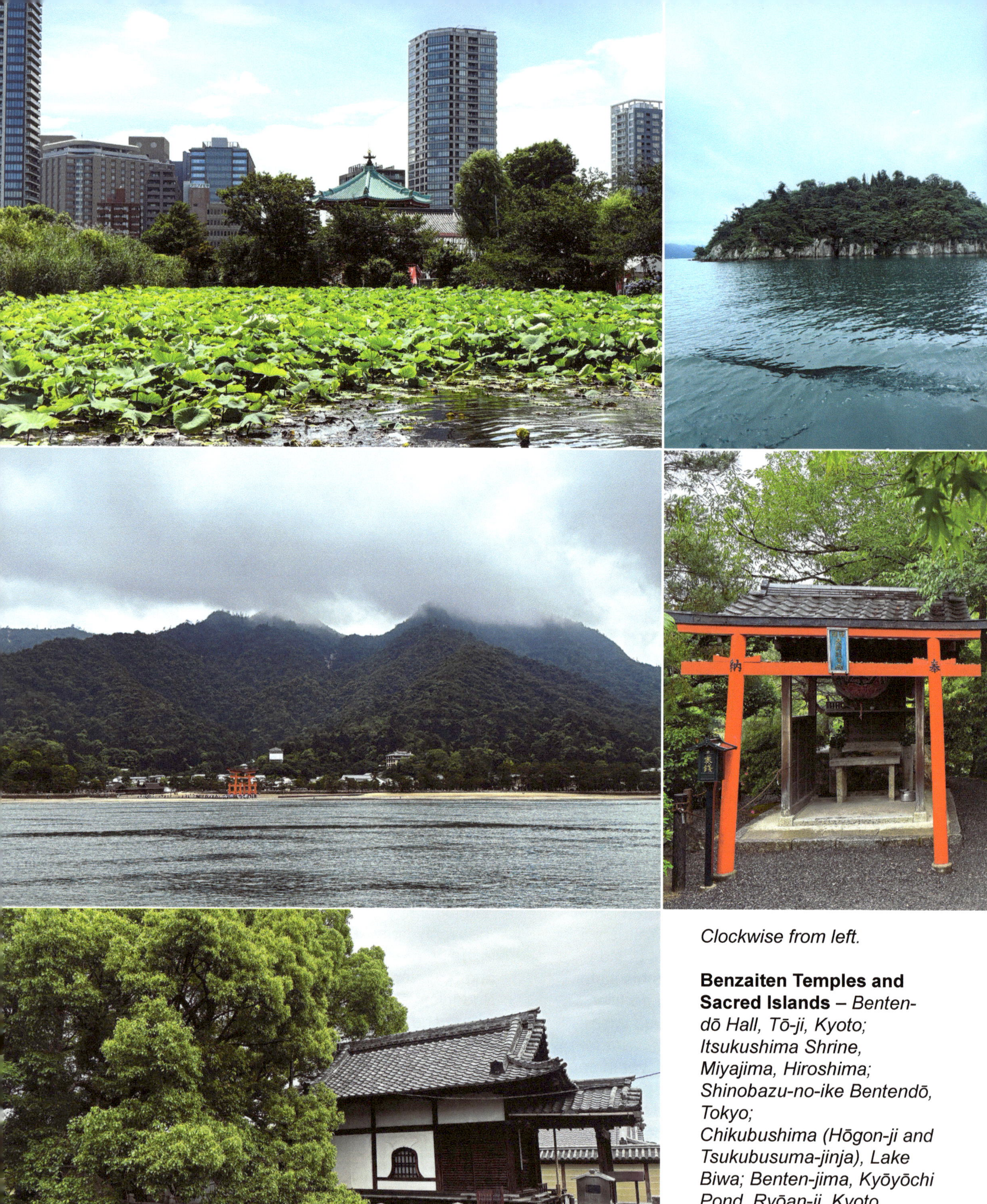

Clockwise from left.

Benzaiten Temples and Sacred Islands – *Benten-dō Hall, Tō-ji, Kyoto; Itsukushima Shrine, Miyajima, Hiroshima; Shinobazu-no-ike Bentendō, Tokyo; Chikubushima (Hōgon-ji and Tsukubusuma-jinja), Lake Biwa; Benten-jima, Kyōyōchi Pond, Ryōan-ji, Kyoto*

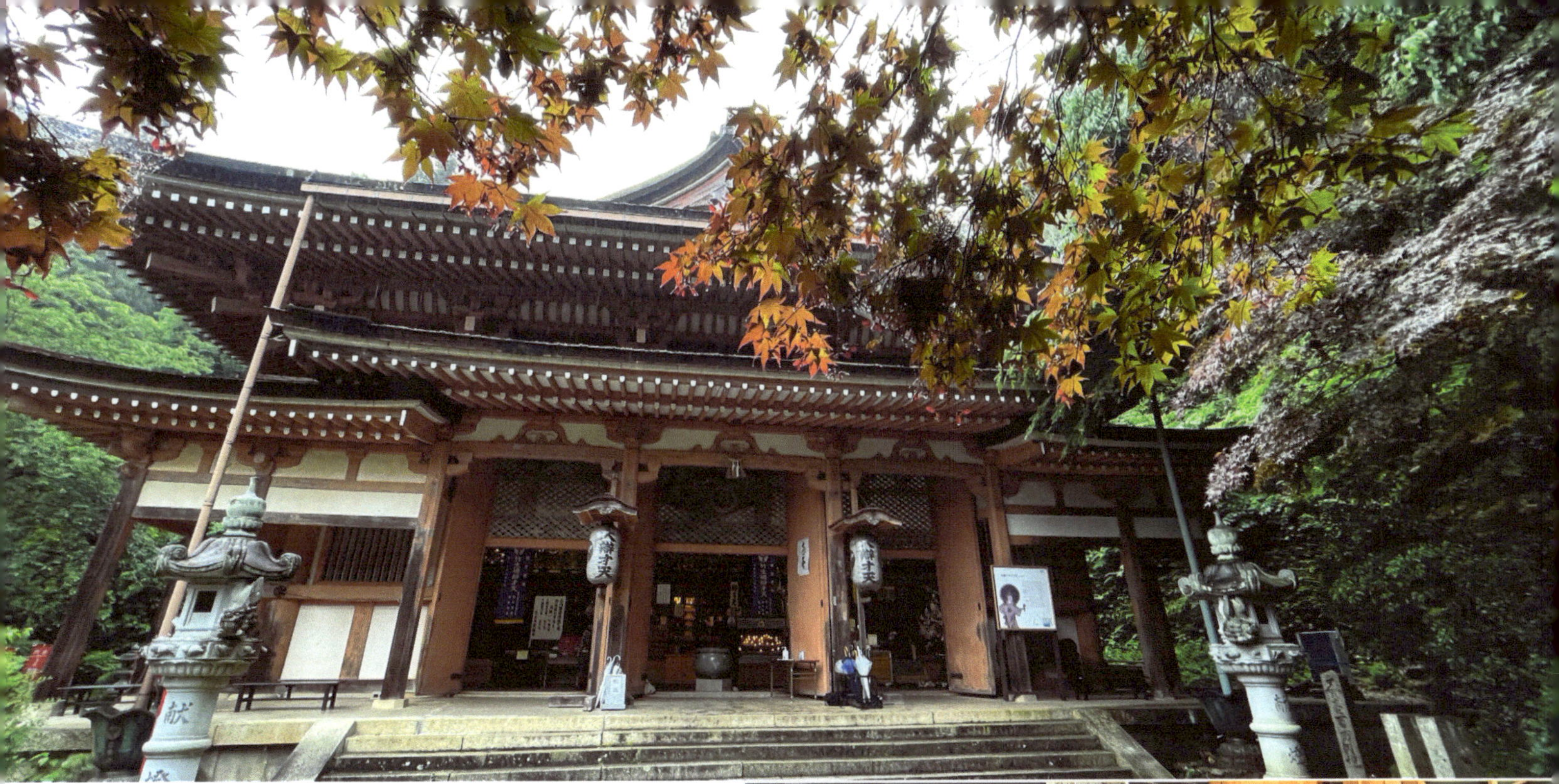

Benzaiten – *Hōgon-ji, Chikubushima*

Emperor Shōmu dreamed of an island sacred to Benzaiten and ordered the monk Gyōki (helped build Tōdai-ji with Bodhisena), to build a temple here (above) in 724 CE. Gyōki carved both a red Benzaiten and a 1,000-armed Kannon (below). Hōgon-ji is on the Saigoku Kannon pilgrimage and is also one of Japan's "three great Benzaiten." The red Benzaiten daruma dolls (right) hold visitors' written wishes, left for the goddess to carry through.

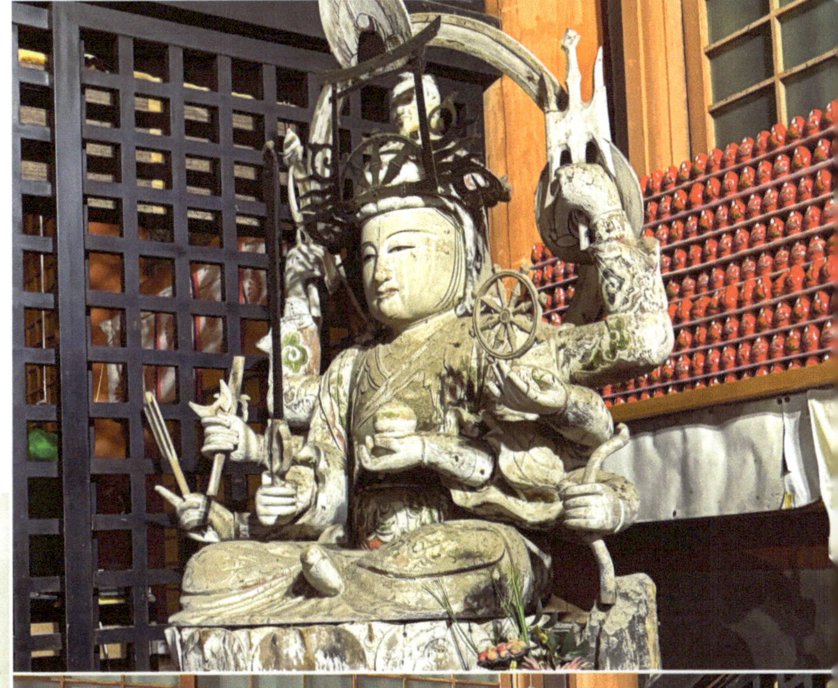

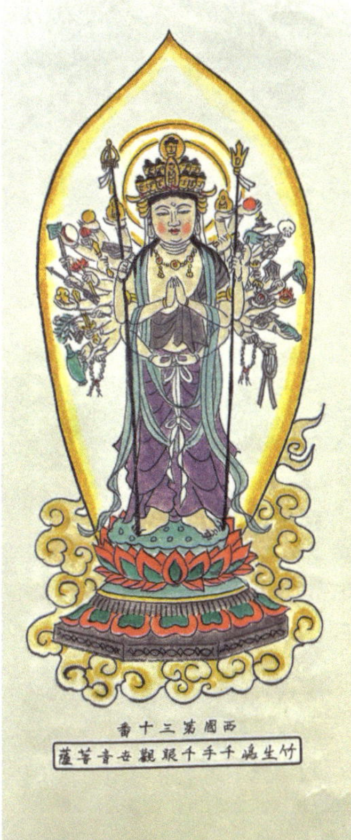

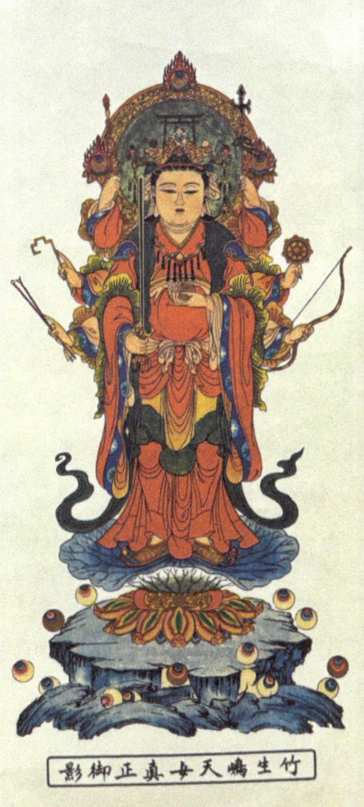

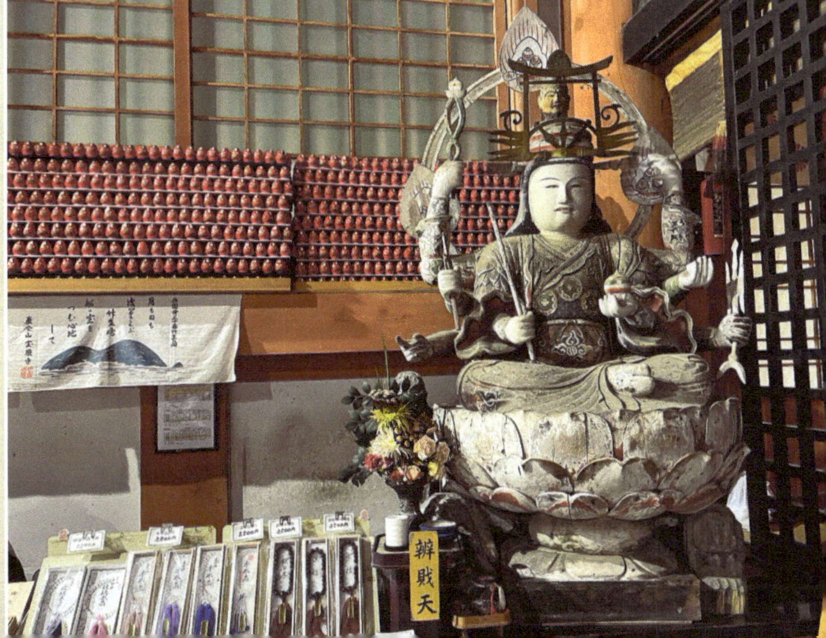

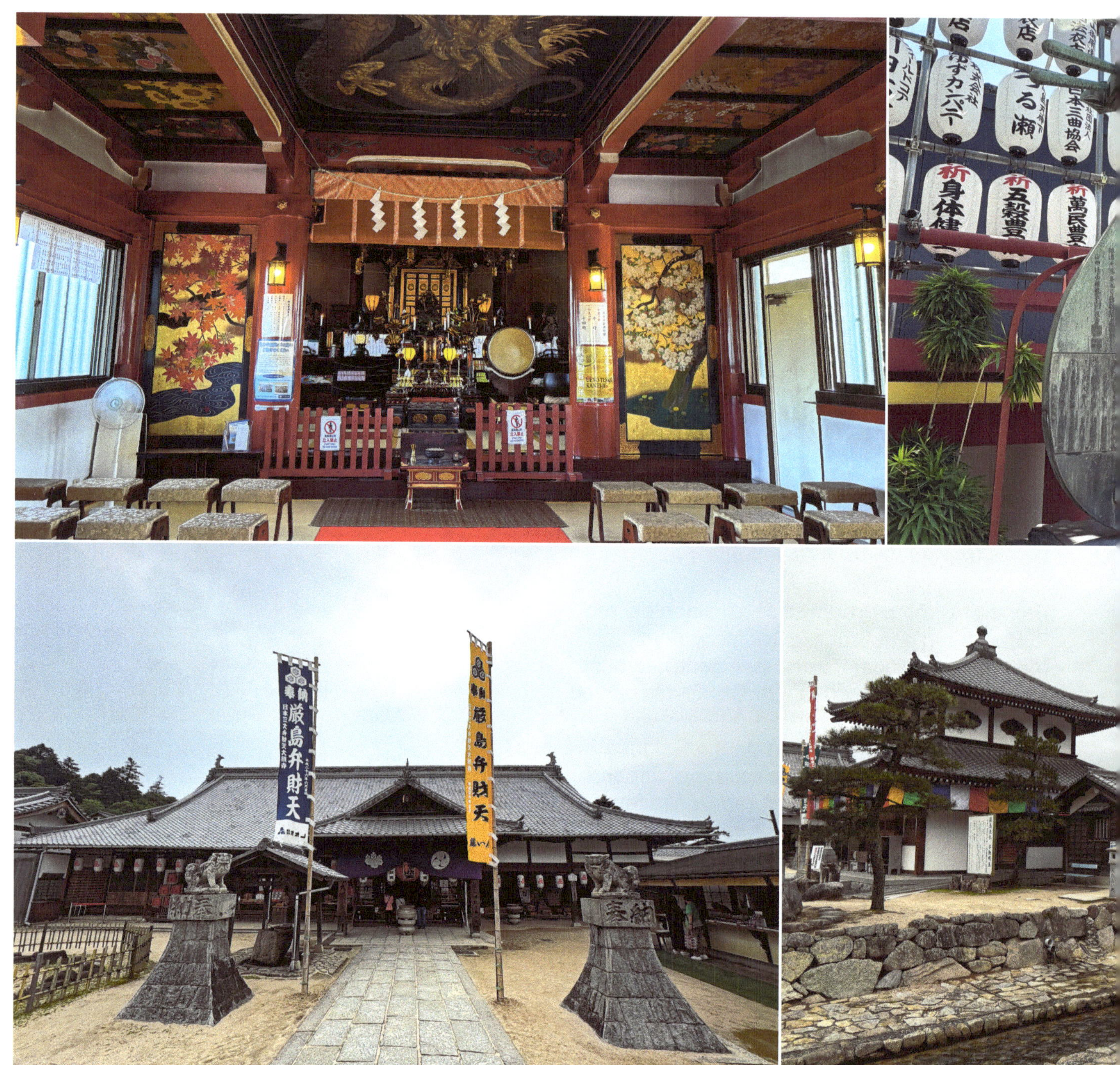

Top row, left to right.
Benzaiten on campus – *Shinobazu-no-ike Bentendō, Ueno Park, Tokyo*

Shinobazu-no-ike Bentendō stands on a small island in Shinobazu Pond, a short walk from the University of Tokyo, so it is popular with students who pray here for good grades. The Benzaiten image in the octagonal hall (left) is said to be a replica of the statue at Hōgon-ji on Chikubushima, made when the monk Tenkai founded the temple in the 1600s. Outside the hall a giant bronze *biwa* (middle; Japanese lute derived from *Sarasvatī's vīṇā*) recalls her role as patron of music. Nearby, visitors write wishes for exam success, artistic skill, and good fortune on *biwa*-shaped wooden plaques and leave them for Benzaiten to bless (right).

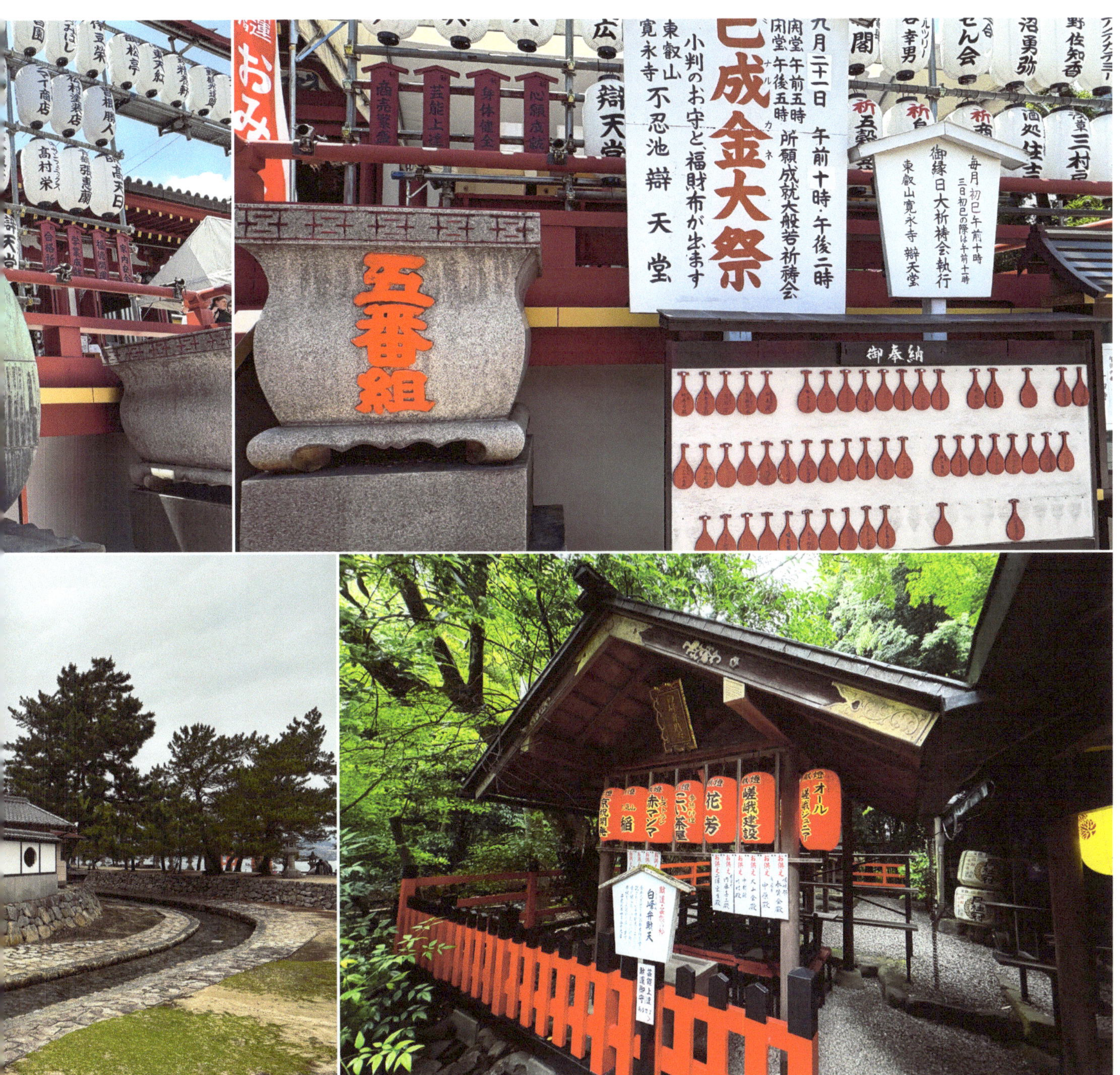

Bottom row, left to right.

Island Temple and Forest Shrine of Benzaiten – *Daigan-ji, Miyajima; Daigan-ji canal, Miyajima; Benzaiten sub-shrine, Nonomiya Shrine, Arashiyama, Kyoto*

At *Daigan-ji* on Miyajima Island, a stream flows around the temple where Itsukushima Benzaiten is enshrined, a statue that Kūkai is said to have carved and is one of Japan's "three great Benzaiten." The temple is closely tied to sea and tide. In Arashiyama bamboo forest, *Shirahine Benzaiten-sha* hides in a mossy corner of *Nonomiya Jinja*, with bright red lanterns and fence, where visitors pray for prosperity and success in the performing arts.

Left to right.

Fūten (Skt. *Vāyu*): वा → vā
Suiten (Skt. *Varuṇa*): व → va
Rasetsuten (Skt. *Nirṛti*): नृ → nṛ
Enmaten (Skt. *Yama*): यं → yaṃ

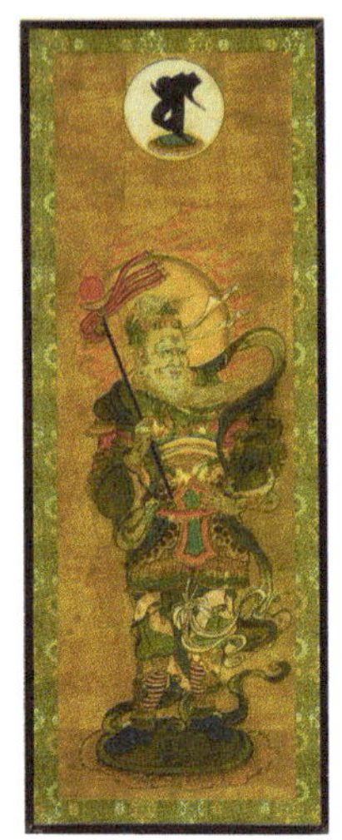
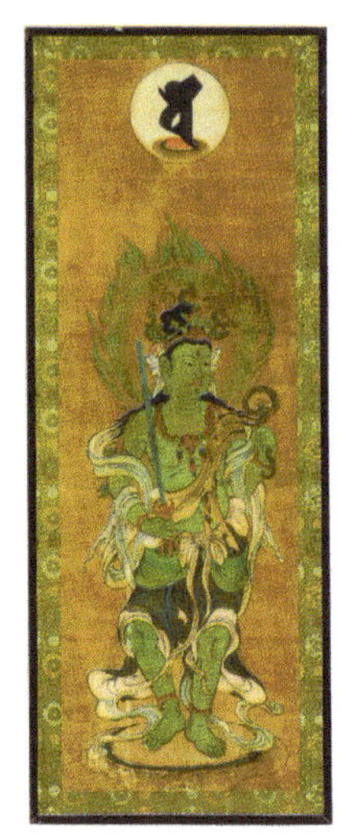
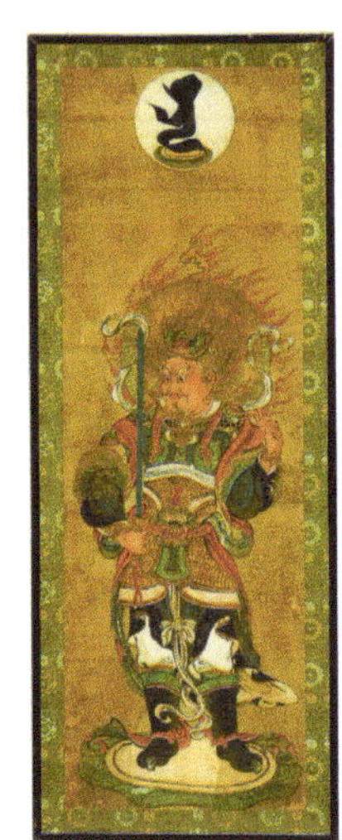
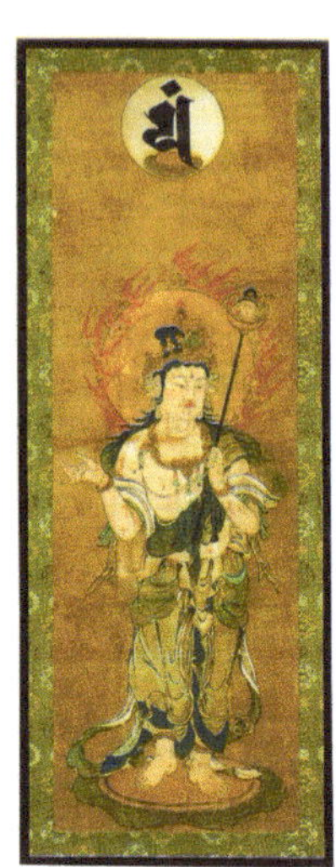

Left to right.

Gatten (Skt. *Candra*): च → ca
Nichiten (Skt. *Āditya*): अ → a
Jiten (Skt. *Pṛthivī*): पृ → pṛ
Bonten (Skt. *Brahmā*): ब्र → bra

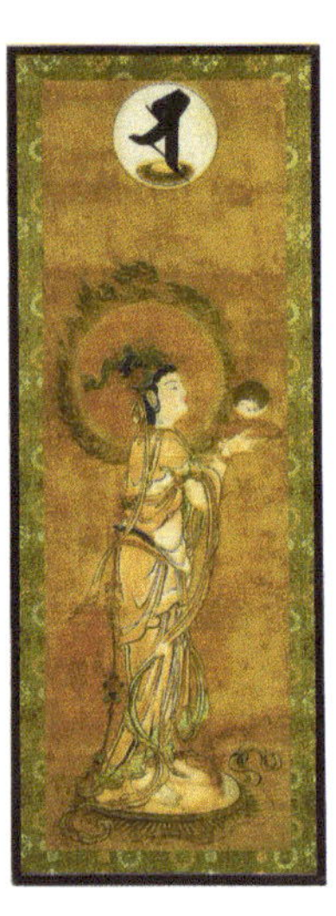
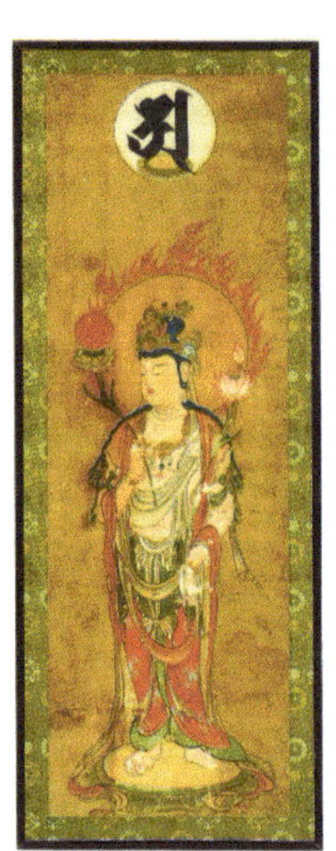
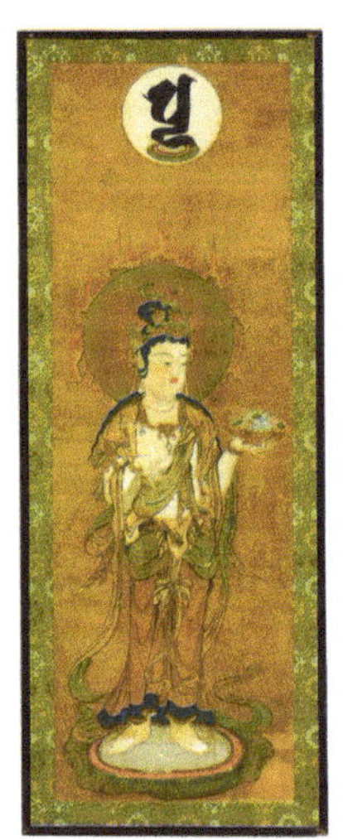
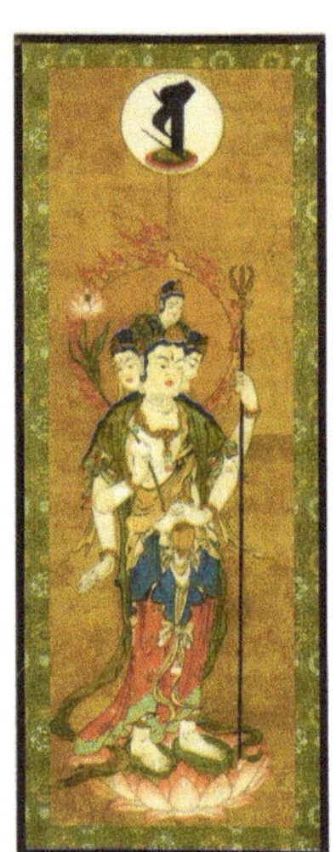

Left to right.

Īshanaten (Skt. *Īśāna*): इ → i
Bishamonten (Skt. *Vaiśravaṇa*): वै → vai
Katen (Skt. *Agni*): अ → a
Taishakuten (Skt. *Indra*): ई → ī

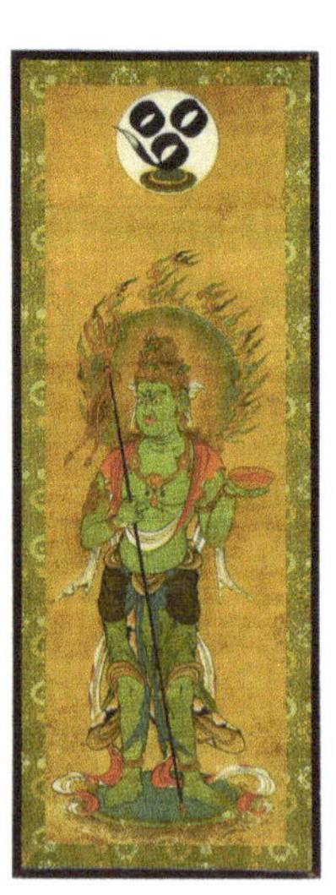
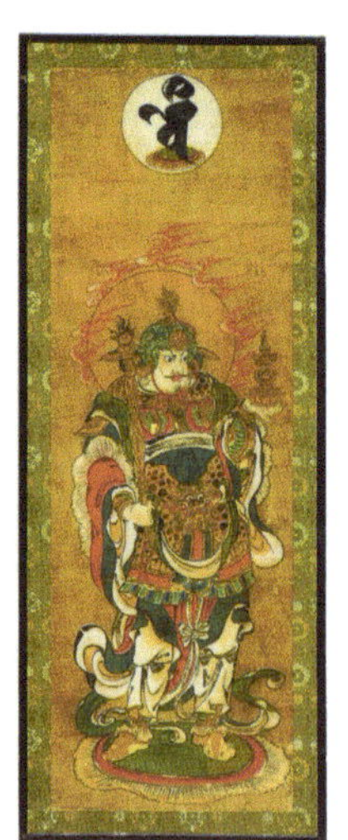
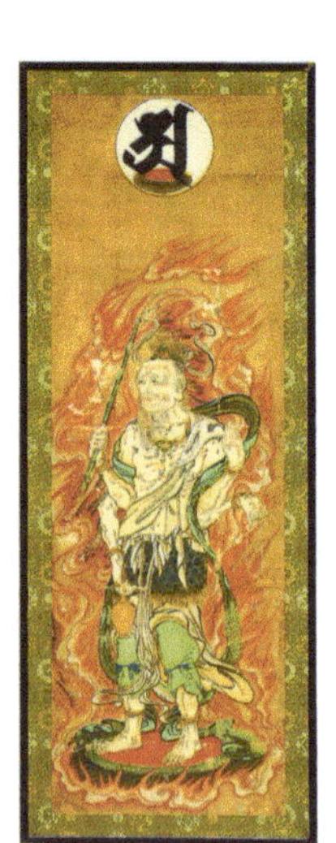
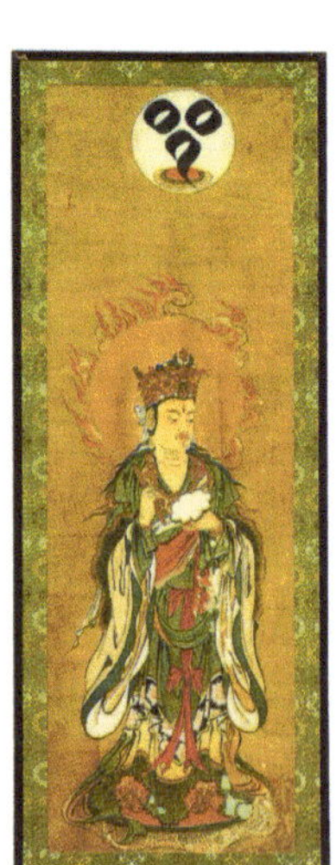

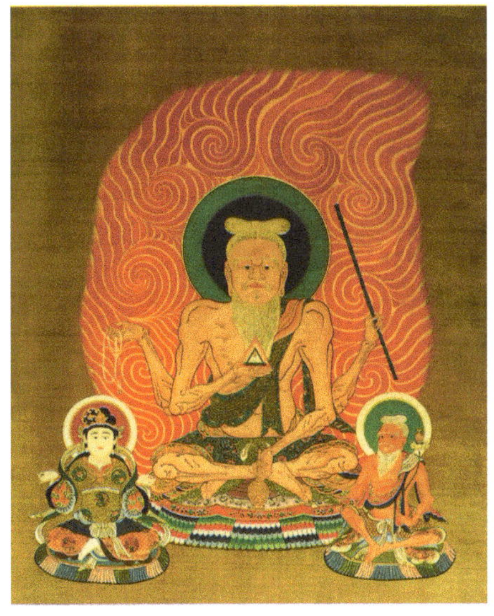

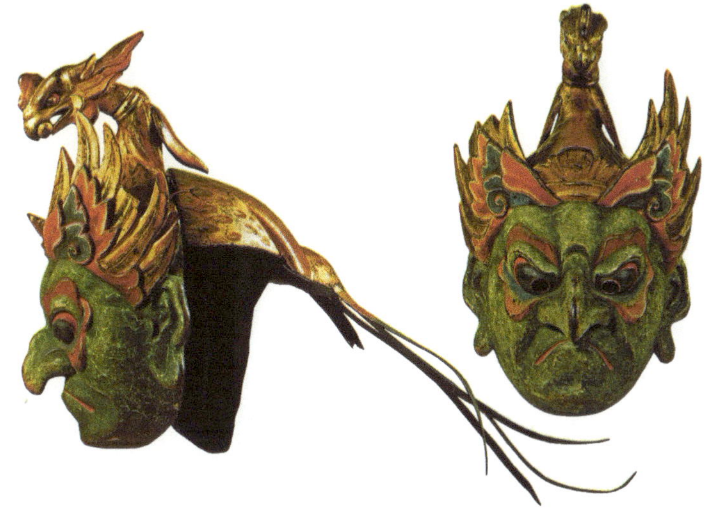

Images on this page and opposite page
Scanned from Tō-ji Temple's Heavenly Being Statues

Opposite Page.
Twelve Devas, Two Kinds of Names

In this set of twelve scrolls, the Japanese names do not always match the Vedic deities whose seed syllables (Skt. *bījākṣara*) are written above them. For the six "nature" deities, Japan already had strong everyday words for sun, moon, wind, water, earth, and fire. When Buddhism arrived, monks described these deities (Skt. *deva*) with Japanese titles such as Nichiten "Sun Deva," Gatten "Moon Deva," Fūten "Wind Deva," Suiten "Water Deva," Jiten "Earth Deva," and Katen "Fire Deva." The images show how their Siddham seed syllables still spell out the Sanskrit deities beneath those titles, such as अ for Agni.

Over time, several of these devas also syncretized with native Shinto kami: Fūten overlaps with the wind kami Fūjin, Suiten with water kami such as Suijin, and others like them. Even though these names are translated into Japanese, the seed syllables retain their Sanskrit origins.

The other six deities are treated more like persons than forces of nature, so their names come straight from Sanskrit: Bonten from Brahmā, Īshanaten from Īśāna, Taishakuten from Śakra/Indra, Bishamonten from Vaiśravaṇa, Enmaten from Yama, and Rasetsuten from rākṣasa.

Many Hindus who perform Skt. *Satyanarayana Puja* will immediately recognize these Twelve Devas as the same directional guardians (Skt. *dikpālaka*): ten protectors of the quarters, with the sun and moon completing the mandala. Japanese esoteric Buddhism assigns these twelve devas in exactly the same way. In Sanskrit texts Vaiśravaṇa (also Skt. *Kubera*) rules from Alakapuri in the Himalayan north of India, and in Japan his form as Bishamonten still stands at the northern edge of the mandala. This shared mapping of directions is one more sign of how deeply Hindu ideas are woven into Japanese Buddhism.

Above Left.
Agni as a Vedic sage

Agni appears as a Vedic ascetic sage (Skt. *ṛṣi*), seated cross-legged before a wall of flame with a staff, water pot (Skt. *kamaṇḍalu*), and rosary (Skt. *akṣamālā*) to count mantras.

Above Right.
Karura (Skt. *Garuḍa*) Gigaku mask

Karura, the Japanese Buddhist form of Viṣṇu's bird vehicle (Skt. *vāhana*), is revered as a protective guardian and appears in masked temple dances (*gigaku*) like this. Garuḍa's avian features and martial divinity continues to shape the visual language of Pokémon and Anime.

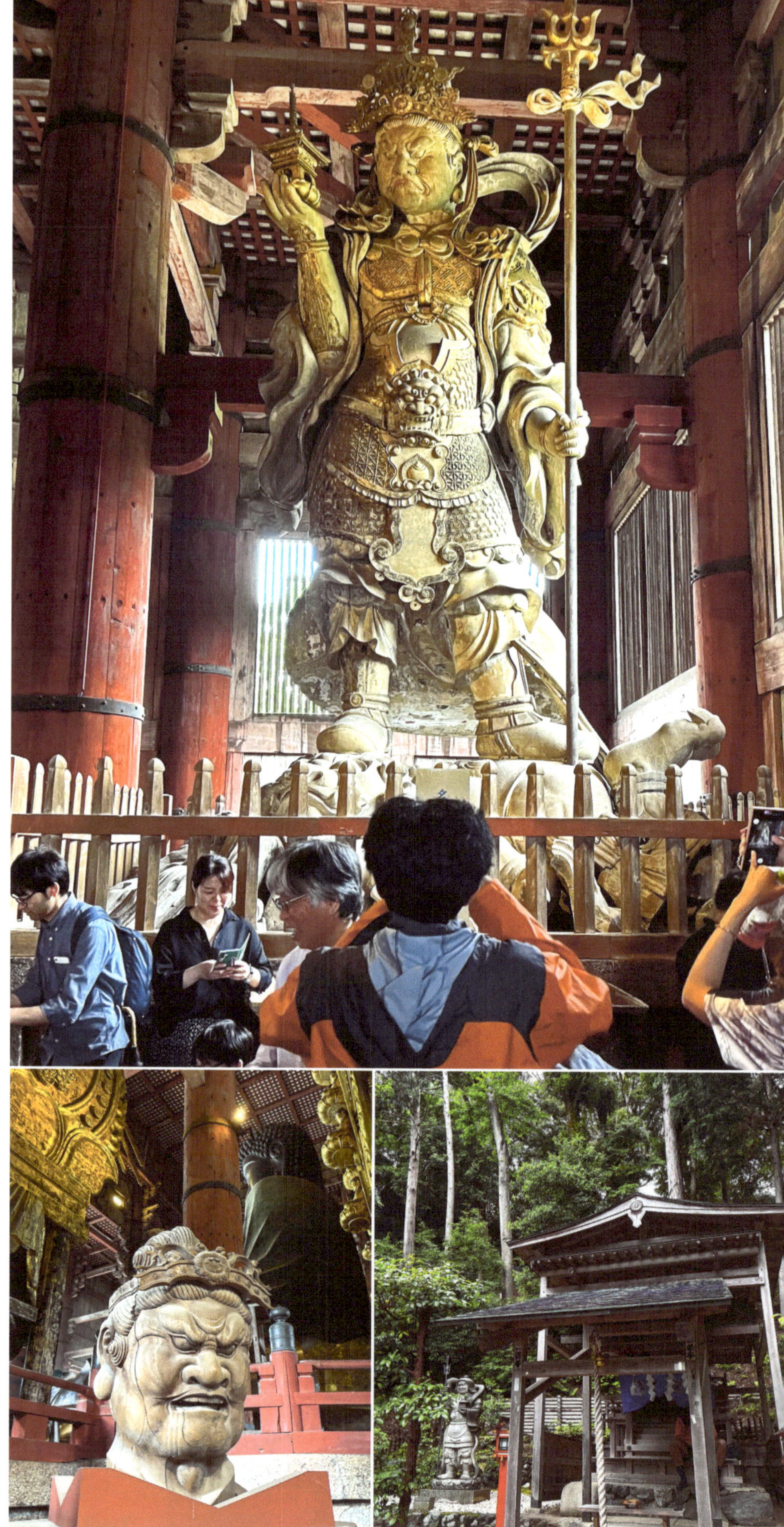

Right, right below.
Bishamonten – *Tōdai-ji, Nara; Wayside Shrine in Arashiyama, Kyoto*

Bishamonten is the Hindu deity of wealth who, in Buddhism, becomes leader of the Four Heavenly Kings protecting temples. He holds a pagoda in one hand and a trident in the other to drive away enemies. At Tōdai-ji this gigantic wooden statue towers inside the Great Buddha Hall, trampling a demon to depict hostile forces under control (similar to Skt. *Māra* beneath Śiva's foot).

Bishamonten is venerated across Japan as a ubiquitous protector. Hindu daily prayers extol him thus *rājādhirājāya prasahya sāhine* | *namo vayaṃ vaiśravaṇāya kurmahe* | *sa me kāmān kāmakāmāya mahyaṃ* | *kāmeśvaro vaiśravaṇo dadātu* | *kuberāya vaiśravaṇāya mahārājāya namaḥ* || (Krishna Yajurveda, TA 1.31), which salutes Vaiśravaṇa as "king of kings" and asks him to grant rightful wishes, prosperity, and protection.

Right.
Jikokuten (Skt. Dhṛtarāṣṭra) – *Tōdai-ji, Nara*

Dhṛtarāṣṭra shares his name with the blind king of the Indian epic Mahābhārata, but here he is one of the Four Heavenly Kings (Jp. *Shitennō*) instead. This fierce carved head once belonged to a massive guardian statue at Tōdai-ji.

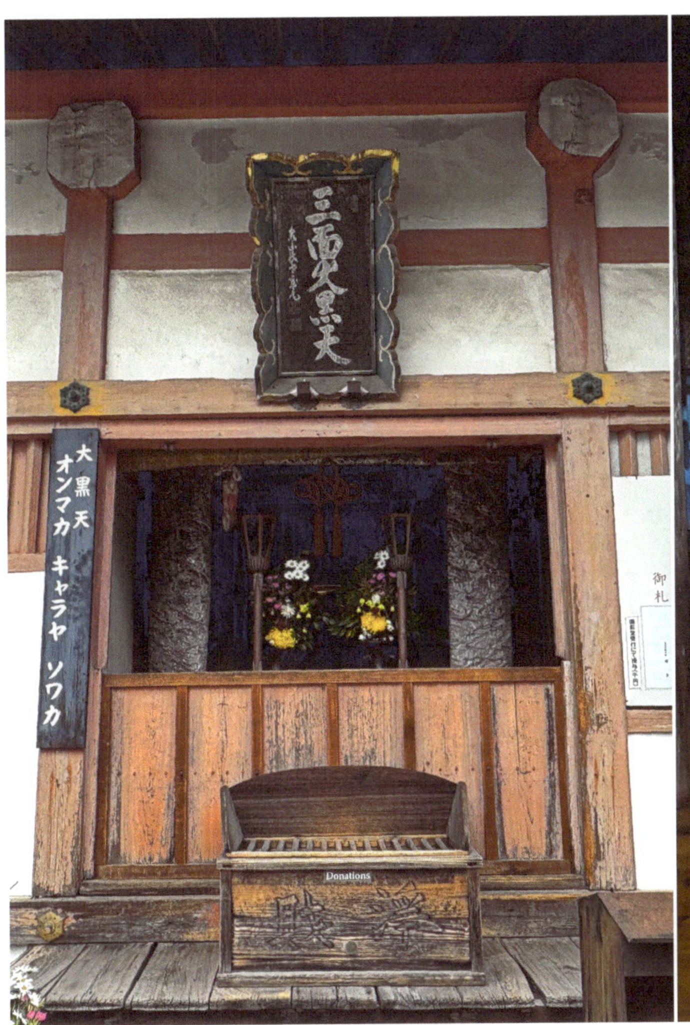

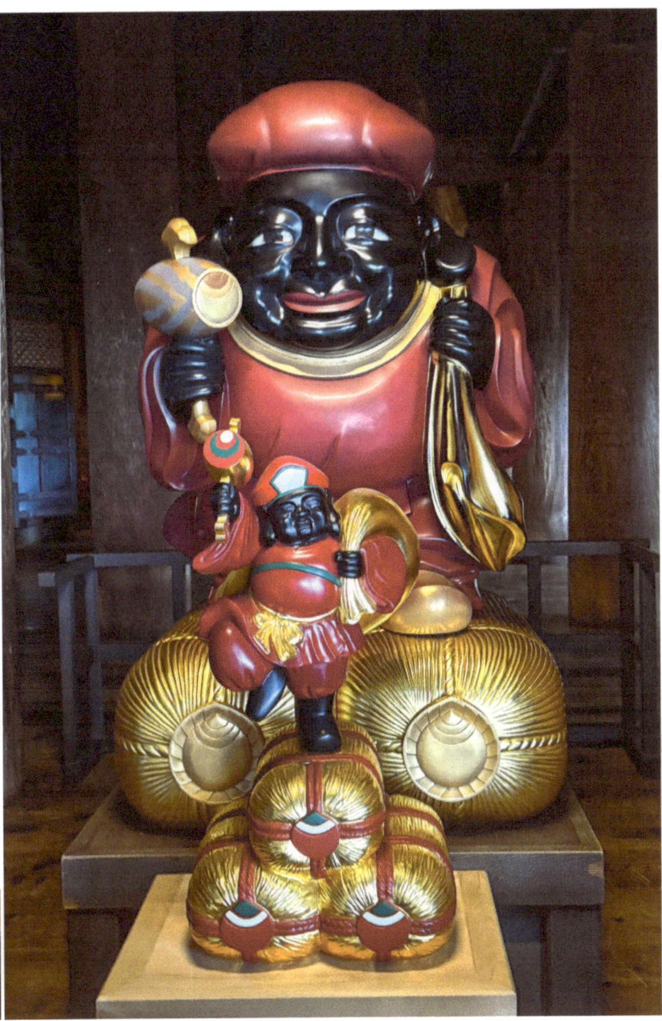

3-Faced Daikokuten (Skt. *Mahākāla*) Mantra "Om makakārāya sowaka" – *Tō-ji, Kyoto*

Mahākāla, Sanskrit for "Great Master of Time," is a name for Śiva as lord of cosmic cycles (*yugas*) who governs creation and dissolution of the universe. This cosmological view of *yugas* required Indian astronomers to track time with extreme precision, and therefore the Mahākāleśvar temple city of Ujjain became a major center of astronomy and mathematics. For over a thousand years, Ujjain time was a de facto "Greenwich Mean Time" for parts of Asia. Mahākāla as the embodiment of time, and the drive to measure that time precisely, made Ujjain a center of astronomy and mathematics. In Japanese Buddhism, however, Mahākāla is adopted with a different emphasis as "Great Dark One," translated as Daikokuten (dai "great," koku "black," ten "deva").

Daikokuten – *Kiyomizu-dera, Kyoto*

Buddhist Daikokuten later syncretized with the Shinto land and grain god *Ōkuninushi*, whose name can also be read "Daikoku" in Japanese. This fusion of Buddhist protector and rice-field *kami* turned him into a guardian of land, harvests, and the household, and later into one of the Seven Lucky Gods, a popular folk pantheon shared by Shinto and Buddhism. Over time, his iconography shifted from a wrathful black deity into a cheerful storehouse lord, still dark in color recalling the original *Mahākāla* but dressed like a prosperous merchant, seated on bales of rice, and holding a wish-fulfilling mallet and a treasure sack that never runs out. Today Daikokuten appears both in formal esoteric rituals in Shingon and Tendai temples and in approachable figures like this one at *Kiyomizu-dera*, where ordinary visitors pray for luck, good harvests, and steady business.

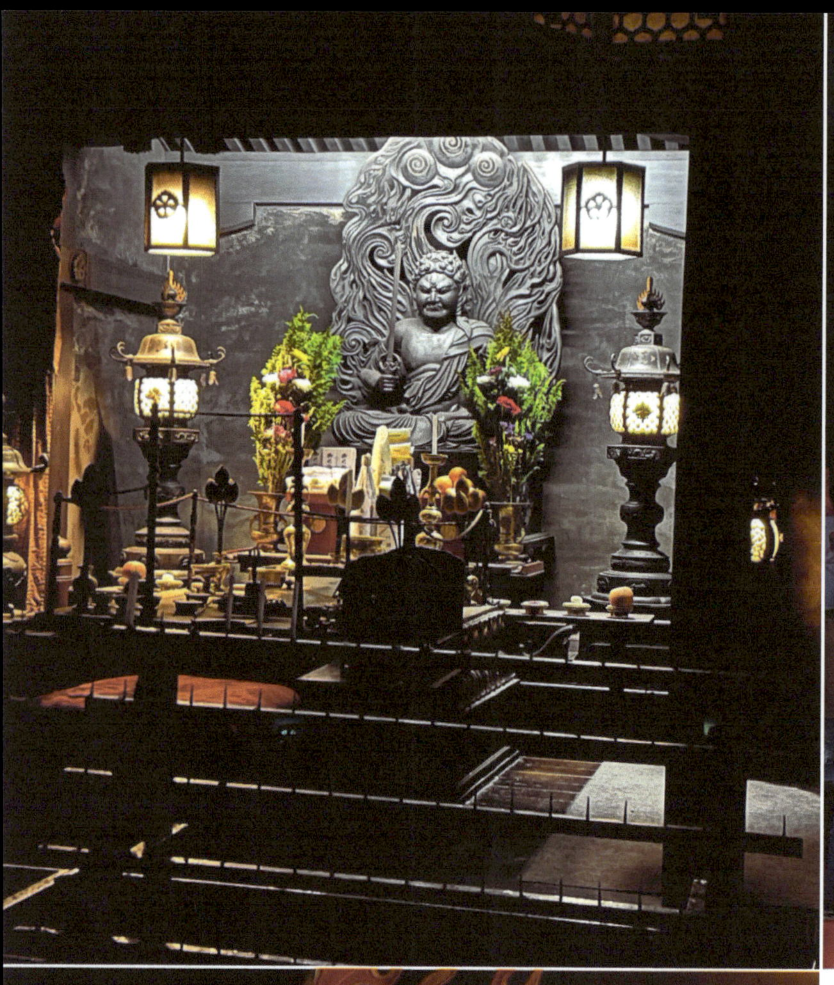

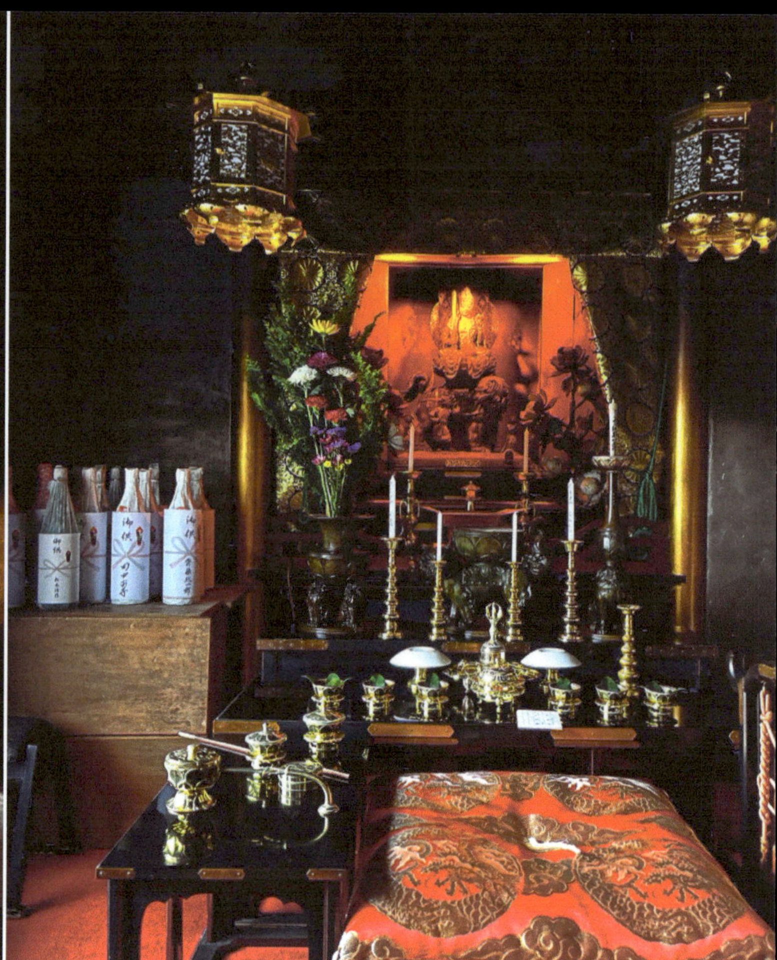

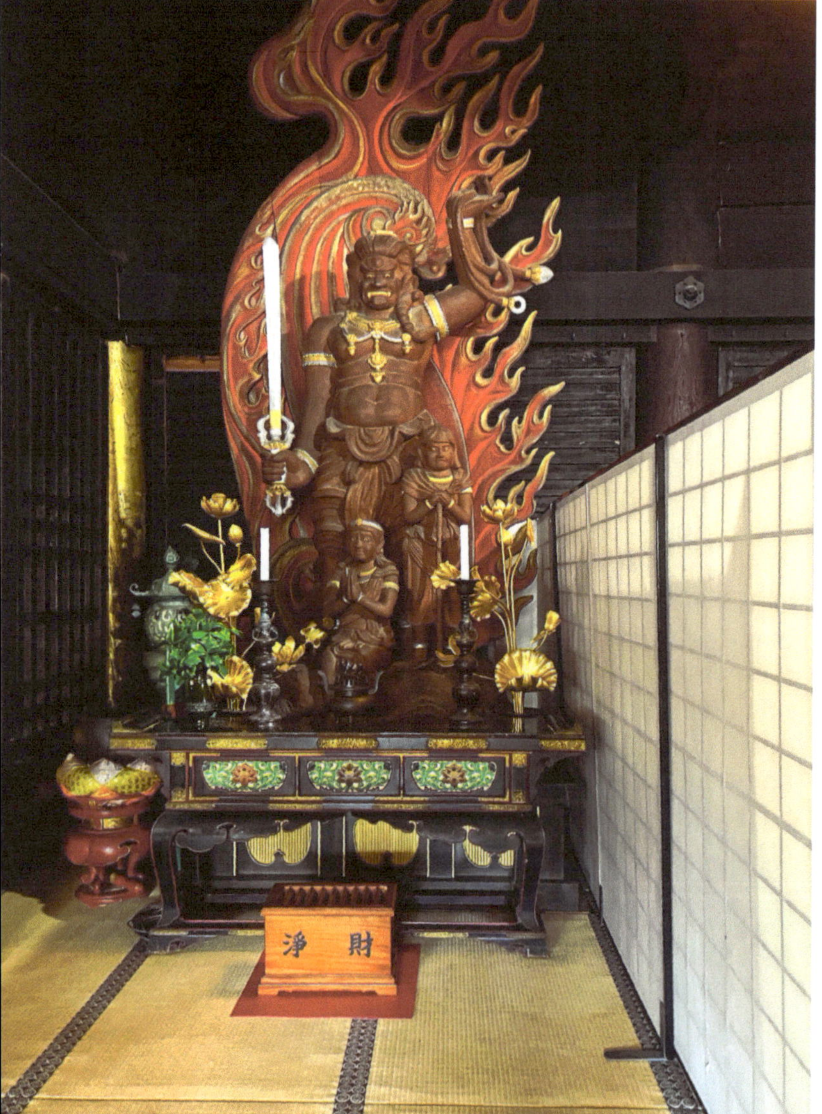

This and opposite page (all images).
Fudō Myōō (Skt. *Acala*) – *Temples across Japan*

Fudō Myōō is a wrathful Buddhist protector derived from Śiva. A popular Sanskrit *śloka* (prayer) praises Śiva in this form:

śāntaṃ padmāsanasthaṃ śaśidharamakutam
pañcavaktraṃ trinetram | śūlaṃ ***khaḍgaṃ*** *ca*
vajraṃ paraśuṃabhayadaṃ dakṣha bhāge
vahantaṃ | nāgaṃ ***pāśaṃ*** *ca ghaṇṭāṃ*
pralaya-hutavahaṃ śāṅkuśaṃ vāma-bhāge
| nānālaṅkāra-yuktaṃ sphāṭika-maṇinibhaṃ
pārvatīśaṃ namāmi ||

In this verse, Śiva holds a **khaḍgam** (sword) in his right hand and a **pāśaṃ** (noose) in his left, exactly as Fudō here before a wall of fire. Acala (meaning the Immovable One), becomes Fu "not" dō "move" Myōō in Japanese, the "Immovable Wisdom King," and his form comes from this multi-armed Śiva who cuts through obstacles and binds ignorance. Samurai sought his blessings to attain *Fudōshin* (Skt. *sthitaprajña,* immovable mind) to remain imperturbable and decisive in battles.

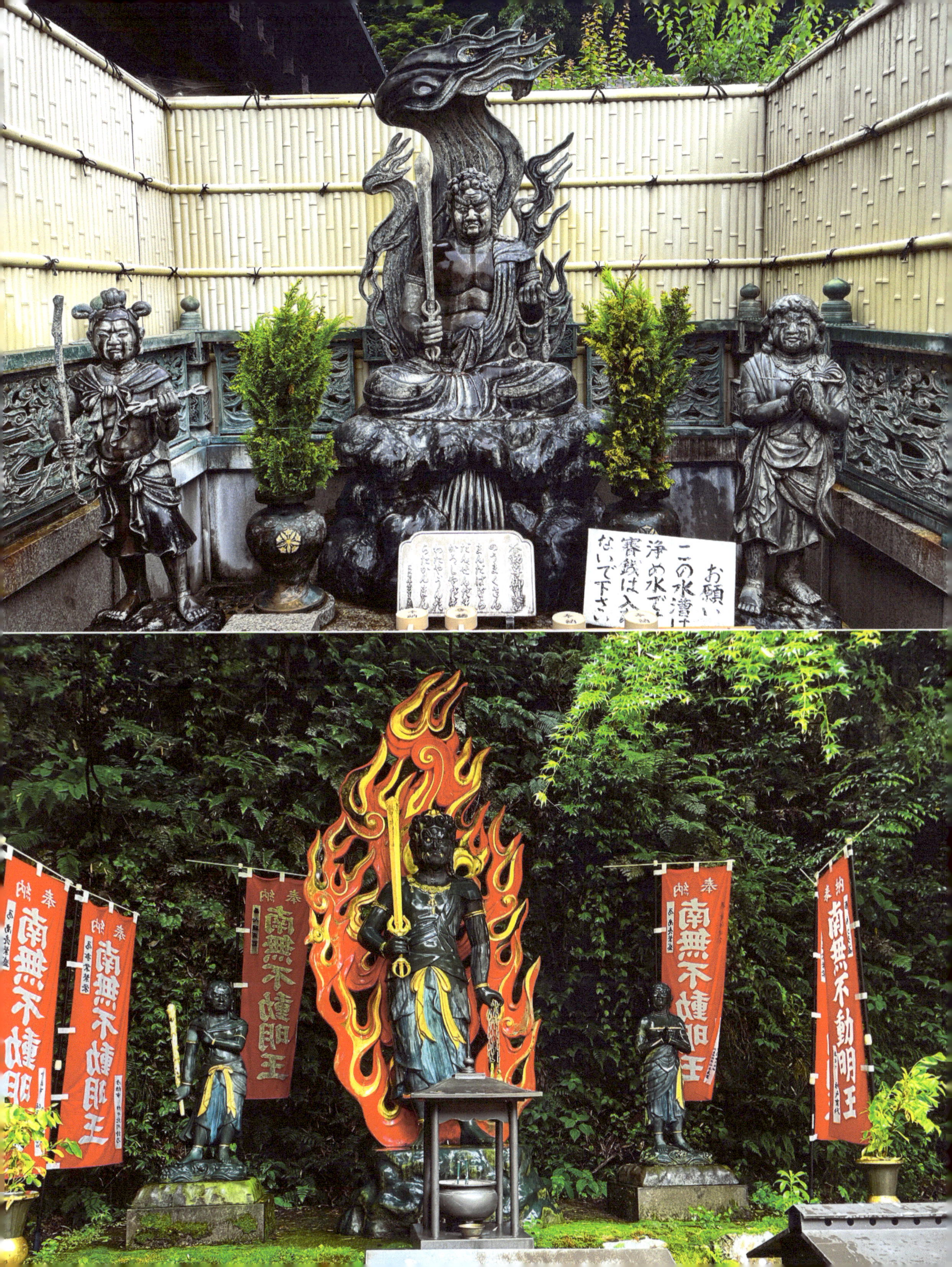
お願い
この水
浄め水で
賽銭は入
ないで下さい
奉納
南無不動明王
奉納
南無不動明王
奉納
南無不動明王
奉納
南無不動明王
奉納
南無不動明王

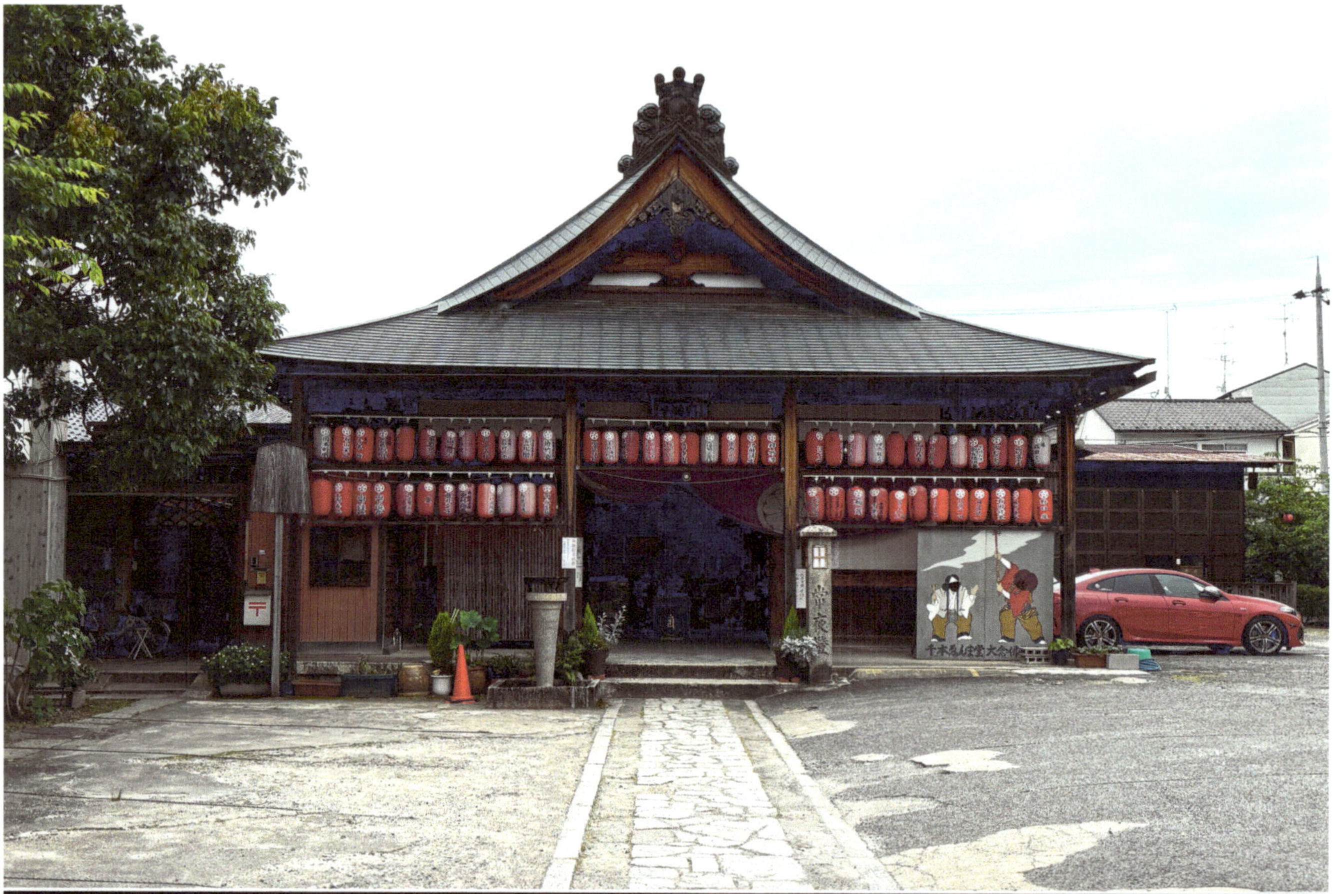

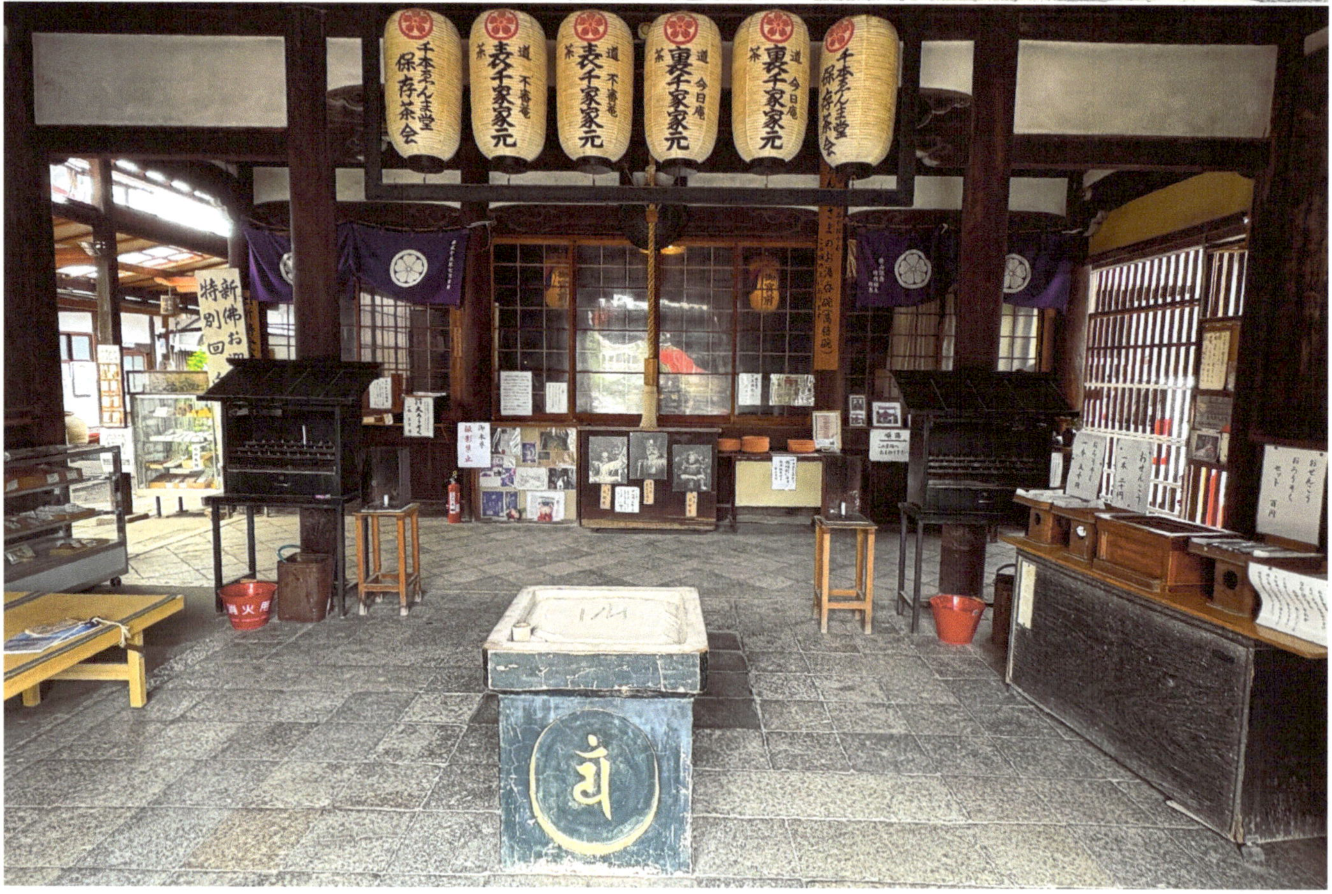

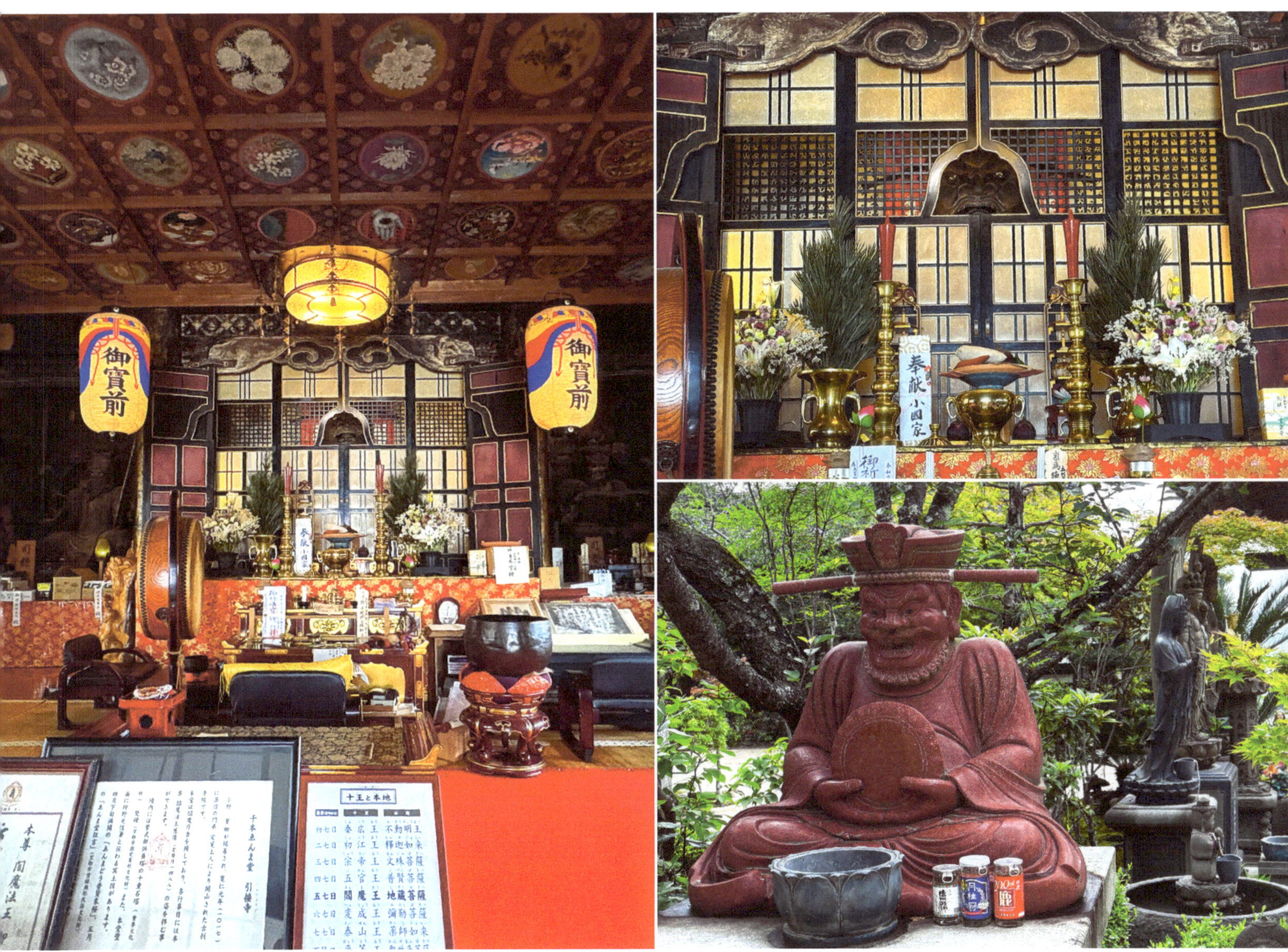

This page and opposite page.
Enmaten (Skt. *Yama*) – *Injō-ji, Kyoto; Daishō-in, Miyajima*

Enmaten is the Buddhist form of the Hindu deity of death and dharma, *Yama*. In the Daishō-in statue (above right bottom) Enmaten holds a round mirror of karma, where each soul must face the true record of its deeds before he assigns their next rebirth. Inside the main hall of Injō-ji, the mantra "oṃ yamāya svāhā" is written in bonji script (above) while his fierce eyes peer through the small opening in the lattice behind the altar (right top). Yama is flanked by *Shiroku* (Skt. *Citragupta*) and *Shimyō* (Skt. *Vicitragupta*). At the entrance, the offering box (left) diplays the Siddham seed syllable *yam* (यं), for Yama.

Next page (both pages).
Binzuru (Skt. *Pindola Bhāradvāja*) –
Temples across Japan

Binzuru gains powerful yogic Skt. *siddhi* abilities in the Buddha's time and shows them off. The Buddha rebukes him and bars him from final nirvāṇa until the next Buddha. In Japan, Binzuru becomes a healer who stays close to ordinary people. His statues sit near temple entrances so anyone can approach, rub the worn wood where they feel pain, and then touch the same place on their own bodies, asking this ubiquitous Indian elder-monk to take on their illness and grant relief.

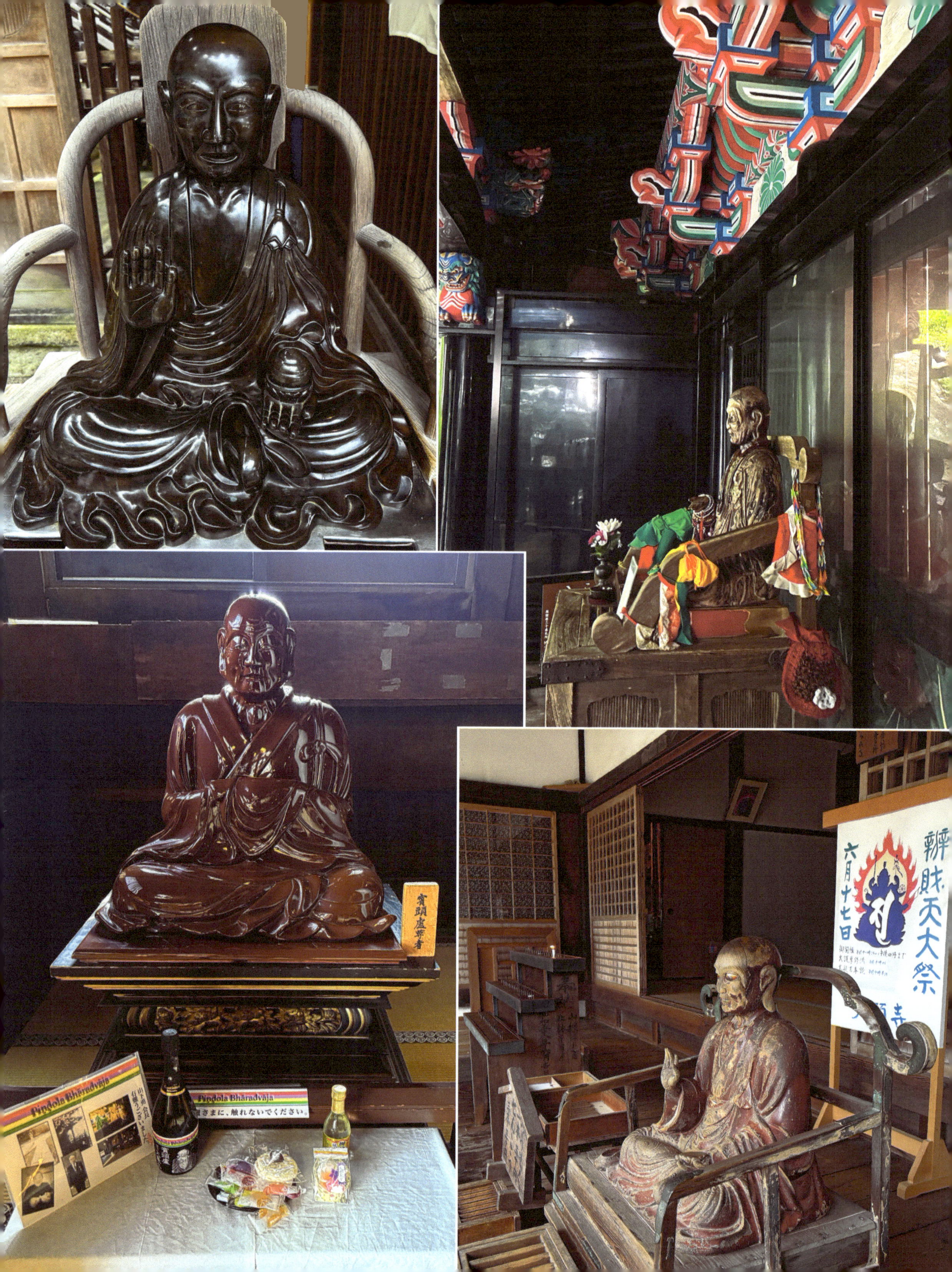

賓頭盧尊者
Piṇḍola Bhāradvāja
Piṇḍola Bhāradvāja
さまに、触れないでください。
辨財天大祭
六月十七日

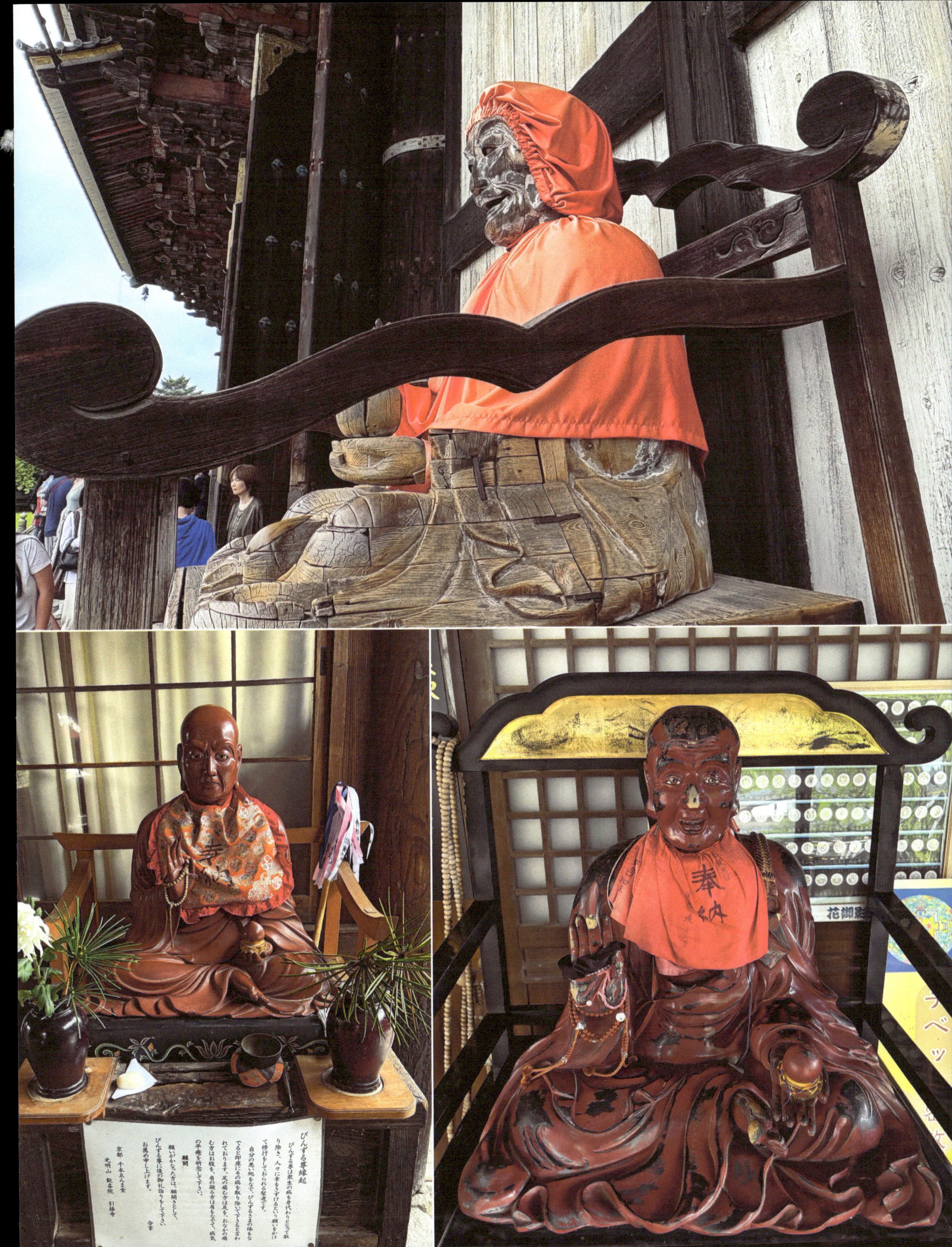
奉納
びんずる尊縁起
びんずる尊は衆生の病を身代わりとなって取
り除き、人々に幸をさずけるという願いをかけ
て修行をしておられる聖者です。
自分の悪い処をなで、びんずるさまの体をな
でると即座にその病を取り除いて下さるといわ
れております。足の痛む方は足を、おなかの痛
む方はお腹を、肩の凝る方は肩をなでて、病気
の平癒を祈念して下さい。
願開
願いがかなった方は、願開きとして、
びんずる尊に後の御礼詣りをして下さい
お薦め申し上げます。
合掌
京都 千本えんま堂
光明山 歓喜院 引接寺

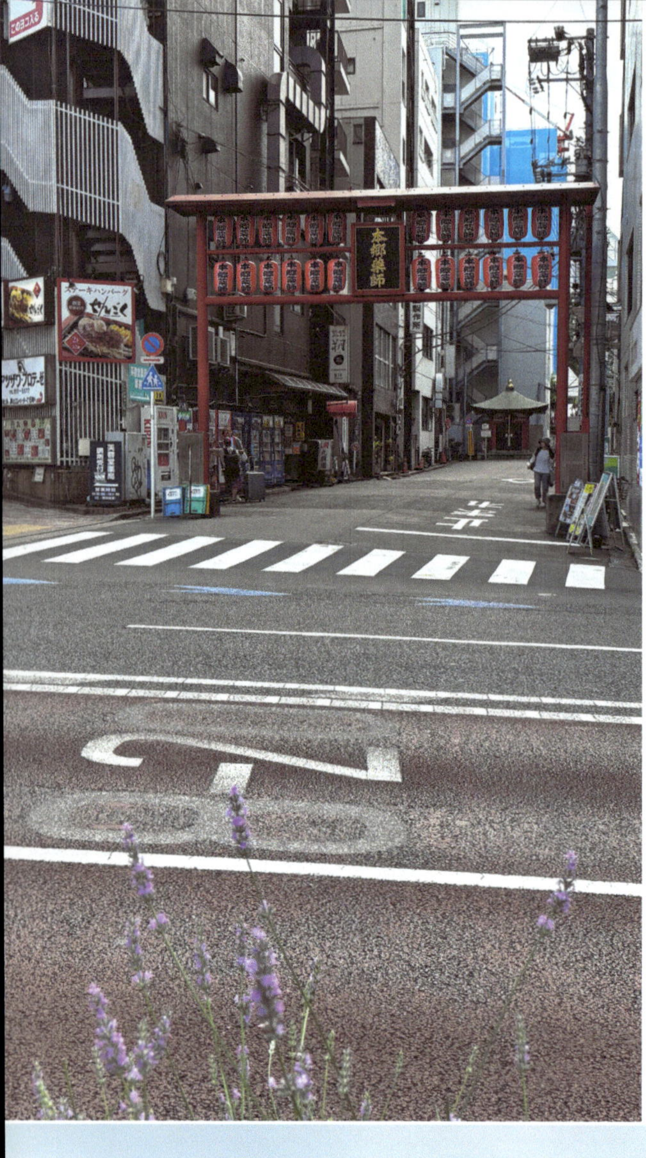

This page (top and bottom).
Yakushi Nyorai (Skt. *Bhaiṣajyaguru*) – *Bunkyō, Tokyo; Tō-ji, Kyoto*

Bhaiṣajyaguru (*bhaiṣajya* "medicine" + *guru* "teacher") becomes *Yakushi* in Japanese. *Skt. tathāgata* meaning *tathā* ("thus") + *gata* ("gone") or *āgata* ("come"), a word that can be read as beyond both coming and going, is often applied to the Buddha. *Nyorai*, derived from this idea, preserves primarily the "thus-come" sense. As such, Yakushi Nyorai is a medicine Buddha. Yakushi's healing function is a Buddhist counterpart to *Dhanvantari*, divine physician in Hinduism: both hold healing substances (*amṛta* in Hindu iconography, a medicine jar in Yakushi's), and both are invoked as givers of health who relieve physical illness while also easing spiritual afflictions.

In a random photo I took near the University of Tokyo, I later noticed a small Yakushi/Dhanvantari temple in the background. At Tō-ji, Yakushi is enshrined in the *Kondō* Hall (built in a blend of styles, including elements described as Jp. *Tenjiku-yō*, literally "Indian style") with his attendants *Nikkō* and *Gakkō* (sun and moon), similar to the Bhagavad Gītā's *viśvarūpa darśanam* vision of the cosmic form as *śaśisūryanetram … paśyāmi tvāṃ* (Bhagavad Gītā 11.19), "with the Sun and Moon as Your eyes … I see You."

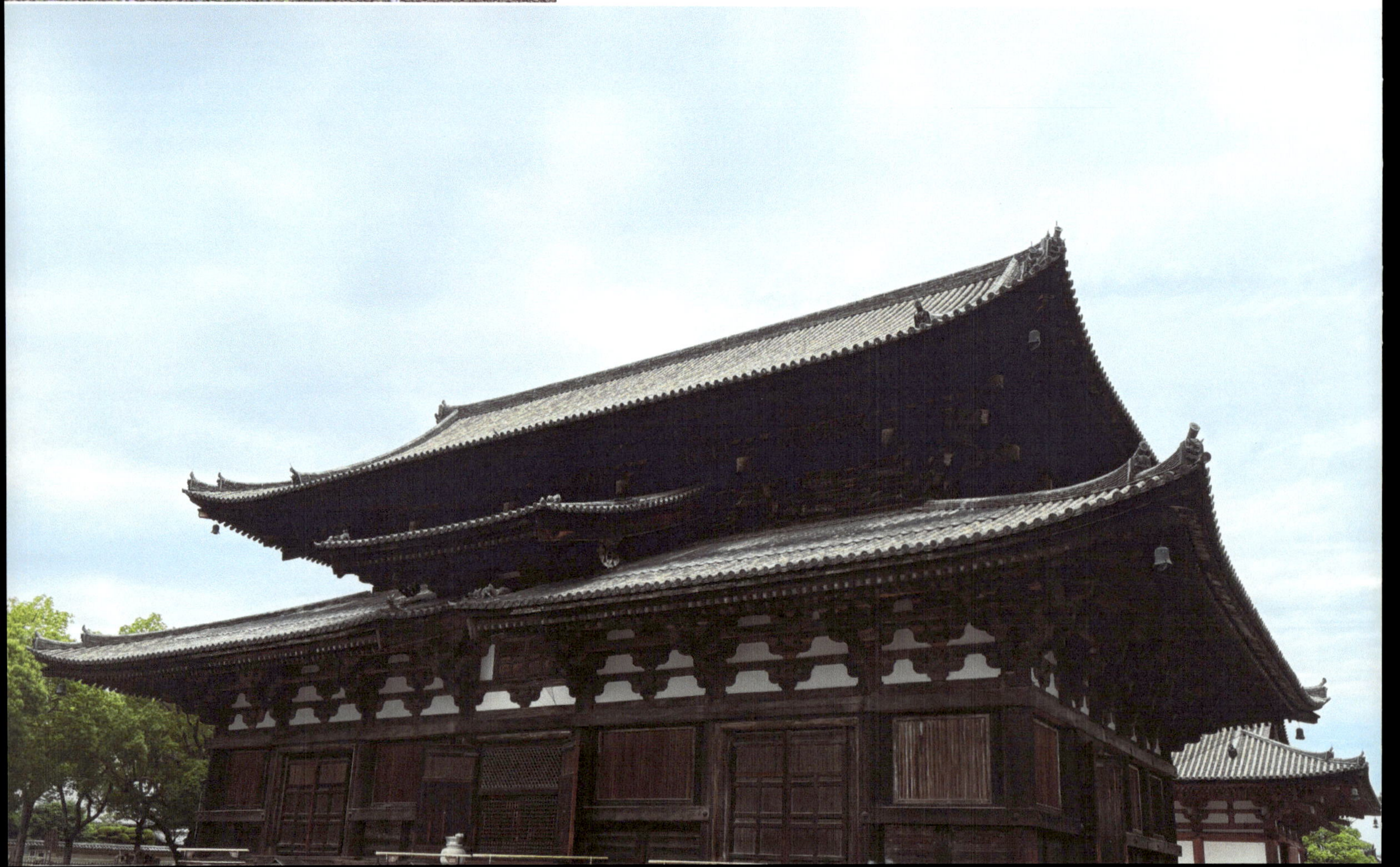

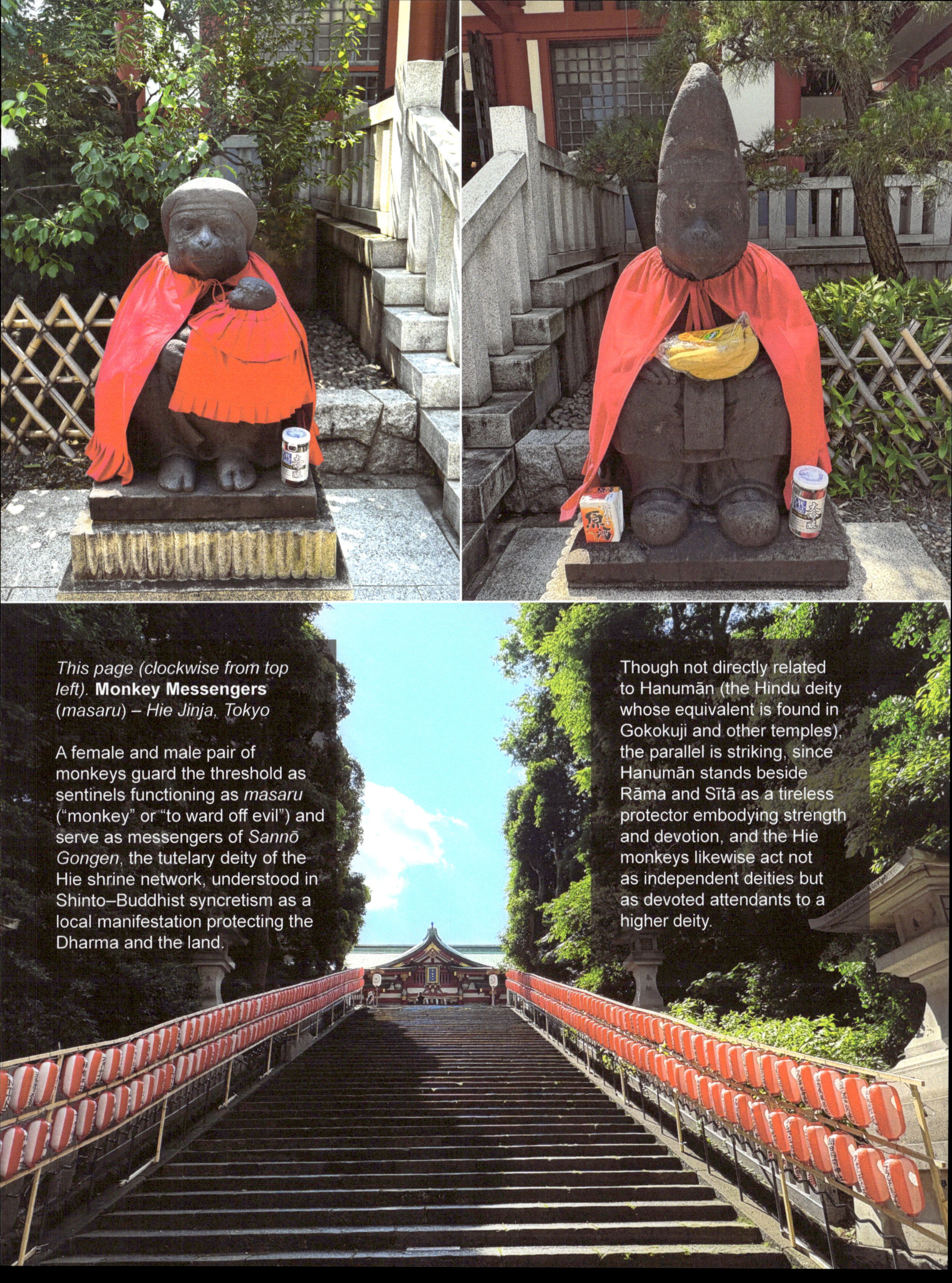

This page (clockwise from top left). **Monkey Messengers** (*masaru*) – *Hie Jinja, Tokyo*

A female and male pair of monkeys guard the threshold as sentinels functioning as *masaru* ("monkey" or "to ward off evil") and serve as messengers of *Sannō Gongen*, the tutelary deity of the Hie shrine network, understood in Shinto–Buddhist syncretism as a local manifestation protecting the Dharma and the land.

Though not directly related to Hanumān (the Hindu deity whose equivalent is found in Gokokuji and other temples), the parallel is striking, since Hanumān stands beside Rāma and Sītā as a tireless protector embodying strength and devotion, and the Hie monkeys likewise act not as independent deities but as devoted attendants to a higher deity.

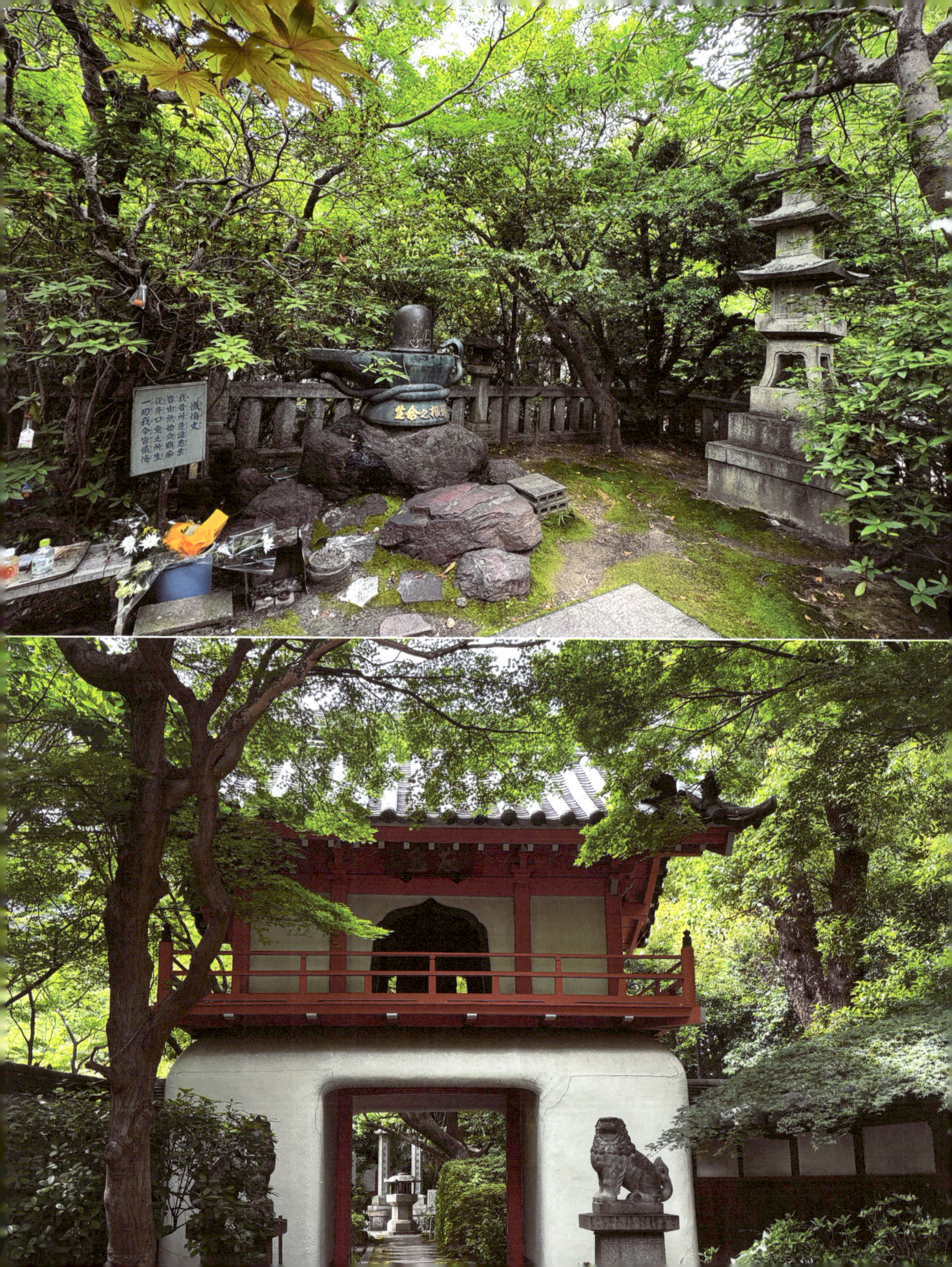
懺悔文
我昔所造諸悪業
皆由無始貪瞋痴
従身口意之所生
一切我今皆懺悔
生命之根

Opposite page (top and bottom).
Śiva-liṅga and Temple Gate – *Tōgan-ji, Nagoya*

At Tōgan-ji, a Sōtō Zen temple built by a samurai, Śiva is described not as a foreign deity, but as the primordial energy of the *hōshin* (Skt. *Dharmakāya*), the cosmic body of the Buddha. In Zen Buddhism, *hōshin* is the formless, ultimate reality. Because the Śiva-liṅga can also be understood in Hindu philosophy as a primordial, unmanifest source, the temple treats the Śiva-liṅga as a physical pointer to the same formless state Zen practitioners seek in meditation.

The gold characters on the base read 生命之根源 (Jp. *seimei no kongen*), meaning "Source of Life." This phrasing helps bridge the gap for Japanese visitors, explaining that the energy of Śiva is the primal vibration that underpins all existence, including the Buddha's own manifestation. The form is a classic Hindu Śiva-liṅga set on a spouted base for libations, and visitors pour water using the ladle (Jp. *Konjō* / Skt. *abhiṣeka*). A coiled serpent wraps the base, reinforcing the Hindu iconography even in a Japanese temple setting.

According to Tōgan-ji's own historical records, a former head priest traveled to India to study the original sources of Buddhism. The Śiva-liṅga here is presented as an attempt to bring Japanese Zen into direct contact with India's Vedic and Tantric roots again, not only through texts, but through a physical object of worship. In that sense, the Skt. *liṅga* functions like a deliberate return to origins, reconnecting with the Indian spiritual source.

This page (below).
Myōken Bosatsu (Skt. *dhruva*) Temple – *Aioi*

This photo is taken from a train window, and only later do I notice a temple in the background. When I looked it up, it turned out to be dedicated to Myōken Bosatsu, the North Star deity. In Sanskrit, *dhruva* means "fixed," and Dhruva is the name given to the North Star, revered as an ardent devotee of Viṣṇu. In Japan, that same idea of the North Star becomes Myōken Bosatsu, a Buddhist deification of the North Star honored for protection and guidance. Even a chance photo like this made me realize how pervasive Vedic and Hindu influences are across Japan.

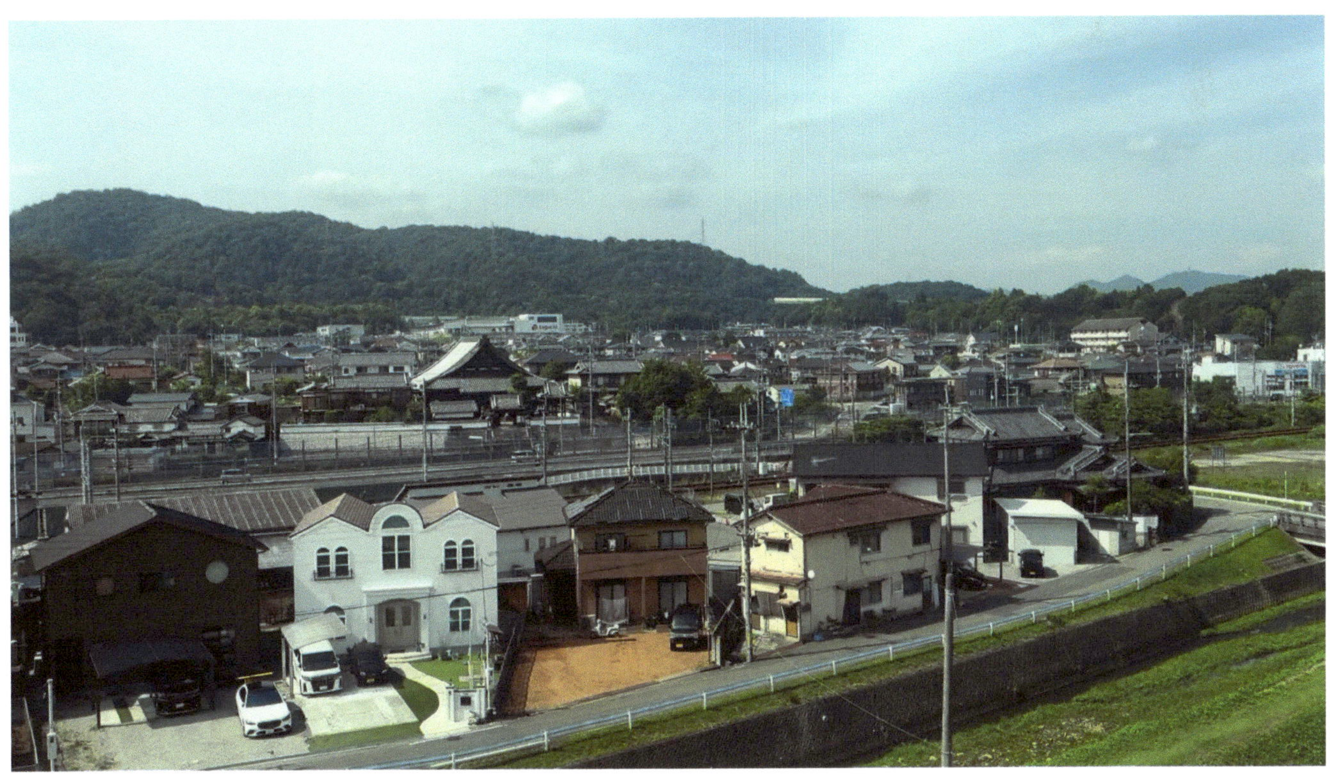

This spread (all images).
Bodhisattvas (Skt. *bodhisattva*) – *Across Japan*

The Sanskrit word bodhisattva means "one whose being is devoted to awakening," a figure who takes a vow to delay his own final nirvāṇa in order to guide others. In Japan, the same word is read as bosatsu, so names like Jizō Bosatsu and Kannon Bosatsu preserve this Sanskrit term even when everyday speech shortens them to just Jizō or Kannon.

Bodhisattvas form a bridge between distant Buddhas and ordinary worshippers. Bronze figures like these appear in city gardens and temples, among rows of children's memorial statues, and in mossy cemeteries such as Kōyasan's Okunoin, watching over both the living and the dead.

Bodhisattvas are typically shown with halos and lotus bases, hands holding lotus buds, jewels, or staffs and making reassuring, gift-giving gestures. The lotus itself comes from Hindu iconography used in art for all deities. Lakṣmī is often shown holding an opened lotus or even a spent lotus heavy with seeds, symbolizing abundance already in bloom, while many Japanese bodhisattvas hold a still-closed bud, suggesting awakening that is just about to unfold.

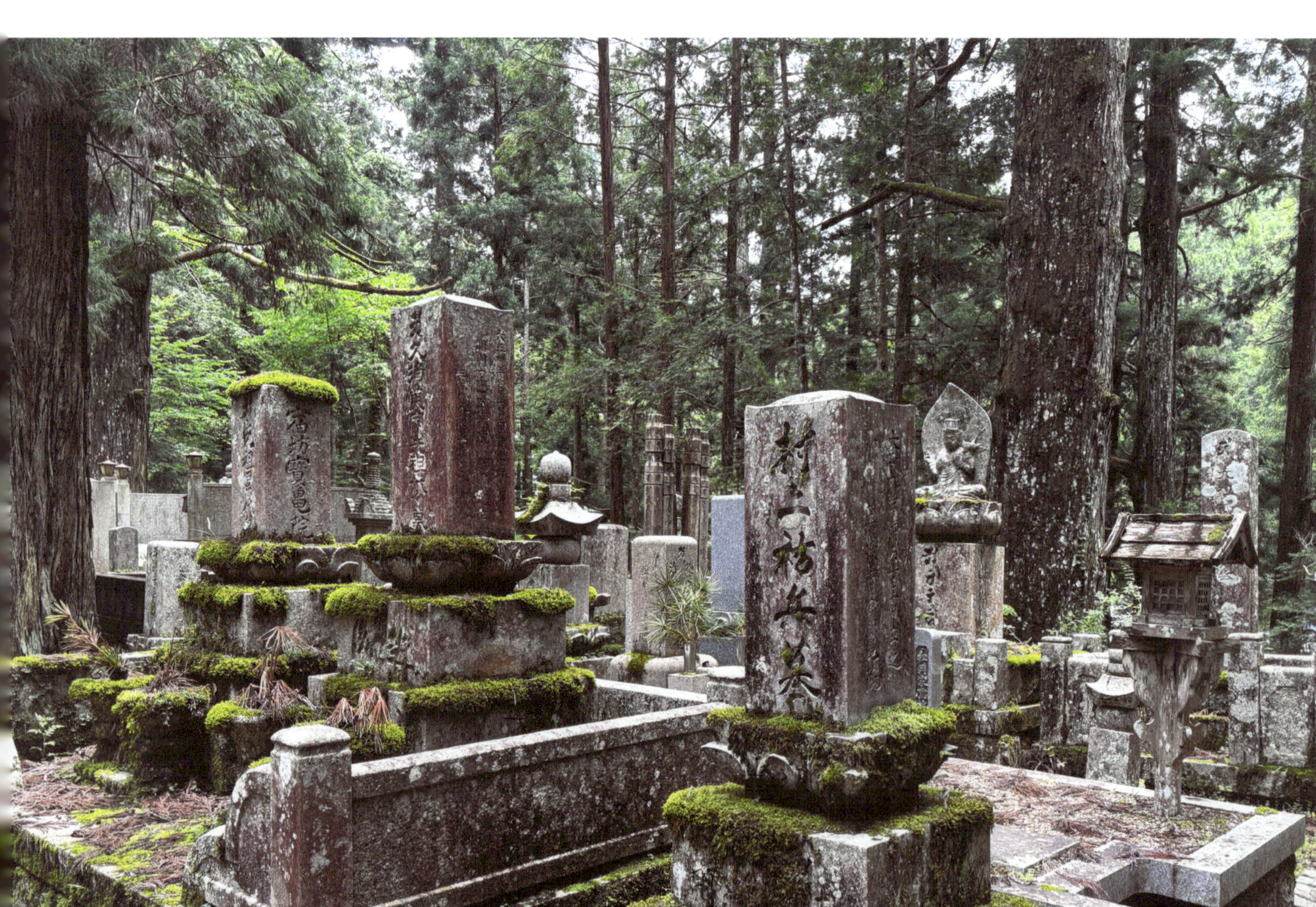

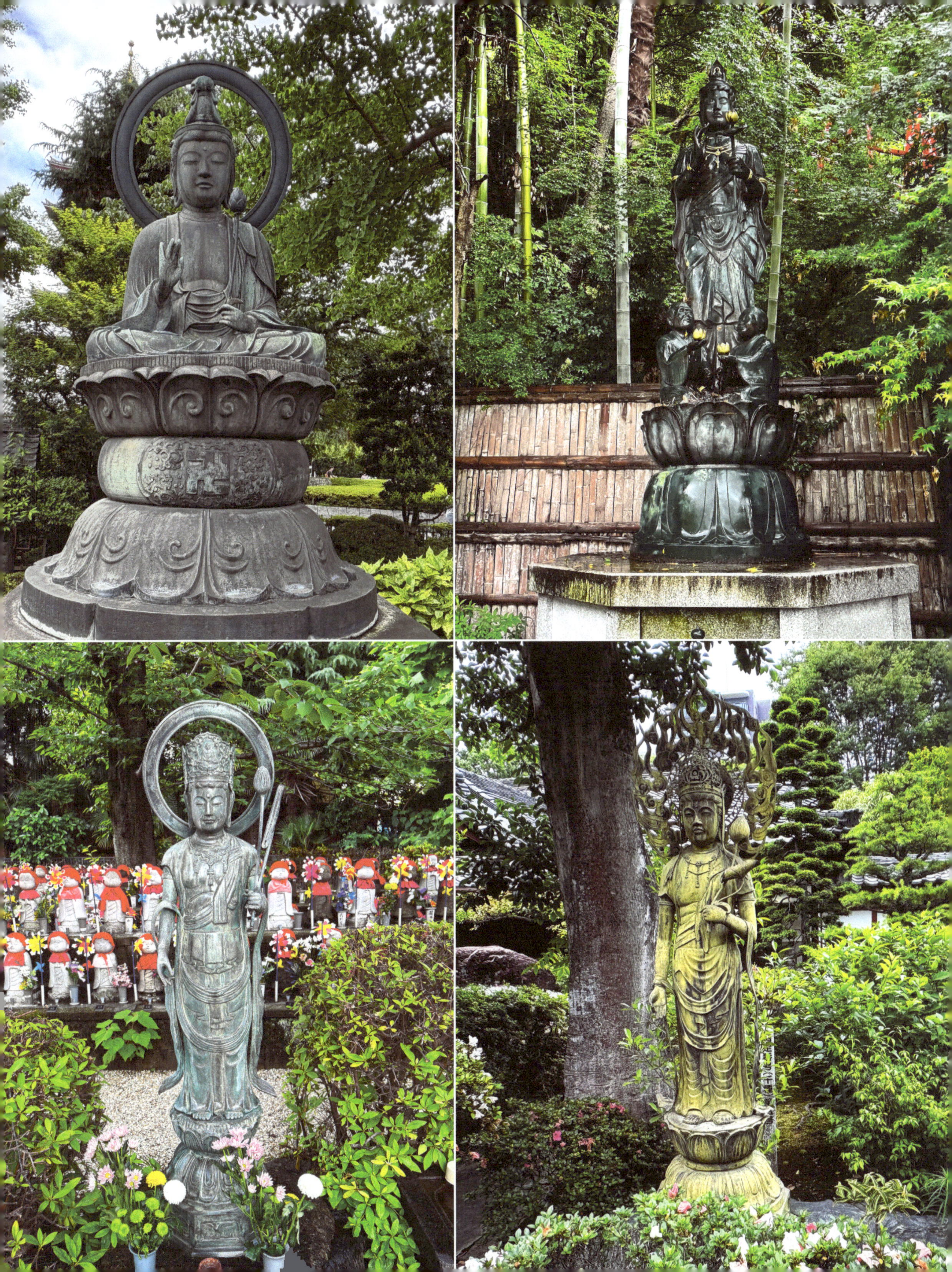

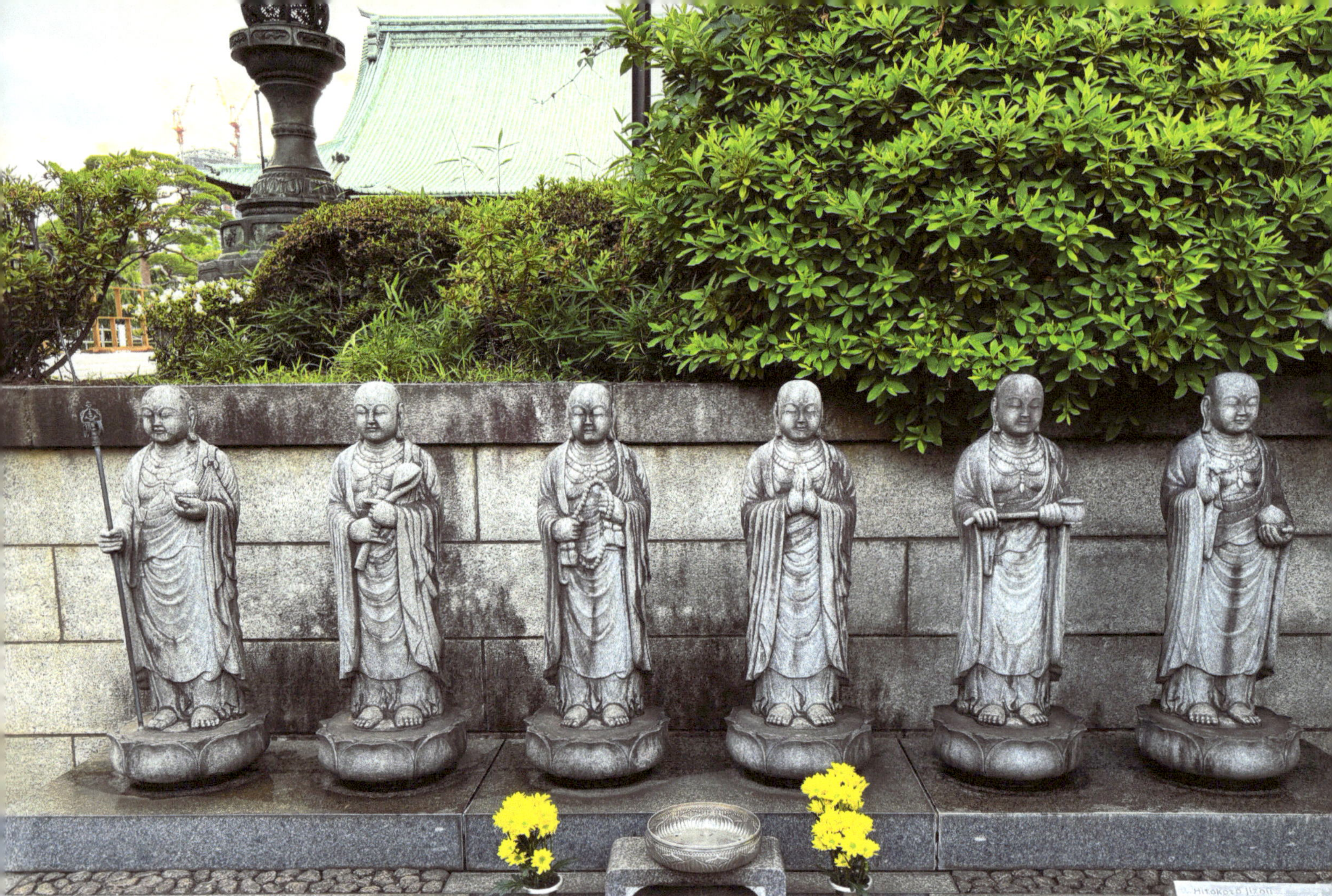

This page and opposite page (clockwise from above).
Jizō Bosatsu (Skt. *Kṣitigarbha*) – *Gokoku-ji, Tokyo; Daishō-in, Miyajima; Okunoin, Kōyasan*

These images show Jizō Bosatsu, one of Japan's most beloved bodhisattvas, in classic groupings of Six Jizō (Jp. *Roku Jizō*). Each figure embodies his promise to guide beings in one of the Six Realms of existence – Skt. *naraka* (hell beings), Skt. *preta* (hungry ghosts), Skt. *tiryag* (animals), Skt. *manuṣya* (humans), Skt. *asura* (jealous gods), and Skt. *deva* (deities) – so that no corner of the Buddhist cosmos is left without a compassionate guide. You can recognize them from their monk's robes, shaven heads, and calm faces; some carry a six ring-topped staff (*shakujō*, from the Skt. *khakkhara*), others a wish-fulfilling jewel (Skt. *cintāmaṇi*), scroll, or begging bowl, showing him by turns as wandering pilgrim, light in the darkness, teacher of scripture, and humble mendicant. Jizō's compassion is sometimes described as so immediate that statues are believed to weep, or even perspire, as they take on the suffering of those who pray to them.

His Sanskrit name *Kṣitigarbha* joins *kṣiti* "earth" with *garbha* "womb/treasure," and early Indian Buddhist ritual texts link him with *Prithvī Devī*, the Earth goddess invoked for agricultural prosperity and the protection of crops, which helps explain the "earth" in his name. In Japan, this "Earth Store" bodhisattva is especially worshipped as the protector of children (including deceased and unborn), travelers, pilgrims, and those suffering in the realms of the dead. At Daishō-in, the hillside paths are lined with small Jizō in knitted red caps and scarves, dressed by local devotees as offerings and prayers for the safety of children and travelers, while at Kōyasan a bibbed Buddha watches over a mound of tiny Jizō and piled stones, a *muen-zuka* or "mound of the nameless," where the forgotten dead, including many unnamed and unborn children, are entrusted to his care.

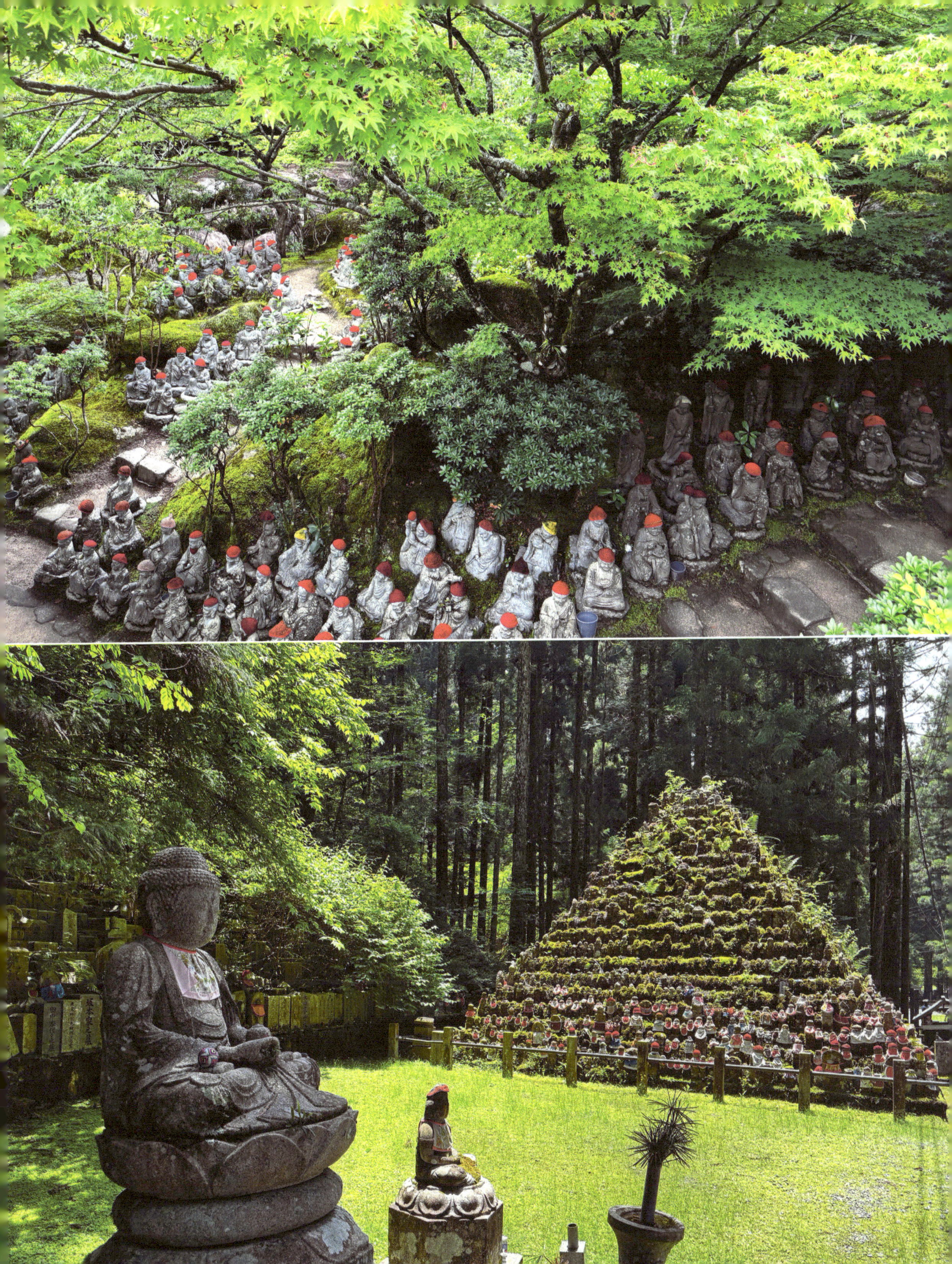

This page (right and below).
Jizō Offerings – *Kinkaku-ji, Kyoto; Matsuchiyama Shōden, Tokyo*

At Kinkaku-ji, three weathered stone Jizō sit beside the path, with coins that visitors toss for luck, in a scene similar to offerings for Hindu deities in India.

At Matsuchiyama Shōden, dedicated to *Kangiten* (Skt. *Gaṇapati*), rows of Jizō line a serene courtyard, each with its own bib, flowers, and inscribed tablet with the prayers of people who come here to offer thanks and to ask for harmony at home. The Skt. *cintāmaṇi* (wish-fulfilling jewel) in Jizōs' hands feels especially apt, since it is originally and still closely associated with *Gaṇapati* in India; the famous Cintāmaṇi temple at Theur in India honors him in this form as a deity of wisdom whose jewel grants spiritual and material fulfillment.

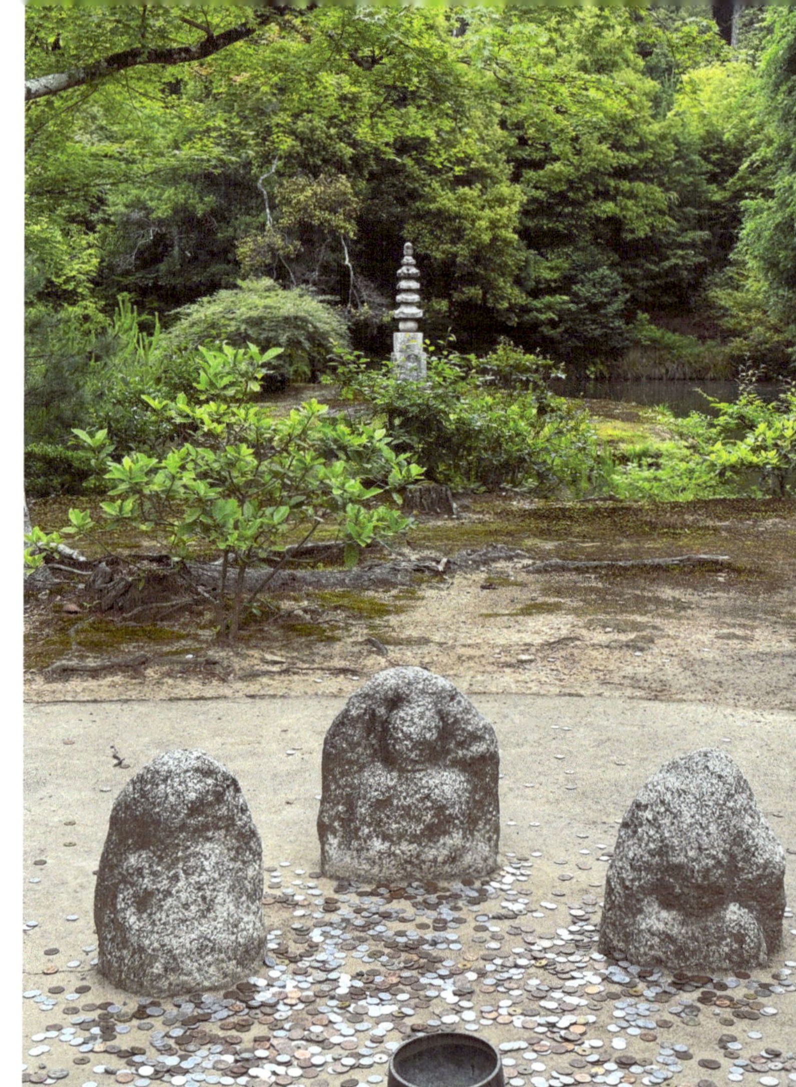

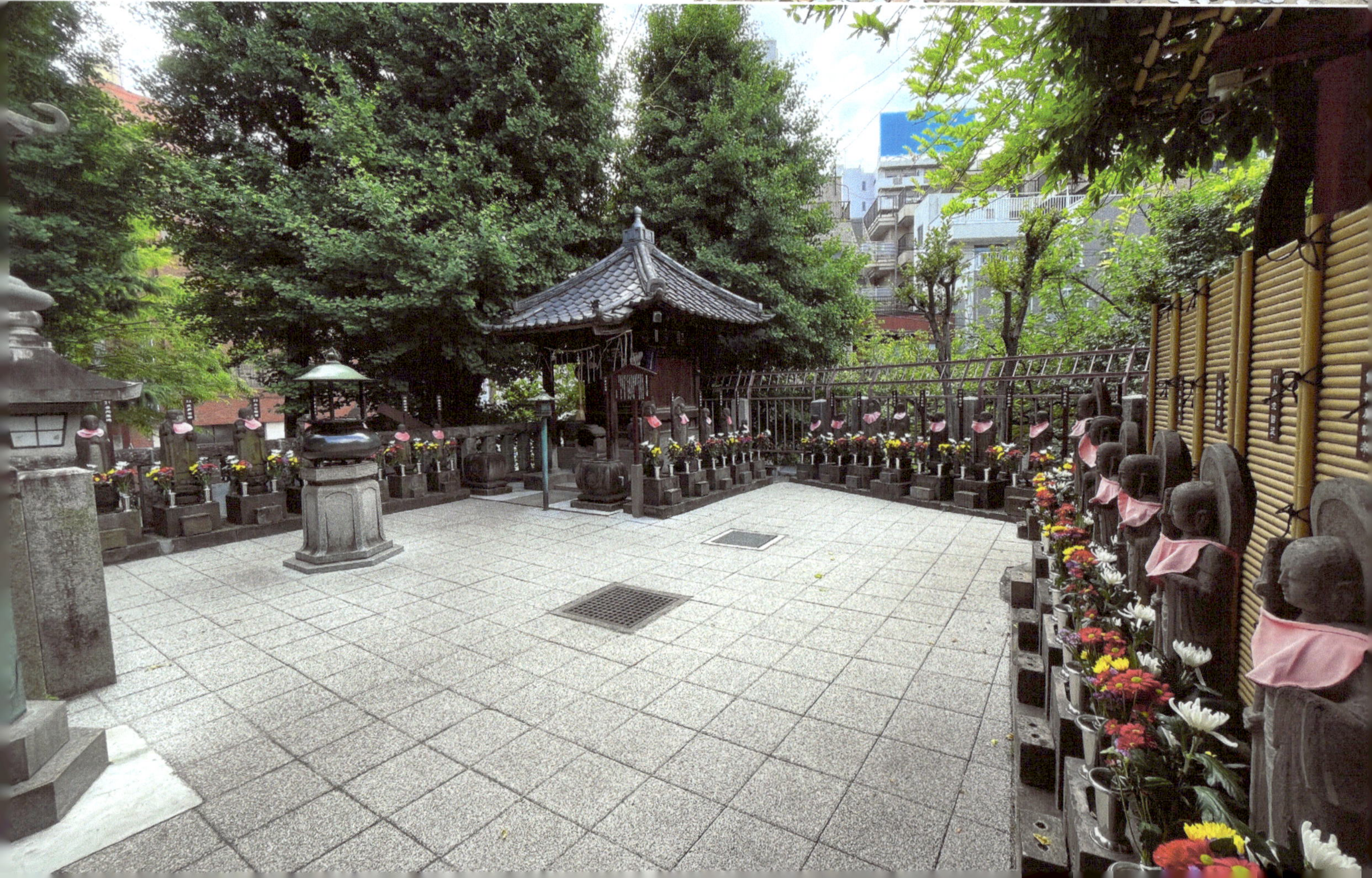

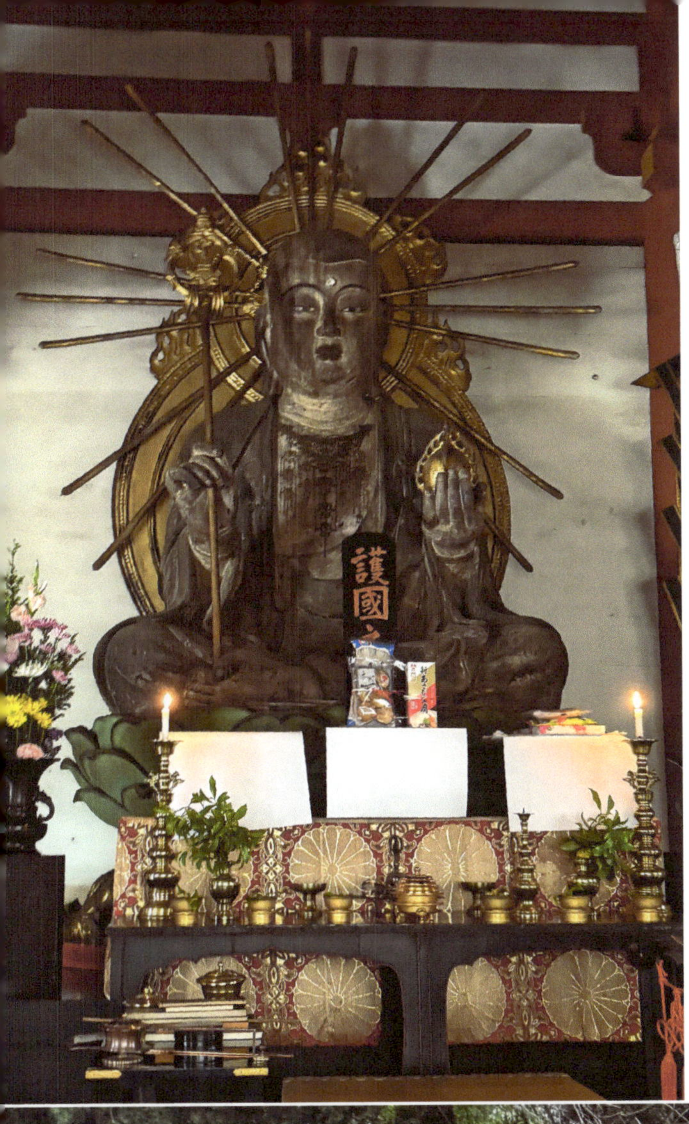

This page (left and below).
Hilltop Jizō Guardians – *Above Tōdai-ji, Nara; Hōzan-ji, Ikoma*

On the hillside above Tōdai-ji, near the great bell tower, a seated Jizō Bosatsu (Skt. *Kṣitigarbha*) holds his staff and wish-fulfilling jewel (Skt. *cintāmaṇi*) while a small plaque reading Jp. *gokoku* ("protecting the nation") leans against his chest, linking him with Tōdai-ji's ancient role as a guardian of the state.

At Hōzan-ji on Mount Ikoma, a steep forest path is lined with standing Jizō, along the way uphill.

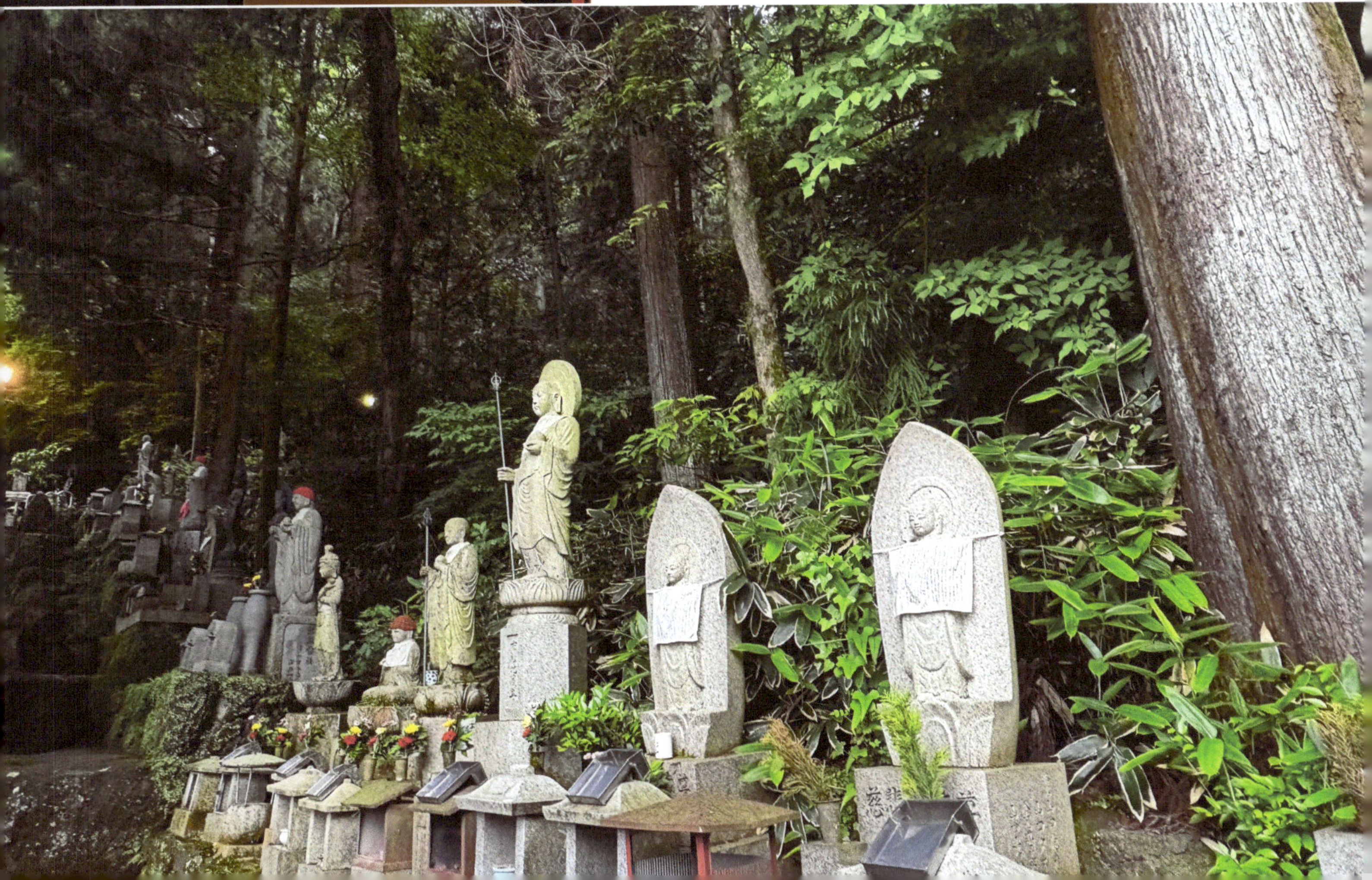

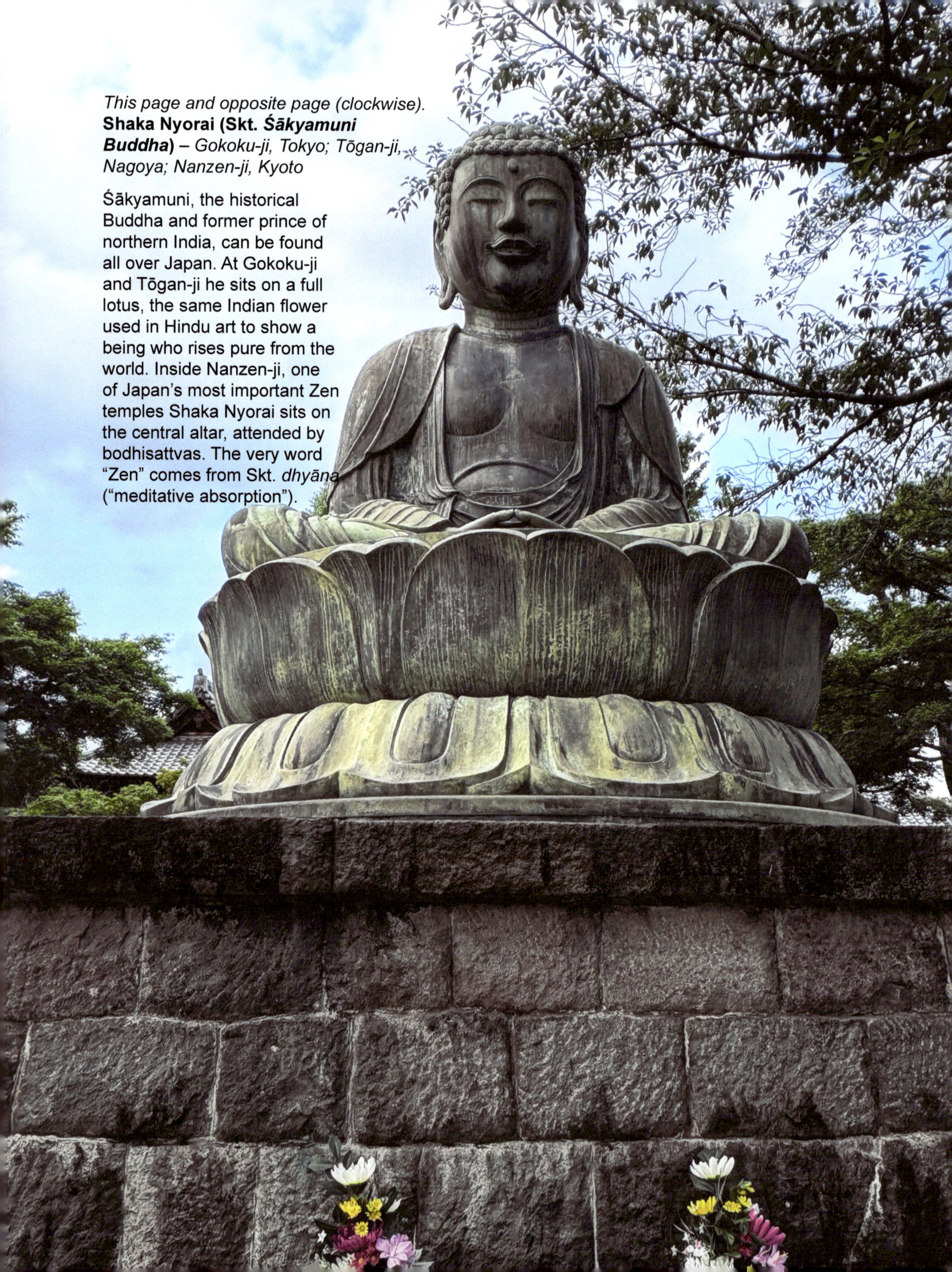

This page and opposite page (clockwise).
Shaka Nyorai (Skt. *Śākyamuni* *Buddha*) – *Gokoku-ji, Tokyo; Tōgan-ji, Nagoya; Nanzen-ji, Kyoto*

Śākyamuni, the historical Buddha and former prince of northern India, can be found all over Japan. At Gokoku-ji and Tōgan-ji he sits on a full lotus, the same Indian flower used in Hindu art to show a being who rises pure from the world. Inside Nanzen-ji, one of Japan's most important Zen temples Shaka Nyorai sits on the central altar, attended by bodhisattvas. The very word "Zen" comes from Skt. *dhyāna* ("meditative absorption").

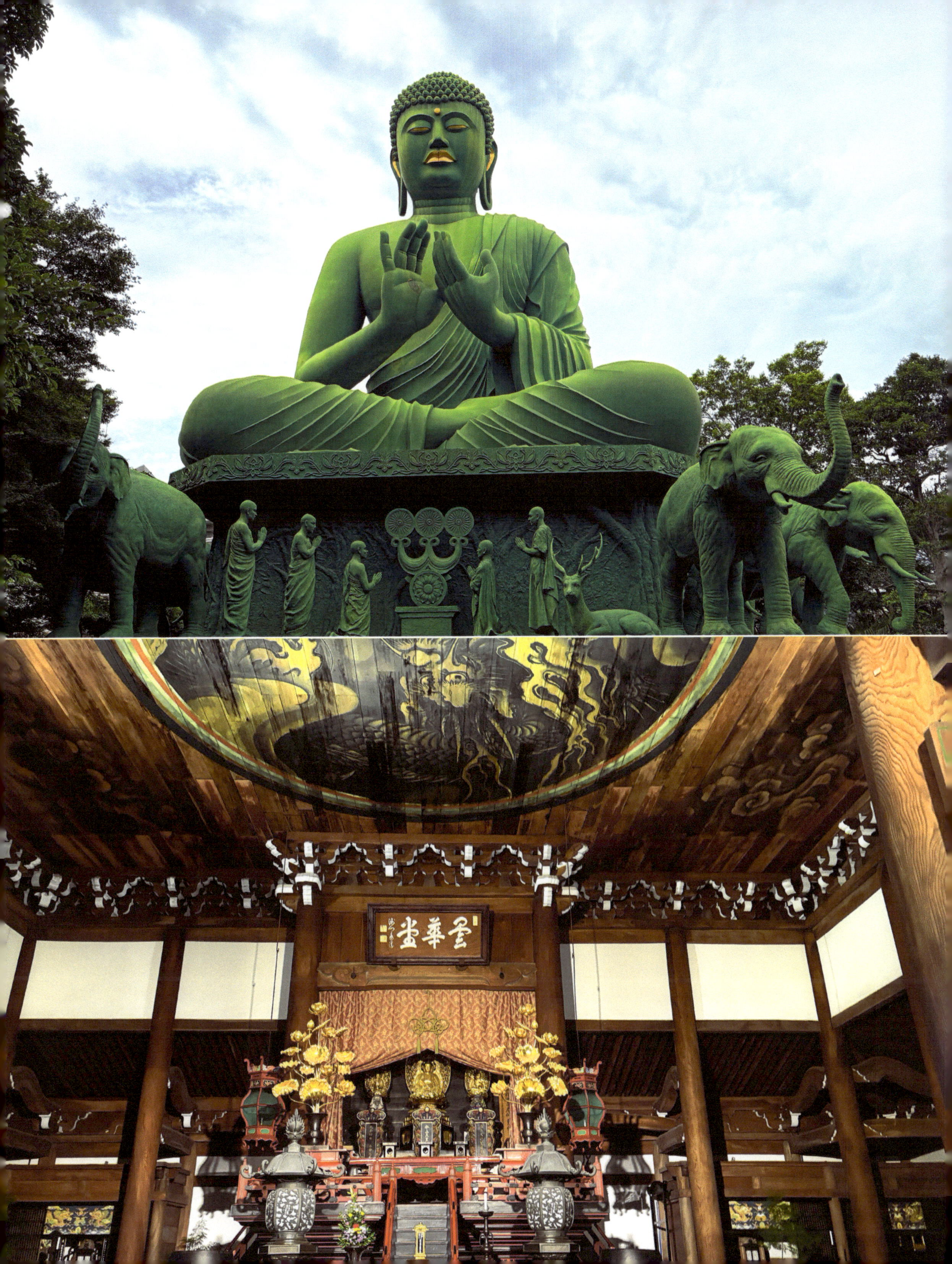

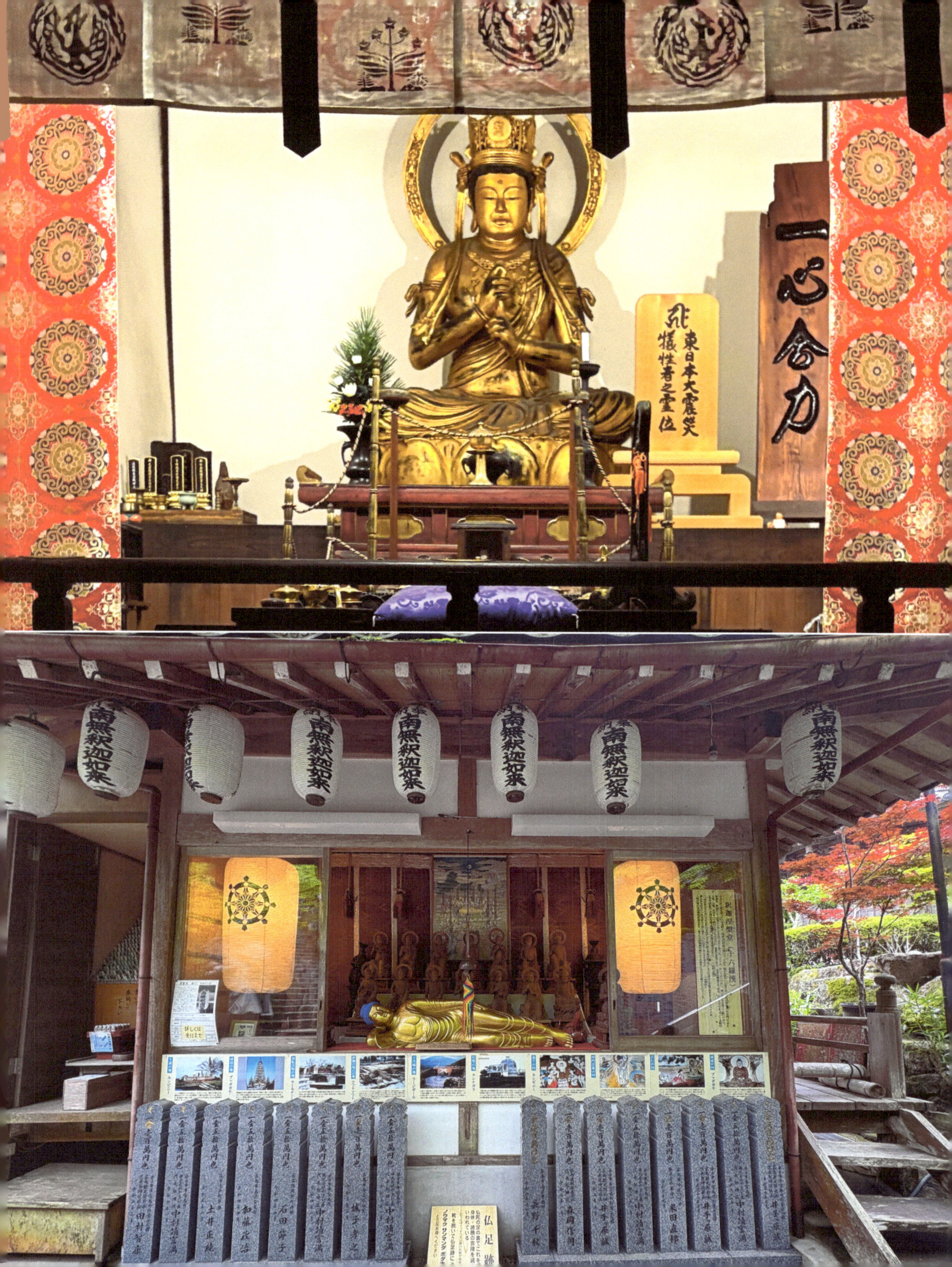
東日本大震災
犠牲者之霊位
一心合力
南無釈迦如来
仏足跡

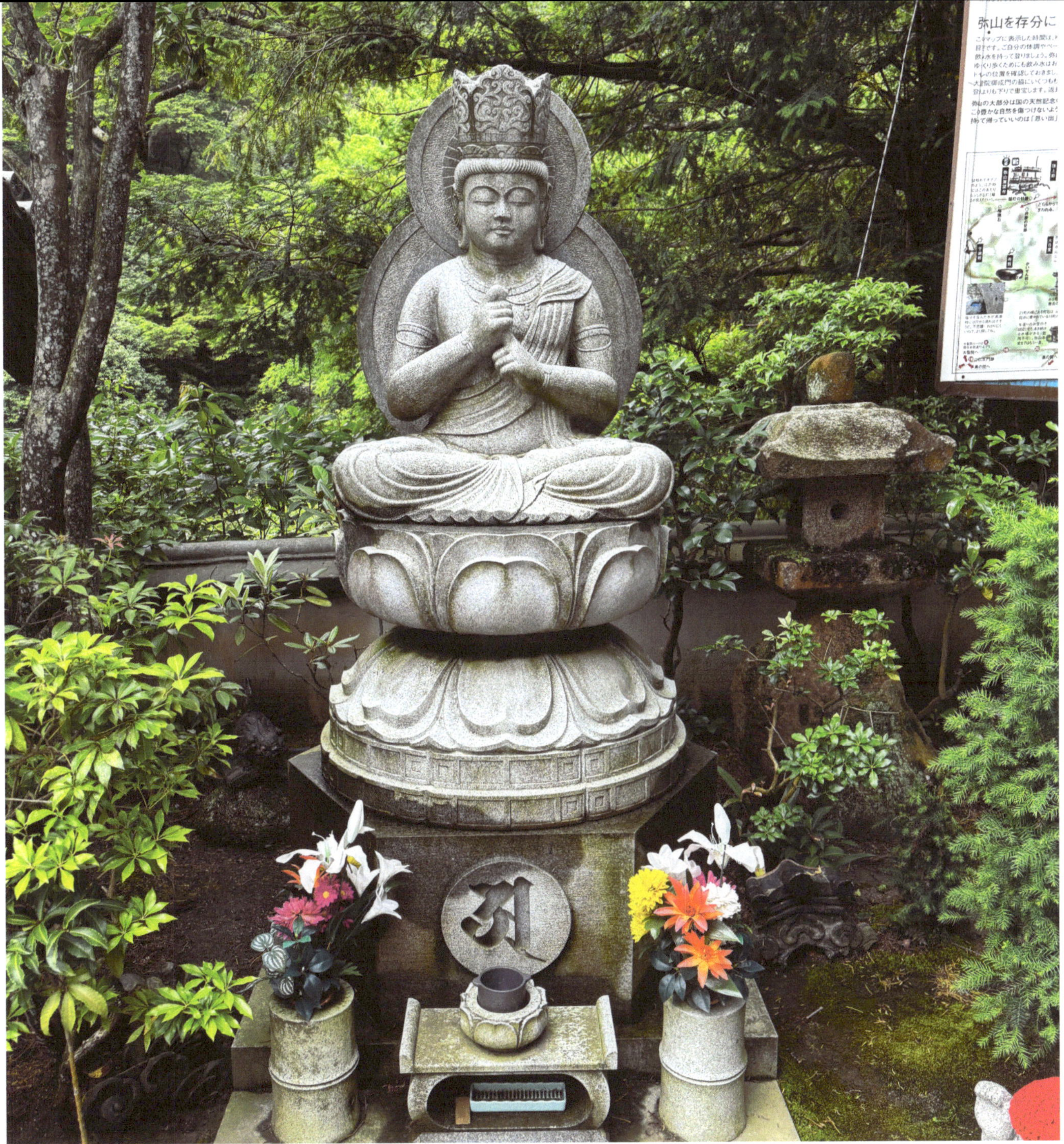

Opposite page (above) and this page (above).
Dainichi Nyorai (Skt. *Mahāvairocana*) – *Near Kiyomizu-dera, Kyoto; Daishō-in, Miyajima*

Dainichi Nyorai, "Great Sun Buddha," is at the center of the cosmic Skt. *maṇḍala*, replacing the historical Buddha as ultimate reality, much like the all-pervading Skt. *brahman* of Hinduism. His hands form the Skt. *vajra mudrā*, uniting the five elements with one consciousness. To realize the unborn Buddha-nature that pervades every being, in *Ajikan* meditators contemplate on his Sanskrit seed syllable, अ (on the base of the pedestal above).

Opposite page (below).
Reclining Buddha (Skt. *Mahāparinirvāṇa* of Śākyamuni) – *Daishō-in, Miyajima*

Here Śākyamuni lies on his right side surrounded by disciples at the moment of Skt. *mahāparinirvāṇa*, his final passing into complete *nirvāṇa*. This pose comes from early Indian depictions of the Buddha's last moments, where the enlightened teacher's death is not a tragedy but a release from further rebirth.

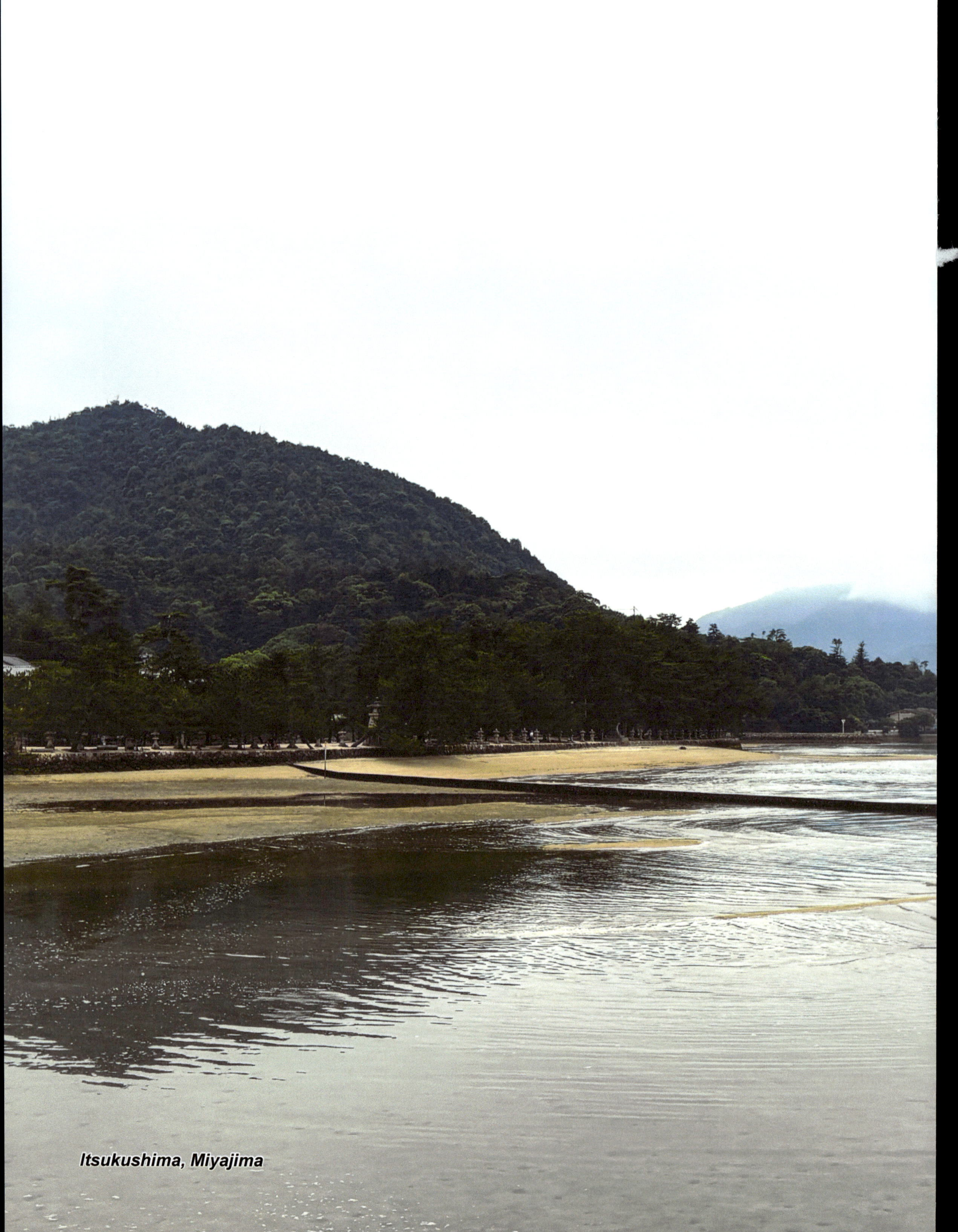
Itsukushima, Miyajima

Sacred Architecture

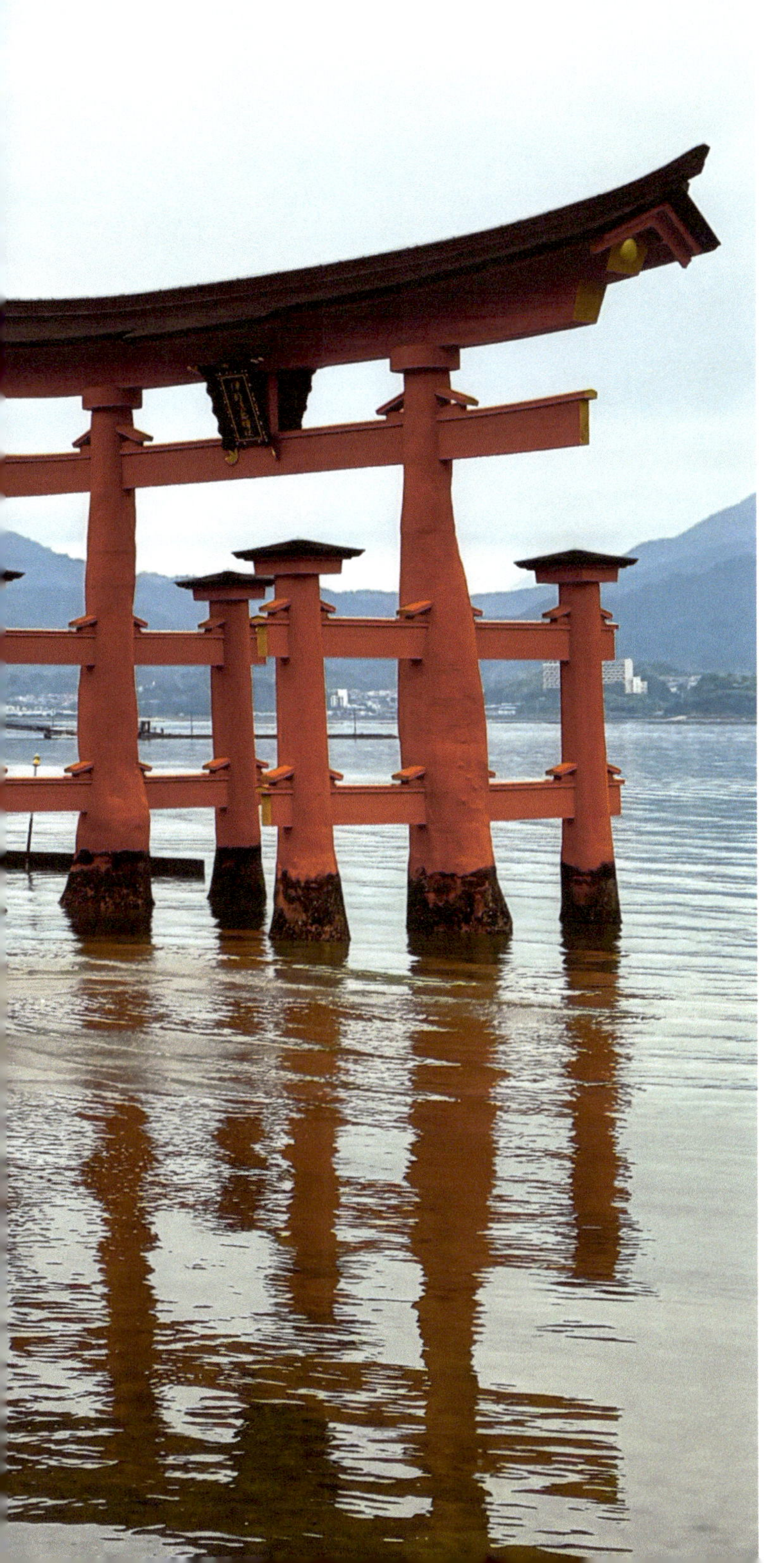

FOUR

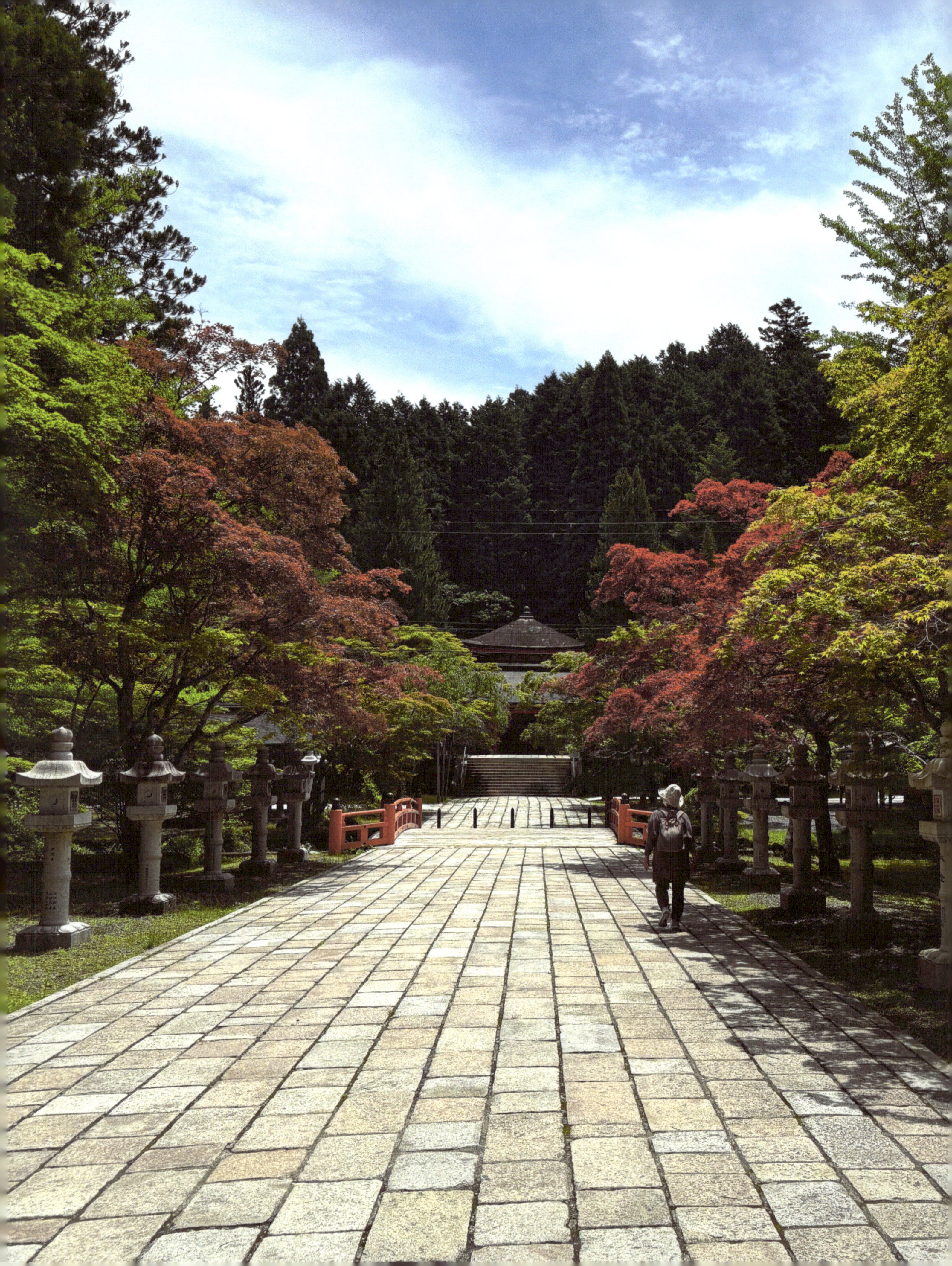

Opposite page and this page.
Next page (clockwise from top left).

Five-Story Forms – *Temples, gardens, castles, and memorials across Japan*

The five-story forms seen across Japan reflect a cosmology articulated in the *Taittirīya Upaniṣad 2.1 (Brahmānandavallī),* which describes the unfolding of the universe through the Skt. *pañca-bhūtas*, the five elements. The text states:

तस्माद्वा एतस्मादात्मन आकाशः सम्भूतः । आकाशाद्वायुः । वायोरग्निः । अग्नेरापः । अद्भ्यः पृथिवी ॥

meaning “From that very Self (*ātman*) arose space (*ākāśa*); from space, air (*vāyu*); from air, fire (*agni*); from fire, water (*āpaḥ*); from water, earth (*pṛthivī*).” The “Self” (Skt. *ātman*) is identified as *Brahman*, defined as Truth, Knowledge, and Infinite (*satyam jñānam anantam,* Taittirīya Upaniṣad 2.1). This fivefold elemental vision traveled across Asia and entered Japanese esoteric Buddhism as the *godai*, where it shaped Shingon ritual, cosmology, and architectural symbolism. Five-story pagodas, lanterns, and towers translate these elements into visible form, embedding the *pañca-bhūtas* into sacred spaces, gardens, castles, and memorials alike.

In Kōyasan Okunoin, there are thousands of 5-story stone lanterns (this page left) and 5-story memorials (right).

On Miyajima (next page top left), a stone lantern on four legs rises to a fifth rounded cap, turning the idea of the five elements into a compact form overlooking the sea. At Shitennō-ji in Osaka, a granite lantern repeats the same five-part structure. Himeji Castle’s great keep rises in five visible stories above its stone base, showing how this elemental structure shaped even military and civic architecture. On the hillside behind Tōdai-ji in Nara, stone lanterns line the path upward. In the garden of Matsuchiyama Shōden in Tokyo, a small moss-covered five story pagoda reduces the same fivefold idea to a garden ornament. In Hiroshima Peace Memorial Park, a modern five-story tower stands as a memorial for students that lost their lives in atomic bombing, adapting the same form for remembrance and mourning. At Hōzan-ji near Nara, an ornate bronze pagoda rises in five decorated stages above lotus forms, offering the five elements back to the Buddha through devotion.

From small garden corners to towering castles, the five-story pattern is woven into the Japanese landscape, reflecting the five elements first expounded in the Upaniṣads.

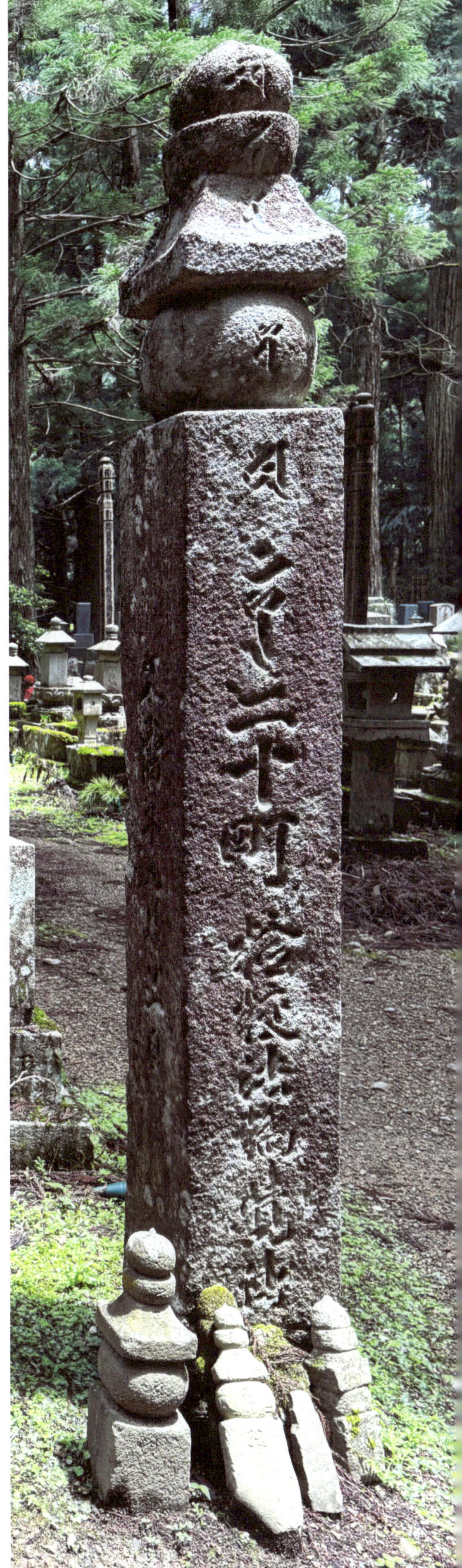

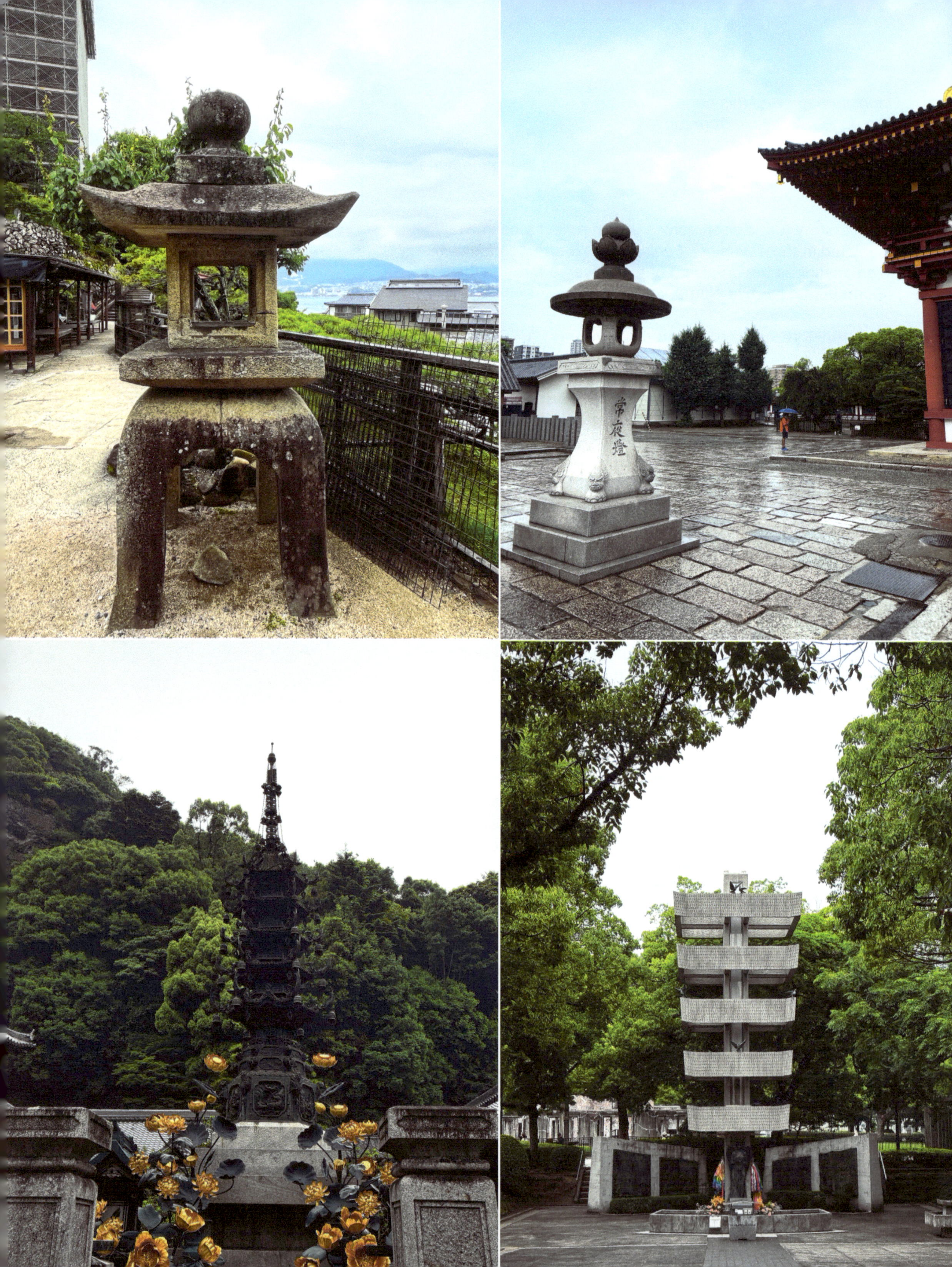
常夜燈

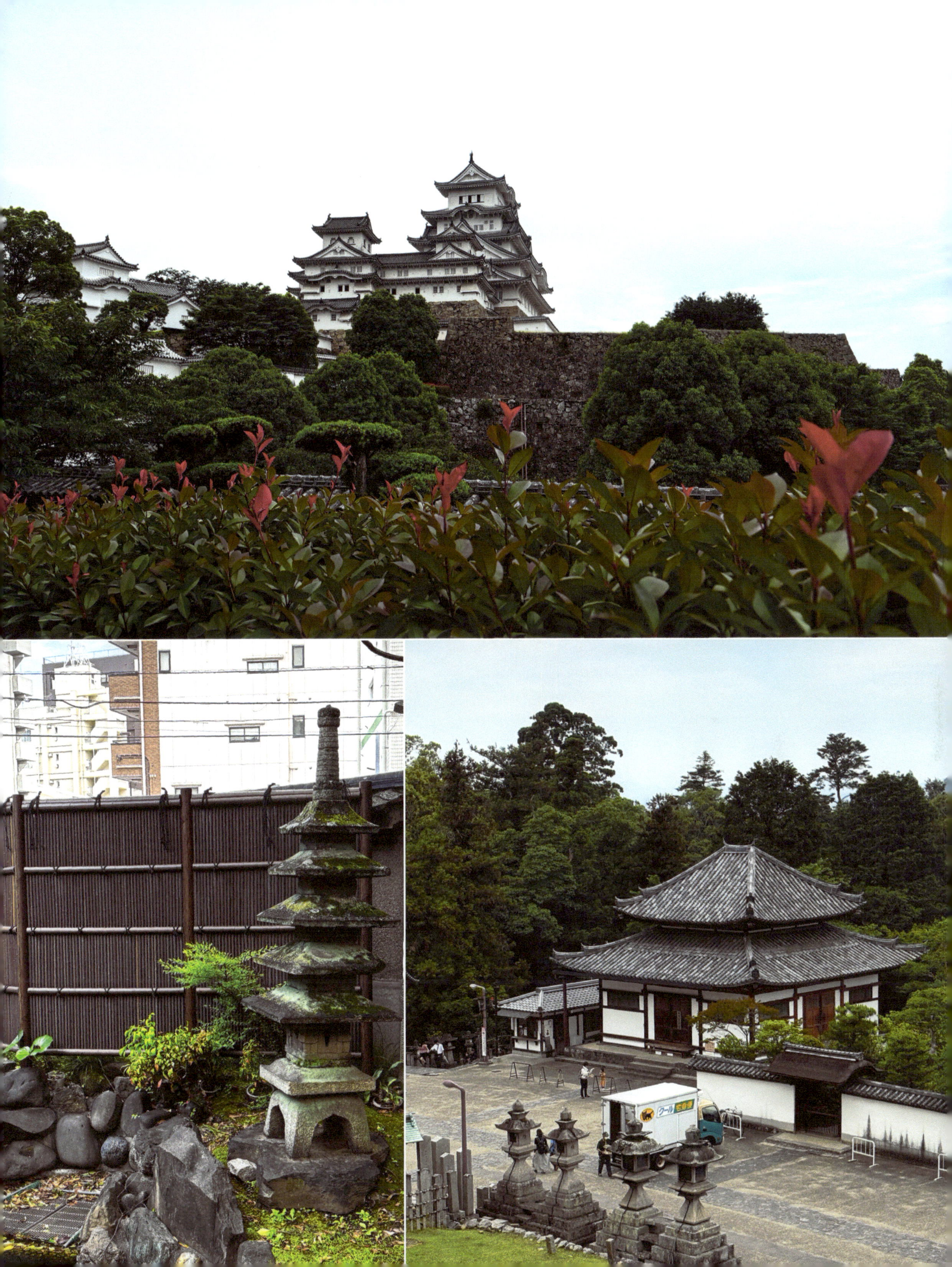
クール

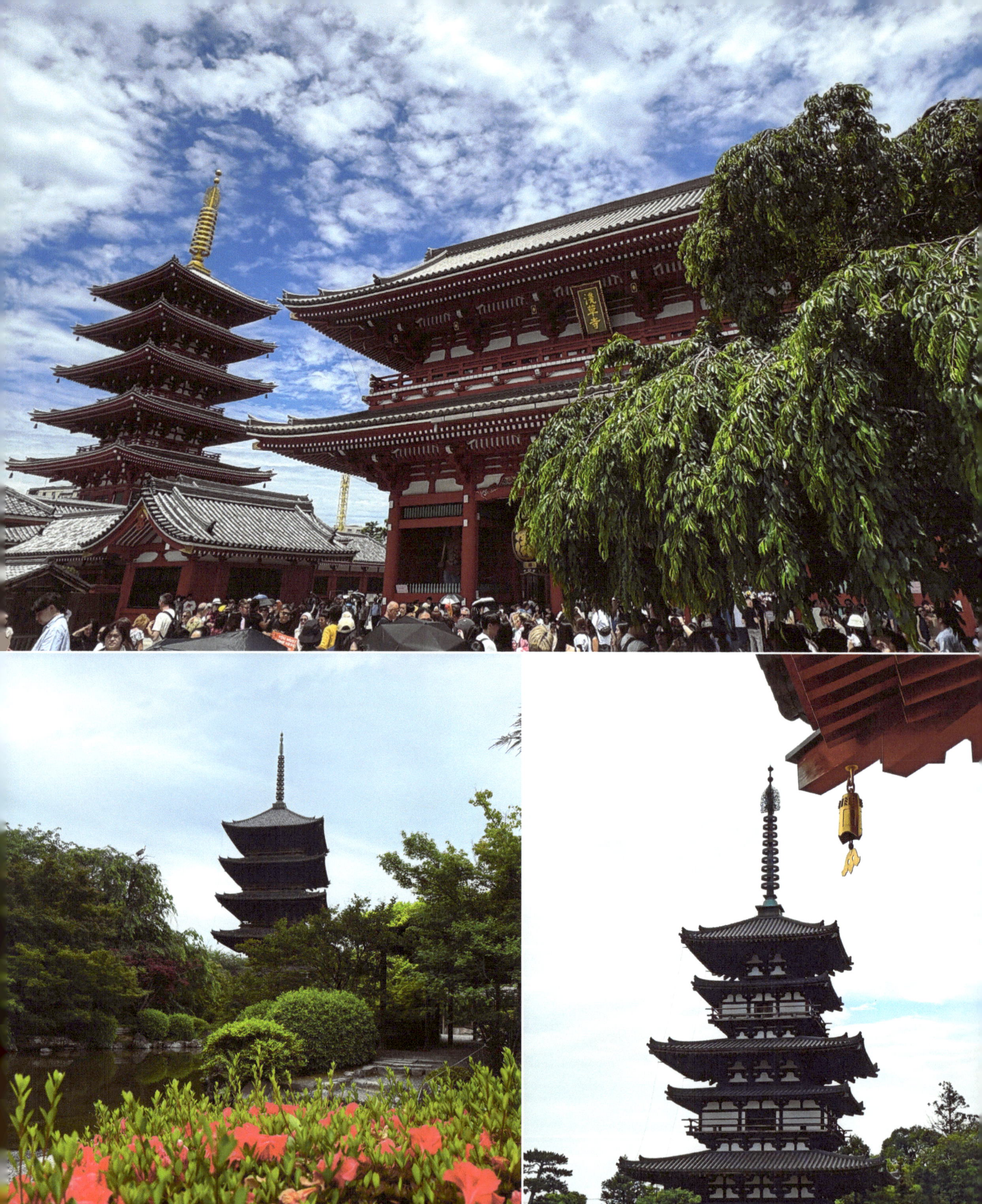
淺草寺

Opposite page and this page (clockwise from left).
Five-Story Pagodas – *Sensō-ji, Tokyo; Shitennō-ji, Osaka; Yakushi-ji, Nara; Yakushi-ji, Nara; Tō-ji, Kyoto*

The pagoda is not a hall for gathering but a symbolic axis linking earth and sky. Among all Japanese Buddhist schools, the five-story pagoda is understood as a vertical map of the cosmos, rising through the five elements from earth to space. The finial (Jp. *sōrin*) above the five stories signals further ascent beyond the material, elemental world, pointing toward liberation (Skt. *nirvāṇa*).

In Shingon Buddhism in particular, this upward movement culminates in realization of Dainichi Nyorai (Skt. *Mahāvairocana*) as the all-pervading cosmic Buddha, with enlightenment understood as attainable in this very body (Jp. *sokushin jōbutsu*). Since Buddhism does not affirm an eternal Skt. *ātman* in the way Hindu traditions do, this invites comparison, though not identity, with Hindu ideas of liberation such as Skt. *sāyujya mokṣa* (union with Brahman) or the Skt. *jīvanmukta* state (liberation while embodied).

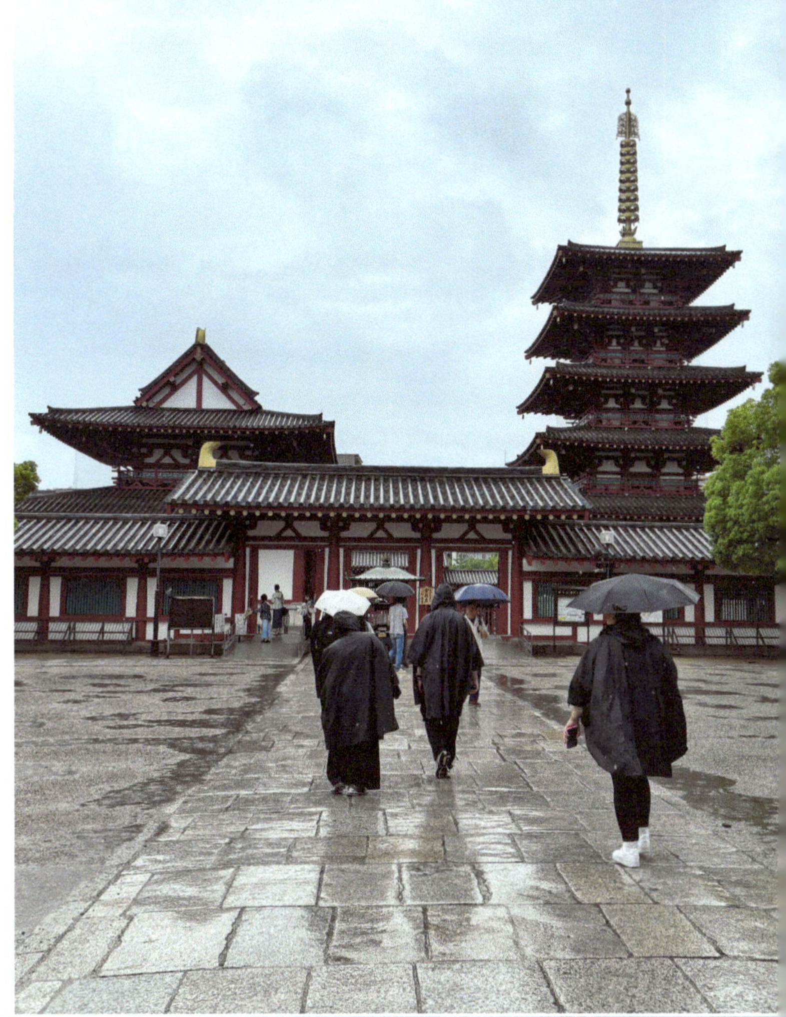

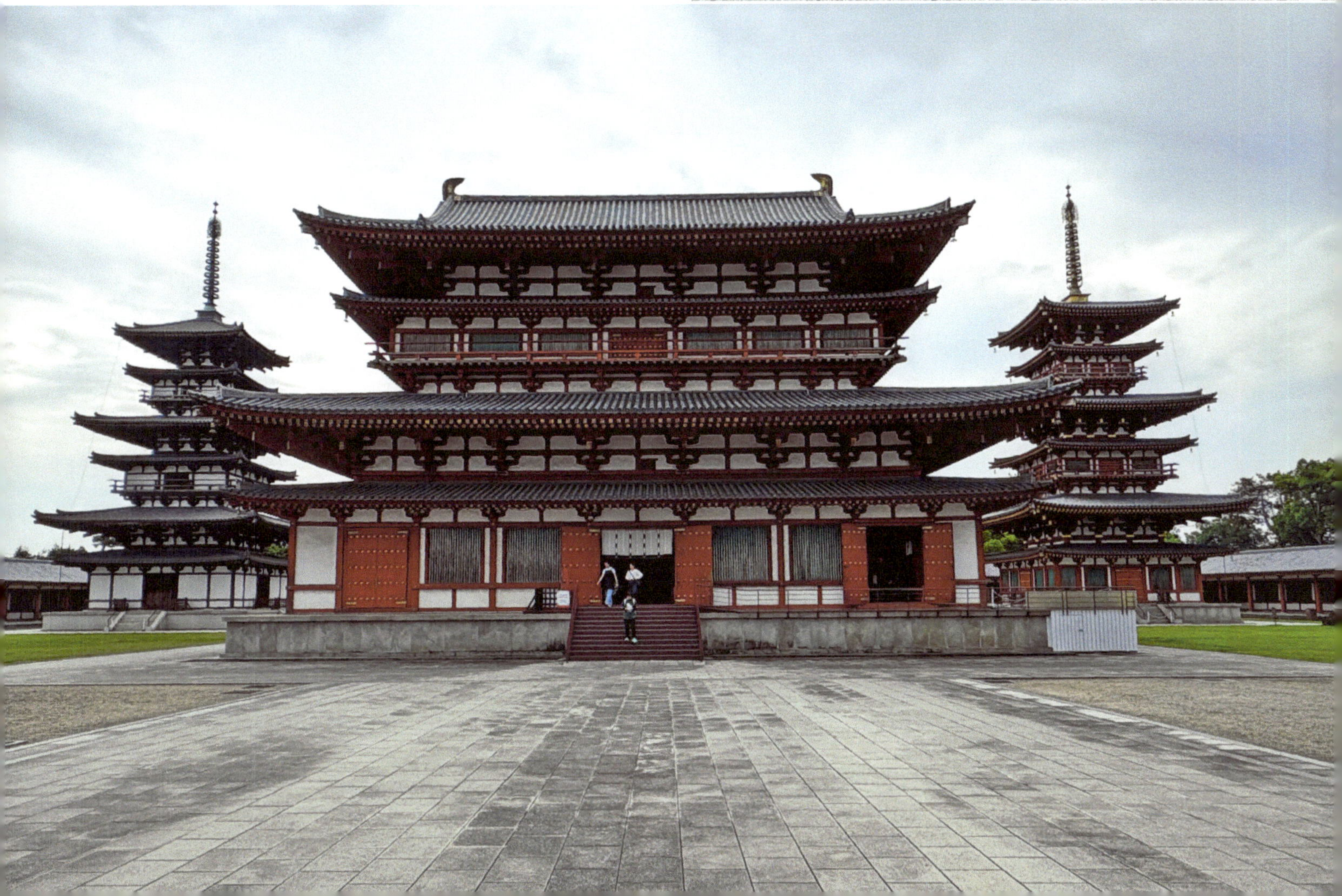

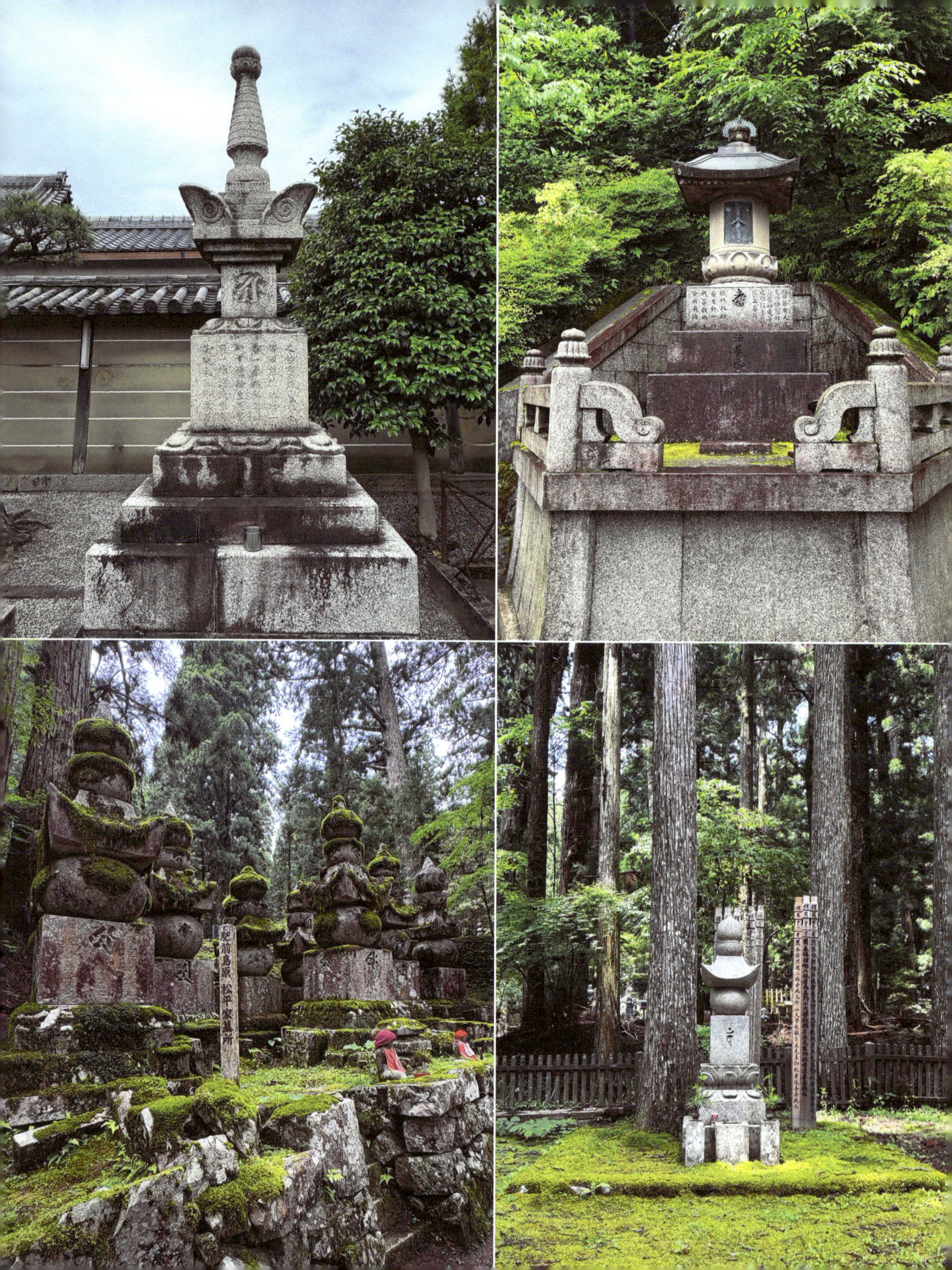
肥前島原 松平家墓所

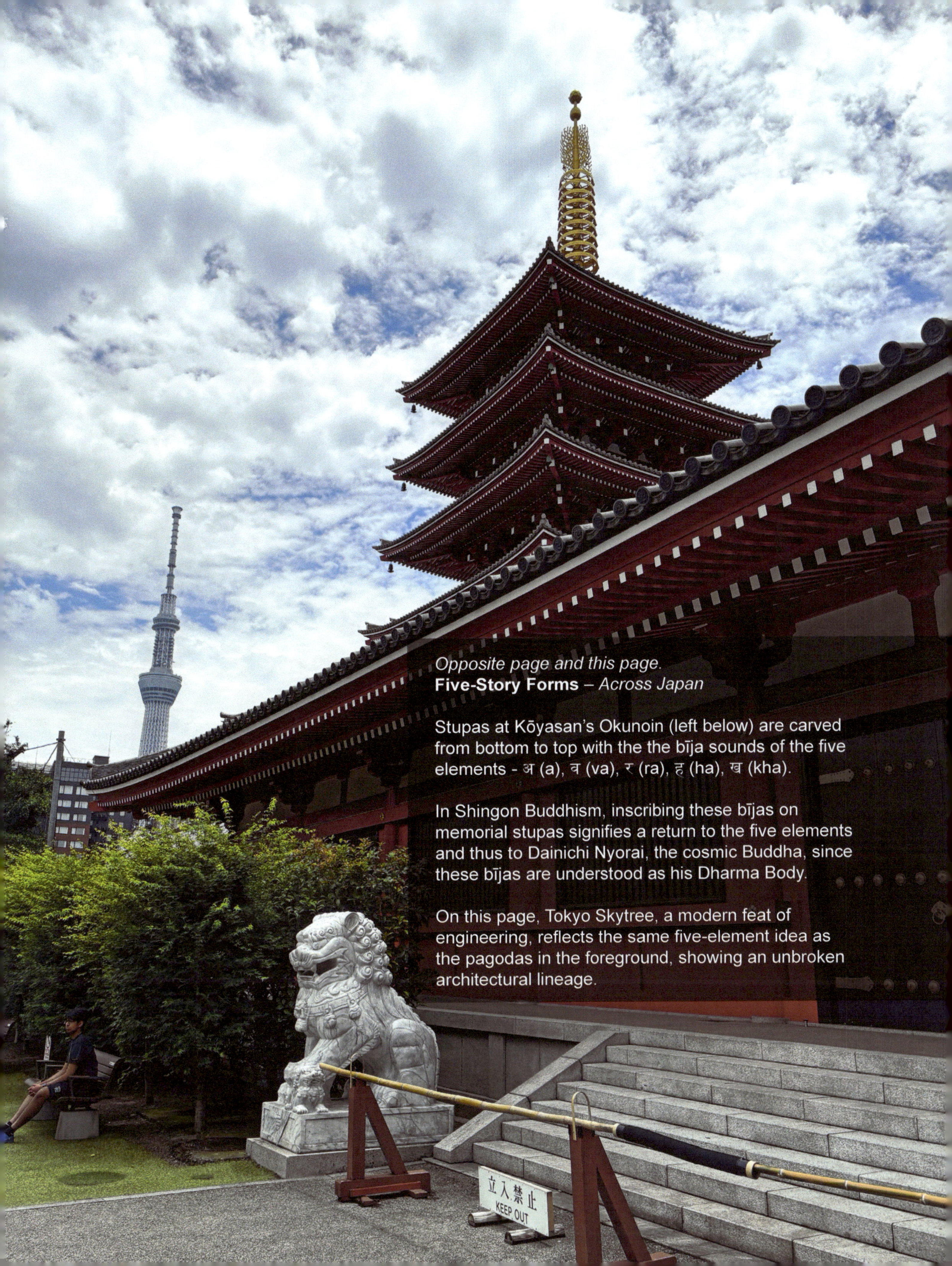

Opposite page and this page.
Five-Story Forms – *Across Japan*

Stupas at Kōyasan's Okunoin (left below) are carved from bottom to top with the the bīja sounds of the five elements - अ (a), व (va), र (ra), ह (ha), ख (kha).

In Shingon Buddhism, inscribing these bījas on memorial stupas signifies a return to the five elements and thus to Dainichi Nyorai, the cosmic Buddha, since these bījas are understood as his Dharma Body.

On this page, Tokyo Skytree, a modern feat of engineering, reflects the same five-element idea as the pagodas in the foreground, showing an unbroken architectural lineage.

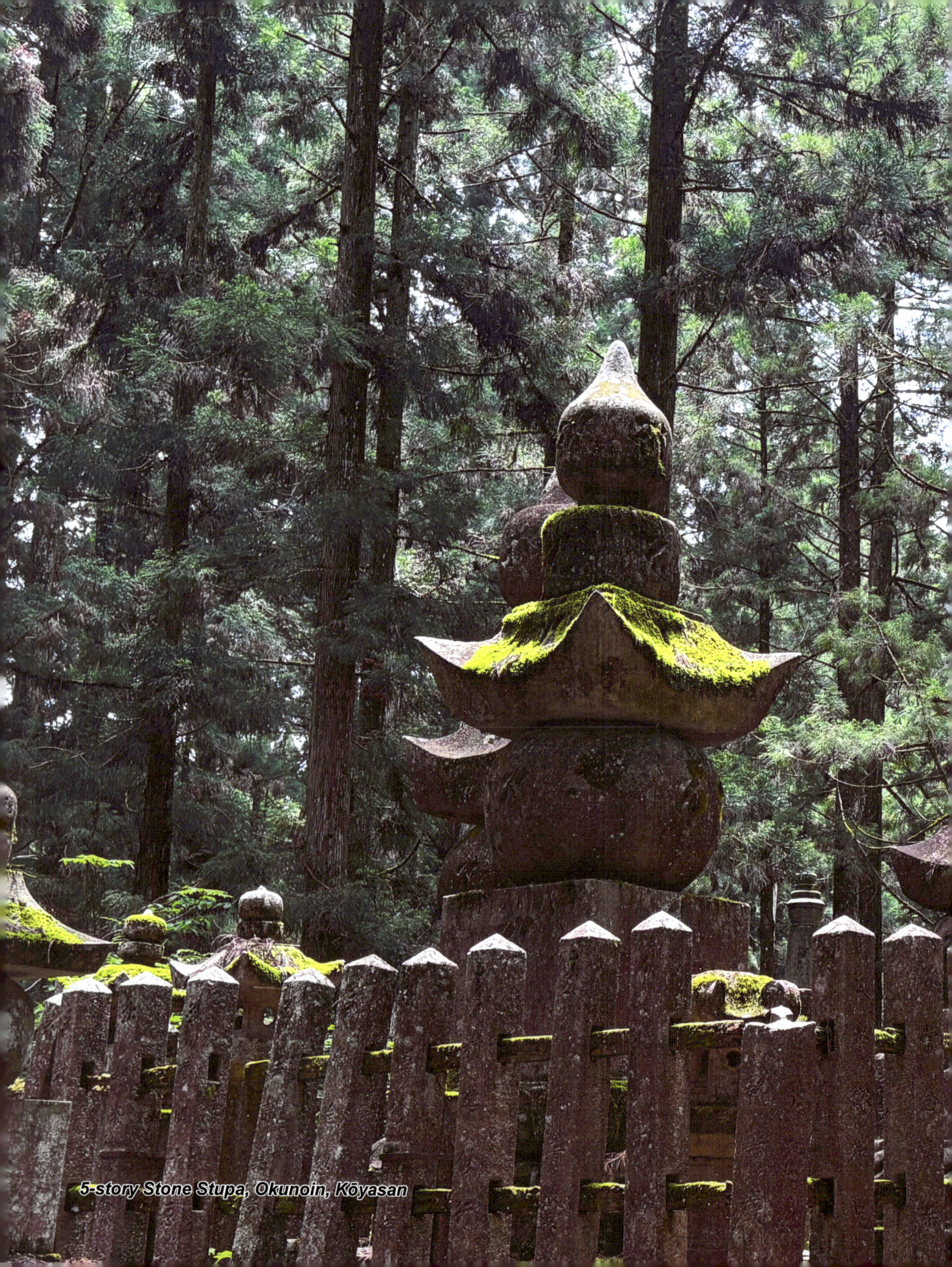

5-story Stone Stupa, Okunoin, Kōyasan

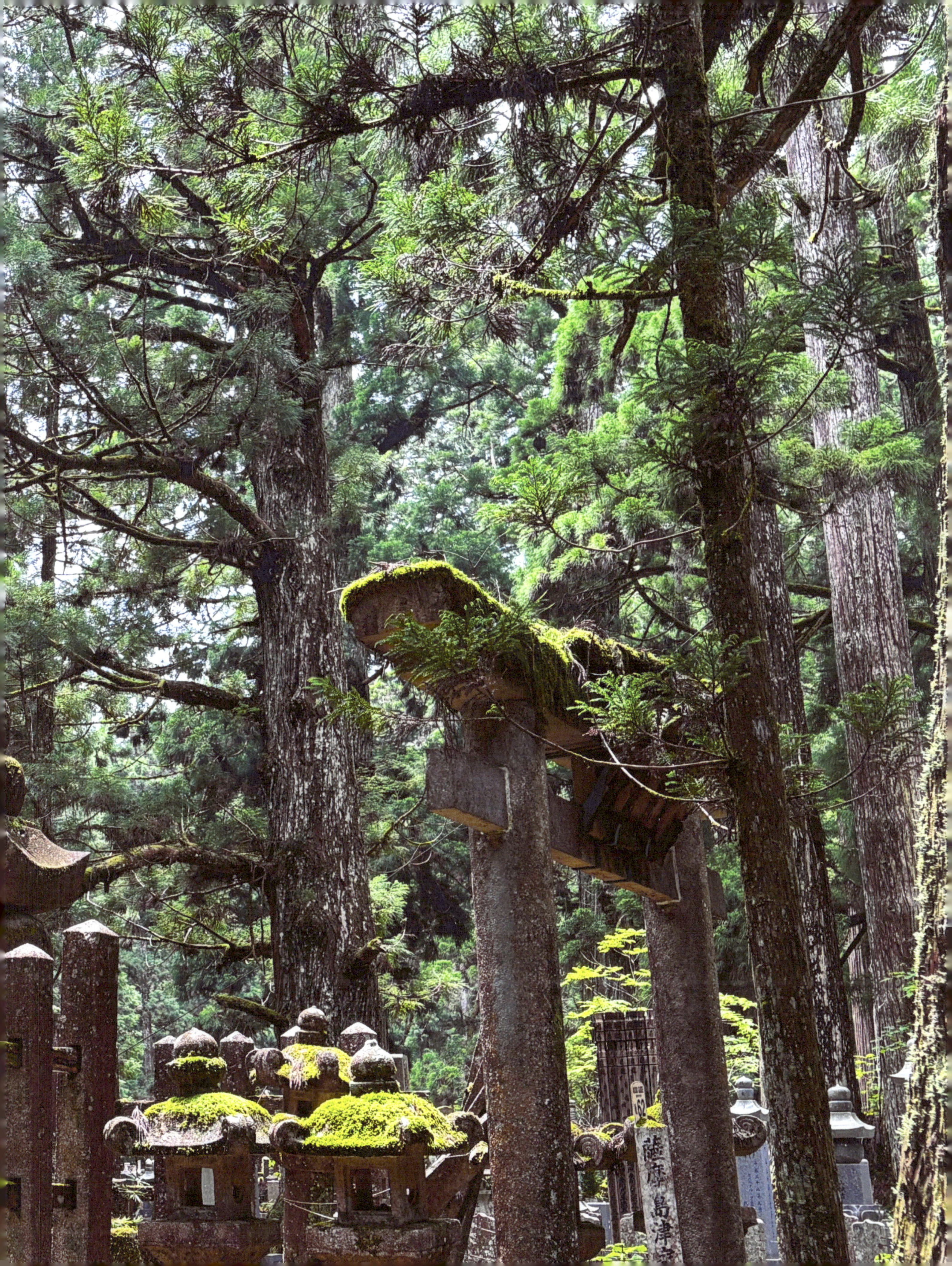
162
薩摩島津

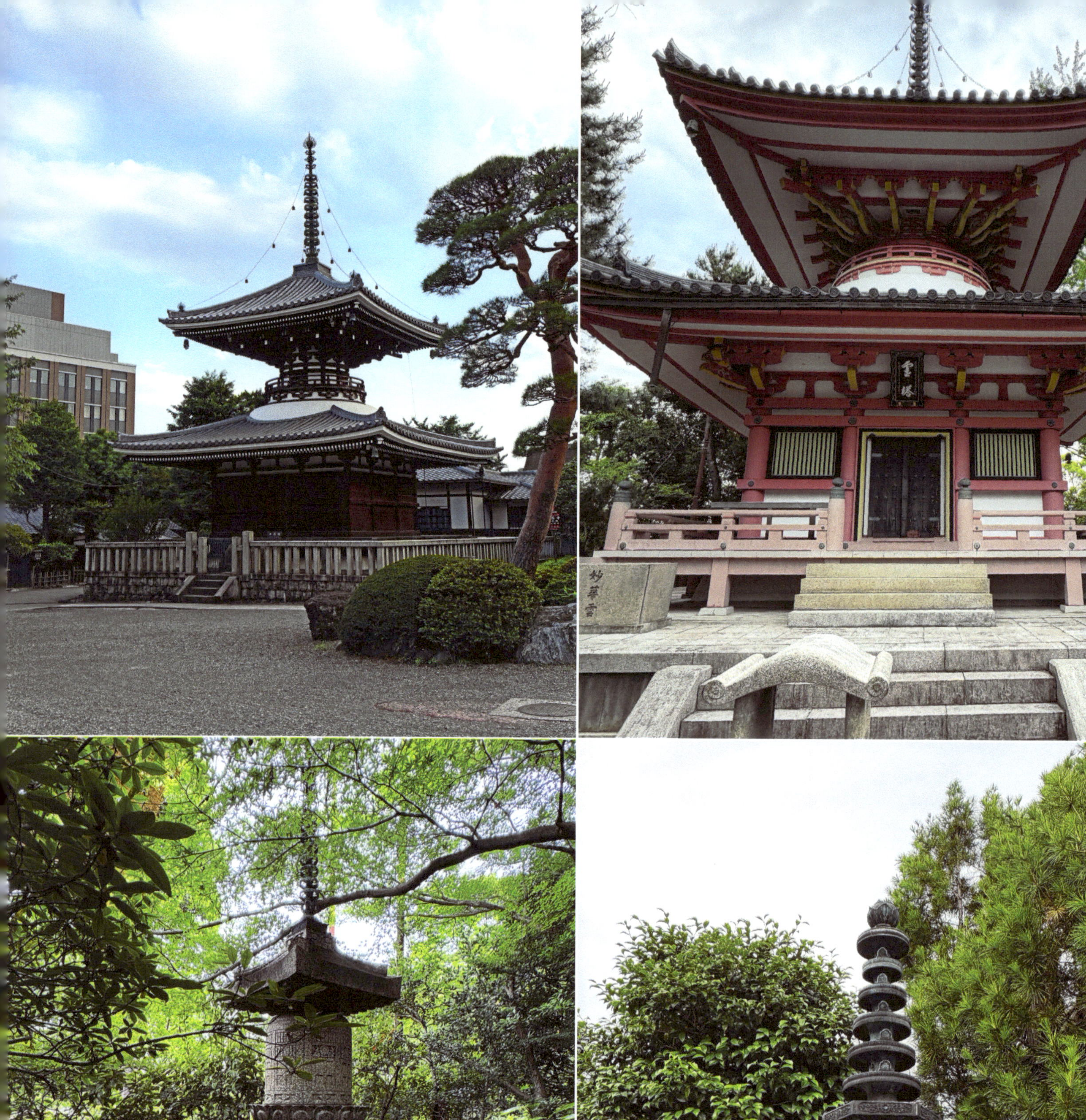

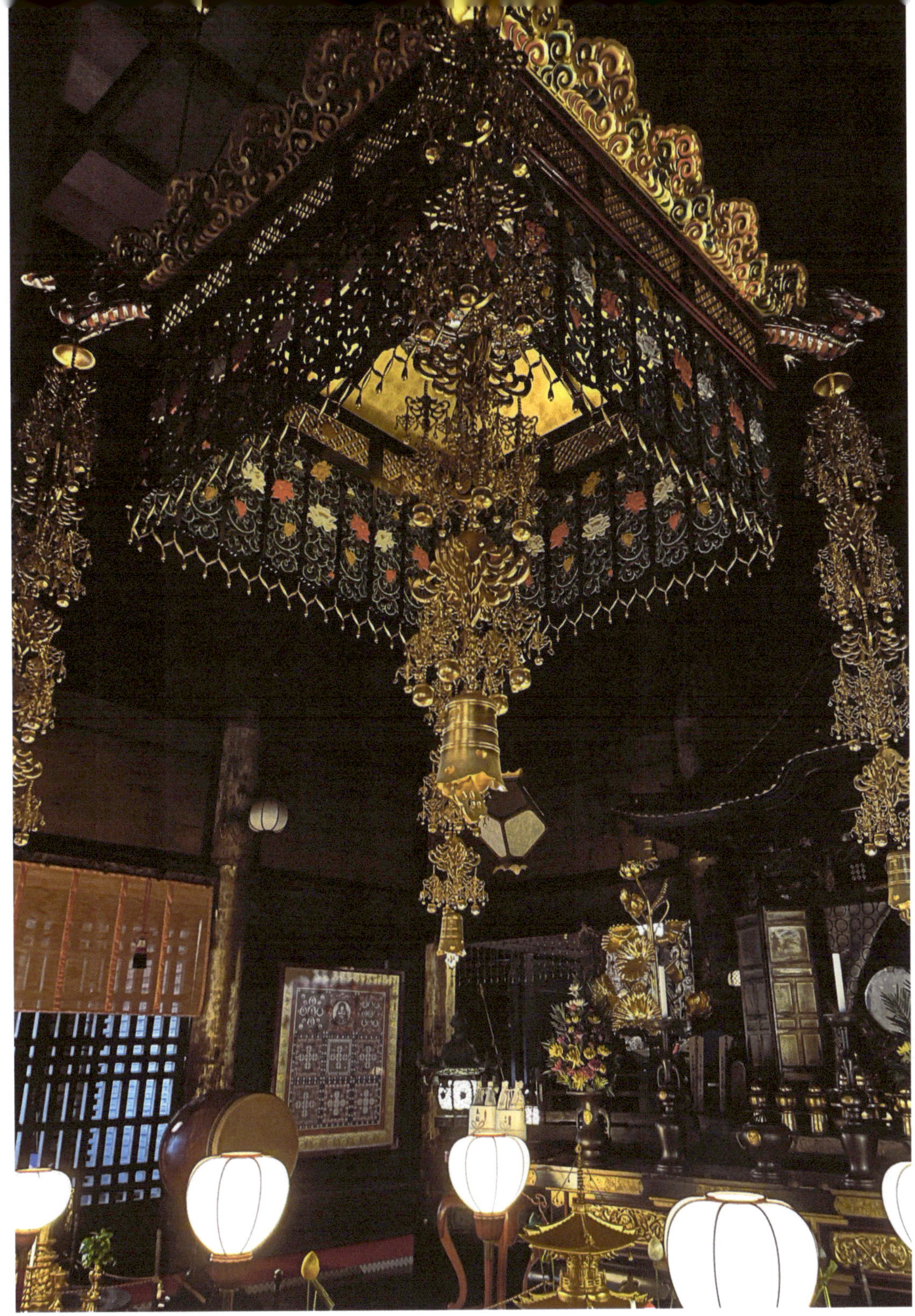

Opposite page (collage).
Stupas from across Japan

After the Buddha's Skt. *parinirvāṇa* (nirvana after death), his remains were enshrined in multiple *stūpas*. In Japan, pagodas and *stūpas* make the Buddha's presence tangible through form. *Sutūpa* is the Japanese form of the Sanskrit word *stūpa*.

This page (above).
Ornate Canopy – *Temple interior, Tokyo*

Above the *shumidan* ("Mount Sumeru" altar), an ornate gold canopy hangs over the temple's principal image. It frames the image much like a Skt. *chatra* in a Hindu temple, creating a threshold that sets this space apart from the rest of the hall.

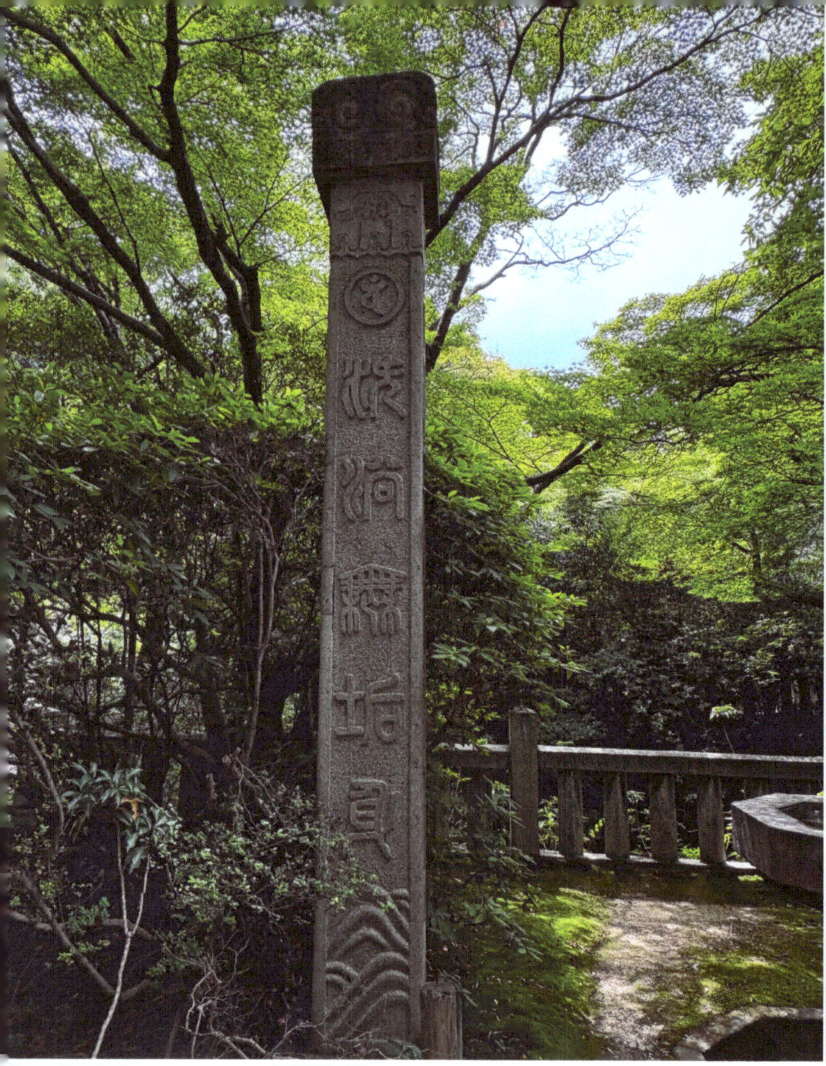

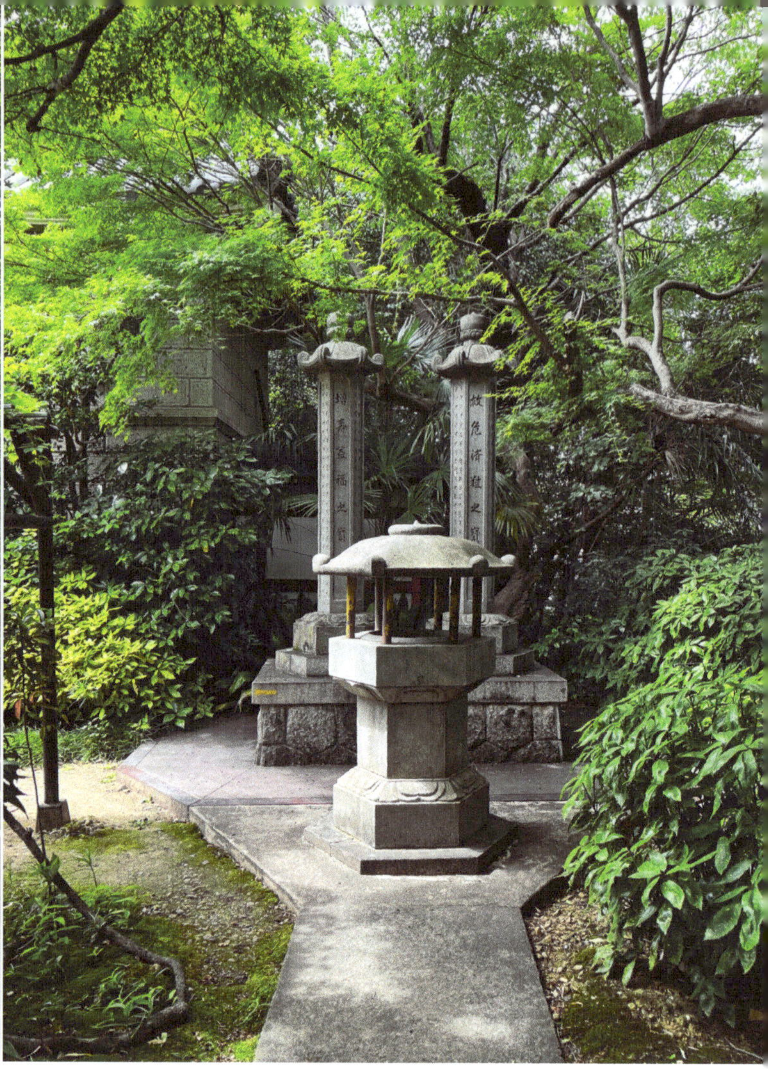

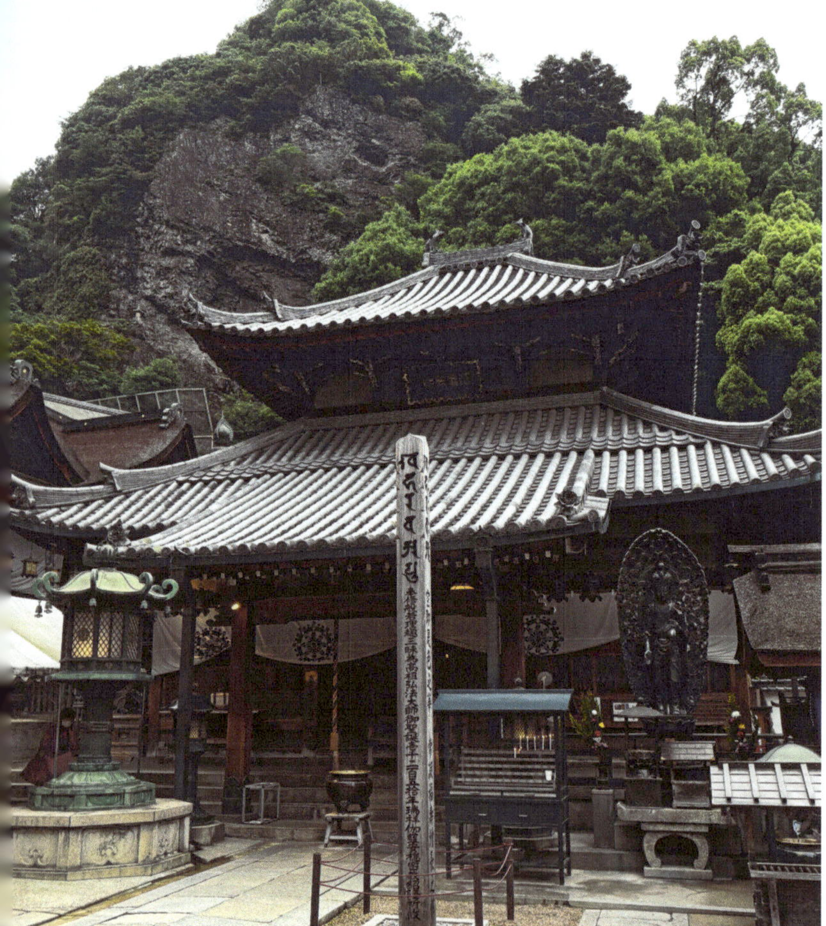

This page (top to bottom).
Inscribed Pillars and Temple Flagstaffs – *Tōgan-ji, Nagoya; Hōzan-ji, Ikoma*

Posts are often carved or painted with the temple's name, prayers, or dedicatory text, functioning more like inscribed vow-pillars than a working flagpole. On the Hōzan-ji pillar (left), you can see the classic five-element mantra, A·VA·RA·HA·KHA, and the bīja for Miroku Bosatsu (Skt. *Maitreya*), यू (yū).

On the Tōgan-ji pillar, you can see a seed syllable commonly associated with Dainichi (Skt. *Mahāvairocana* - वँ vaṃ). This is like a "single-syllable icon" you can bow to, recite with, or treat as the deity's presence in condensed form.

In Hindu temples, a *dhvaja-stambha* ("flag pillar") is set on the central axis before the sanctum, and is used to raise a temple banner on festival days and to signal the deity's presence from a distance. These Japanese posts play a similar visual role, but a different functional one.

Sacred Roof Finials and the Wish-Fulfilling Jewel – *Across Japan*

On top of many temples sits the Jp. *hōju*, a flame-wreathed "sacred jewel" that crowns the temple like a seal of blessing. In Buddhist symbolism, it is closely tied to the idea of the wish-fulfilling jewel, *hōju* (Skt. *cintāmaṇi)*, which confers protection, spiritual power, and auspicious fulfillment.

Skt. *kalasha* placed on top of Hindu temples look similar. A *kalasha* is a vessel that holds life, water, prosperity, and is used to welcome the deities.

Both occupy the highest point as an architectural "crown," marking the structure as ritually charged. *Kalasha* is a vessel of prosperity and life, while the *hōju* is a jewel of blessing and attainment. Both traditions regard the finial as not just decoration but a sign of sanctity.

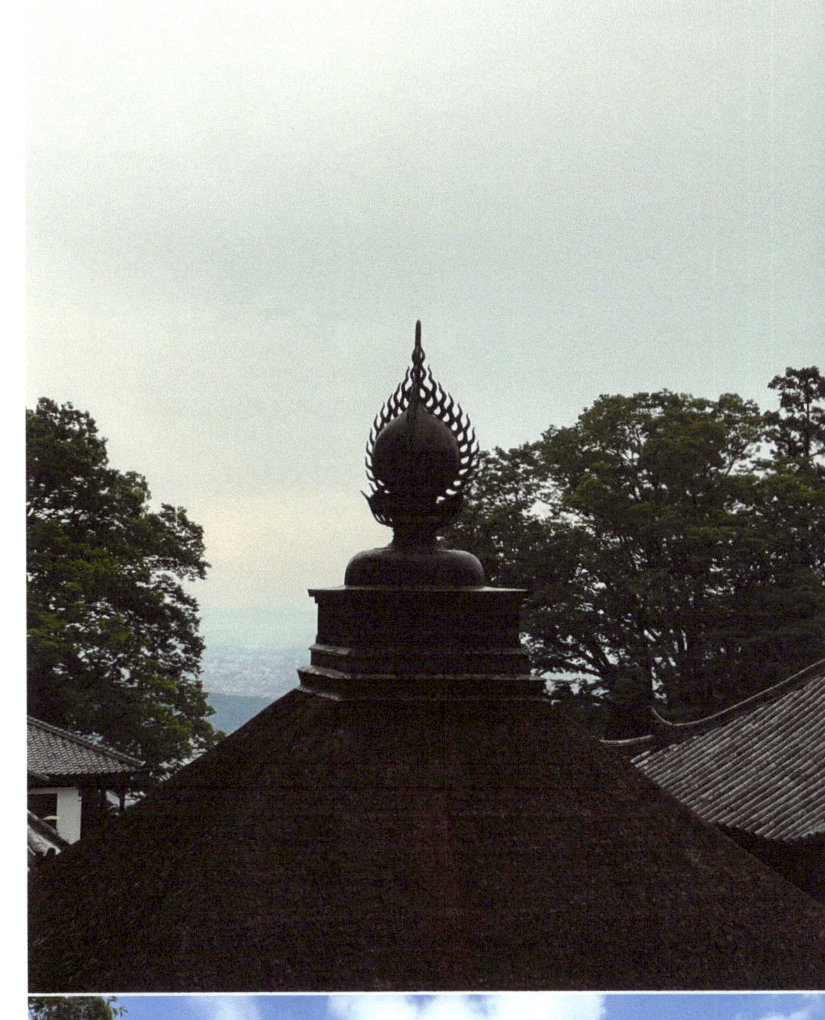

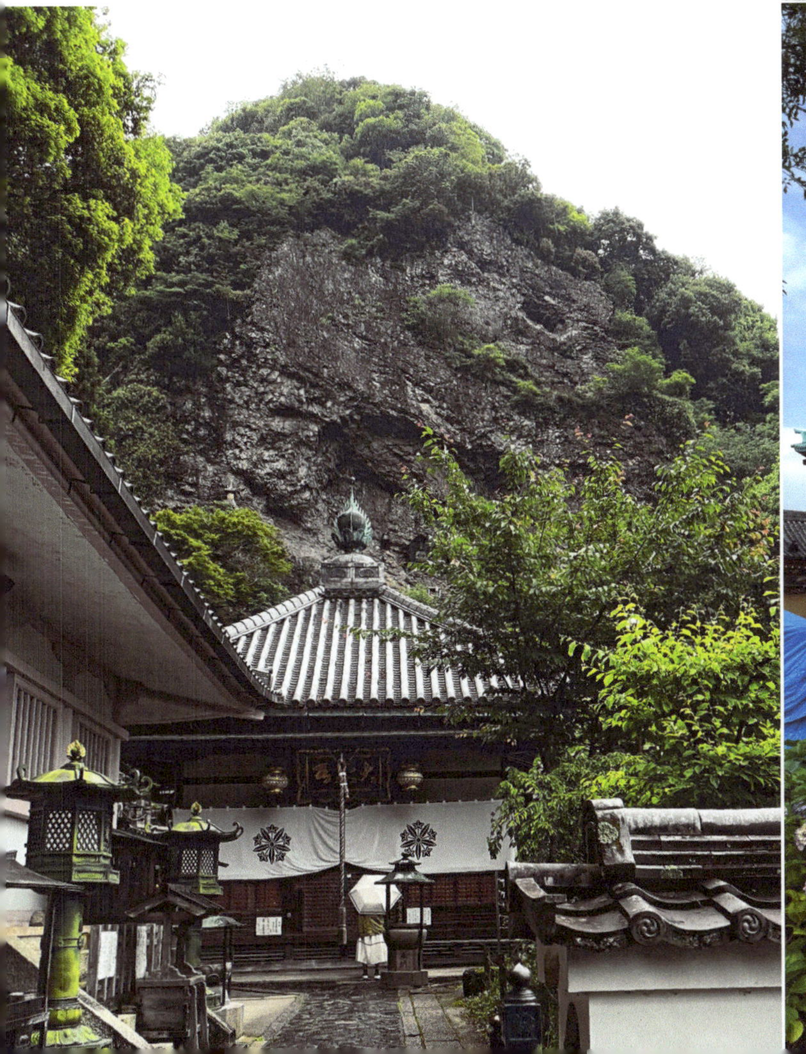

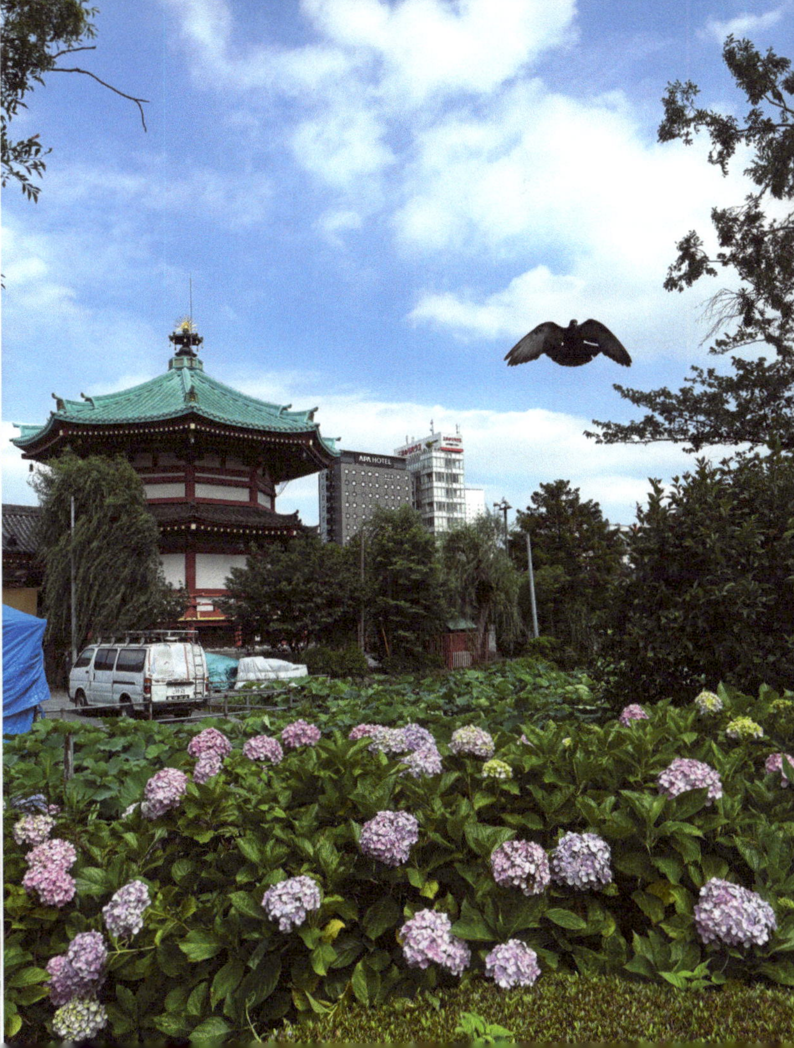

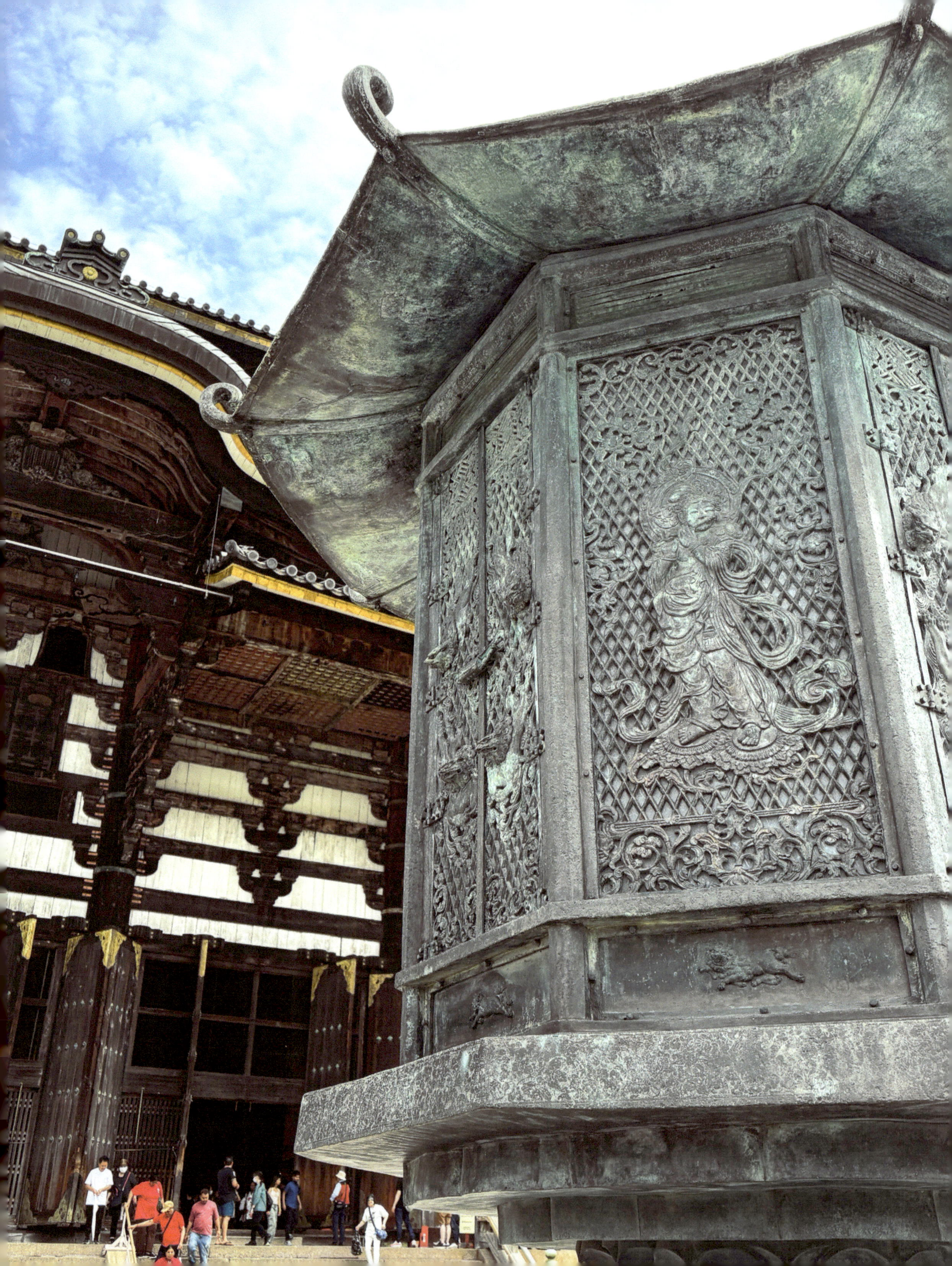

Opposite page and this page, left to right.
Temple Lamp Posts (Skt. *dīpa-stambha*) – *Tōdai-ji and Yakushi-ji, Nara; Tōgan-ji, Nagoya*

Tall bronze lamp posts like these stand in front of the main hall or pagoda at many Japanese temples for holding a lamp, much like the tall *dīpa-stambha* "pillar of lamps" at the entrances of Hindu temples. In many Hindu temples, stone or metal Skt. *dīpa-stambhas* are placed just inside the outer gate or beside the path to the sanctum, with tiers of small niches that are filled with oil lamps on festival nights, which is also prevalent in Japan. The famous octagonal lantern at Tōdai-ji is covered with openwork panels of celestial musicians, including a flute-playing bodhisattva with one leg slightly bent and the torso curved; at Yakushi-ji another musician wearing a *dhoti*-like garment sits in Skt. *padmāsana* with a long flute, and similar flute-players appear again on the Tōgan-ji lamp post.

In the eighth century, the South Indian monk Bodhisena came to Tōdai-ji. He is remembered for introducing Indian music and dance forms that later helped shape the court tradition now known as *gagaku*. The triple-bent stance (Skt. *tribhaṅga*) of the Tōdai-ji flute-player figure looks like Śrī Kṛṣṇa, and the seated flute-player at Yakushi-ji also looks like Indian musicians.

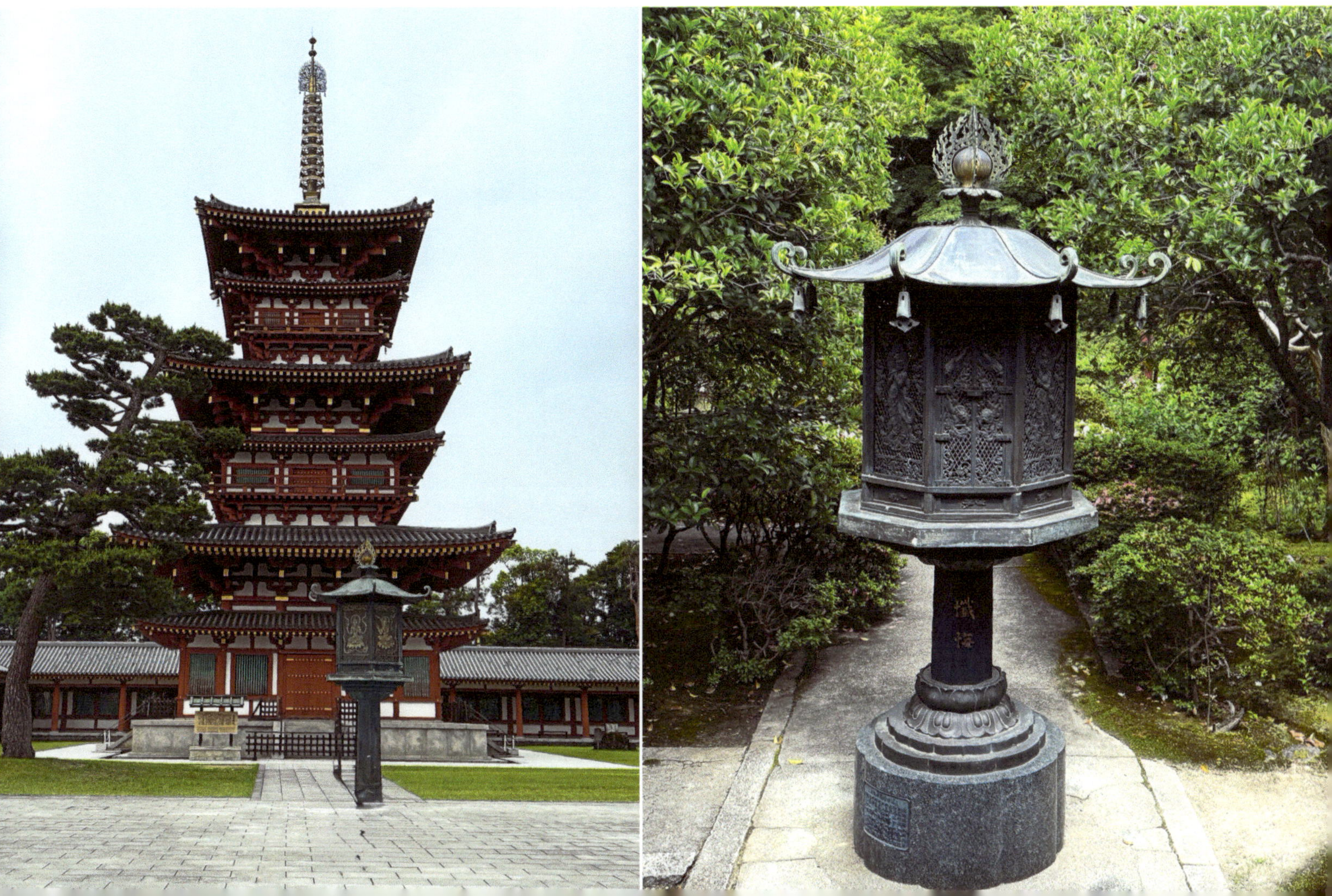

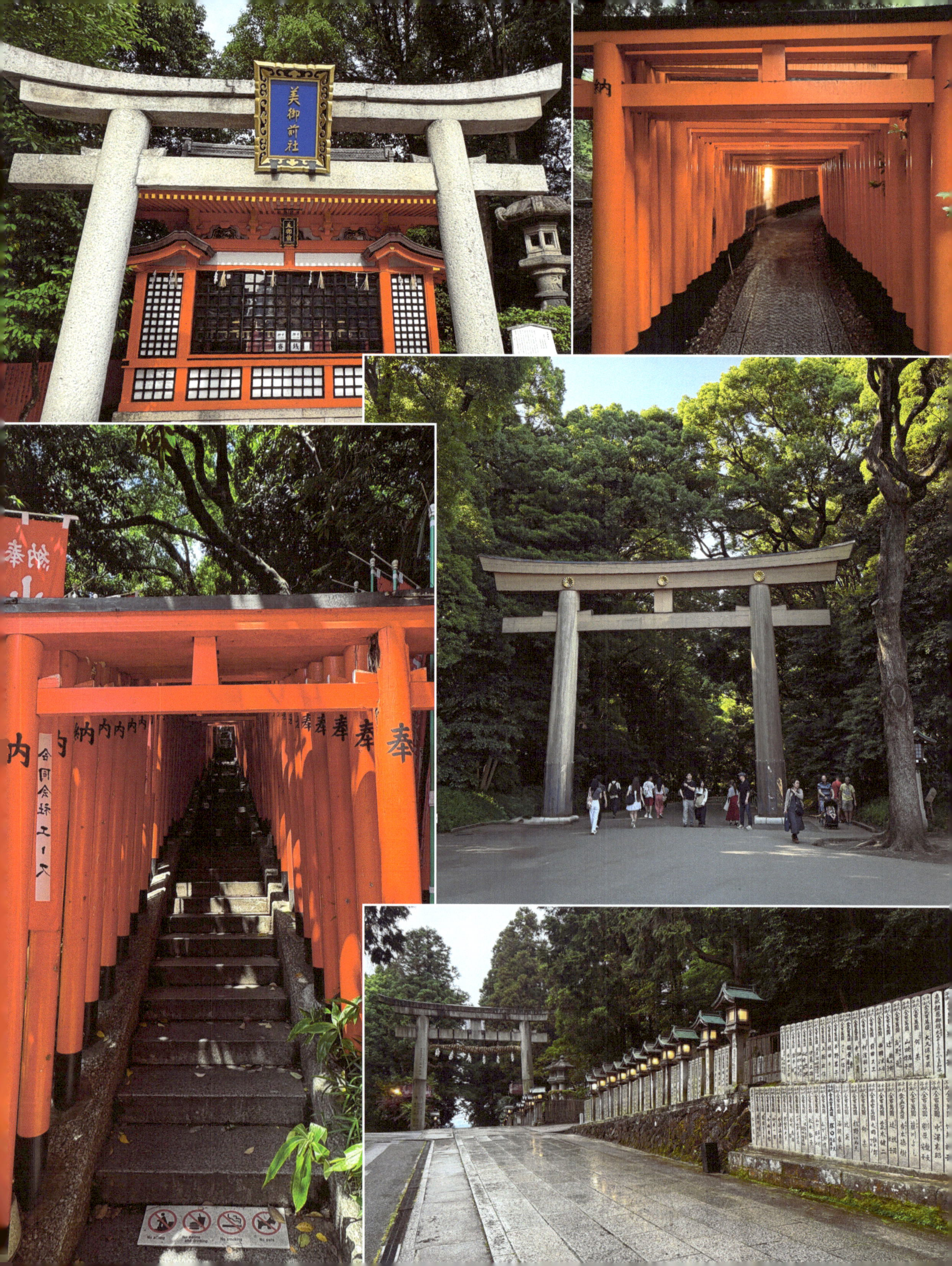
美御前社

Opposite page (collage).
Torii Gates and Sacred Thresholds – *Shrines across Japan*

Torii gates stand at the threshold between ordinary and sacred space. In India, Skt. *toraṇa* gateways stood at the entrace to the Buddhist stupas. The Great Stupa at Sanchi has *toraṇas* dating back over 2,000 years. When Buddhism arrived in Japan, these architectural ideas arrived too. Interestingly, the torii later becomes a prominent icon of Shinto. Several scholars suggest that *torii*, both etymologically and architecturally, derives from *toraṇa*.

This boundary also shows up inside esoteric Buddhist ritual. Kūkai introduces a torii-like marker to demarcate sacred space for the *goma (*Skt. *homa)* fire ceremony, and related forms can still be seen around a *goma-dan* fire altar. In a fire ritual, the priest sets up a *kekkai* (Skt. *sīmā*), a protected boundary around the hearth using posts and sacred ropes or wooden beams. The small gate-like frame at the front of the fire space separates the priest's working area from the consecrated "wisdom fire." In Shingon and Tendai settings, it is often described as intentionally torii-shaped, because the fire is treated as a portal through which the deity, such as Fudō Myōō (Skt. *Acala*), is invited to appear.

Following page (top to bottom).
Temple Ponds and Purification – *Shitennō-ji, Osaka; Tōgan-ji, Nagoya*

Ponds are also part of the sacred architecture of some Japanese temples. In Hindu temples, a ritual pond called a puṣkariṇī is often placed in the northeast of the temple complex. Vāstu (Vedic principles for spatial design) suggests the temple plot be slightly lower in the northeast so water naturally collects there, an idea mirrored in *sakuteiki* (traditional Japanese principles for spatial design). These ponds support Skt. *snāna*, a full ritual bath before entering the temple, and they also supply water for daily worship such as konjō (Skt. *abhisheka,* ritual bathing of the deity, which is also performed in Japanese temples).

Japanese temples also use water to prepare the visitor, but the practice is different. Temple ponds are not used for bathing. Instead, purification is performed through *temizu*, washing hands and mouth before approaching the hall. Both traditions emphasize cleaning with water before worship, helping the body and mind transition from the everyday into the sacred.

Page after the following page (clockwise from top).
Lotus and Sacred Meaning – *Yakushi-ji, Nara; Temples across Japan*

Lotus is one of the most sacred flowers in Hindu and Buddhist traditions. It grows from mud and remains rooted in water, yet it stays clean and dry. This physical quality supports its symbolic meaning: living fully in the world without being stained by it. At Yakushi-ji, for Kichijōten (Skt. *Lakṣmī*), visitors often meditate near the lotus pots. This feels especially fitting when Lakṣmī is praised in the *Śrī Sūktam* of the Vedas as *padma-priye, padminī, padma-haste, padmālaye, padma-dalāyatākṣi*, "she who loves the lotus, is lotus-born, holds it, dwells in it, and has lotus-petal eyes."

Lotus imagery also appears as a surface for mantra where *bonji* seed syllables Skt. *gaḥ gaḥ* are placed. These syllables are associated with Dual-Bodied Vināyaka. Lotus motifs are widespread in Japan, appearing even at the base of lamp pedestals carved as blooming lotuses.

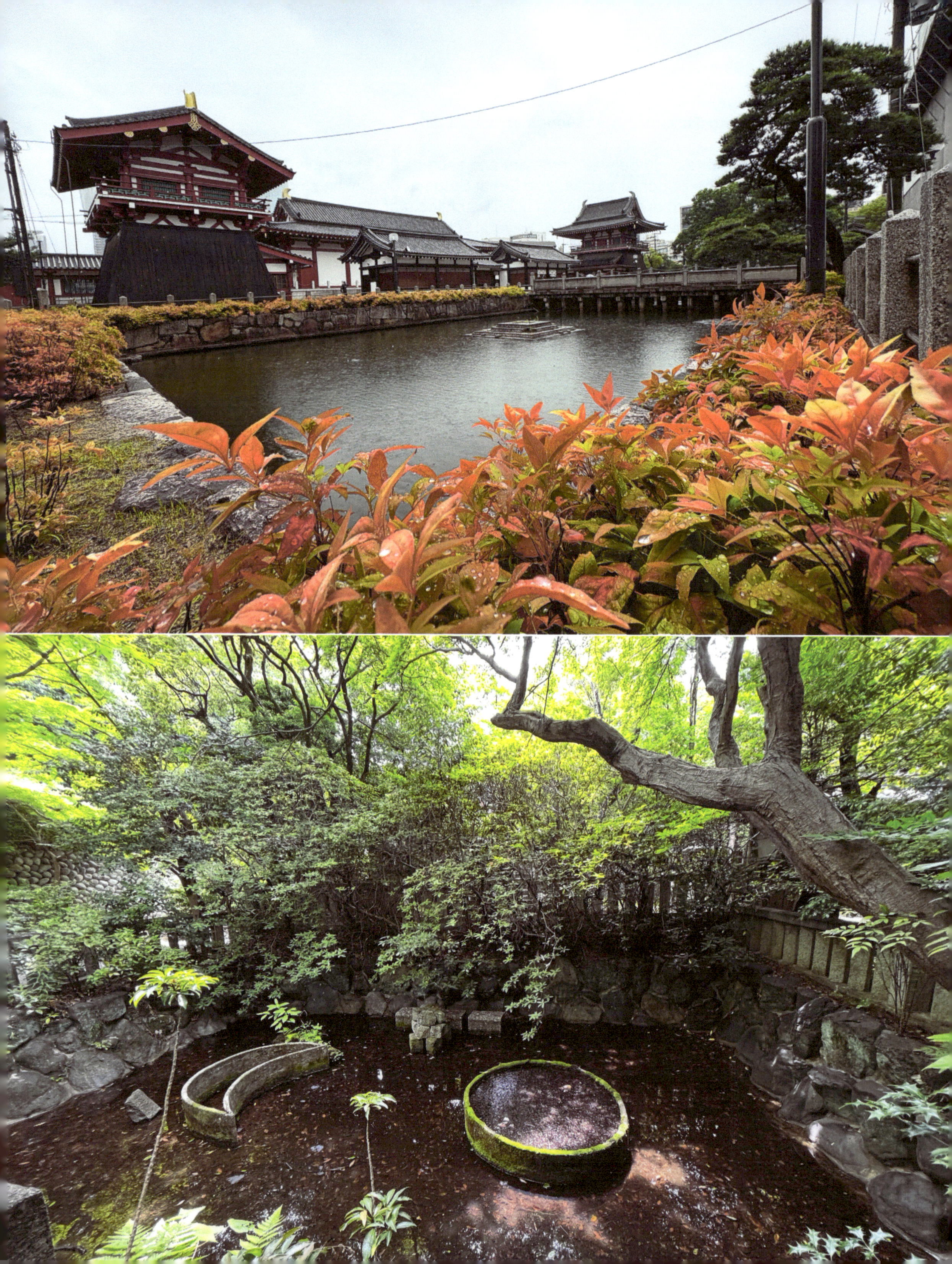

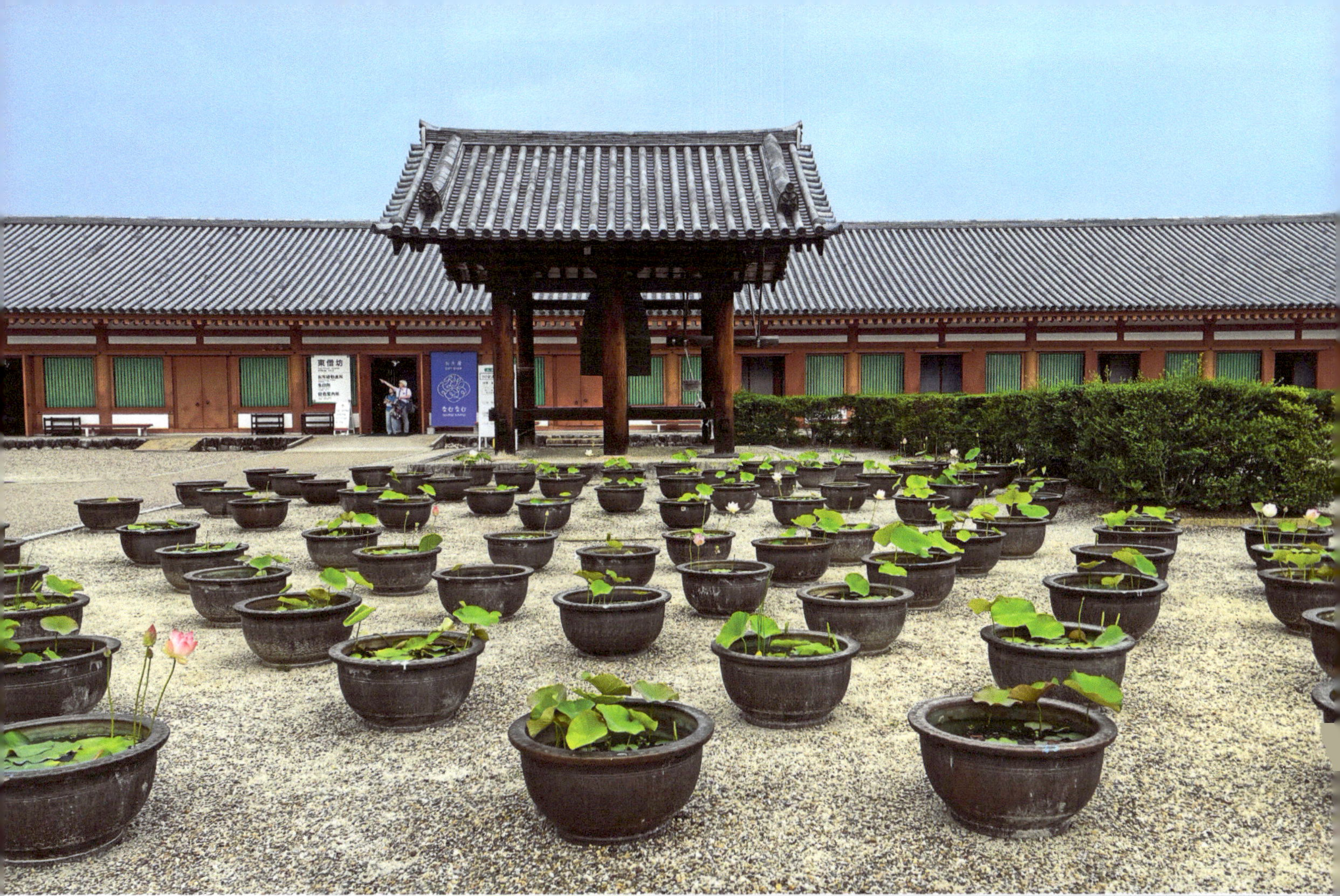

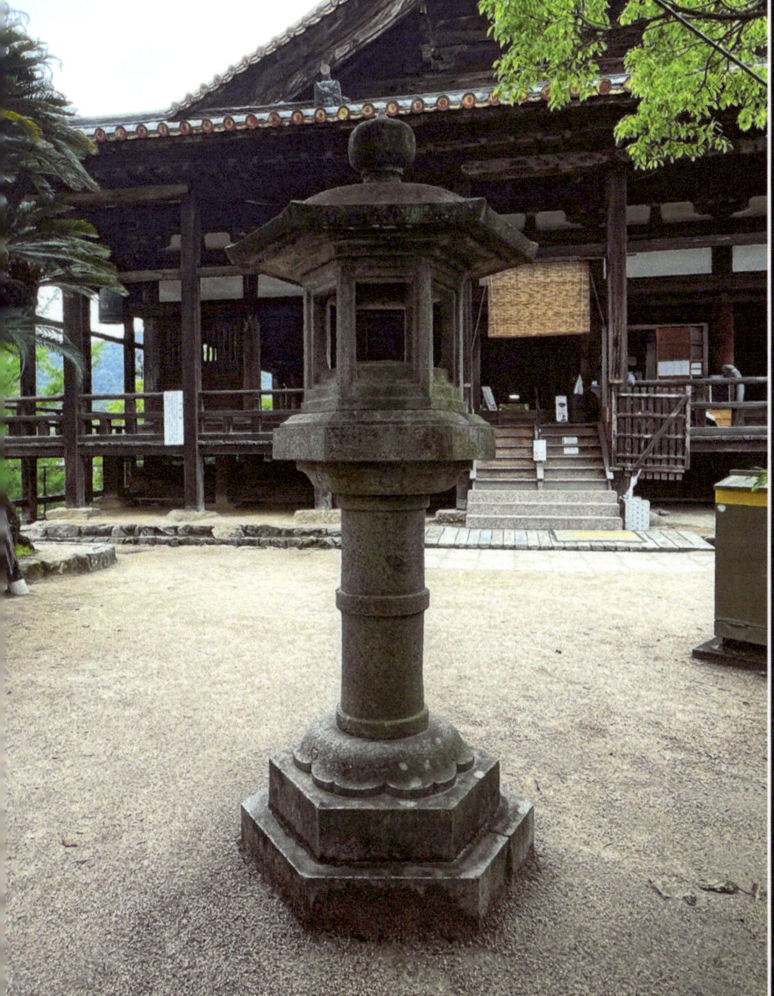

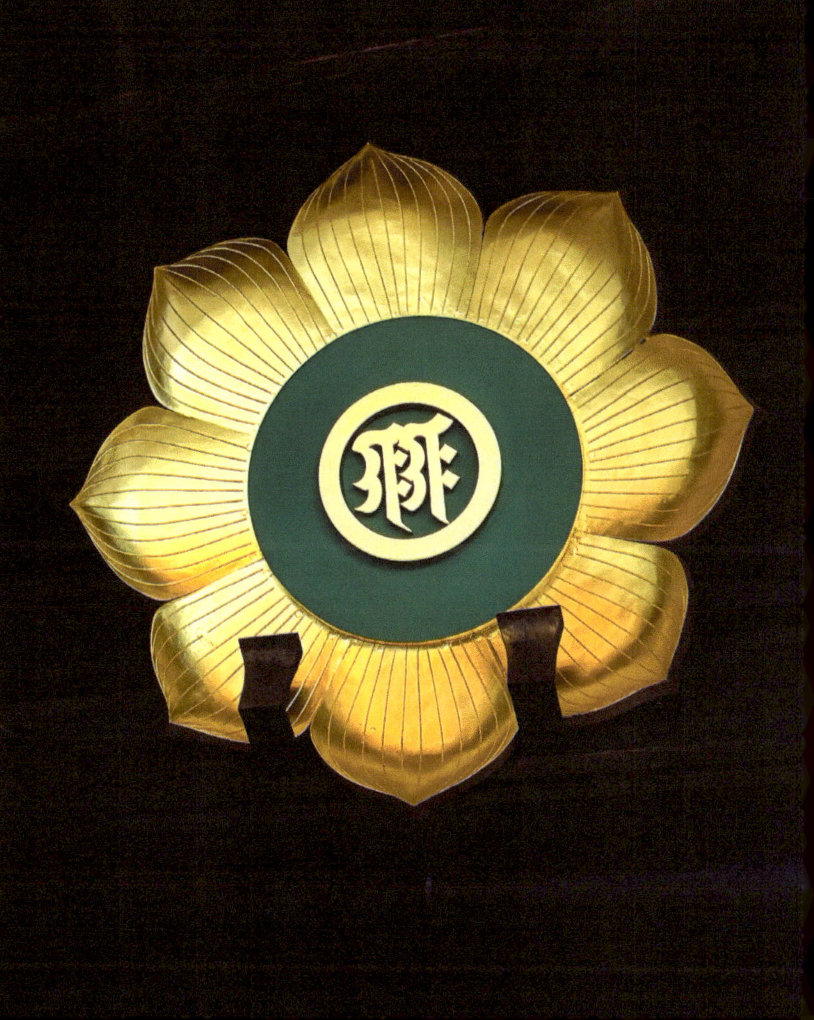

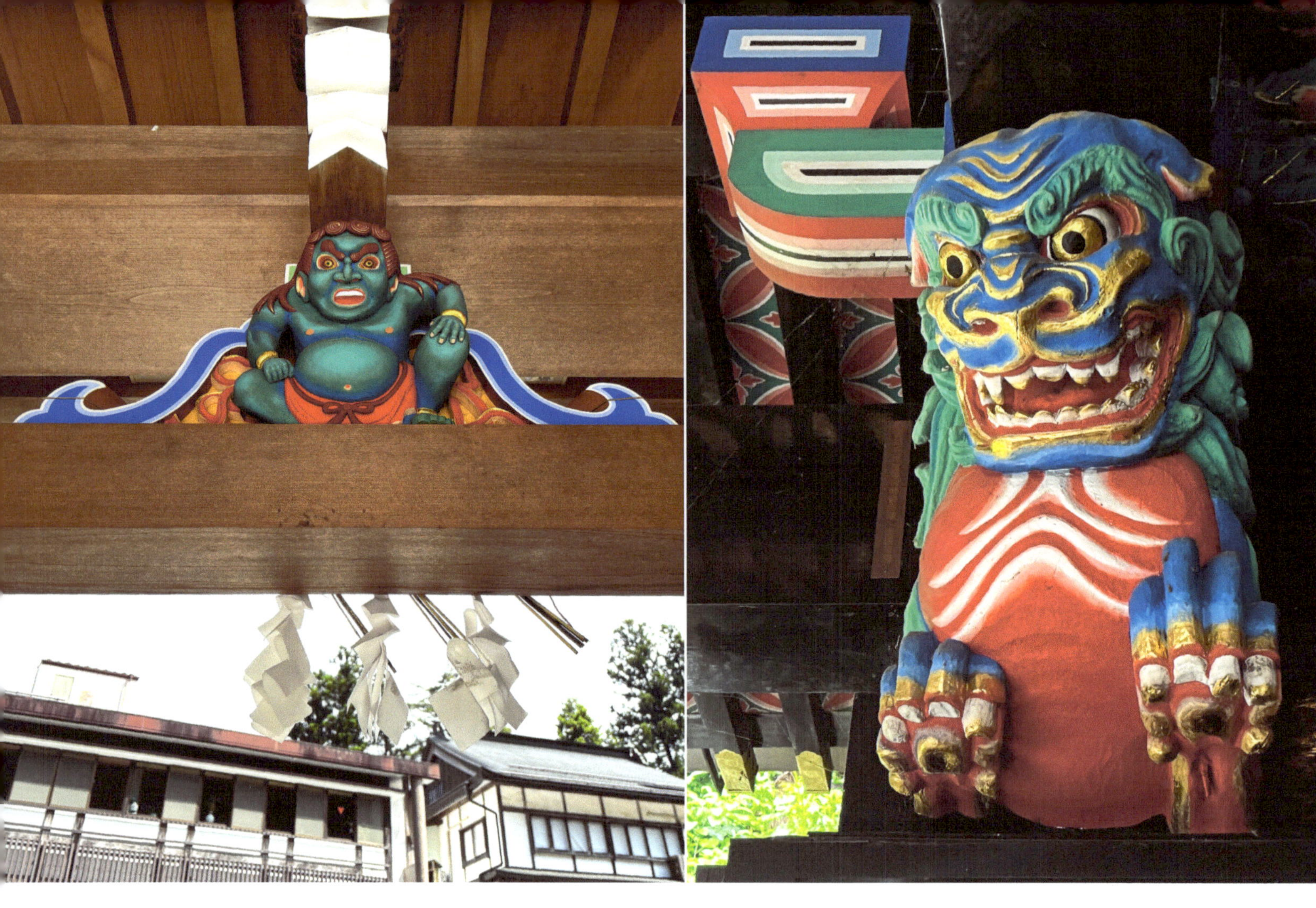

This page and opposite page (clockwise from above left).
Temple Guardians – *Shōjōshin-in, Kōyasan; Hōgon-ji, Chikubushima; Renkō-ji, Tokyo; Daishō-in, Miyajima*

High under the entrance beam, a squat, pot-bellied, impish *oni* figure keeps watch where visitors pass beneath. In form and mood it resembles the stout, mischievous *gaṇas* of South Indian temples, dwarf-like attendants placed on corners of spires (Skt. *gopuram*) and pillar-bases with bulging eyes and exaggerated features. In both contexts, small guardian figures are positioned at architectural joints and entry points to help guard the sacred space.

Alongside these impish warders are larger guardian animals. A painted *shishi* lion bares its teeth and grips with its claws. In South Indian temple architecture, Skt. *yāli & vyāla* figures, lion-bodied with elephant or other hybrid features, appear on brackets and pillar shoulders in a similarly protective role. Japanese temples also feature dragon (*ryū*) carvings in beams and brackets. Whether lion, hybrid beast, or dragon, these figures stand at thresholds and are meant to ward off misfortune.

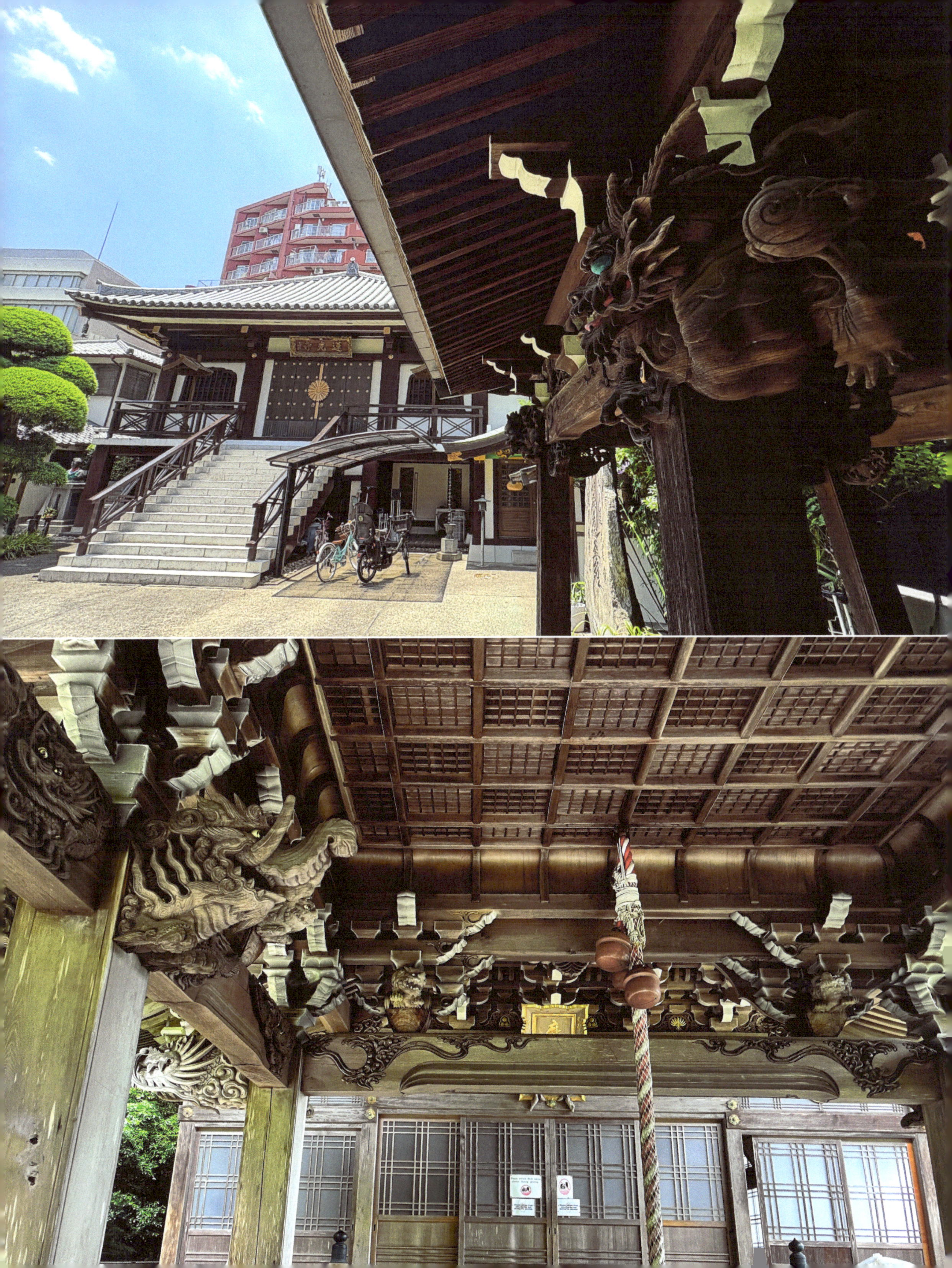

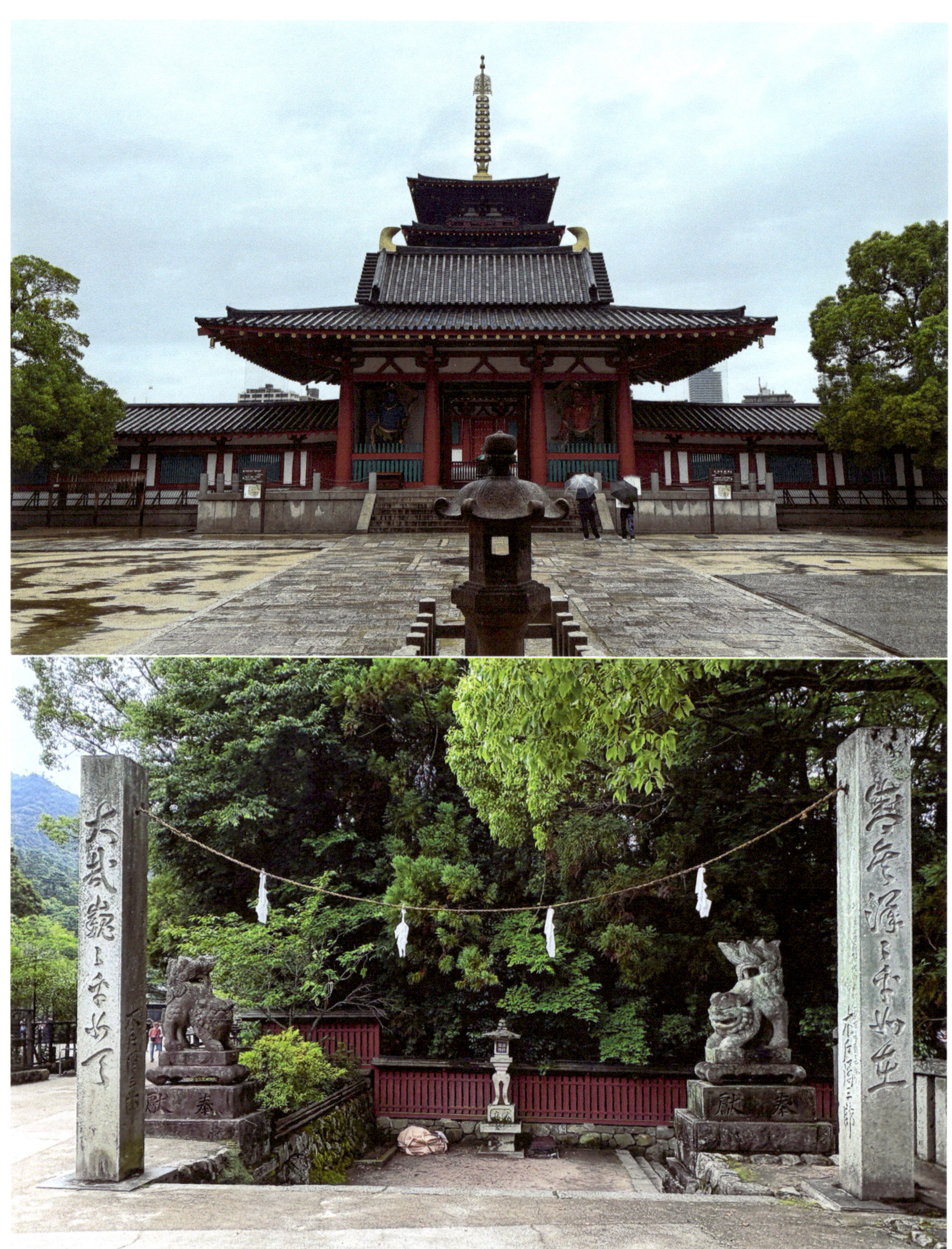

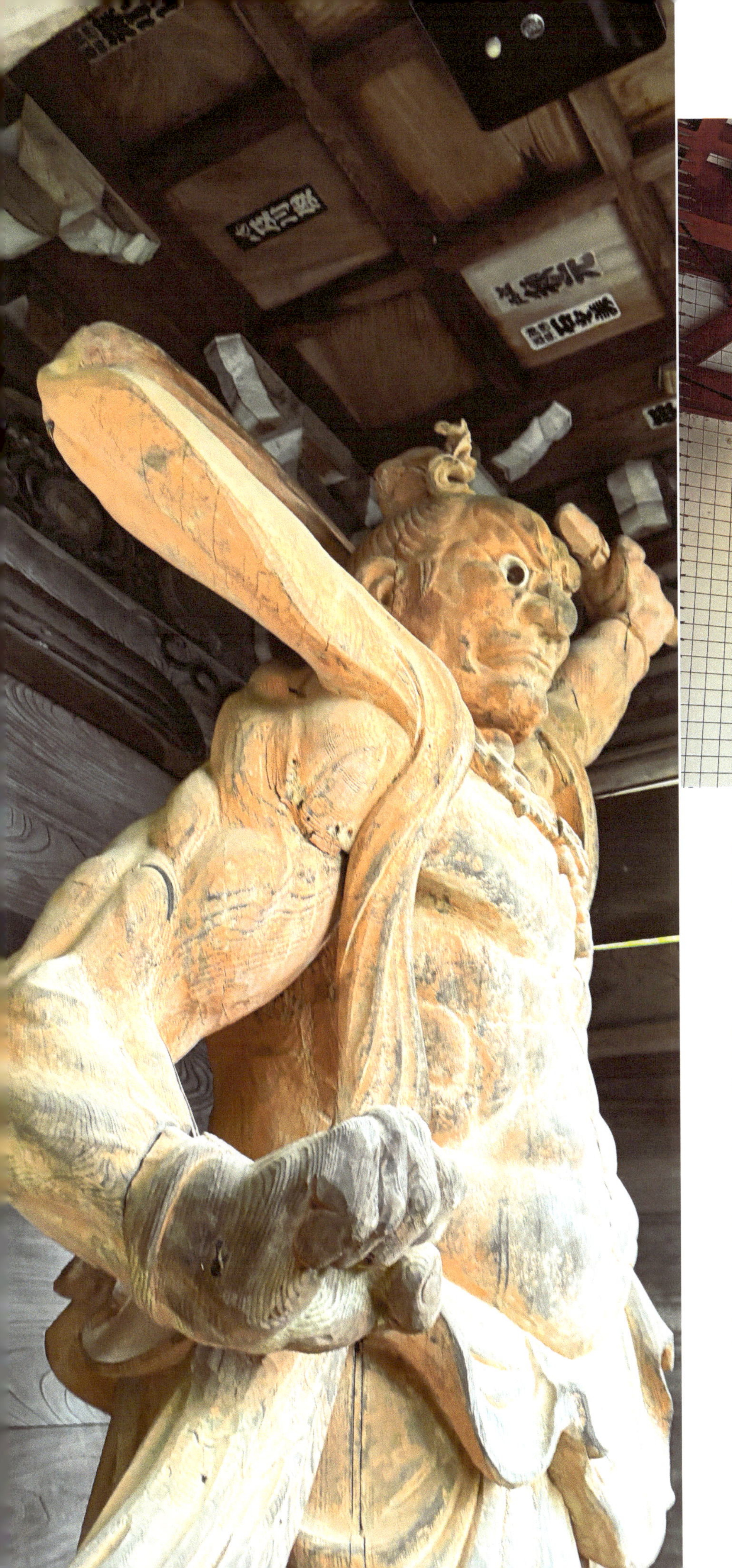

Opposite page (top and bottom); this page left and above.
Gatekeepers at Sacred Thresholds – *Shitennō-ji, Osaka; Itsukushima, Miyajima; Daishō-in, Miyajima; Shitennō-ji, Osaka*

In both Buddhist temples and Shinto shrines, the entrance is a transition from ordinary to sacred space and these thresholds are guarded.

At Buddhist temples, powerful guardian figures called *Niō* stand at the main gate. At Shinto shrines, paired stone animals known as *komainu* serve a similar role. Although they belong to different religious traditions, both function as protectors, standing at the entrance to keep harmful influences out.

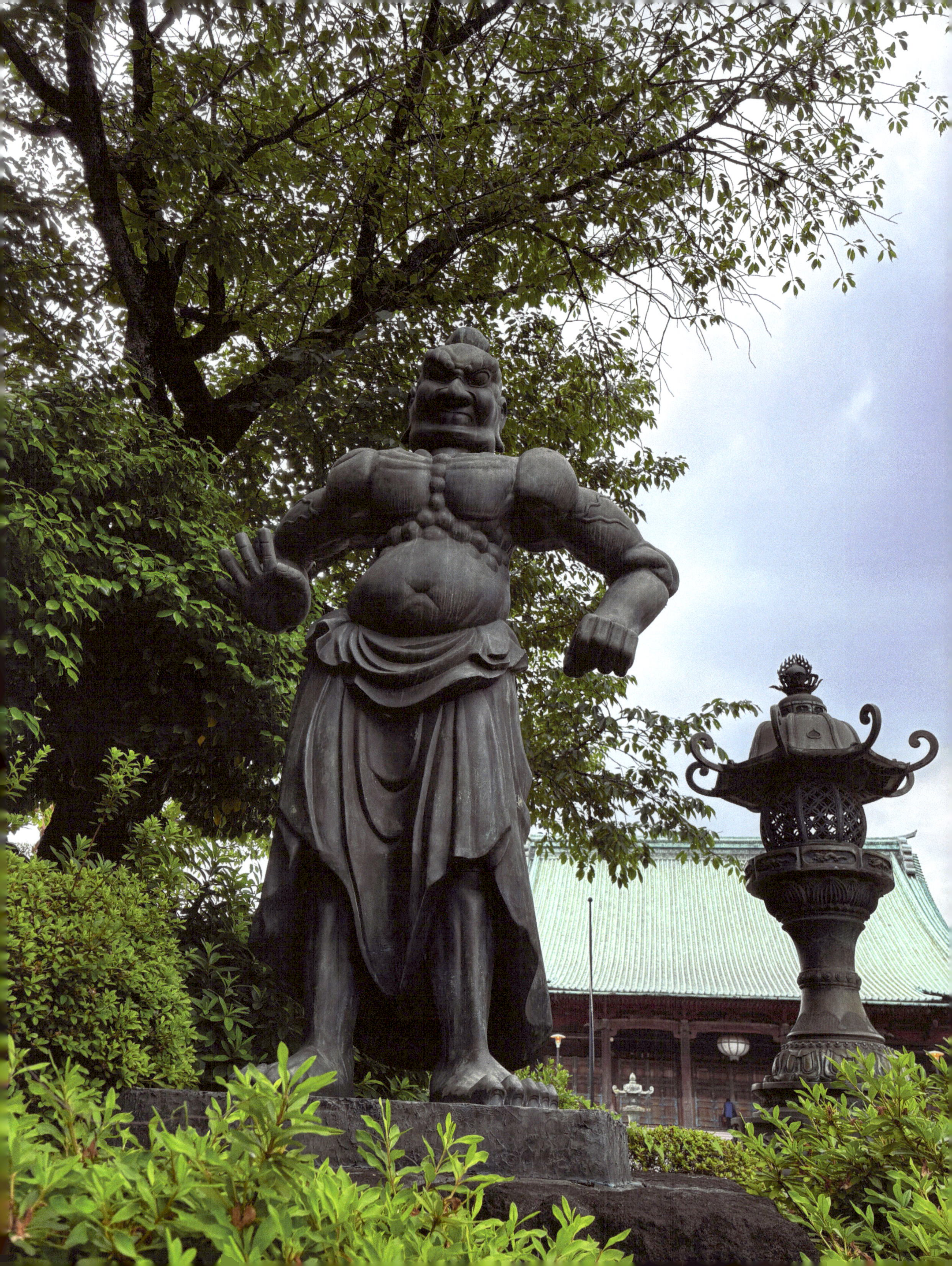

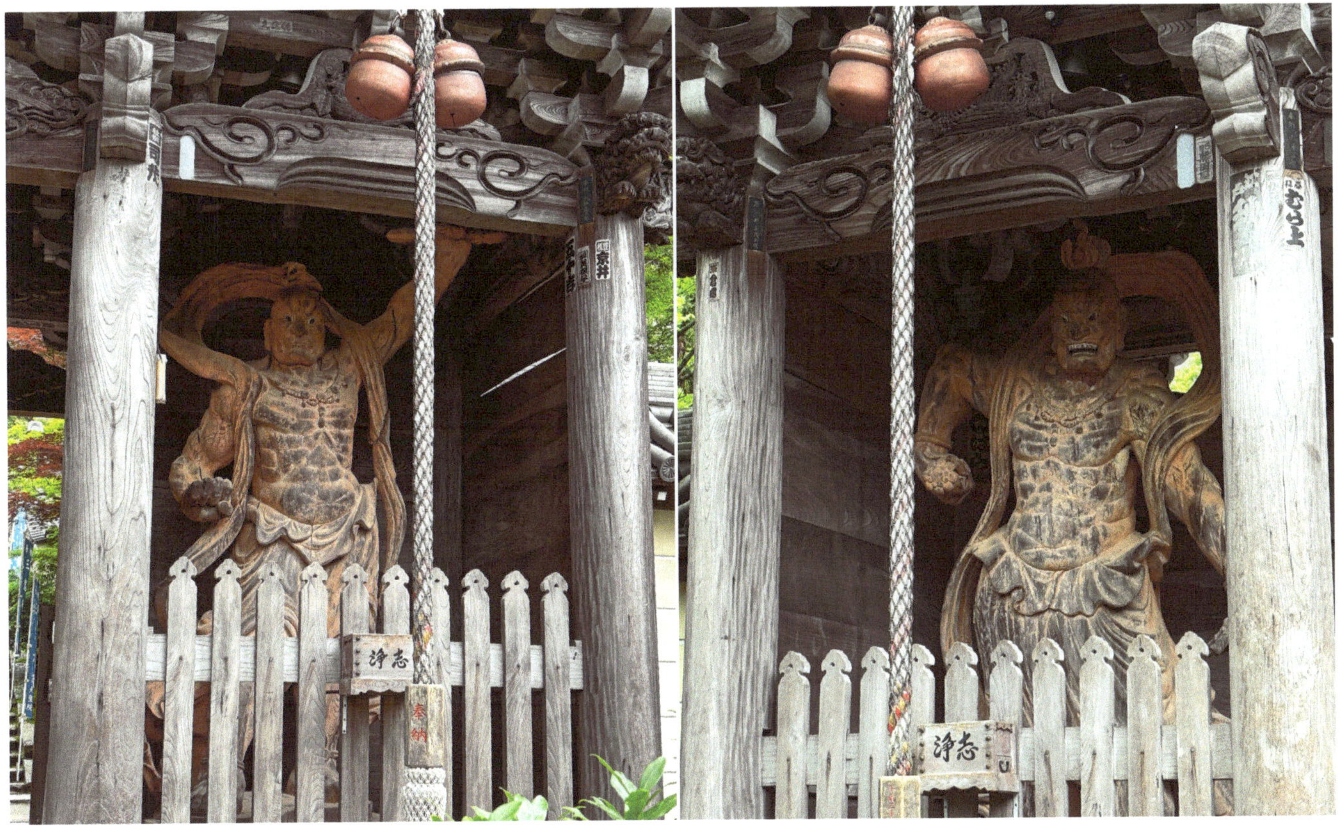

Opposite page (left); this page left and right.
Temple Gate Guardians (Niō) – *Gokoku-ji, Tokyo; Daishō-in, Miyajima*

Niō are fierce guardian figures placed at the main gate of Buddhist temples to protect the sacred space within. They are shown in dynamic poses, with twisted torsos, raised arms, and flying drapery, conveying active force. Often, a small subdued figure appears beneath their feet, signaling the suppression of chaos or ignorance. Their exaggerated muscles and forceful stance reflect an emphasis on physical energy as a form of protection. Niō appear as a paired set: one with an open mouth (*A-gyō*) and anther with a closed mouth (*Un-gyō*).

The Vedas state, *"The sound 'a' is indeed all speech"* (Skt. *akāro vai sarvā vāk; Aitareya Āraṇyaka II. iii. 7. 13*). In Sanskrit, *a* (like the *a* in *ago*) is understood as the most fundamental sound and the first letter of the alphabet. Interestingly, *kana*, which is also developed by Kūkai, has the same structure. When the mouth opens naturally to speak, *a* is produced without any effort of the tongue or lips. Because it begins deep in the throat, it is said to pervade all other sounds, which are understood as modifications of this first sound as breath moves outward. This idea carries into Shingon Buddhism, where *a* is the most sacred syllable and represents Mahāvairocana Buddha and the principle of original unproducedness: all phenomena arise from a primordial source. One Niō guardian with the open mouth embodies this *a*, while his closed-mouth counterpart completes the sound as *Un*. Together, they show how the Vedic *aum/oṃ* is visually expressed in Japan as A–Un, the full cycle of sound and existence.

In Hindu temples, *dvarapālakas* have a similar role in guarding the thresholds but they are usually shown standing upright and composed, emphasizing presence and authority rather than explosive movement.

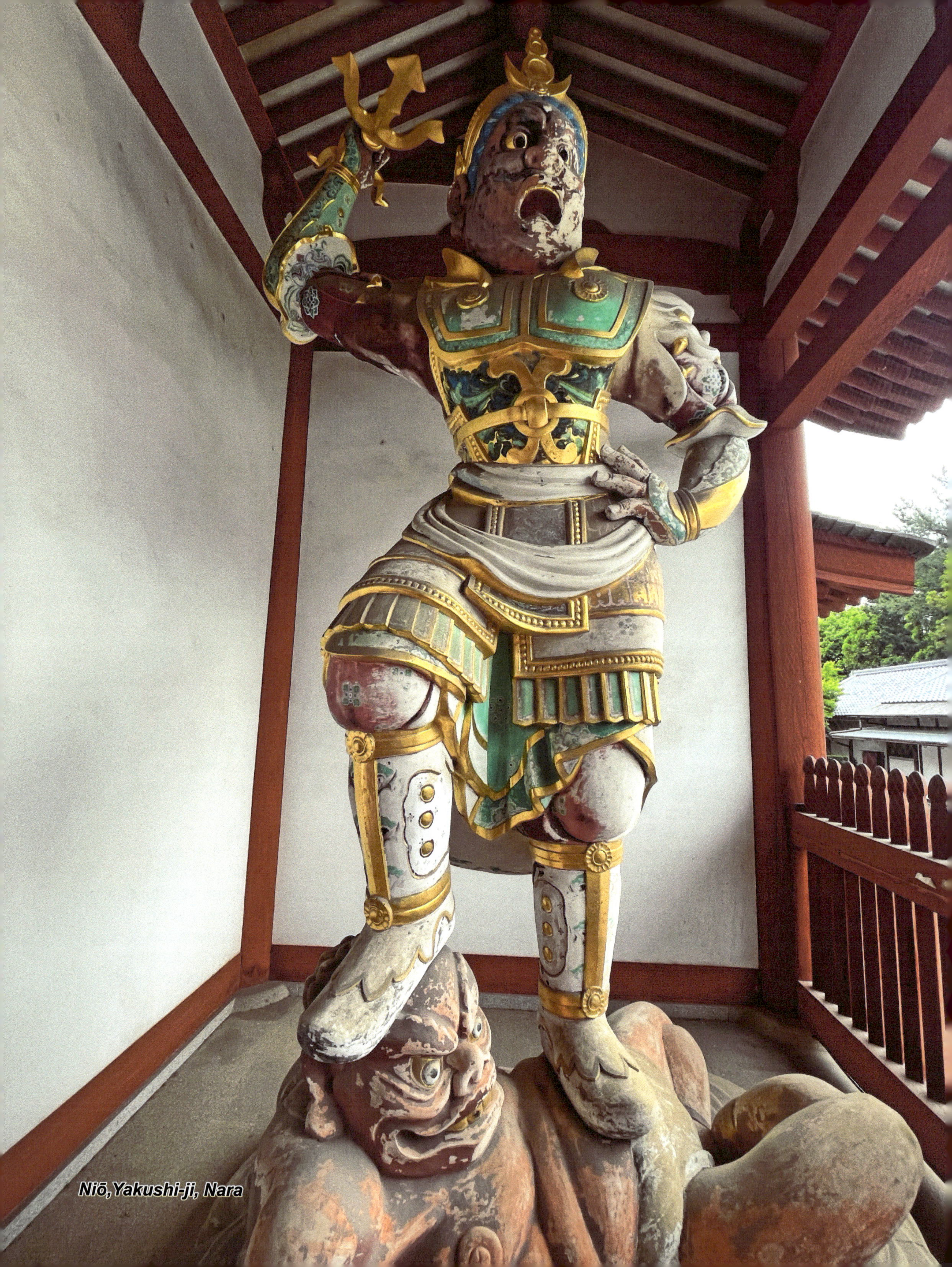

Niō,Yakushi-ji, Nara

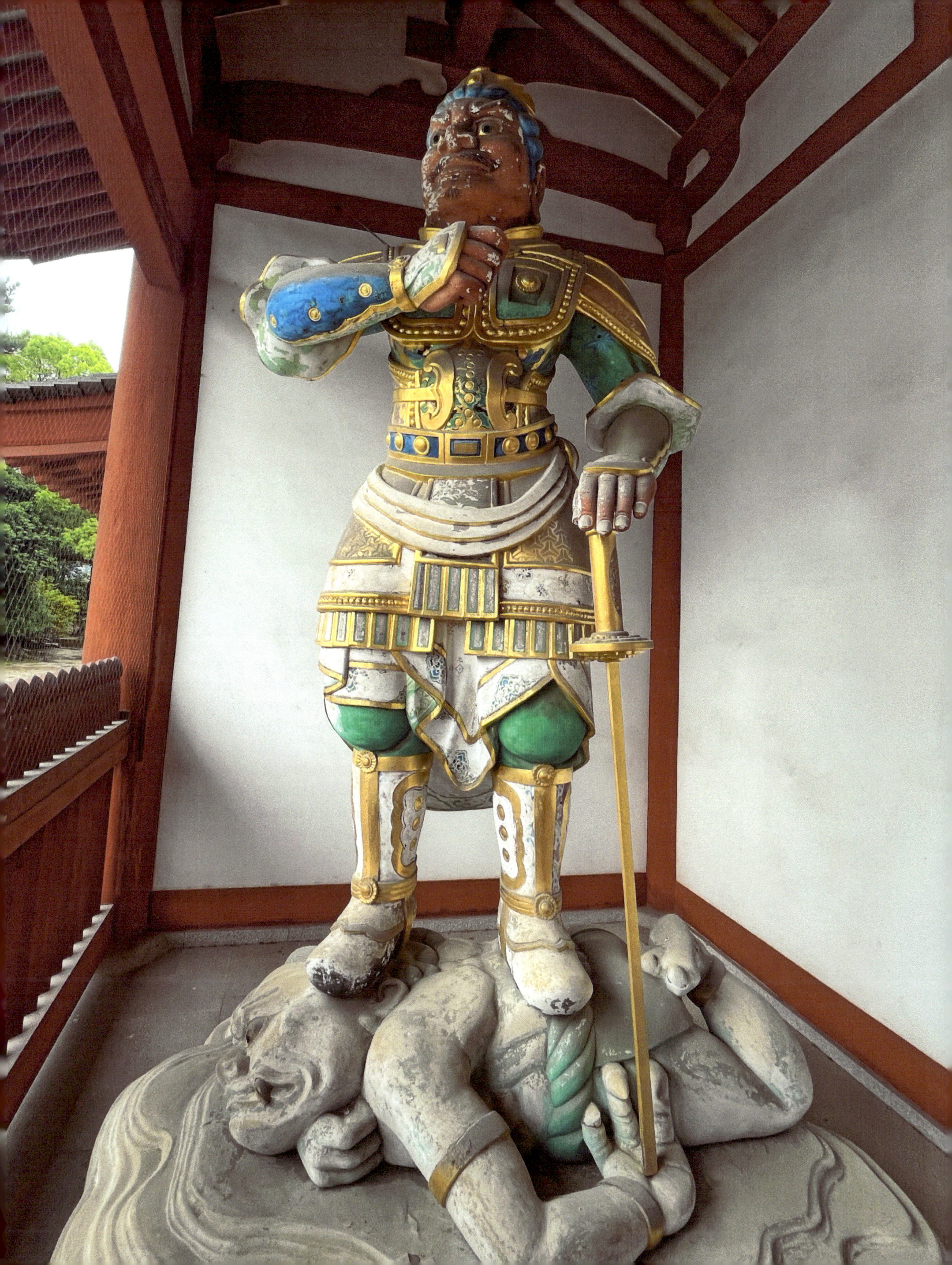

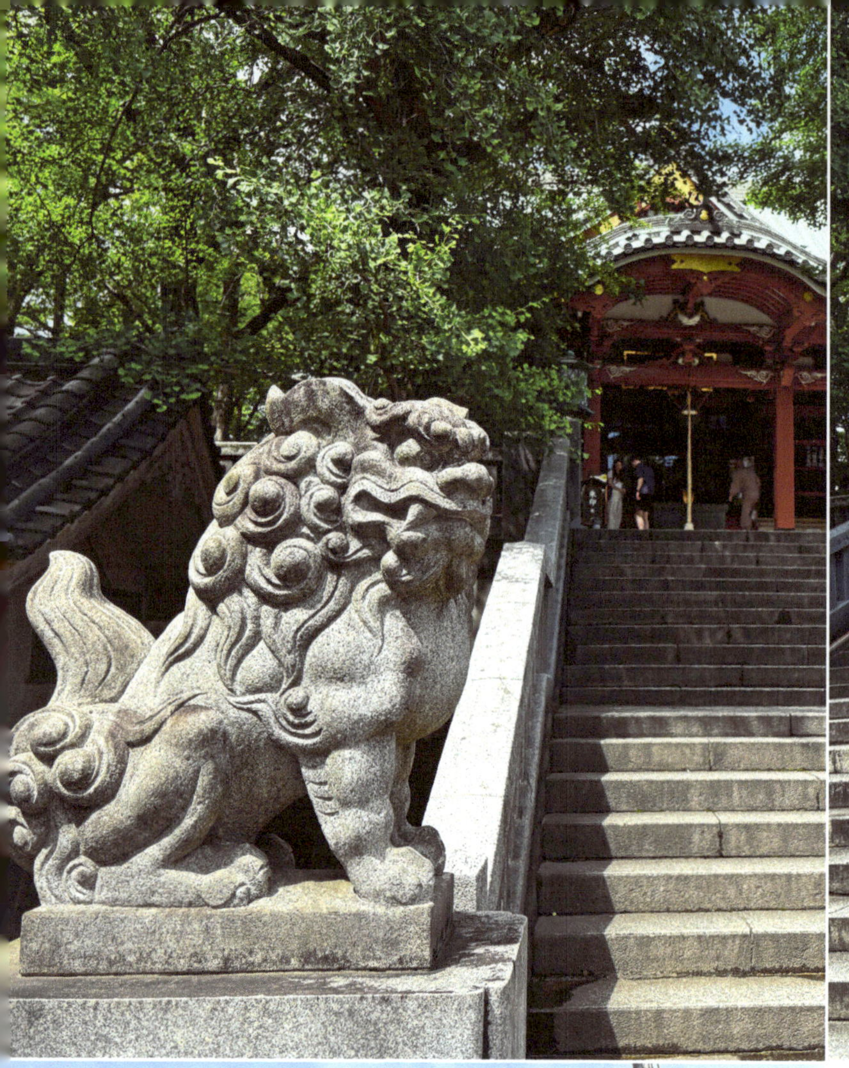

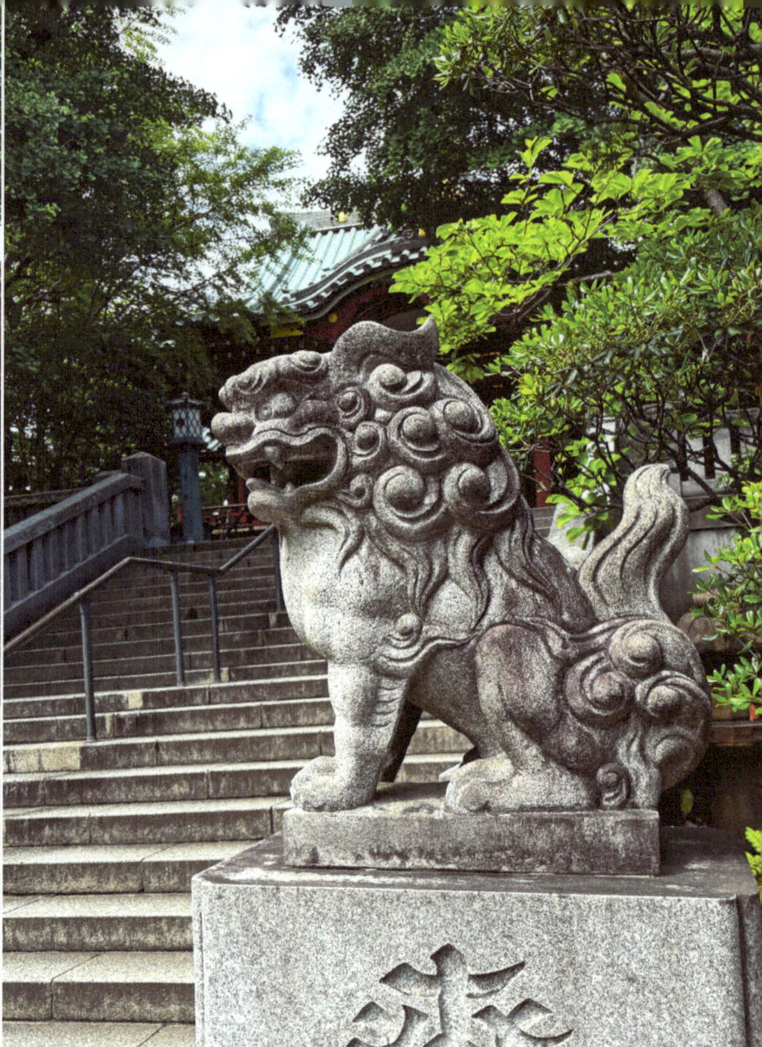

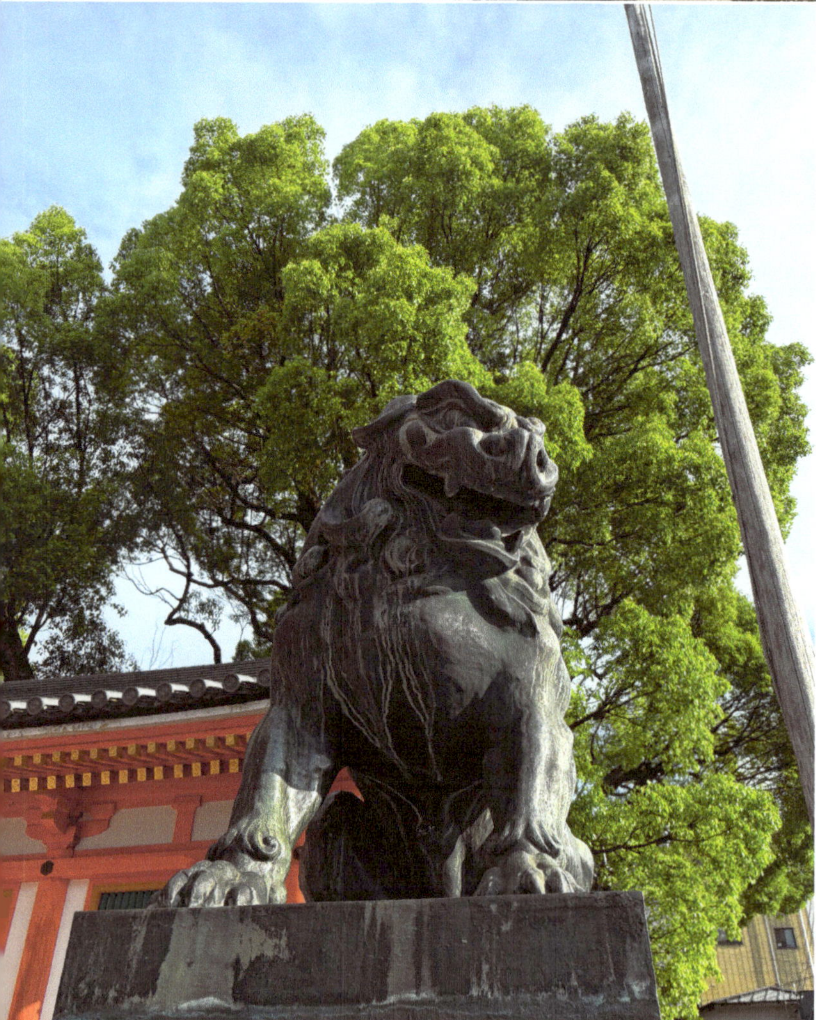

This and opposite page (clockwise from left). **Komainu (Shrine Gate Guardians)** – *Yasaka Jinja, Kyoto; Matsuchiyama Shōden, Tokyo; Sensō-ji, Tokyo; Hōzan-ji, Ikoma*

Komainu are paired guardian animals placed at the entrance of temples and shrines. Like temple *Niō*, they are set as a contrasting pair: one with an open mouth (*A-gyō*) and another with a closed mouth (*Un-gyō*). This *A-Un* pairing draws on the idea of first and last sound, often compared to the full range of sound expressed in Skt. *aum/oṃ*. *Komainu* vary by shrine in style and species, but they all express the *A-Un* form of *aum*.

In Śrī Ādi Śaṅkara's (a philosophical giant in India, often dated to the 8th century CE) commentary on Māṇḍūkya Upaniṣad 8-11, he explains *aum* as a compendium of all sounds because its **a** (like the *a* in *tusk*) starts in the open throat, **u** (like the *u* in *cook*) moves through the mouth cavity, and **m** closes at the lips, showing that all individual words are merely fragmented deconvolutions and combinations of this single, foundational resonance.

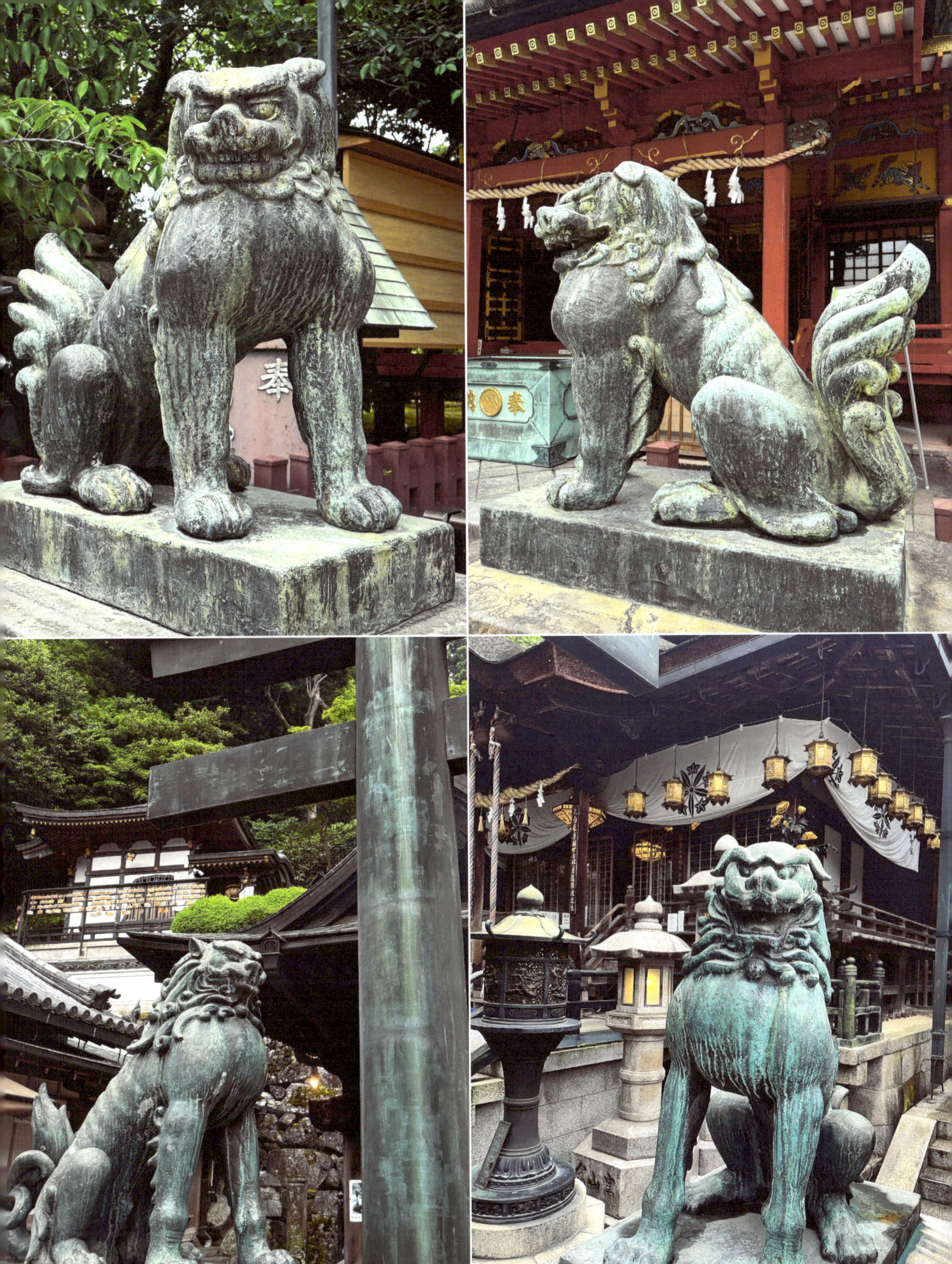
奉
奉

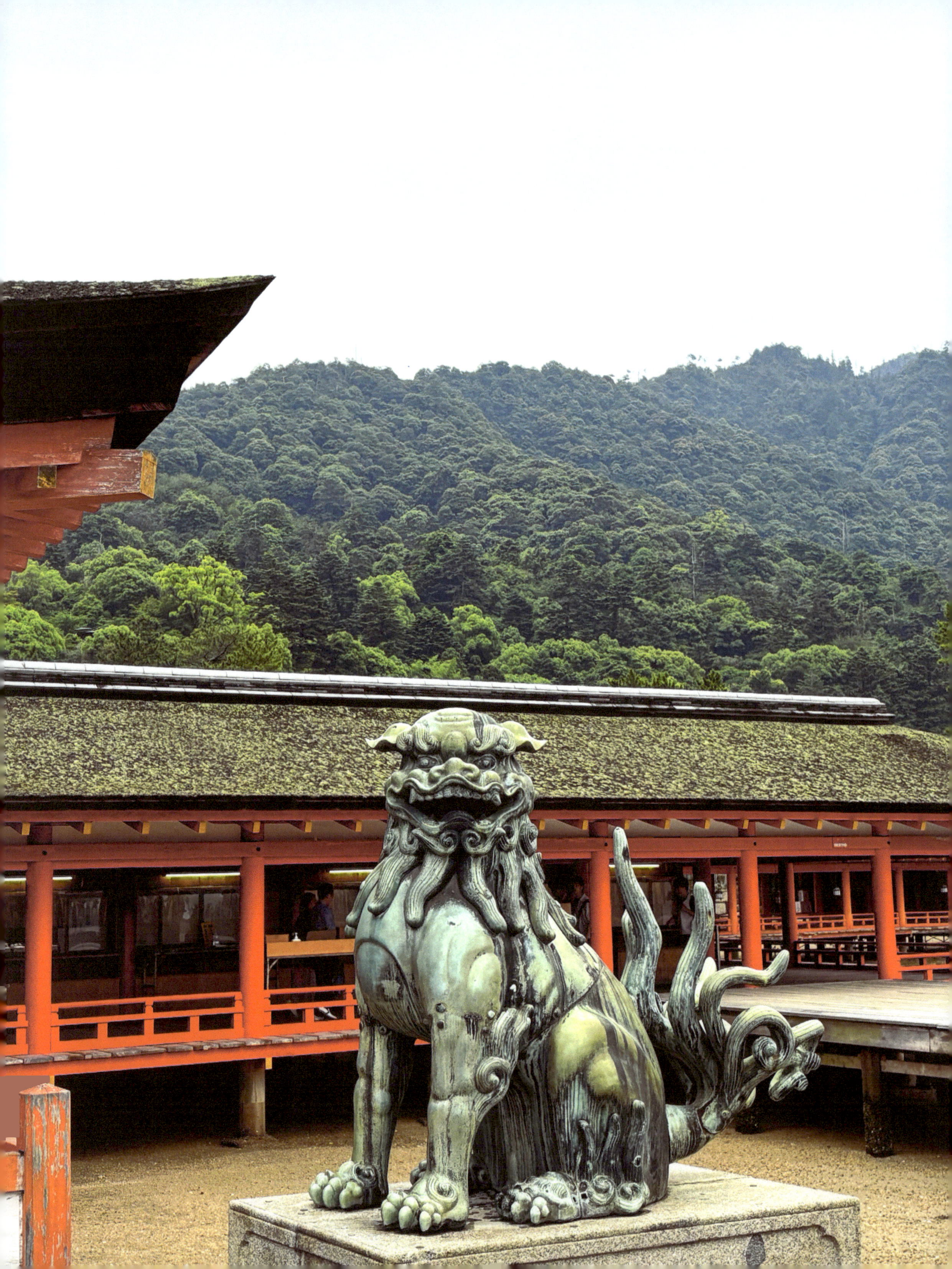

This page and opposite page (clockwise from right).
Animal Gate Guardians – *Hie Jinja, Tokyo; Fushimi Inari Taisha, Kyoto; Itsukushima Shrine, Miyajima*

While *komainu* (lion dogs) are the most common shrine guardians, many Shinto shrines use other animals connected to the resident deity. At Hie Jinja, the guardians are monkeys (*masaru*), sacred to the shrine and associated with protection and warding off misfortune. At Fushimi Inari, foxes (*kitsune*) serve as messengers of Inari, the *kami* (Shinto deity or spirit) of rice, fertility, and prosperity. At Itsukushima, more familiar *komainu* guard the shrine complex.

Despite their different forms, these animal guardians still follow the *A-Un* pattern. The open-mouth figure (*A-gyō*) often holds a *hojū* (Skt. *cintāmaṇi*, wish-fulfilling jewel), symbolizing abundance and divine power, while the closed-mouth figure (*Un-gyō*) holds a key, representing access to storehouses and protection of what lies within. The species may change but the meaning remains consistent.

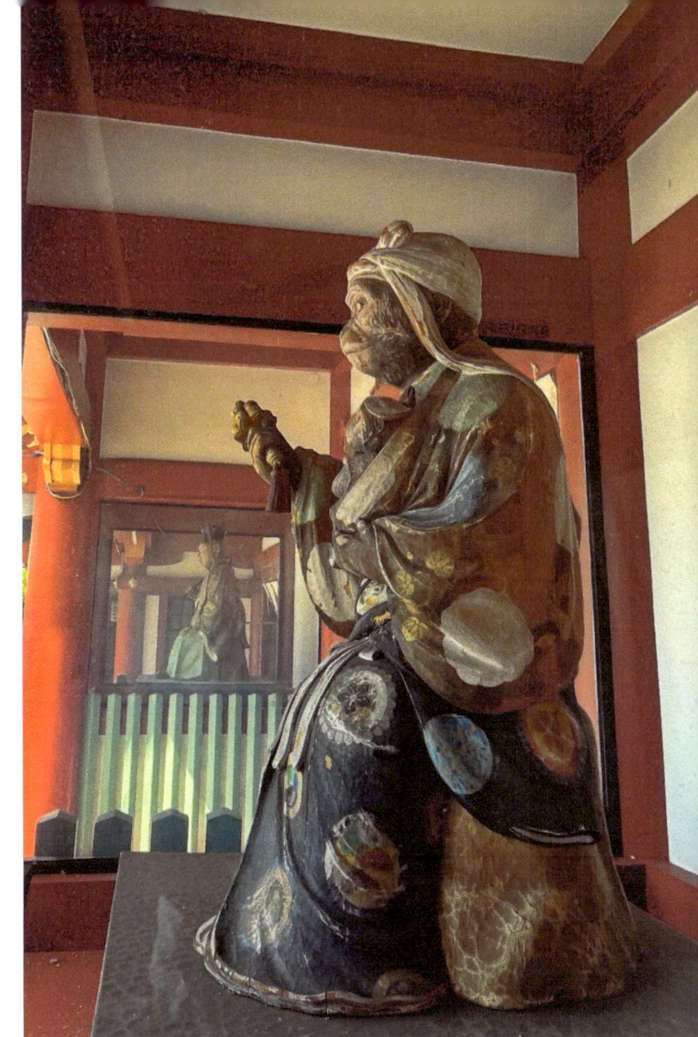

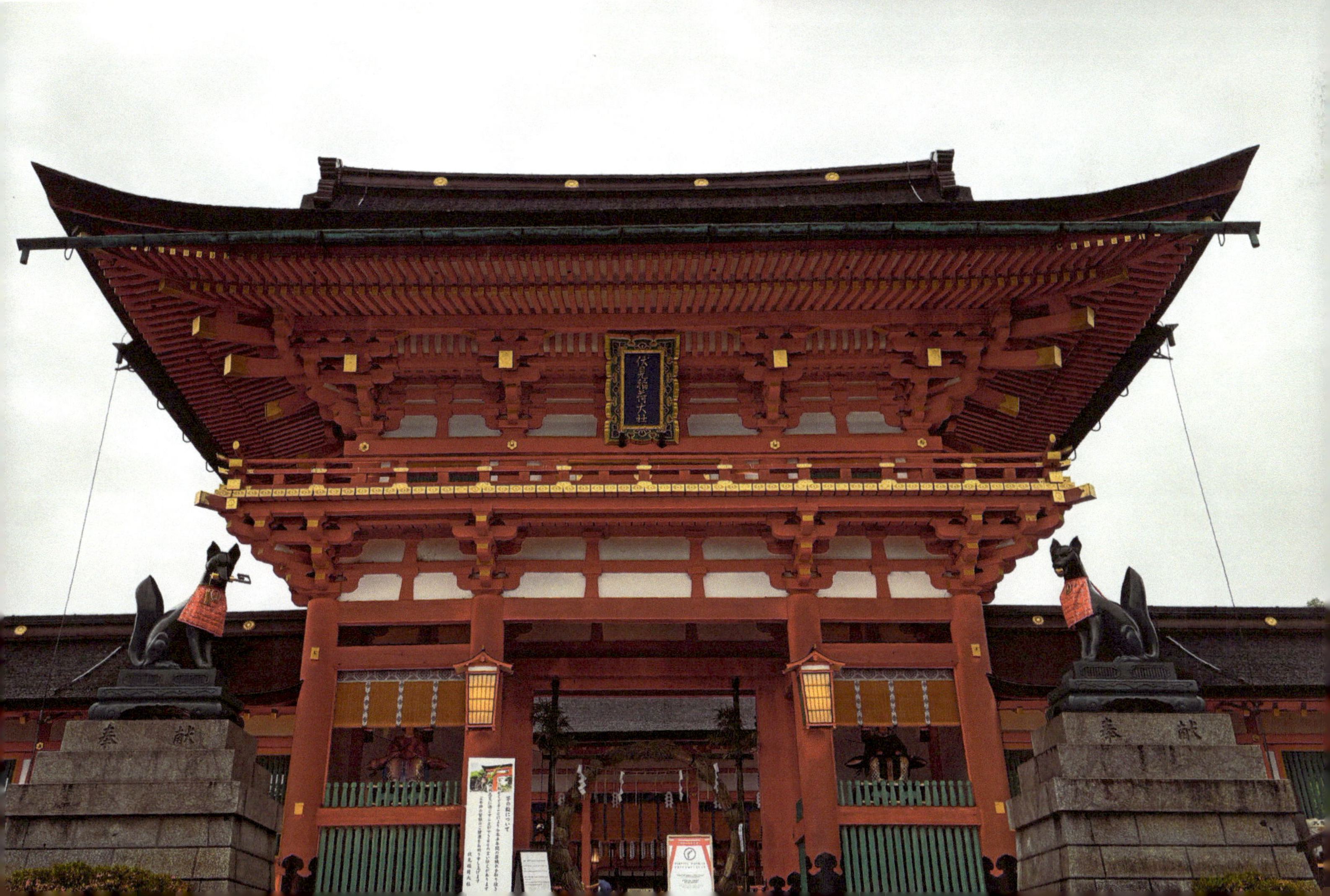

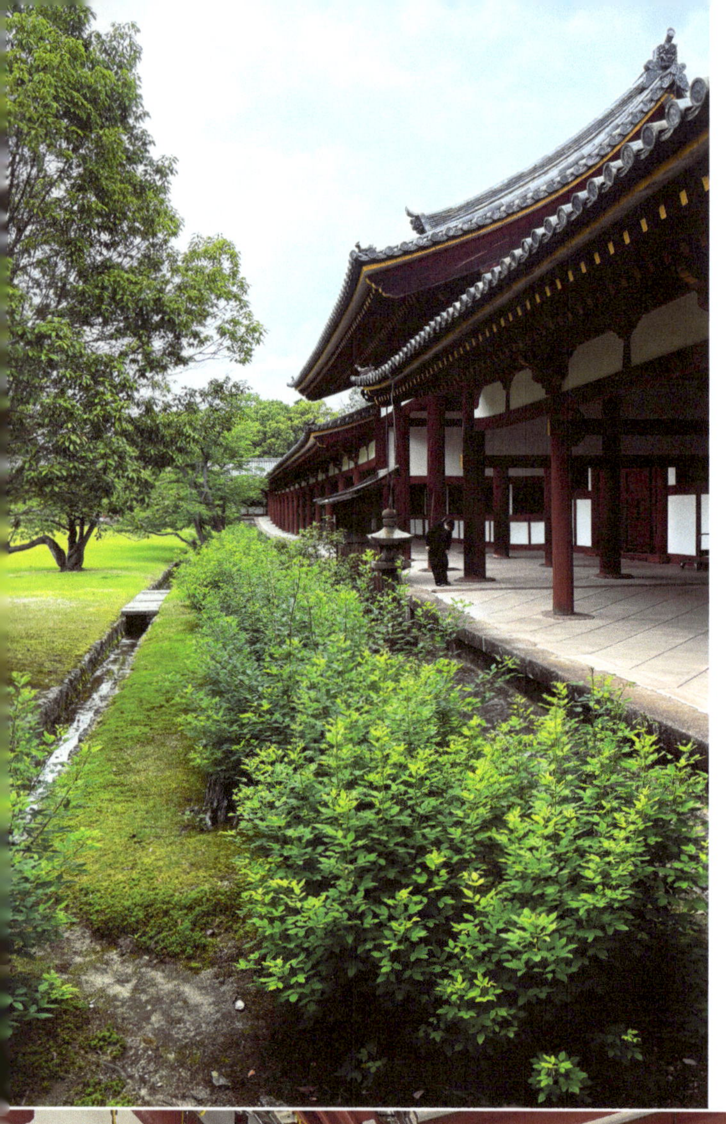

This page and opposite page (clockwise from top right). **Red and White Stripes** – *Itsukushima Shrine, Miyajima; Hie Shrine, Tokyo; Shitennō-ji, Osaka; Tōdai-ji, Nara*

In Japan, red and white carry protective and purifying meanings rooted in material and ritual practice. The red used on shrines and temples is *shu* (vermilion), historically made from cinnabar and valued for preserving wood, which led to its association with protection and the warding off of harmful forces. White represents ritual purity in Shinto. Together, red and white form Jp. *kōhaku*, an auspicious pairing widely used to mark sacred and secular events, and it appears across both Shinto shrines and Buddhist temples.

In South India, temple compound walls are often painted with alternating red and white vertical stripes that mirror the Skt. *nāmam* marks worn by devotees. Here, red signifies life force (Skt. *Śakti*), and white signifies purity and divine order (*Śiva / Viṣṇu*). The striped walls signal that the temple is active, protected, and consecrated.

Although the traditions developed independently, both use red and white in strikingly similar ways to mark sacred space.

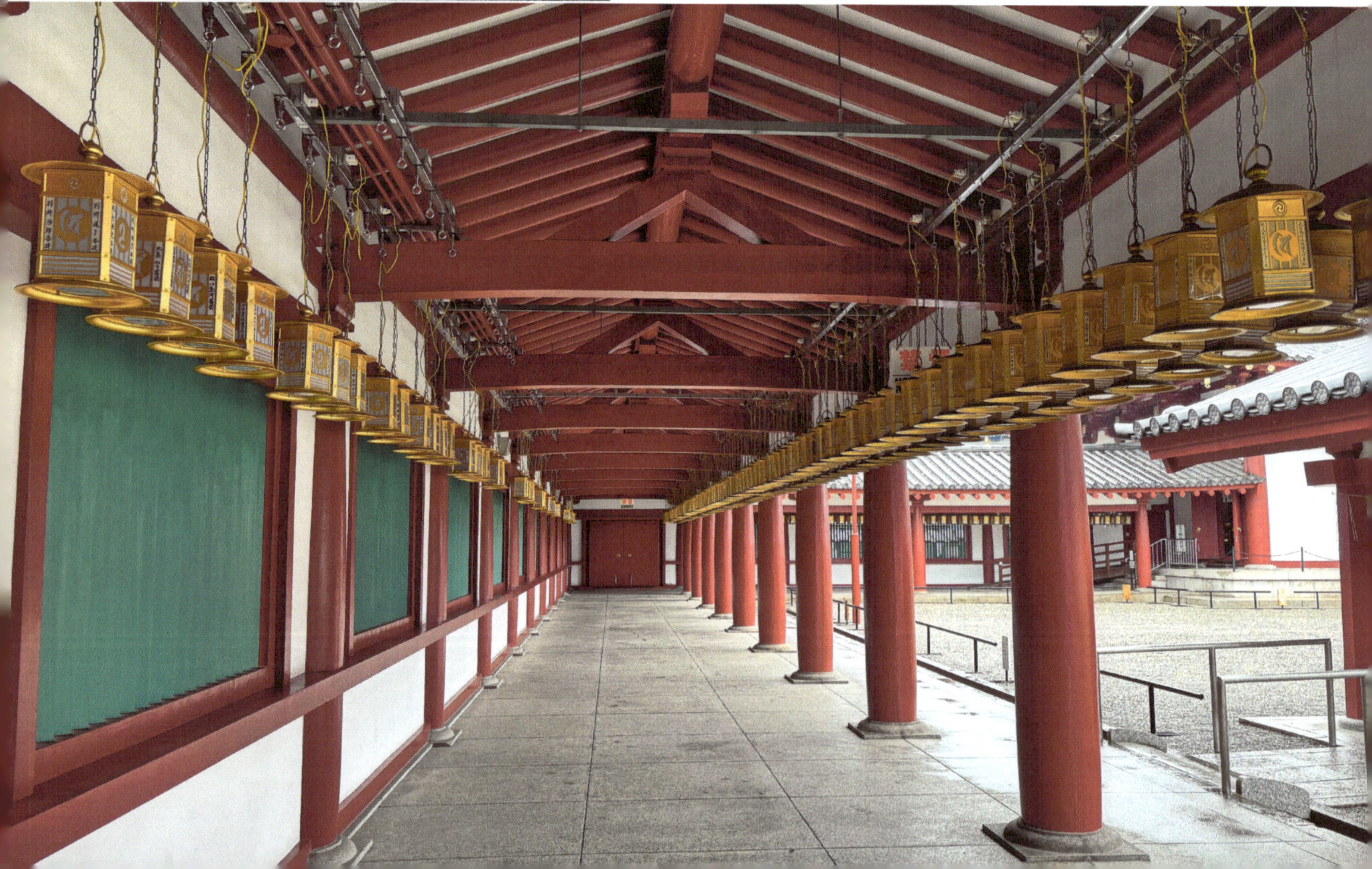

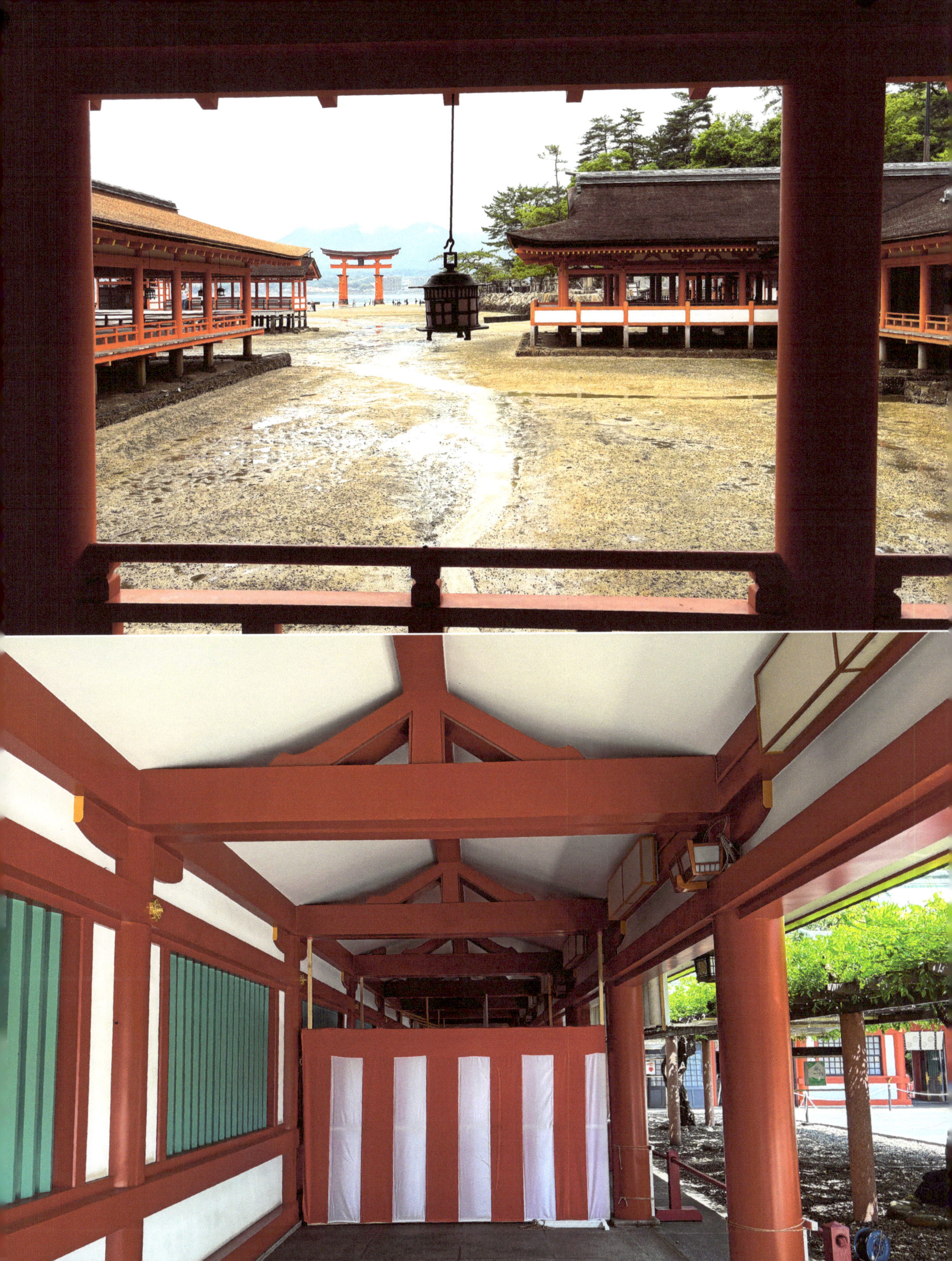

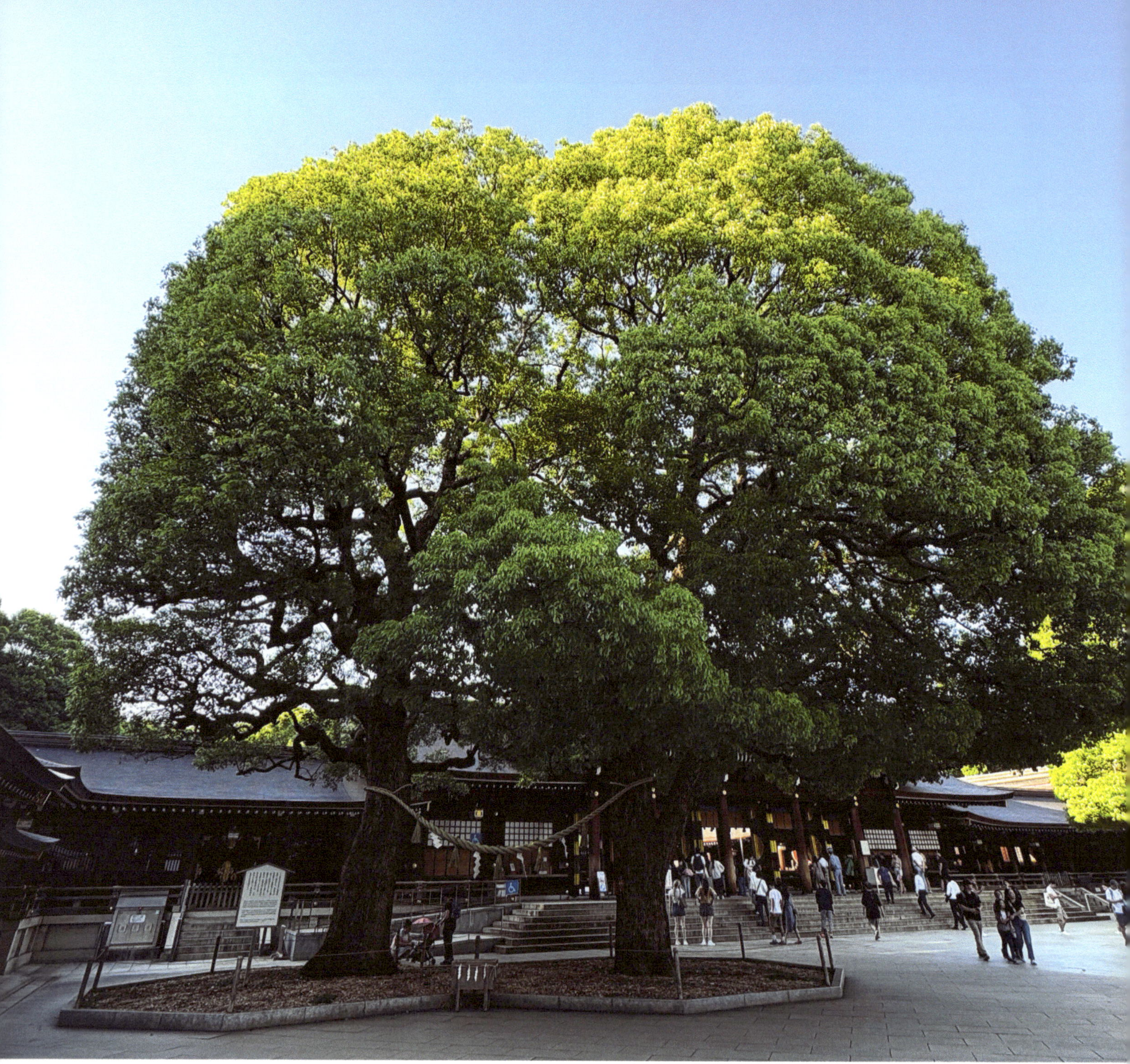

This page (above).
Meoto Kusu ("Married Trees") – *Meiji Jingū, Tokyo*

Two camphor trees stand here as a sacred pair standing for the emperor and empress. I was reminded of the ancient *Aśvattha–Nīm* tree-pair in my ancestral village in India that has been watching over our family for centuries. Vedic weddings are performed there too, and like these "married trees," they are approached as a divine couple seeking prosperity and a harmonious home.

Opposite page, above and below.
Zen Gardens, Stone and Moss –
Ryōan-ji, Kyoto; Arashiyama, Kyoto

Ryōan-ji (founded in 1450 CE), known for its rock garden, where stones are set amid raked white gravel, is meant to be viewed for meditation. In Arashiyama, moss gardens use shade and time itself to create the same quiet focus.

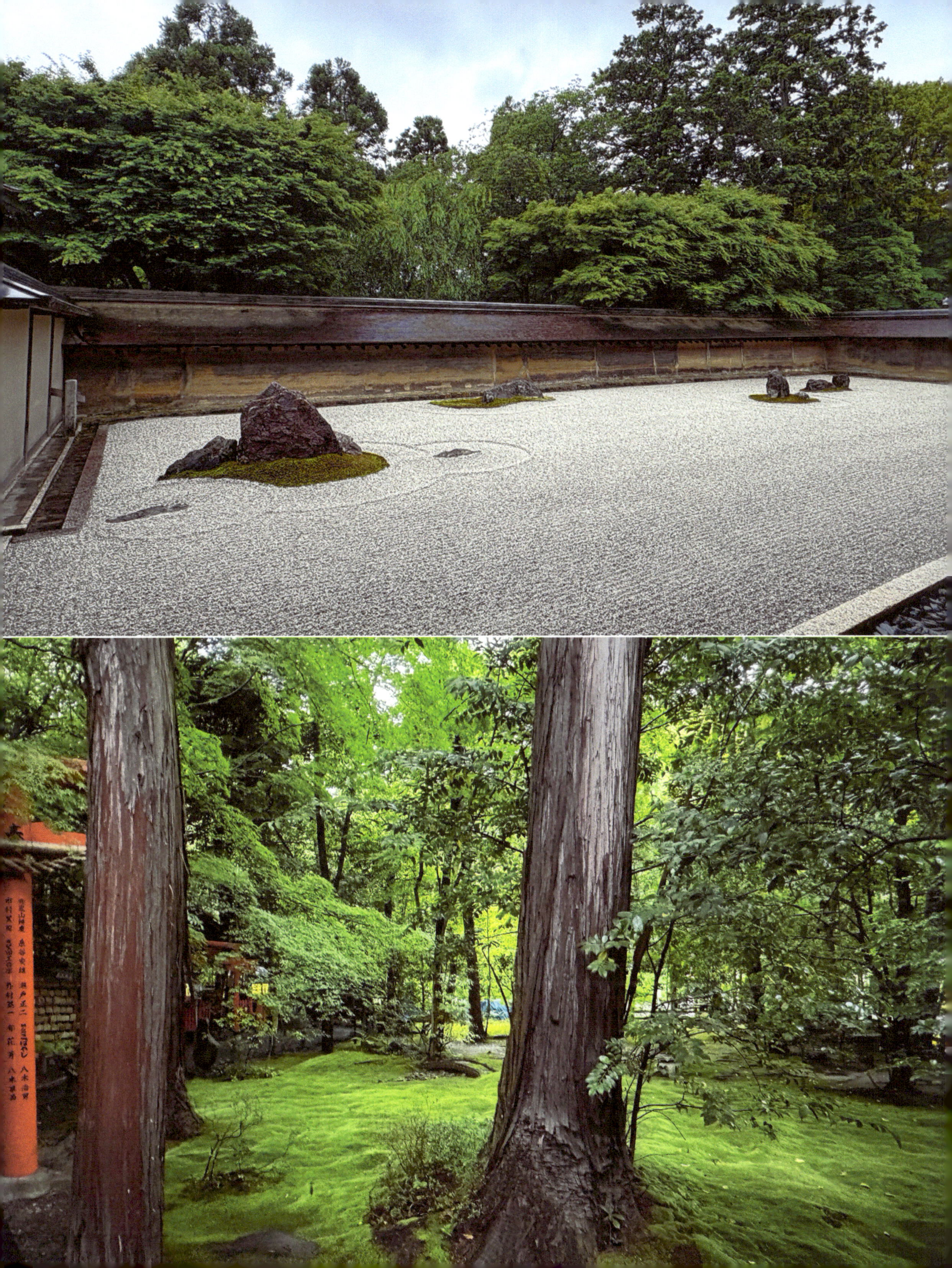

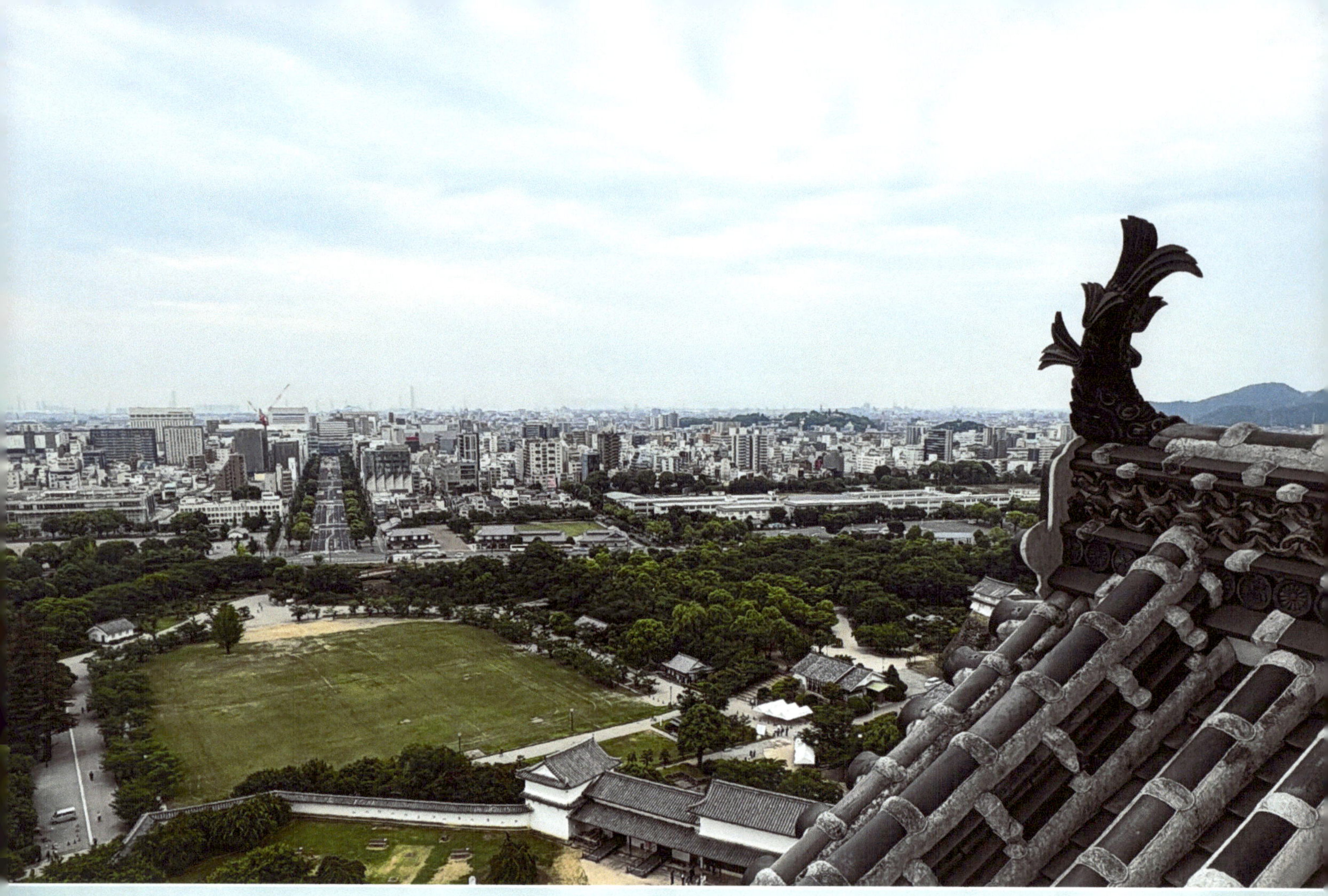

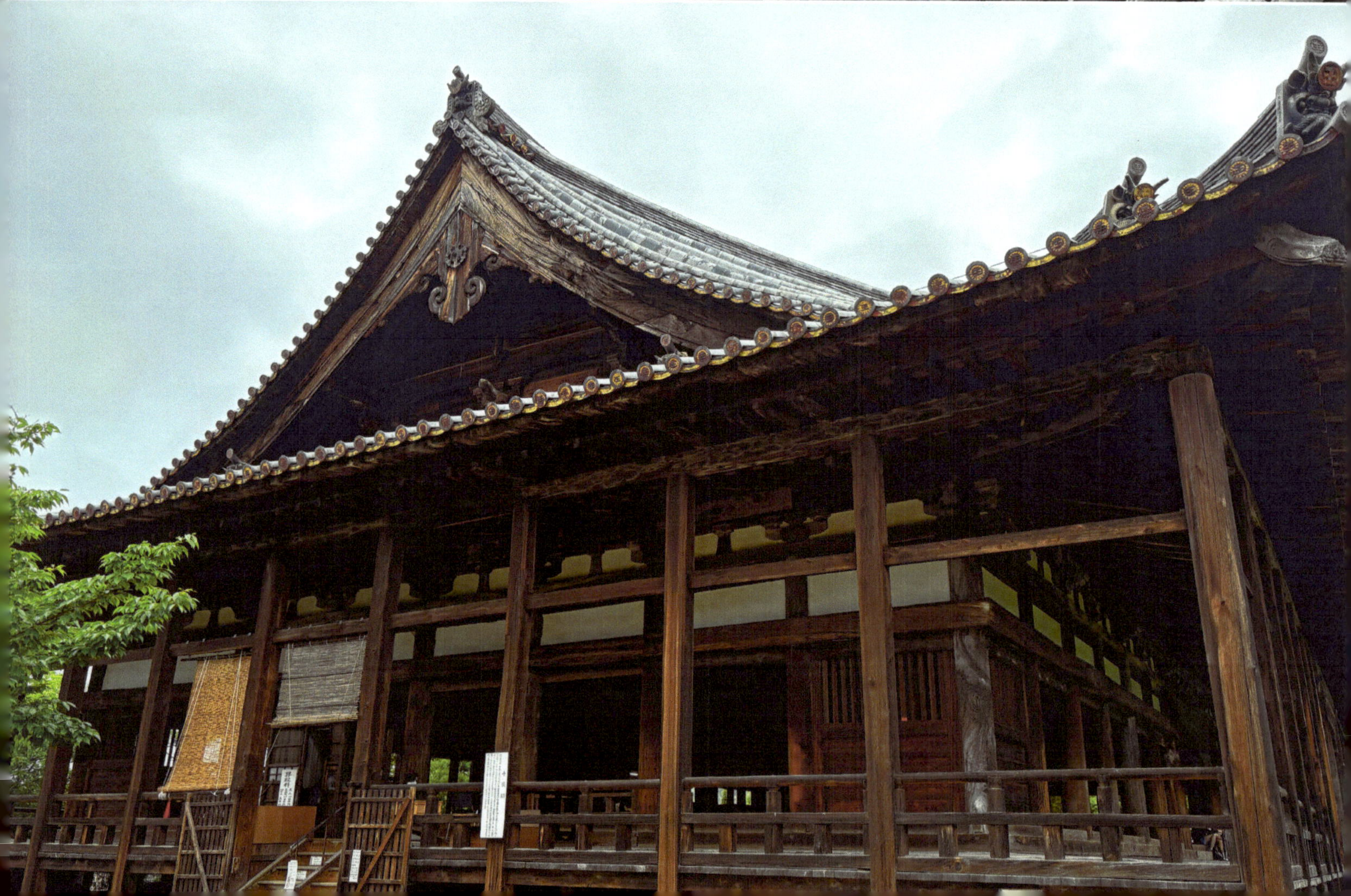

Opposite page (above).
Shachihoko (roof-ridge fish-beast) – *Himeji Castle, Himeji*

A *shachihoko* is placed on the roof ridge as a water-linked guardian believed to summon rain and protect wooden structures from fire. It descends from the older *makara* motif on Hindu temples, with both using a mythic water creature as a protective emblem set high on a sacred structure.

Opposite page (below).
Senjōkaku (Hall of One Thousand Tatami Mats) – *Miyajima*

Senjōkaku is a vast wooden hall, where the Buddhist *sangha* gathers to recite sutras. South Indian temples also have monumental "1,000-pillared halls," such as at Rameshwaram, which are used as a congregation and resting space for pilgrims.

This page (right).
Lion Capital of Aśoka (replica) – *Tōdai-ji, Nara*

This is a modern replica of the famous Lion Capital from Sarnath in India (3rd century BCE), the site of the Buddha's first sermon, set on a lotus base, with lions facing outward like the spread of Buddha's teaching in all directions. It was installed at Tōdai-ji in 1988 for the "Hana Matsuri Thousand-Priests' Service," and it is described as a visible tribute to the historical and spiritual debt Japanese Buddhism owes to India.

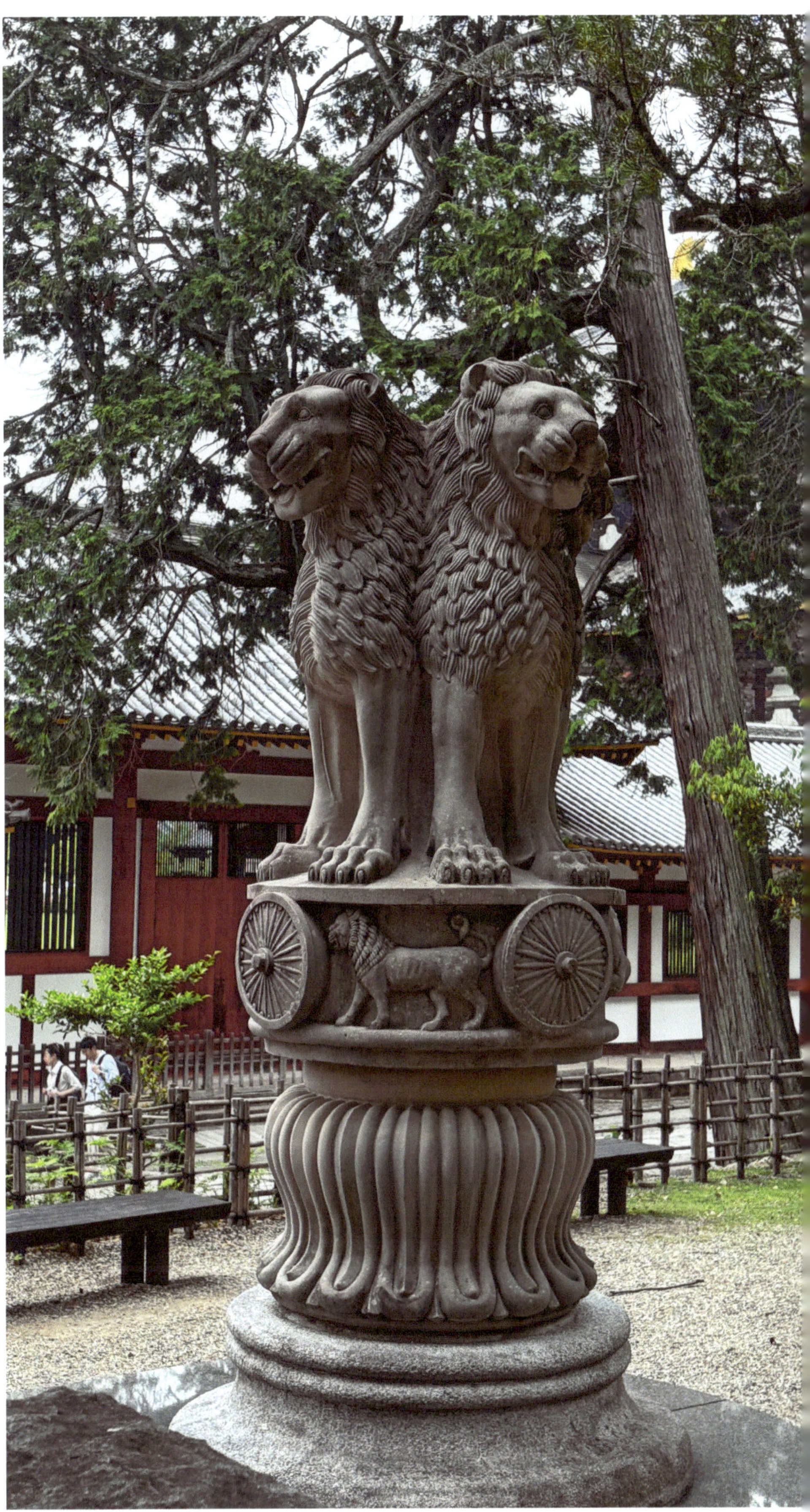

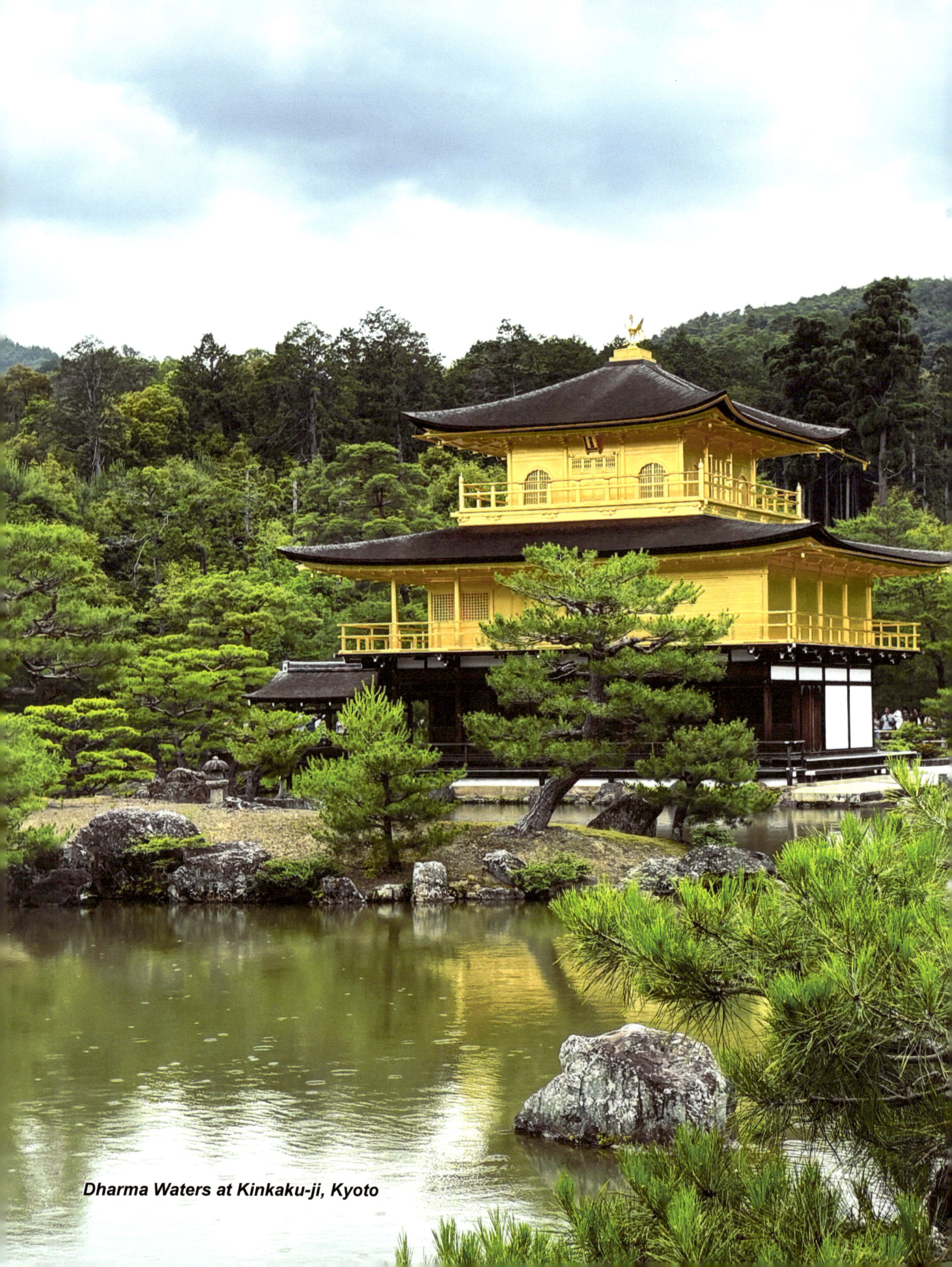

Dharma Waters at Kinkaku-ji, Kyoto

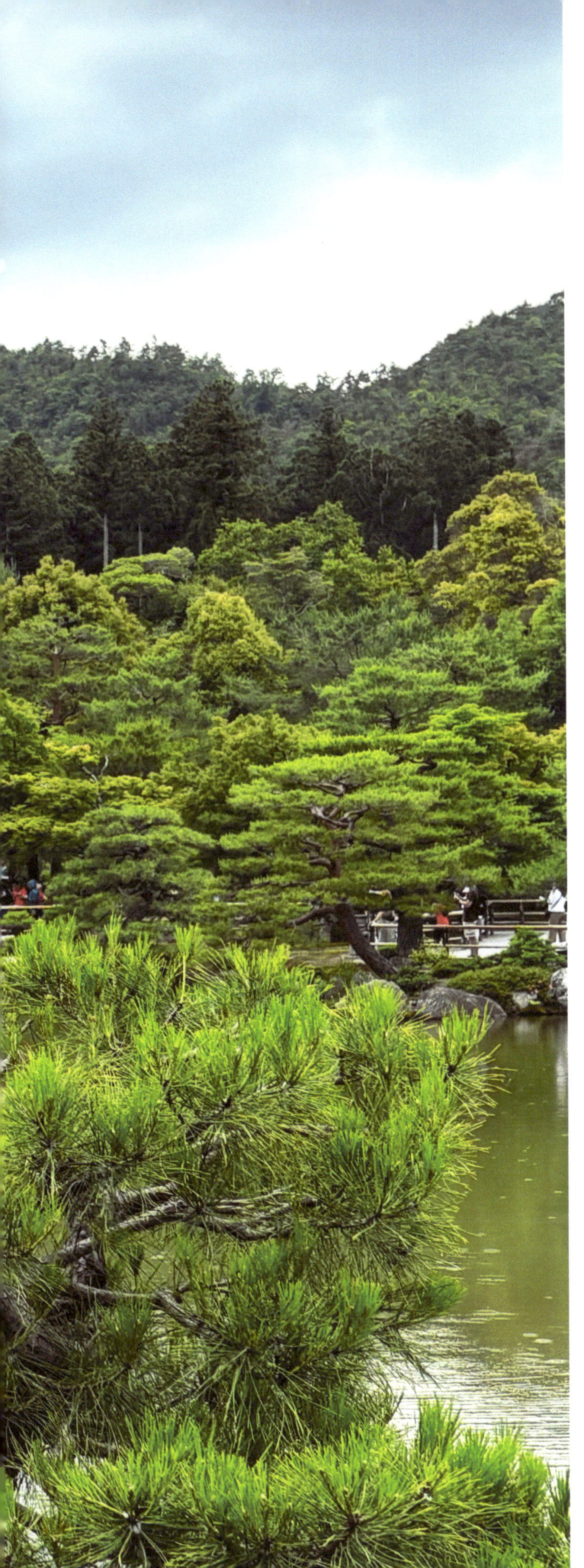

Rituals

FIVE

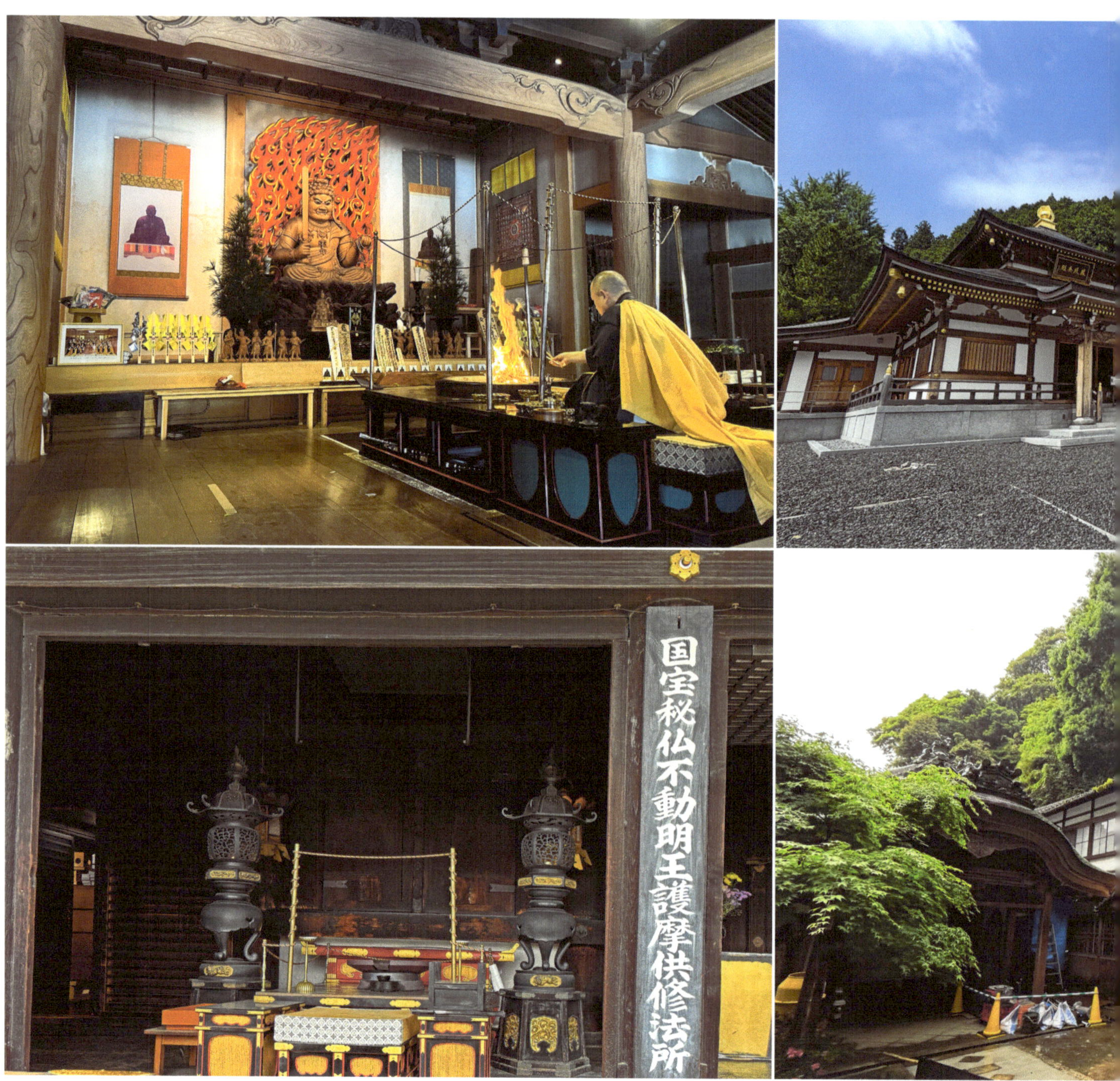

Clockwise from top left. **Goma (Skt. *homa*)** – *Shōjōshin-in, Kōyasan;* **Goma halls** – *Shōjōshin-in, Kōyasan; Shinobazu no Ike, Tokyo; Kanchi-in near Tō-ji, Kyoto; Hōgon-ji, Lake Biwa; Tō-ji, Kyoto*

Goma is the Japanese form of Vedic *homa*, the fire offering performed by Hindus for thousands of years. A square fire altar (*goma-dan*) with its metal hearth plays the role of the *homa kuṇḍa*, with vessels for offerings that work like a *pañcapātra* in a Hindu ritual. Long-handled ladles (*goma-shaku*) carry sesame oil and water into the flames just as *sruk*, *sruva*, and *darvī* carry ghee in a *homa*, while slim wooden prayer sticks (*gomagi*), each inscribed with a person's name and wish, substitute for *samidha* twigs. Before the fire is kindled the priest sprinkles sanctified water on altar, similar to Skt. *prokṣaṇī*, then chants mantras of the deity in Sanskrit but pronounced in Japanese.

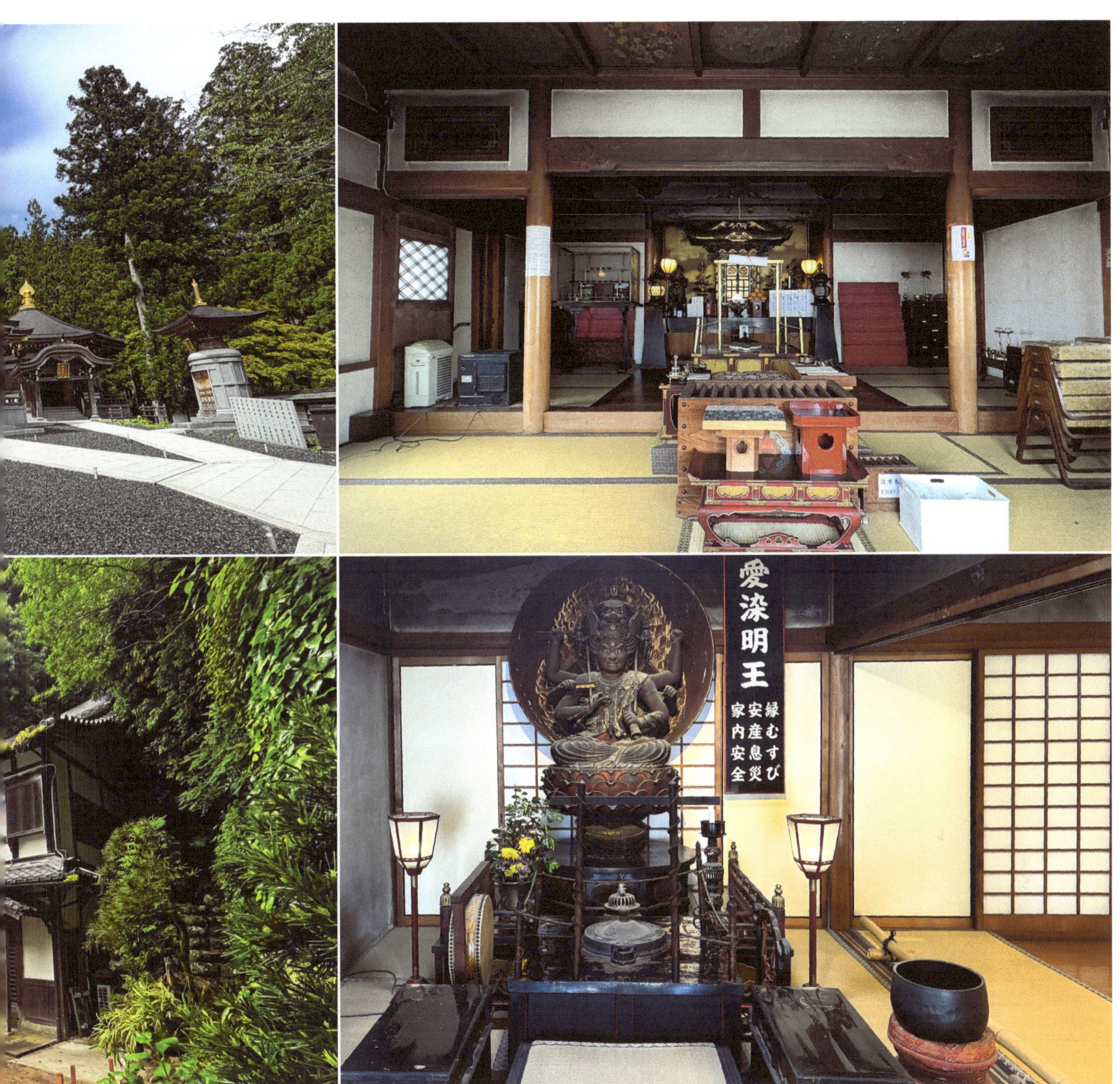

These *goma* halls across Japan retain the same basic form of Vedic *homa* but set in Japanese setttings with *tatami* mats and *shōji* screens.

At Shōjōshin-in, a Shingon monk performs *Fudō goma*, dropping each *gomagi* stick into the *goma-dan* along with sesame oil and grains while chanting Sanskrit *mantra* in Japanese style. A small *vajra* rests on the altar as a sign of indestructible wisdom and the power to smash obstacles, and the monk touches or lifts it at key moments to seal the offerings. People sponsor these rites for protection, exam success, safe childbirth, healing, and the peace of their ancestors, with faith that whatever is written on the wooden sticks is carried by the fire to the deity. Shingon teachers describe this rite as joining speech, body, and mind: *mantra* for speech, *mudrā* and ritual tools for the body, and the blazing fire altar as a living *mandala* for the mind.

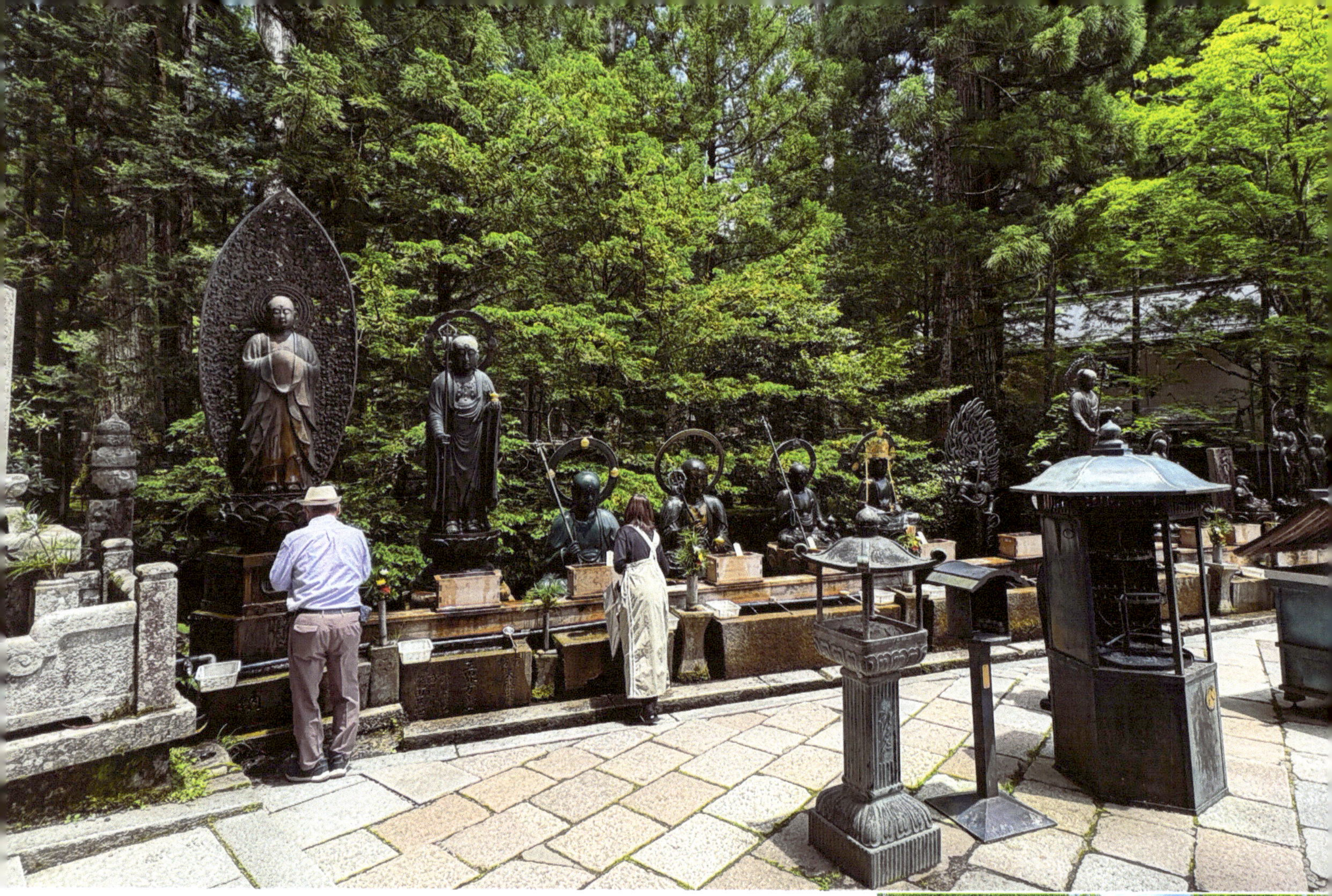

This page and opposite page (clockwise from above).
Prayers, Sponsorships, and Ritual Offerings – *Temples in Kōyasan, Miyajima, Ikoma, and Tokyo*

At Kōyasan, visitors pour water over rows of deities in a form of *kanjō (*Skt. *abhiṣeka)*, the ritual bathing of the deity also seen in Hindu temples. At Daigan-ji, votive candles are labeled for good health, exams, business, and more, so each person can choose a specific wish. At Matsuchiyama Shōden, a detailed *kuyō (*Skt. *puja)* sponsorship list for car blessings, monthly oil-bath prayers for the deity, and large memorial rites, with fixed donations is very much like *puja* sponsorships in Hindu temples. The oil-bath prayer includes small talismans mailed to the sponsor afterward, just as it is done by Hindu temples. In Ikoma, a separate temple is devoted entirely to traffic-safety prayers, while outside Matsuchiyama *senkō* (incense sticks) are burned in the open air, smelling just like Skt. *dhūpa* in Hindu temples.

Moving from temple to temple, these practices feel instantly familiar to anyone who has visited temples in India, with the same mix of sponsored rites, specific-purpose prayers, bathing the deity, incense offerings, and even mailed talismans, all carried across cultures in slightly different forms.

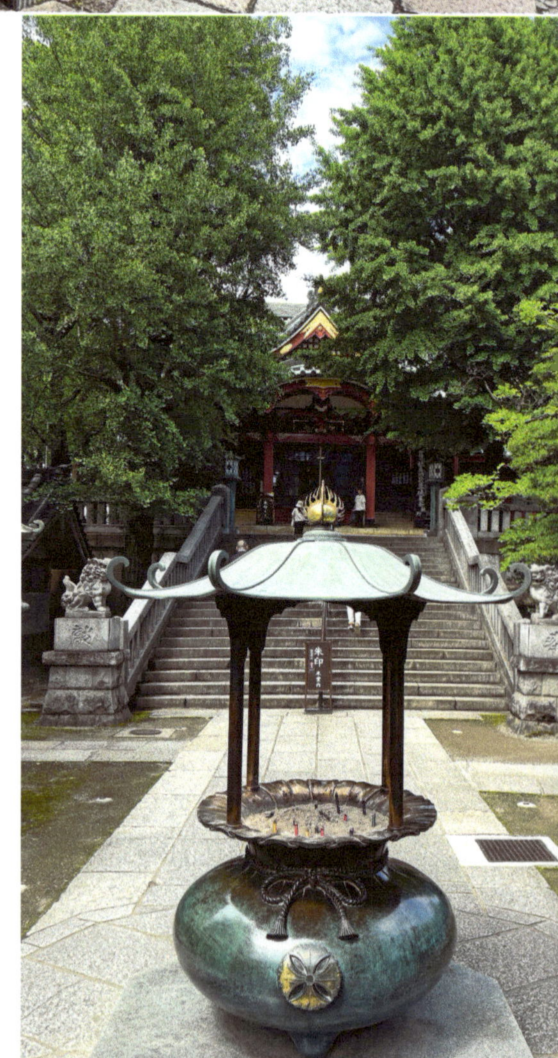

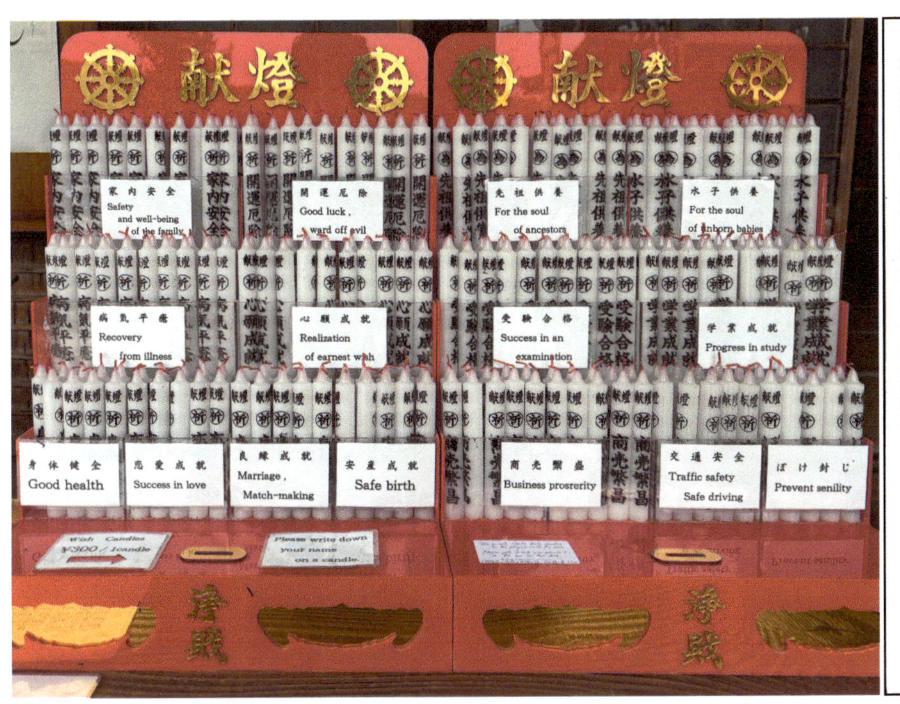

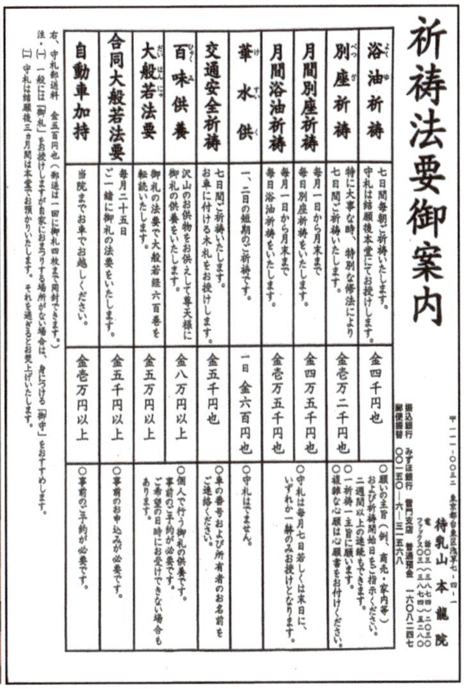

祈祷法要御案内

<table>
<tr><td>浴油祈祷</td><td>七日間毎朝ご祈祷いたします。守札は結願後本堂にてお授けします。</td><td>金四千円也</td><td rowspan="2">○願いの主旨（例、商売・家内等）および祈祷開始日をご指示ください。二週間以上の連続もできます。
○一祈祷一主旨に願います。
○複雑な心願は心願書をお付けください。</td></tr>
<tr><td>別座祈祷</td><td>特に大事な時、特別な修法により七日間ご祈祷いたします。</td><td>金壱万二千円也</td></tr>
<tr><td>月間別座祈祷</td><td>毎月一日から月末まで毎日別座祈祷をいたします。</td><td>金四万五千円也</td><td rowspan="2">○守札は毎月七日若しくは末日に、いずれか一躰のみお授けとなります。</td></tr>
<tr><td>月間浴油祈祷</td><td>毎月一日から月末まで毎日浴油祈祷をいたします。</td><td>金壱万五千円也</td></tr>
<tr><td>華水供</td><td>一、二日の短期のご祈祷です。</td><td>一日 金六百円也</td><td>○守札はでません。</td></tr>
<tr><td>交通安全祈祷</td><td>七日間ご祈祷いたします。お車に付ける木札をお授けします。</td><td>金五千円也</td><td>○車の番号および所有者のお名前をご連絡ください。</td></tr>
<tr><td>百味供養</td><td>沢山のお供物をお供えして尊天様に御礼の供養をいたします。</td><td>金八万円以上</td><td rowspan="2">○個人で行う御礼の供養です。事前のご予約が必要です。ご希望の日時にお受けできない場合もあります。</td></tr>
<tr><td>大般若法要</td><td>御礼の法要で大般若経六百巻を転読いたします。</td><td>金五万円以上</td></tr>
<tr><td>合同大般若法要</td><td>毎月二十五日
ご一緒に御礼の法要をいたします。</td><td>金五千円以上</td><td>○事前のお申込みが必要です。</td></tr>
<tr><td>自動車加持</td><td>当院までお車でお越しください。</td><td>金壱万円以上</td><td>○事前のご予約が必要です。</td></tr>
</table>

右、守札郵送料　金五百円也（郵送は一回に御札四枚まで同封できます。）

注・(一) 一般には「御札」をお授けしますが自宅におまつりする場所がない場合は、身につける「御守」をおすすめします。

(二) 守札は結願後三ヵ月間は本堂でお預かりいたします。それを過ぎるとお焚上げいたします。

〒一一一-〇〇三二 東京都台東区浅草七-四-一
待乳山 本龍院
電話〇三（三八七四）二〇三〇
ファックス〇三（三八七四）五二八〇
振込銀行 みずほ銀行 雷門支店 普通預金 一六〇八二四七
郵便振替 〇〇一五〇—六—三一二五六八

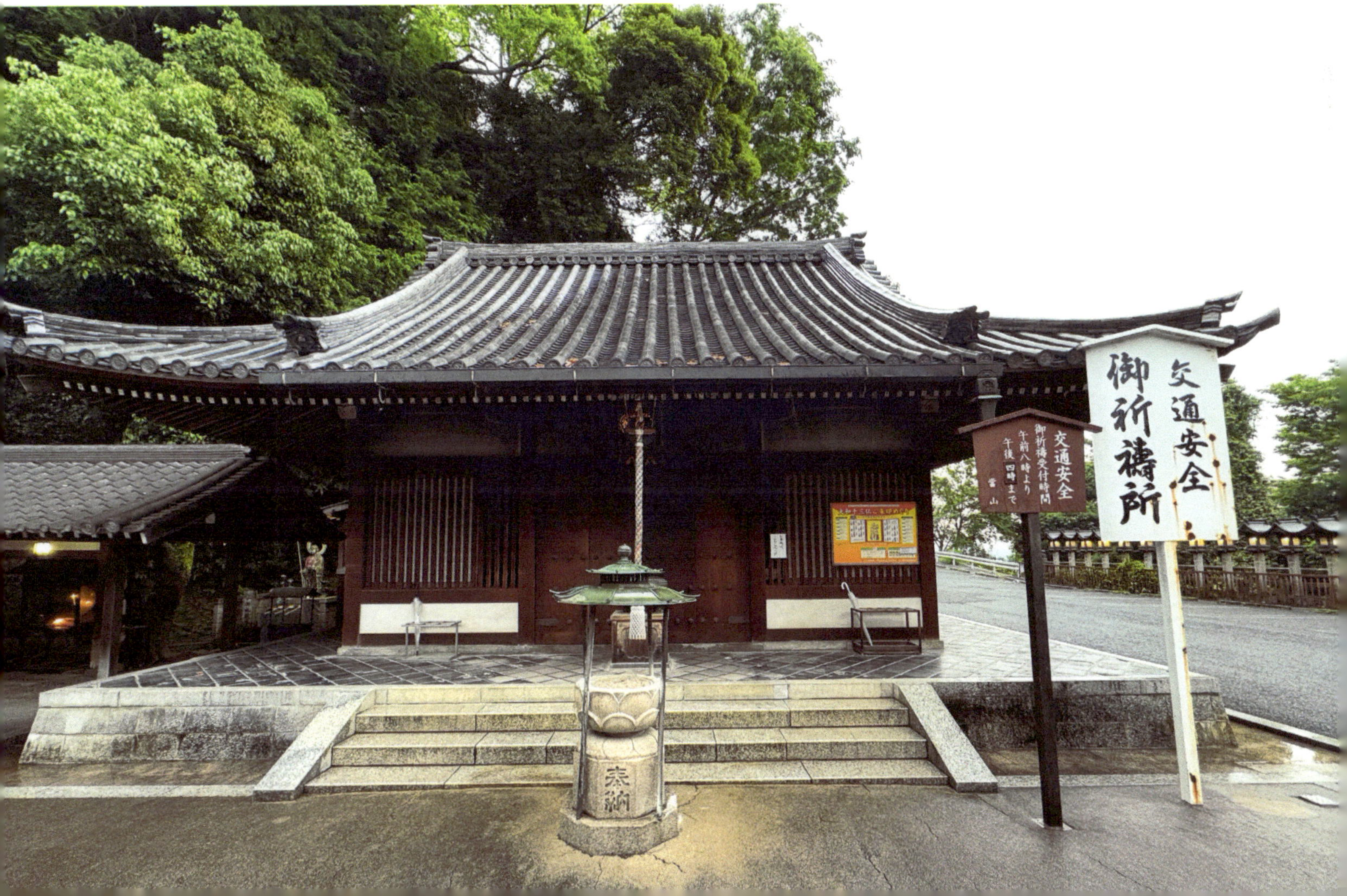

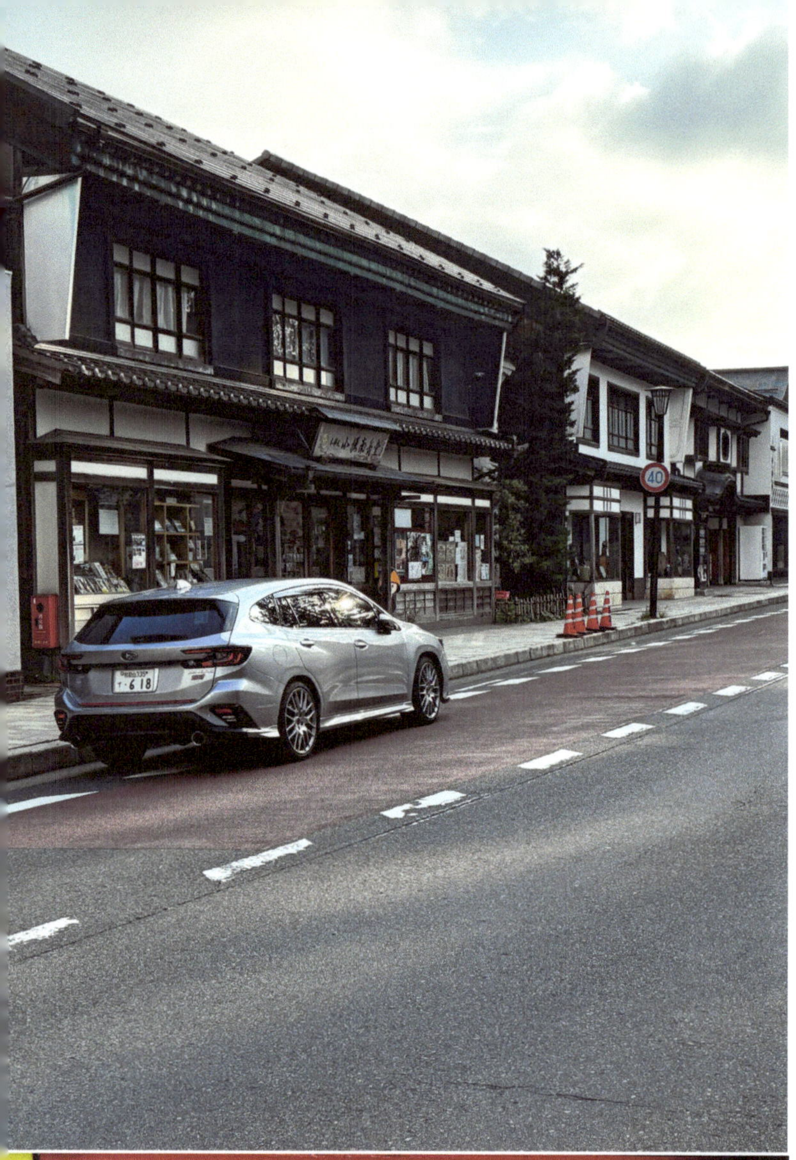

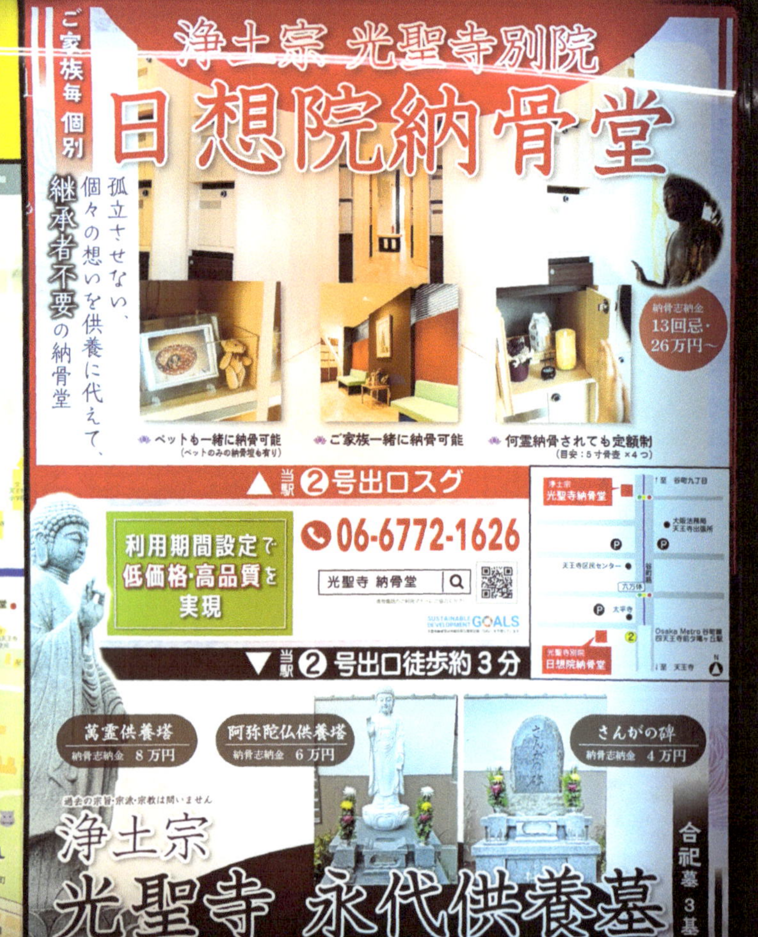

This page top to bottom.
Butsudan (Buddhist Home Altars) – *Kōyasan; Tanimachiyonchōme Station, Osaka*

Butsudan, household Buddhist altars, are common across Japan. Most modern Japanese homes have one, with many standard suburban home models even including a built-in area specifically designed for a butsudan.

In Japanese homes, the butsudan serves as a daily site of reverence for ancestors, Buddhist deities, and memorial tablets (*ihai*, often inscribed with the Buddhist names of ancestors, sutra text, or bonji seed syllables), with offerings of incense, light, flowers, and vegetarian food without *gokun* (5 pungent roots). A typical butsudan is a cabinet with opening doors that reveals an intricate sacred interior, often centered on the family's main bodhisattva image, with shelves for *ihai* and a set of ritual fittings such as a bell, lantern stands, flower vases, and incense burners arranged like a small temple altar.

Kōyasan is regarded as one of the most authoritative places to commission a butsudan, reflecting its role as a living center of Buddhist practice and ancestral veneration. At Kōyasan, a butsudan is not treated like ordinary furniture: families often choose it in consultation with their temple and sect, since the images and layout inside (*Amida, Dainichi, Kannon, Daikokuten, ihai*) must match a living ritual tradition, not just a design preference. After it is brought into the home, a priest may perform a consecration rite, *kaigen kuyō*, "opening" the altar so it becomes a functioning space for offerings and ancestral remembrance, rather than an empty cabinet.

The advertisement seen in the Osaka metro explicitly presents compact altars designed to fit downtown apartments, alongside supplies for ancestral veneration, showing how domestic worship remains embedded in everyday urban life.

Seen comparatively, the butsudan closely parallels the Hindu Skt. *pūjā maṇḍapam* or home shrine: a fixed domestic space for daily worship, ancestor reverence, and ritual continuity, often planned into house construction itself.

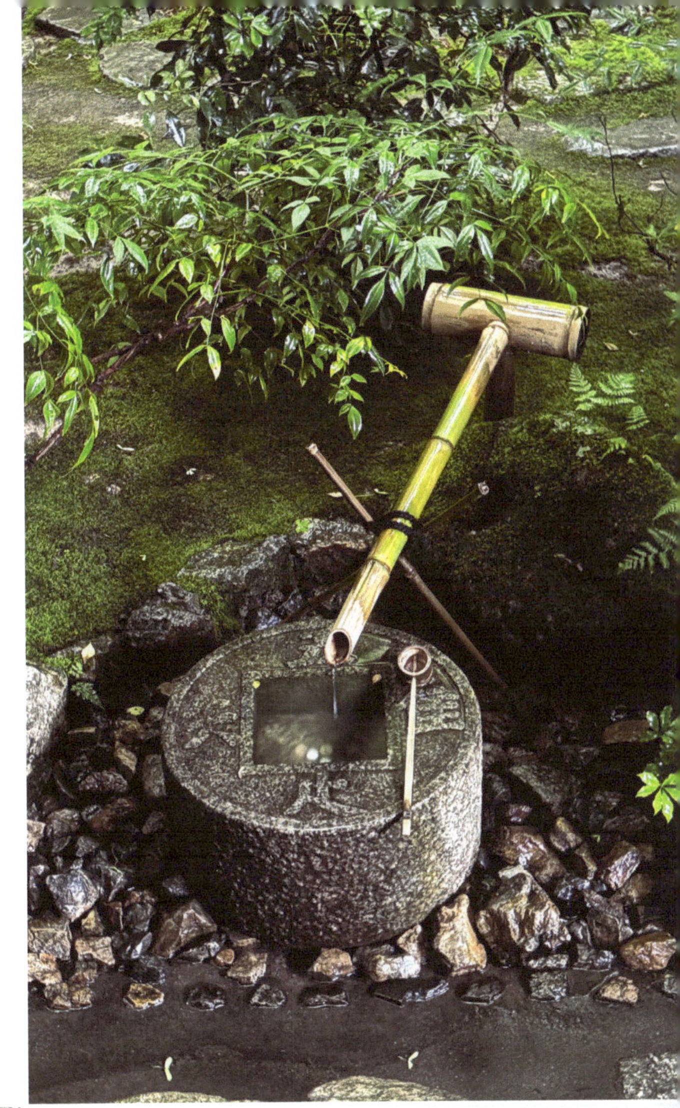

This page (right and below).
Temizu Purification Basins – *Ryōan-ji, Kyoto; Hōzan-ji, Ikoma*

Temizu literally means "hand-water," a brief act of purification before entering a sacred space. At Ryōan-ji in Kyoto, the basin sits quietly in a moss garden, while at Hōzan-ji in Nara, a larger covered *temizu-ya* serves crowds of pilgrims. Visitors rinse left hand, right hand, mouth, then the ladle handle, in a choreographed sequence meant to cleanse both outer action and inner speech. Washing the mouth signifies purifying speech itself, shared across both Buddhist and Hindu traditions, and the quiet trickle of water is a reminder to slow down before stepping into the sacred.

In many Hindu temples, worshippers also wash their feet and hands to remove the dust of the world before Skt. *darśana*, but mouth rinsing is rarely part of the entry ritual. Japanese *temizu* favors stone, bamboo, and stillness, while Hindu temples often use more functional taps in place of what used to be flowing rivers or temple tanks. Both traditions treat purity as physical and moral rather than hygienic alone, part of Skt. *pavitrīkaraṇa*: arriving with respect, clear intention, and an awareness of crossing a threshold between ordinary and sacred space.

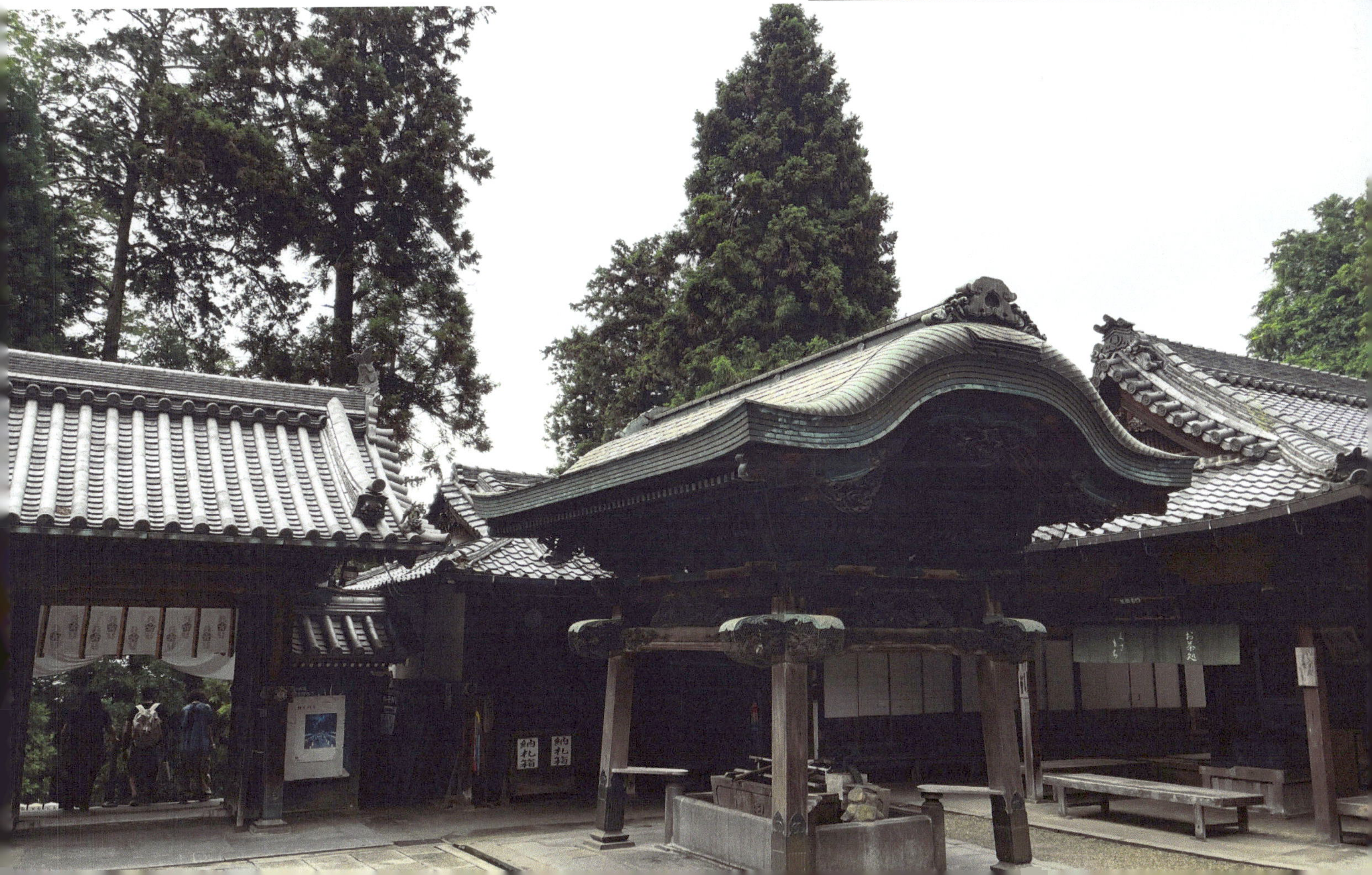

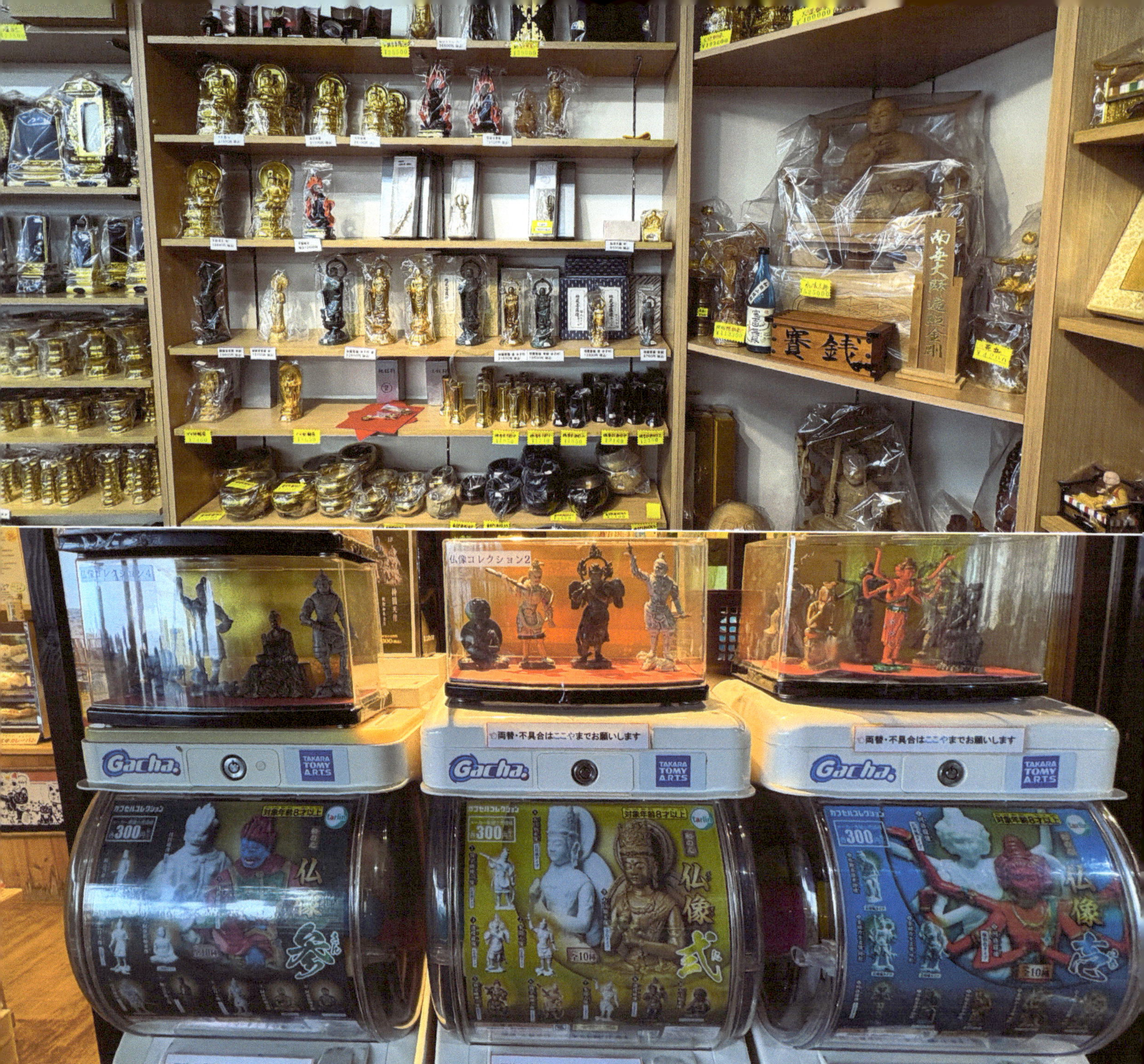

This page above and top.
Shopping Around Temples

Gacha vending machines at Chikubushima dispense miniature Buddhist deities, giving pilgrims small souvenirs to carry home. In Kōyasan, temple shops sell home altar items, continuing a long tradition of laypeople bringing ritual practice back into home.

Opposite page clockwise from top left.

Kyoto's Nishiki Market grew as a provisioning street closely tied to temple and court demand, where trading houses once dealt in imported ritual materials such as incense woods. Along the approach to Sensō-ji, shops line the temple road much like bazaars leading to major temples in India. Modern department stores sell origami kits for building famous temples, allowing people to build and learn from sacred architecture. At Injō-ji, zodiac amulets marked with bonji shuji Skt. *bīja-akṣaras* link astrology, mantra, and protection.

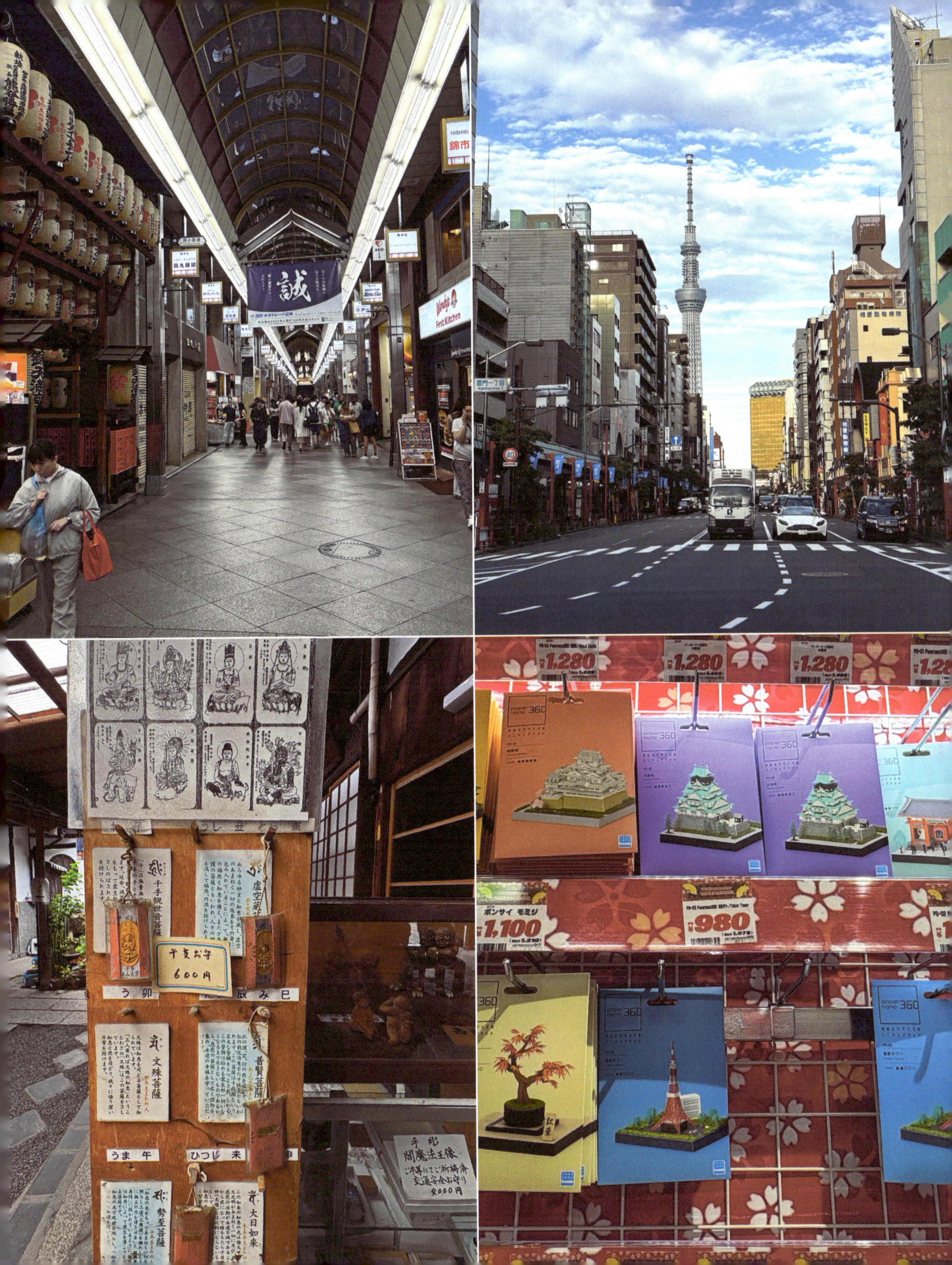

誠
錦市
First Kitchen
千支お守
600円
う 卯
辰 み 巳
文殊菩薩
普賢菩薩
うま 午
ひつじ 未
勢至菩薩
大日如来
千手観世音菩薩
虚空蔵菩薩
手彫
閻魔法王像
6000円
1,280
ボンサイ モミジ
1,100
980

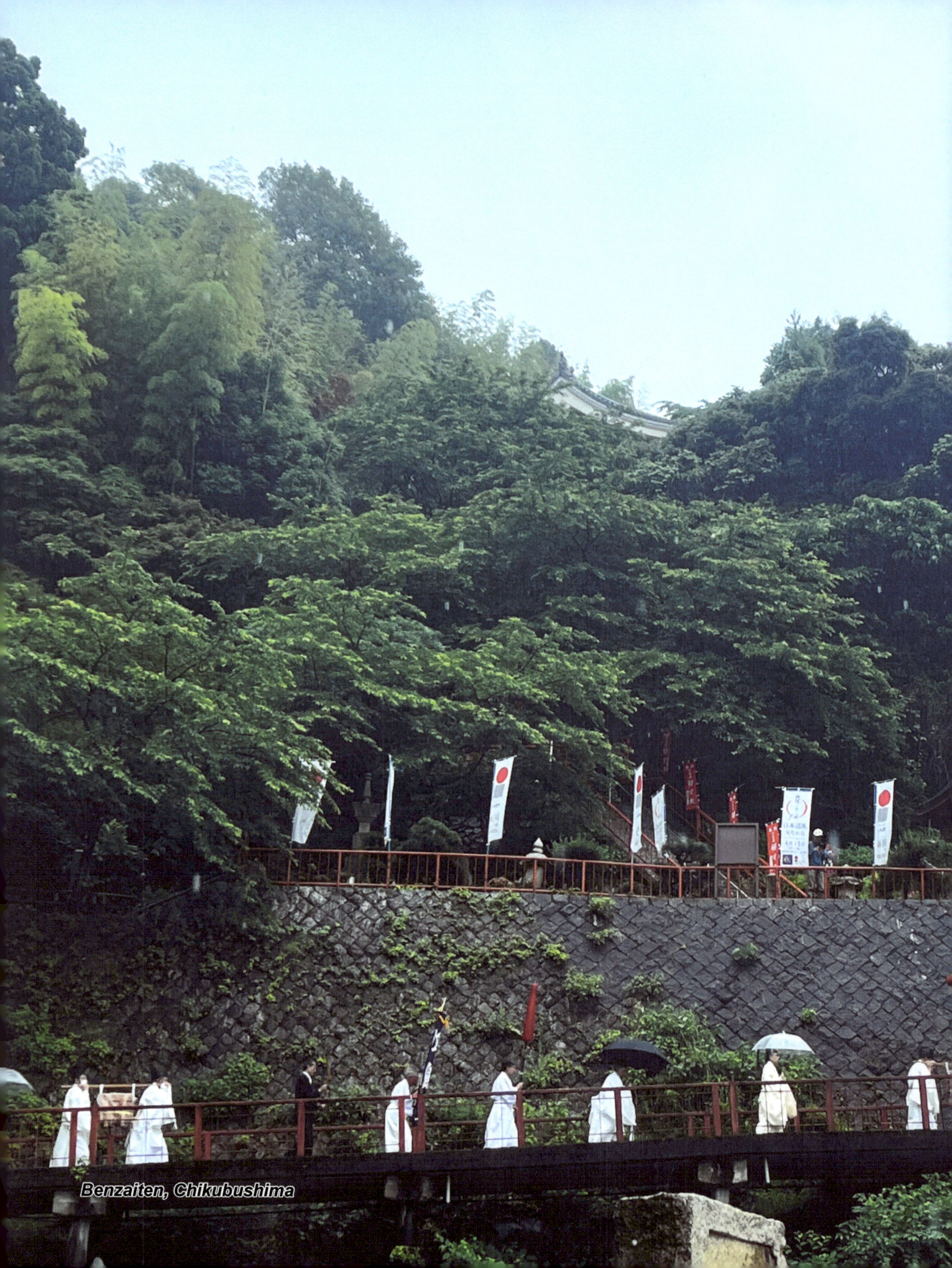

Benzaiten, Chikubushima

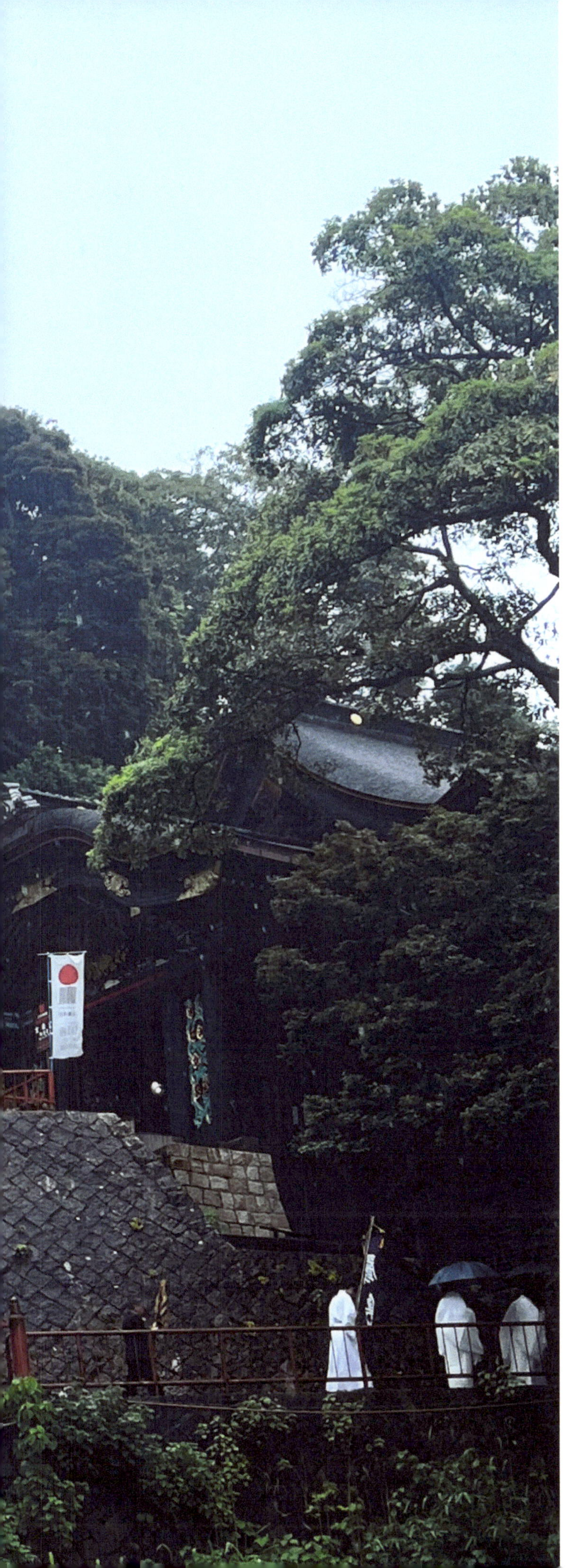

Festivals

SIX

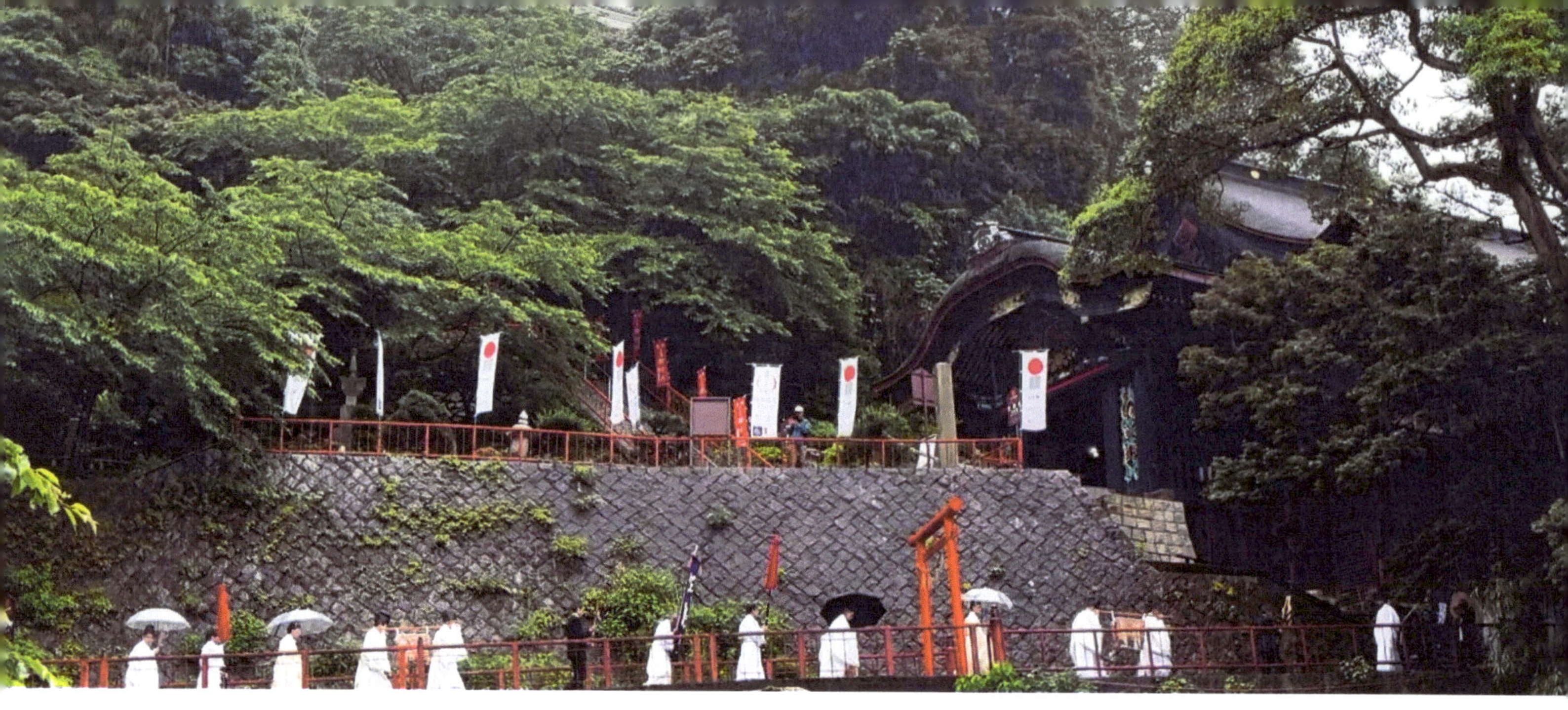

This page (above).
San Dai Benzaiten Matsuri (Festival of the Three Great Benzaiten) – *Hōgon-ji, Chikubushima*

As we boarded the boat to Chikubushima, we were surprised to see it packed to the brim with pilgrims dressed in festive kimonos and *rakusu*s. After talking with them, we learned we had arrived, seemingly by chance, on June 10 for the *San Dai Benzaiten Matsuri* (Festival of the Three Great Benzaiten). In the rain, a white-robed procession ascended the hill to the sound of *gagaku* as the processional deities (*gobunrei*) and priests from Enoshima and Itsukushima joined at Chikubushima. A *bugaku* (court dance) performance is offered to the deities. I felt blessed to be the only non-Japanese among hundreds of Japanese pilgrims to take part in this sacred once-a-year "meeting" of Japan's Three Great Benzaiten (Skt. *sarasvati*).

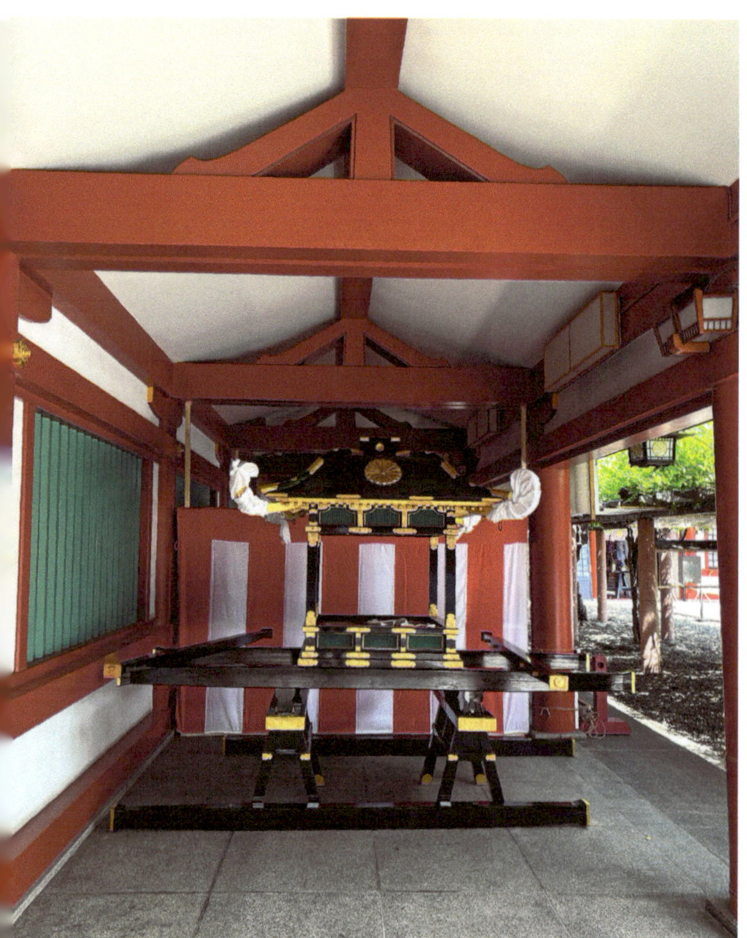

This page (left).
Mikoshi – *Hie Jinja, Tokyo*

A *mikoshi* is a miniature shrine that serves as a portable seat for the Shinto *kami*, so the deity can "tour" the neighborhood and bless the streets. Before it moves, it is ritually purified with water, then lifted onto long beams and carried shoulder-high by local devotees as a coordinated community act. It is similar to Hindu processions of Skt. *utsava mūrtis*, where bronze deities are carried through the community and devotion is expressed through mantra chanting and sheer physical effort. In both traditions, the procession itself is part of the ritual, not just a mode of transport. This *mikoshi* at Hie Jinja is being prepared for Sannō Matsuri. Kyoto's famous Gion Matsuri looks like a *ratha yātrā* ("chariot journey") in Hindu practice. The English word "juggernaut" comes from Puri Jagannātha's *Ratha Yātrā*, the world's oldest and largest Hindu chariot procession, with over a million devotees participating.

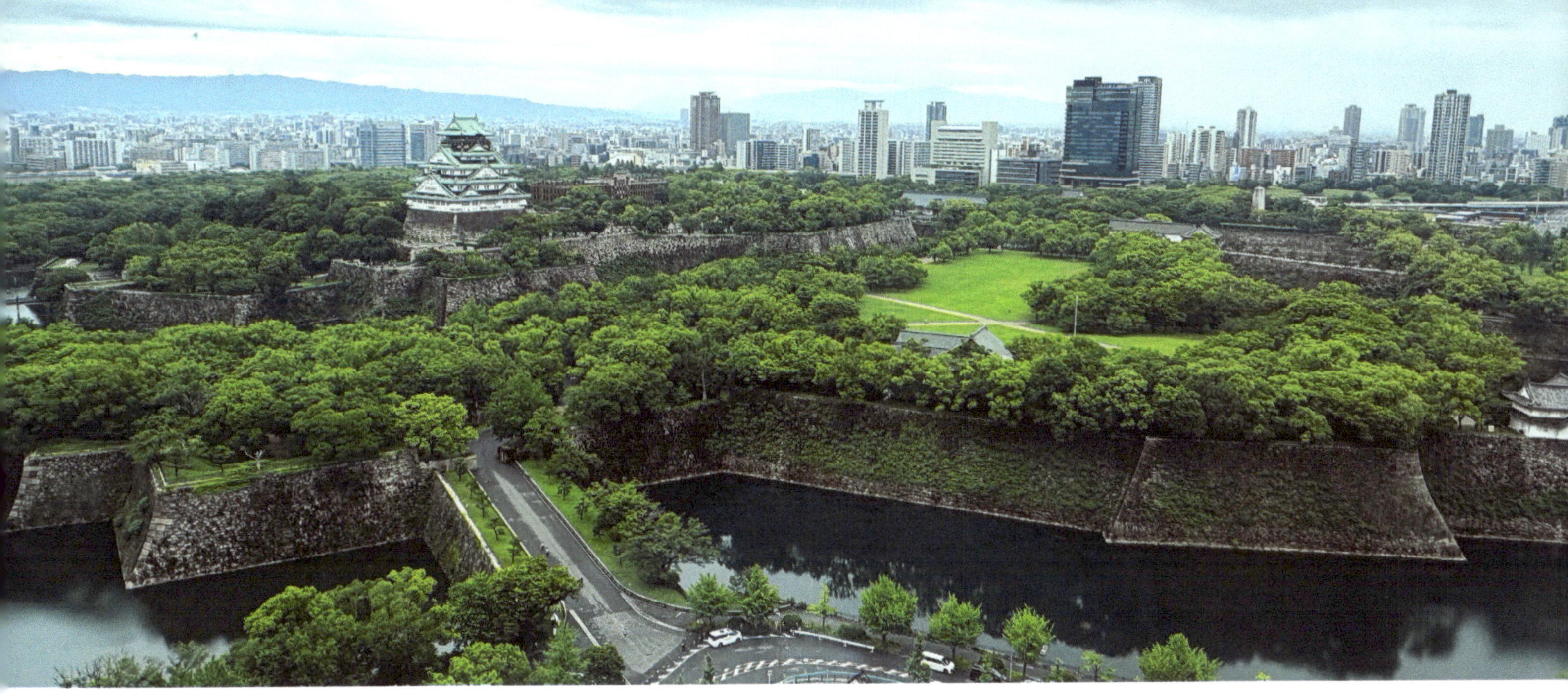

This page (above and below).
Tenjin – *Osaka Castle, Osaka; Hōzan-ji, Ikoma*

Tenjin was a 9th-century CE courtier who was deified after his death as the Shinto deity of learning. Many traditions see him as a human manifestation of Benzaiten. Students pray to him at his shrines, often alongside Benzaiten at the same site, asking for sharp focus, eloquence, and success in studies. He is closely associated with bulls, said to be the animal he rode, so bull statues and bull offerings are made such as these below at Hōzan-ji, where local tradition says Tenjin often came to meditate. Tenjin was also a renowned poet and a master of Japanese, Chinese, and Indian calligraphy styles. Tenjin Matsuri, an annual festival is held in his honor in Osaka on the Yodo River, starting at his shrine near Osaka Castle, where mikoshi are loaded onto boats and carried down the river as lanterns are lit along its banks.

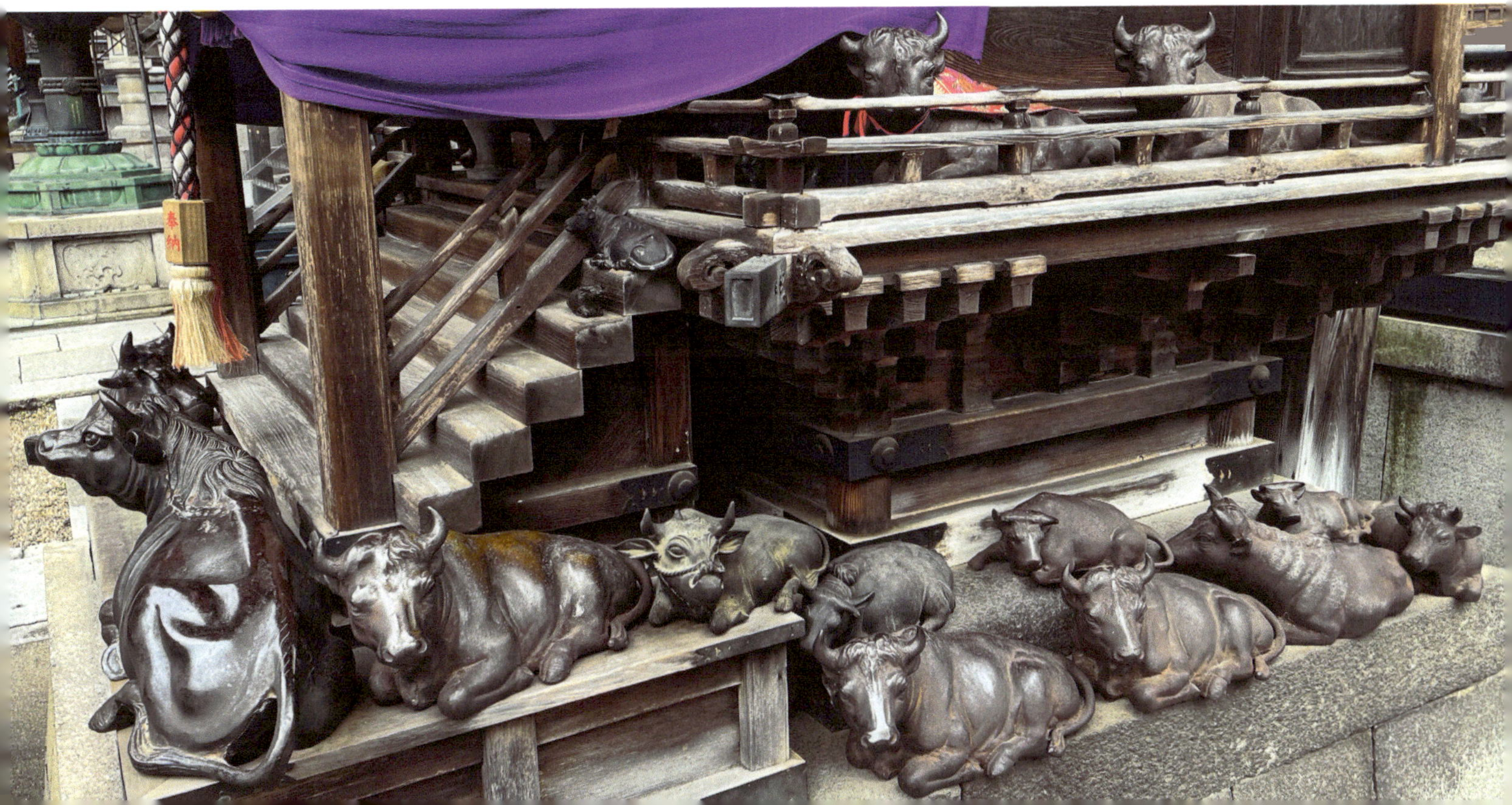

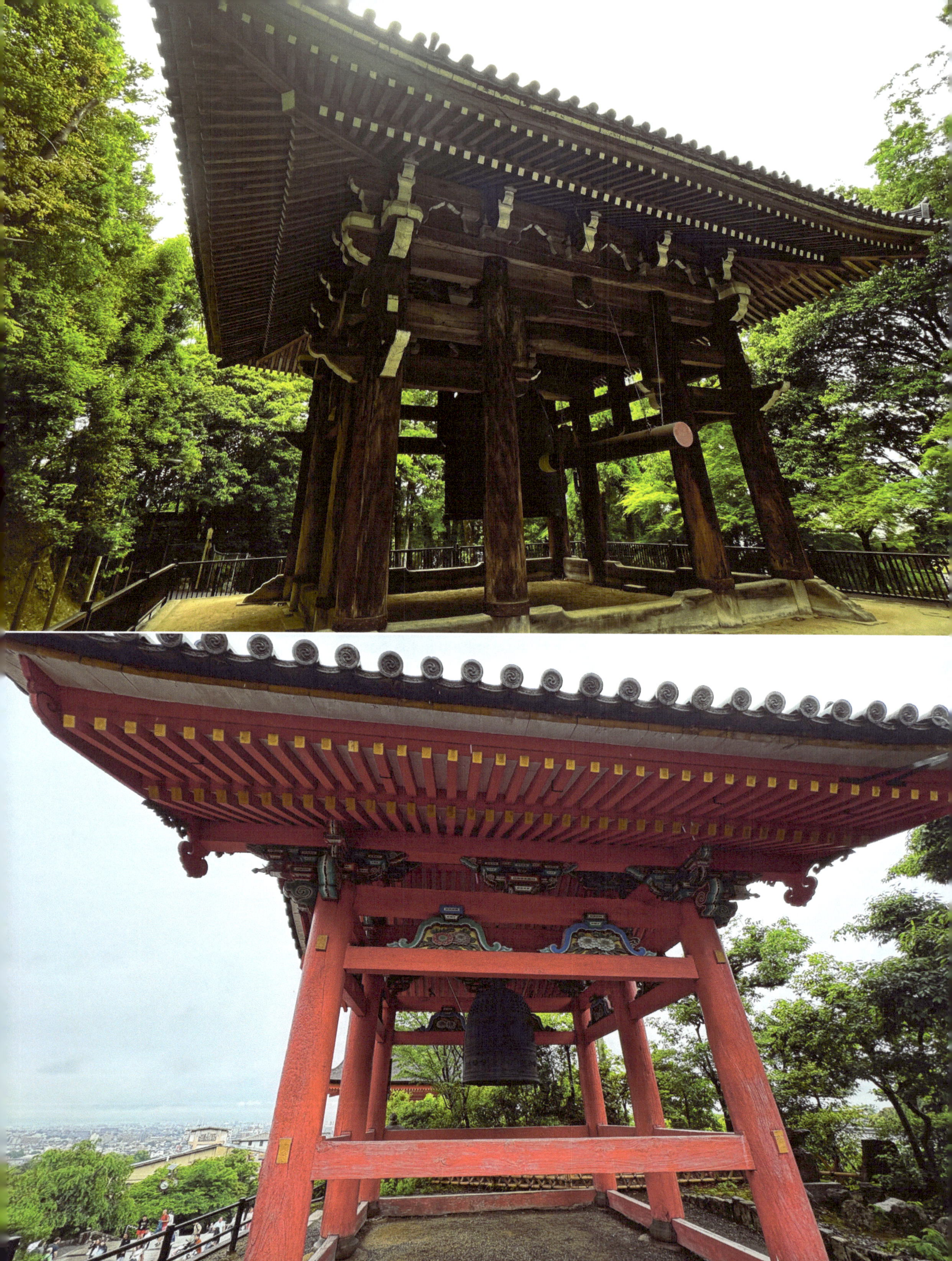

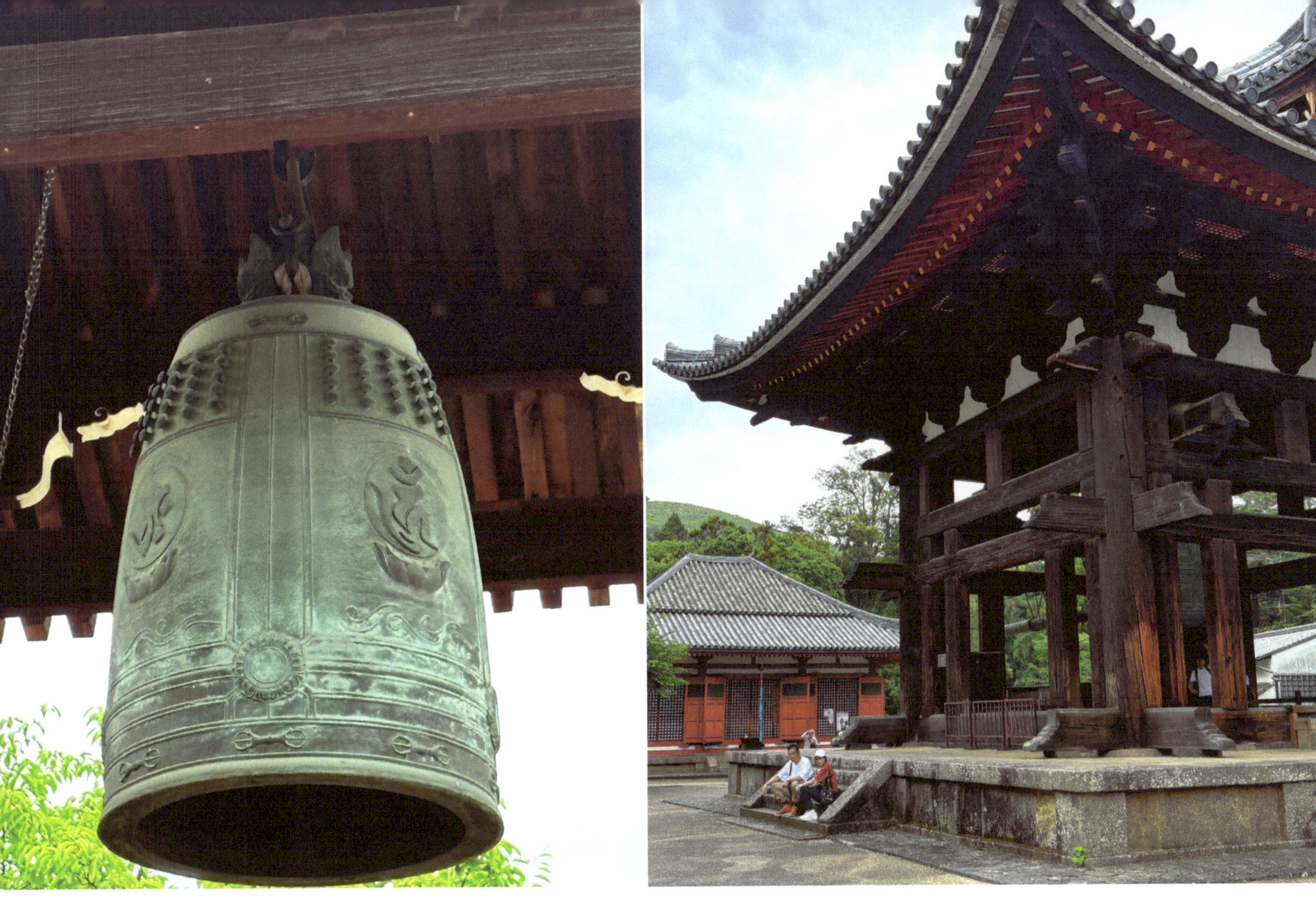

Opposite page and this page, clockwise from bottom left.
Temple Bells (Bonshō) – *Kiyomizu-dera, Kyoto; Chion-in, Kyoto; Tō-ji, Kyoto; Tōdai-ji, Nara*

Large temple bells (*bonshō*, "dharma bells") hang in open wooden towers and are struck from the outside with a suspended log rather than an internal clapper, producing a deep, slowly resonating sound. Like the bronze bells of Hindu temples, they are cast with sacred motifs and inscriptions, but Japanese bells often carry *bonji* Siddham seed syllables, visible here on the Tō-ji bell above.

Hindu temple bells are usually smaller and rung directly by devotees to announce their presence to the deity, focus the mind, mark the transition into worship, and sound during Skt. *ārati* (the waving of lamps) at the conclusion of a Skt. *pūjā*. In Japanese temples, devotees may pull a rope to ring small bells before their prayer, while during services struck instruments such as gongs and bowls punctuate the chanting and offerings.

The large Japanese bells shown here, by contrast, are typically sounded in single measured strikes by monks to mark the monastic day, though on New Year's Eve the public may be invited to ring them during *Jōya no Kane.* During this ritual the bell is struck 108 times, each toll standing for one of the 108 human delusions that obscure awakening. The slow sequence, often stretching to about an hour, creates a feeling of purification as the old year recedes. Many temples understand the bell's deep vibration itself as dharma, a sound-offering that can reach even the realm of departed spirits and bring them comfort.

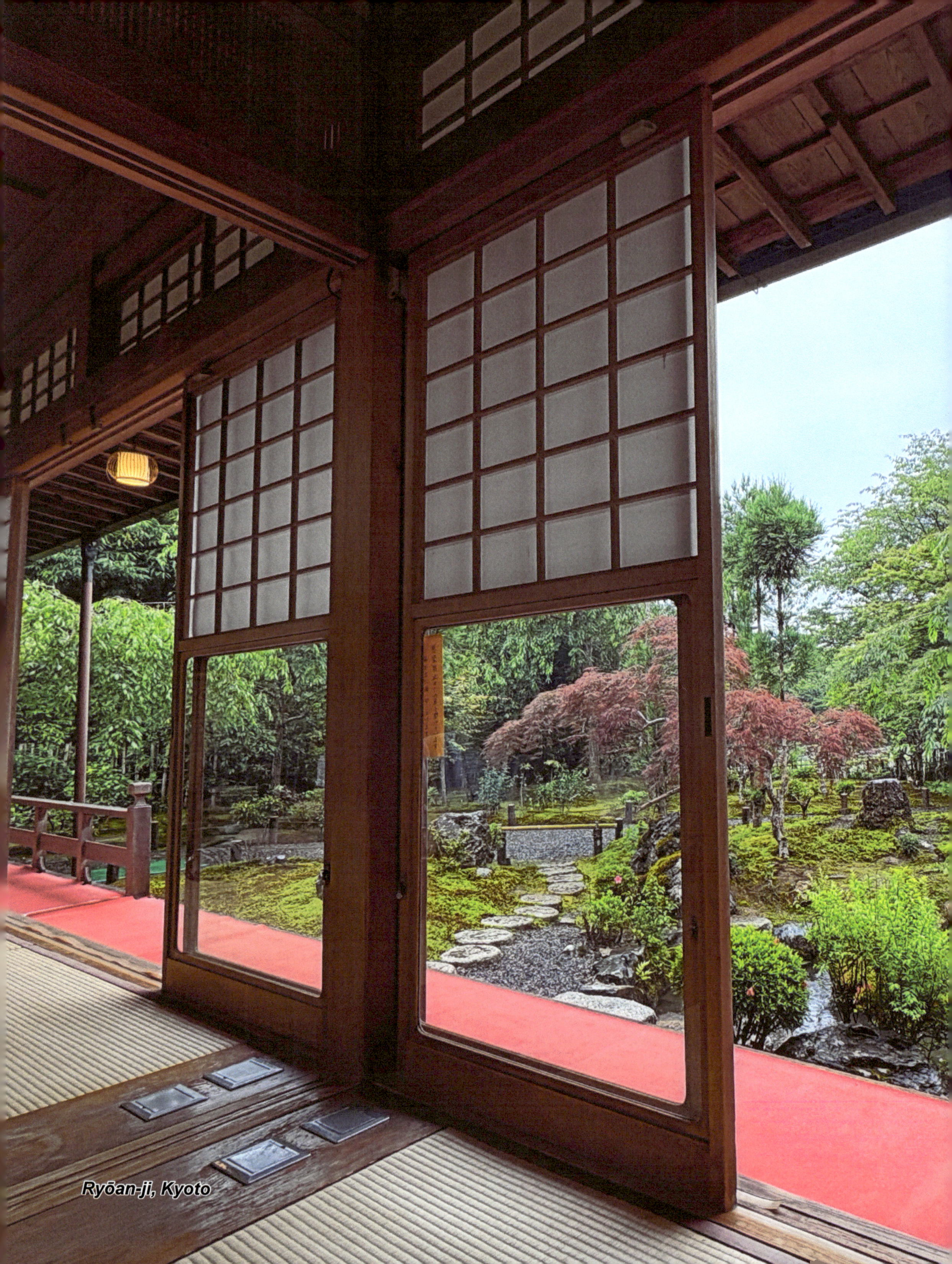

Ryōan-ji, Kyoto

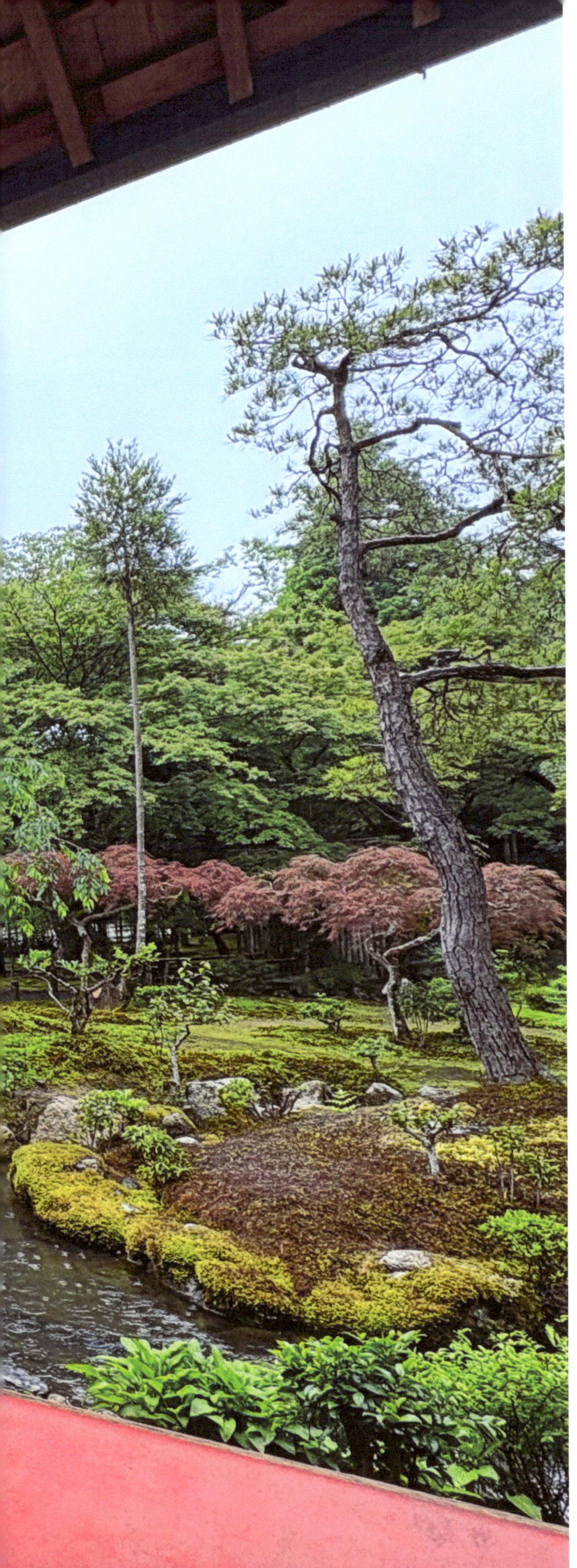

Food

SEVEN

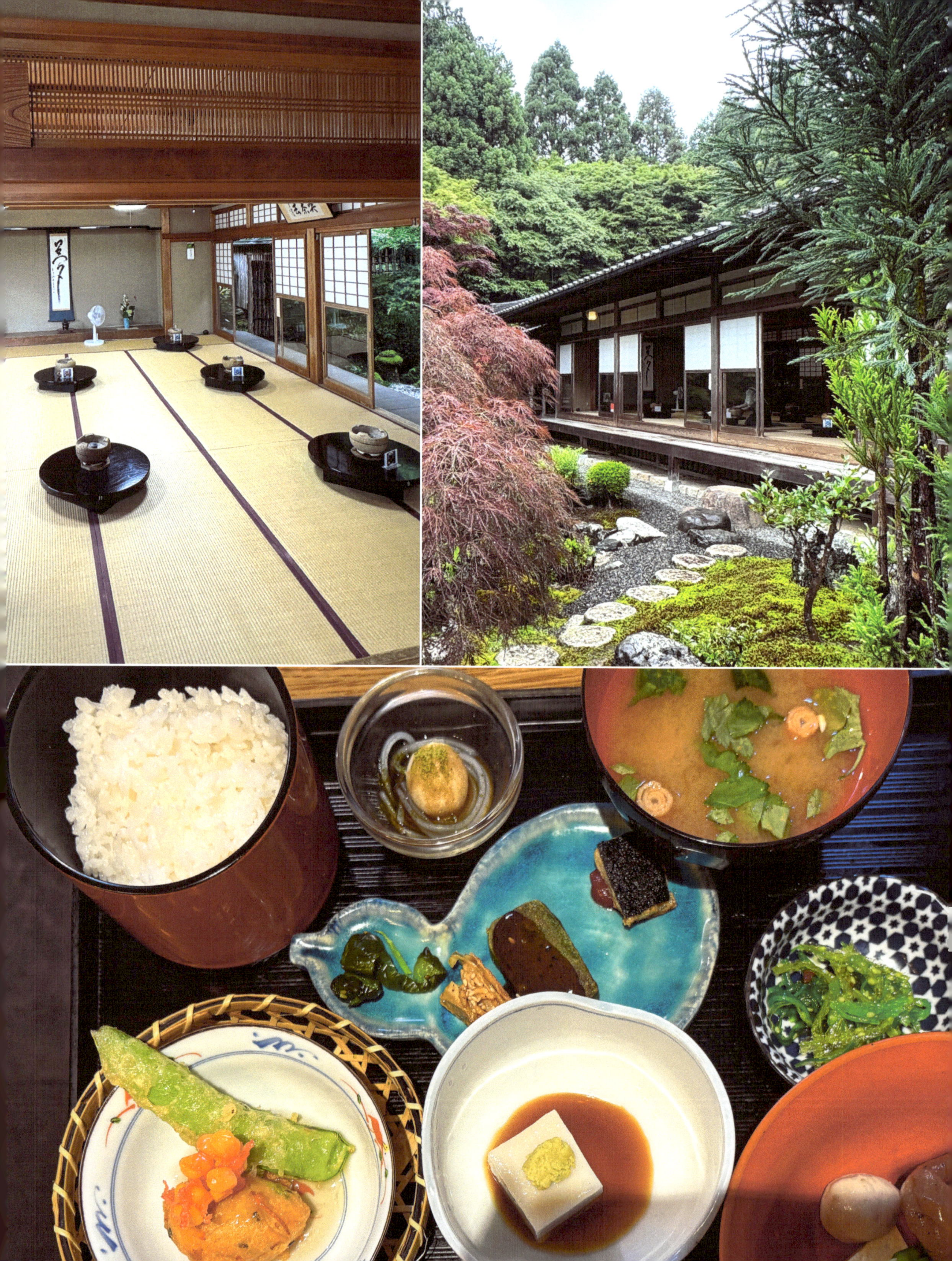

Opposite page (top to bottom).
Shōjin Ryōri – *Seigen-in (Ryōan-ji), Kyoto; Kōyasan*

At Seigen-in, within Ryōan-ji temple grounds, you dine on *tatami* in a traditional building that looks out onto a quiet garden and pond. *Shōjin* is the Japanese term used for the Sanskrit *vīrya*, meaning "diligence," and *ryōri* simply means "cooking," so *shōjin ryōri* is not just "vegetarian food," but cuisine shaped by disciplined practice.

Kōyasan is famous for *goma-dōfu* (white square in white bowl in left bottom picture), a sesame "tofu" traditionally made through hours of slow, careful grinding. Eating this becomes an offering into the inner fire that sustains the body for meditation, reminiscent of Bhagavad Gītā 15.14 (Skt. *Ahaṃ vaiśvānaro bhūtvā…*), "I am the fire of digestion…".

This page (top to bottom).
Kangidan (Seijō-kankidan) – *Kameya Kiyonaga, Kyoto*

Kangidan (Kangi (歓喜) literally means "Bliss" and Dan (団) means a "ball") is a "moneybag" sweet and is derived from Skt. *modaka* ("that which brings joy"), which has been offered to Kangiten for over 1,000 years in Japan and to Gaṇapati in Hindu temples for thousands of years. Kameya Kiyonaga has a 400+ year old lineage of making this sweet and supplying it to the temples whose names are written above the chef.

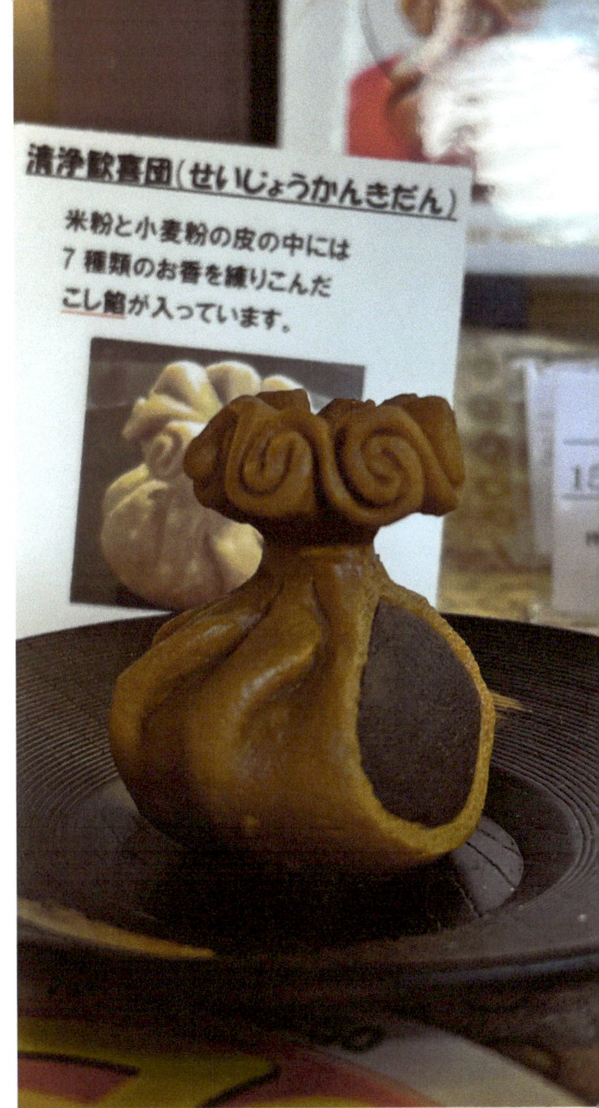

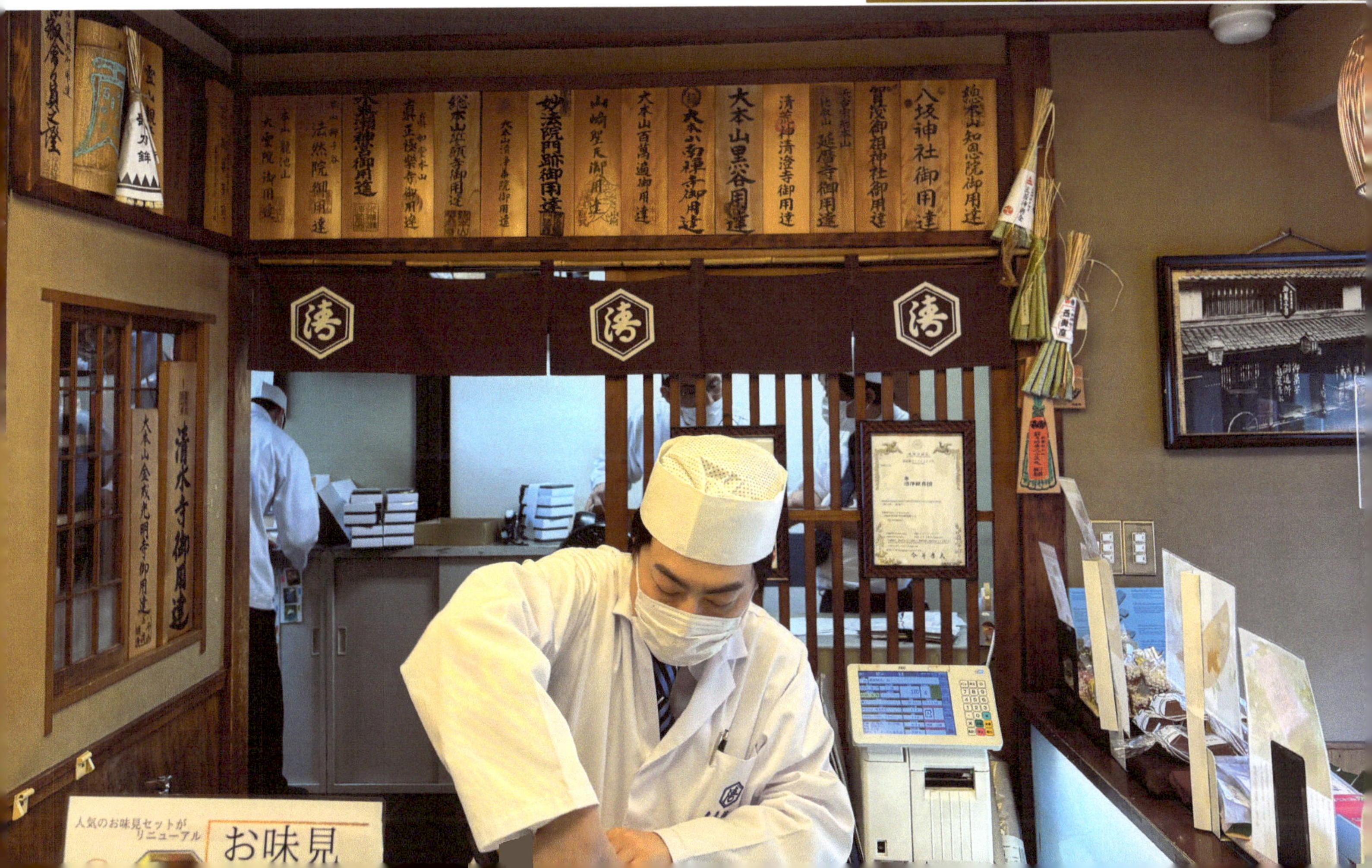

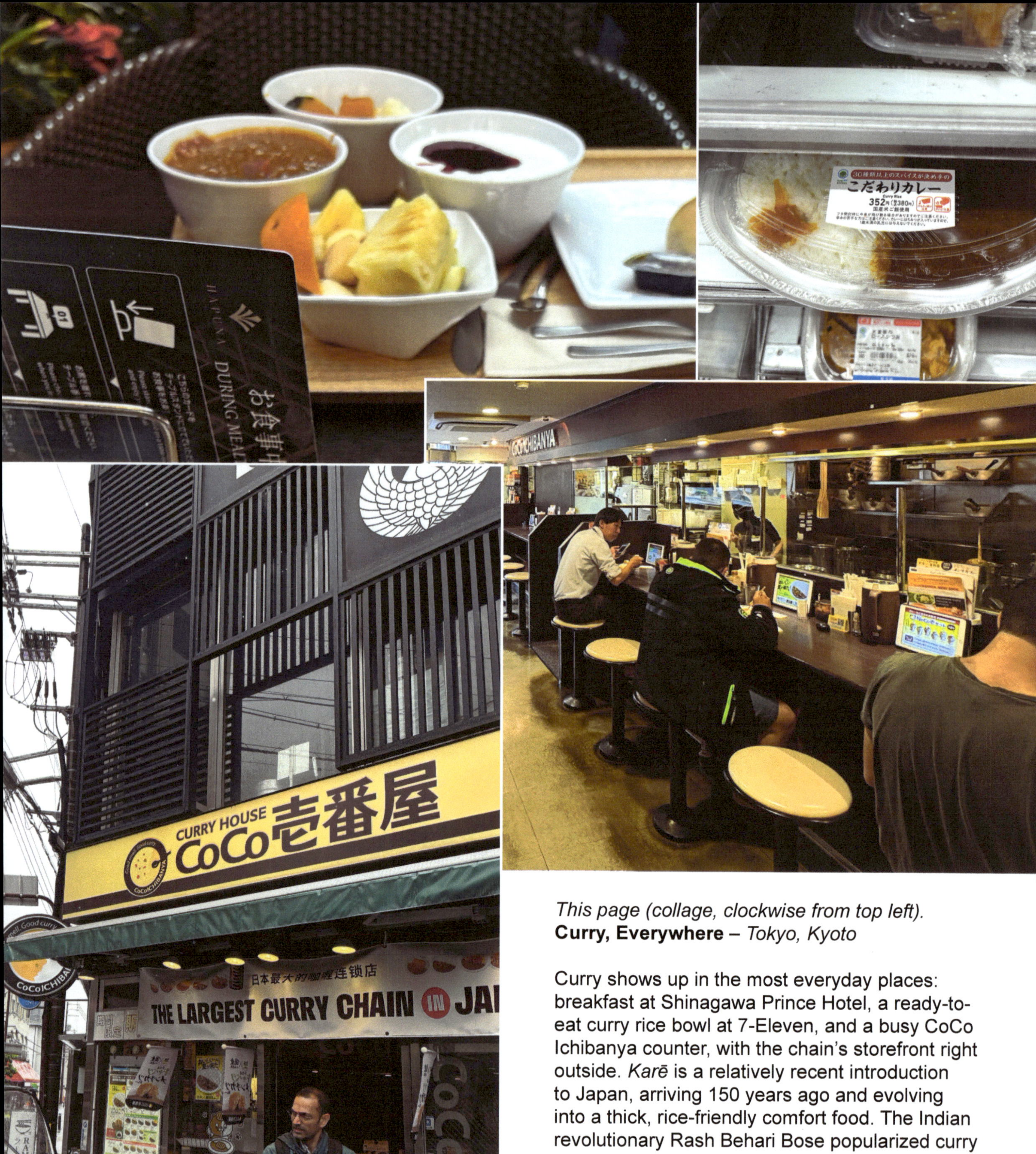

This page (collage, clockwise from top left).
Curry, Everywhere – *Tokyo, Kyoto*

Curry shows up in the most everyday places: breakfast at Shinagawa Prince Hotel, a ready-to-eat curry rice bowl at 7-Eleven, and a busy CoCo Ichibanya counter, with the chain's storefront right outside. *Karē* is a relatively recent introduction to Japan, arriving 150 years ago and evolving into a thick, rice-friendly comfort food. The Indian revolutionary Rash Behari Bose popularized curry in Japan in 1927 through Nakamuraya, a famous Tokyo bakery. Japan is famous overseas for sushi but curry is more commonly consumed. For vegetarians, that ubiquity is a gift as vegetarian curry is easy to find almost anywhere you stop.

This page (right).
Tea House and Garden – *Meiji Jingu, Tokyo*

Tea was first brought to Japan by Buddhist monks. In tea ceremony, each small movement is deliberate, a Zen practice of training attention. Matcha, the powdered green tea originally used in monasteries, helped monks stay awake through long sessions of *zazen* (seated zen meditation).

This page (below).
Vegetarian Burger Without Onion & Garlic – *MOS & CAFE, Nagoya*

The inset menu calls out a detail: "no Five Pungent Roots" (Jp. *gokun*): garlic, onions, scallions/leeks, chives, and shallots. In Hindu *sāttvika* food, onion and garlic are often avoided for ritual and meditative clarity, and *shōjin ryōri* follows a similar tradition. Because MOS is a nationwide chain, it becomes one of the easiest "safe" finds for travelers, including monks, who avoid onion and garlic.

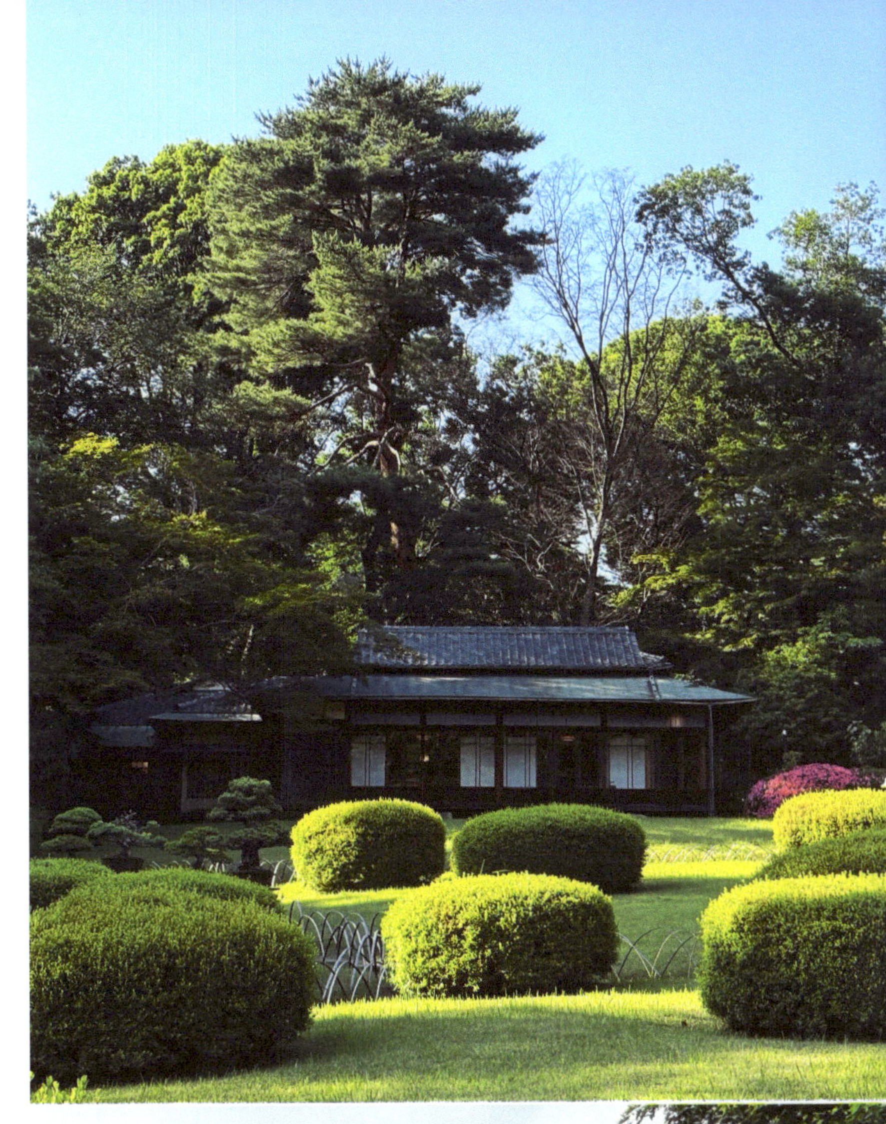

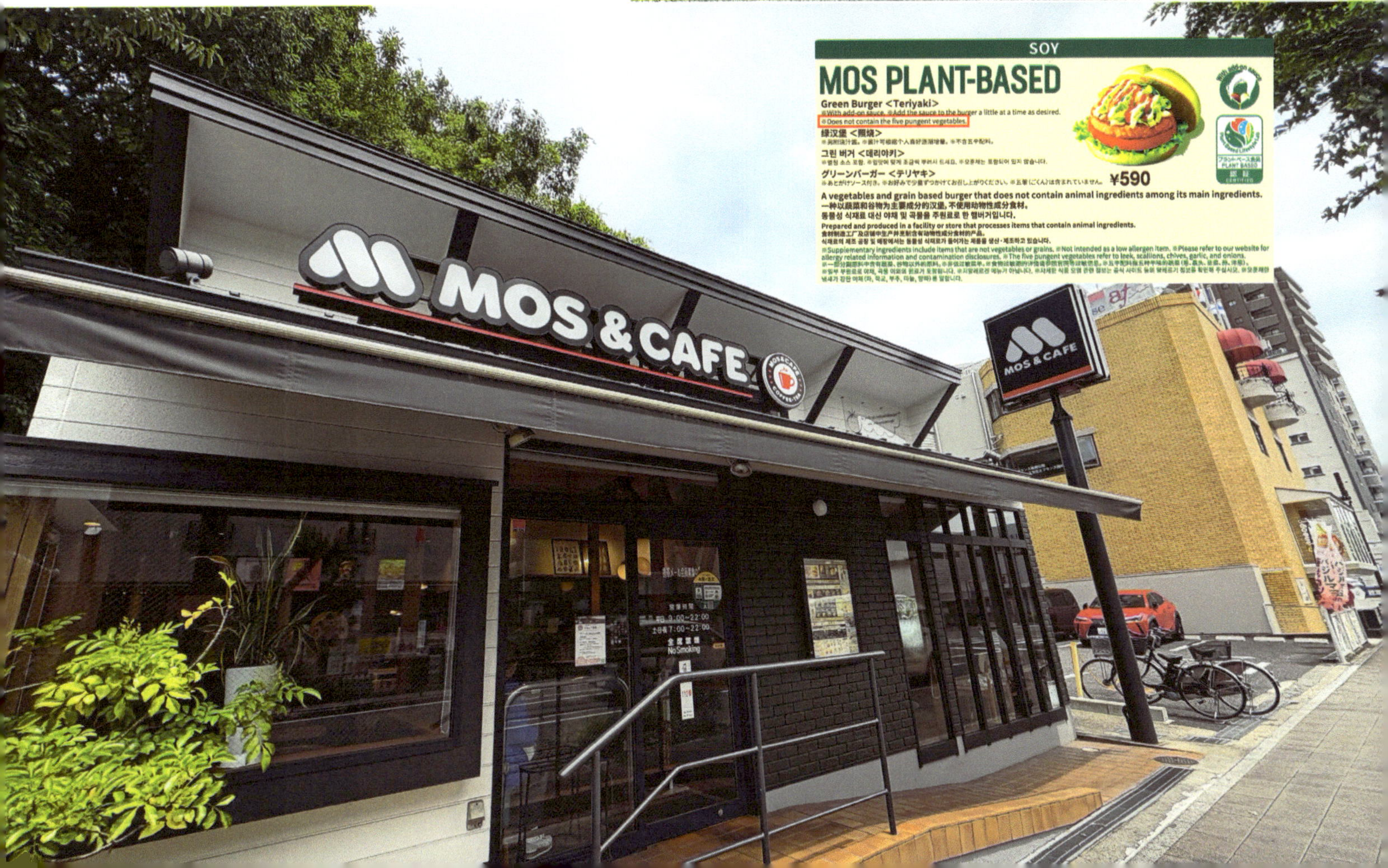

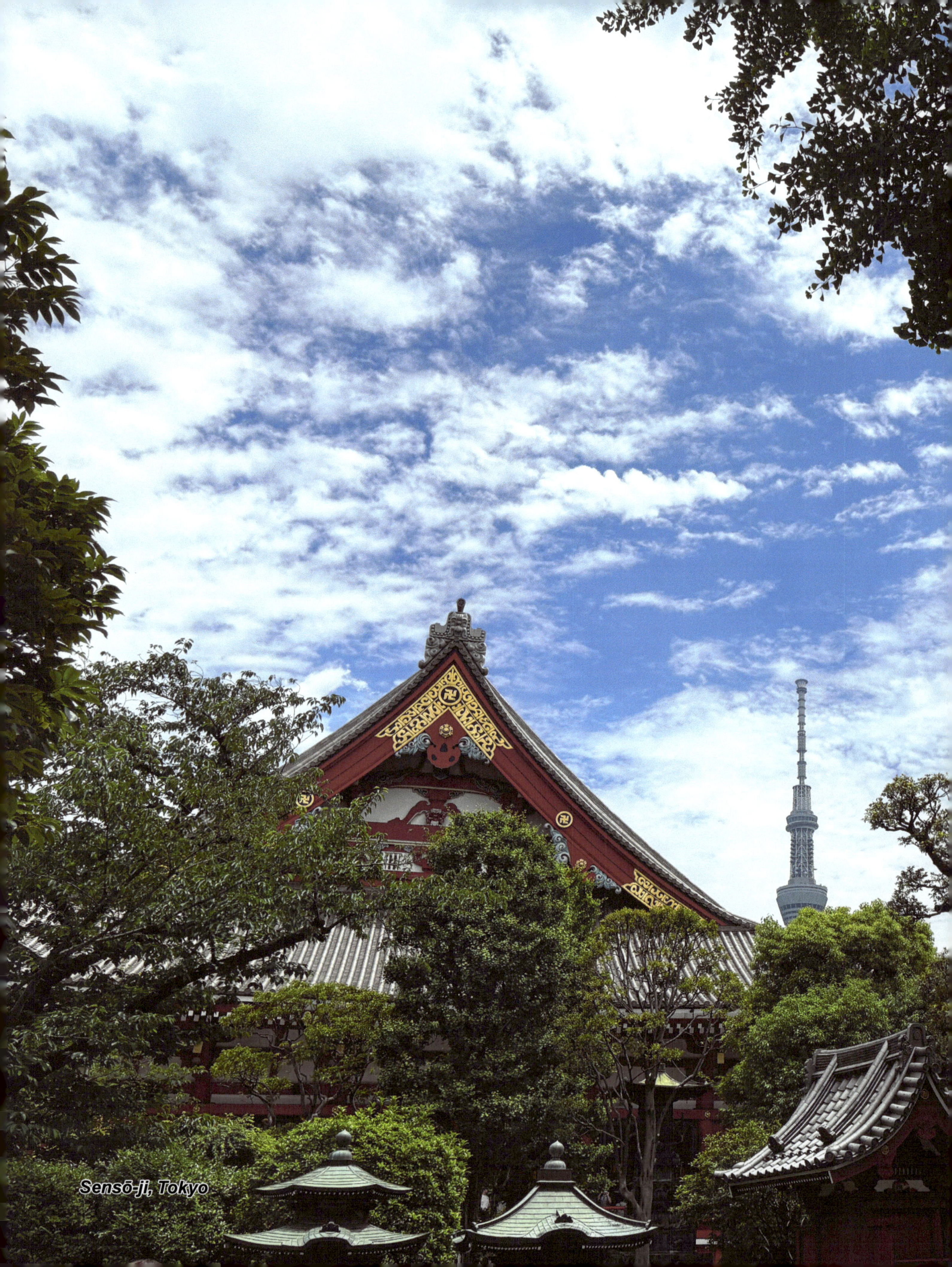

Sensō-ji, Tokyo

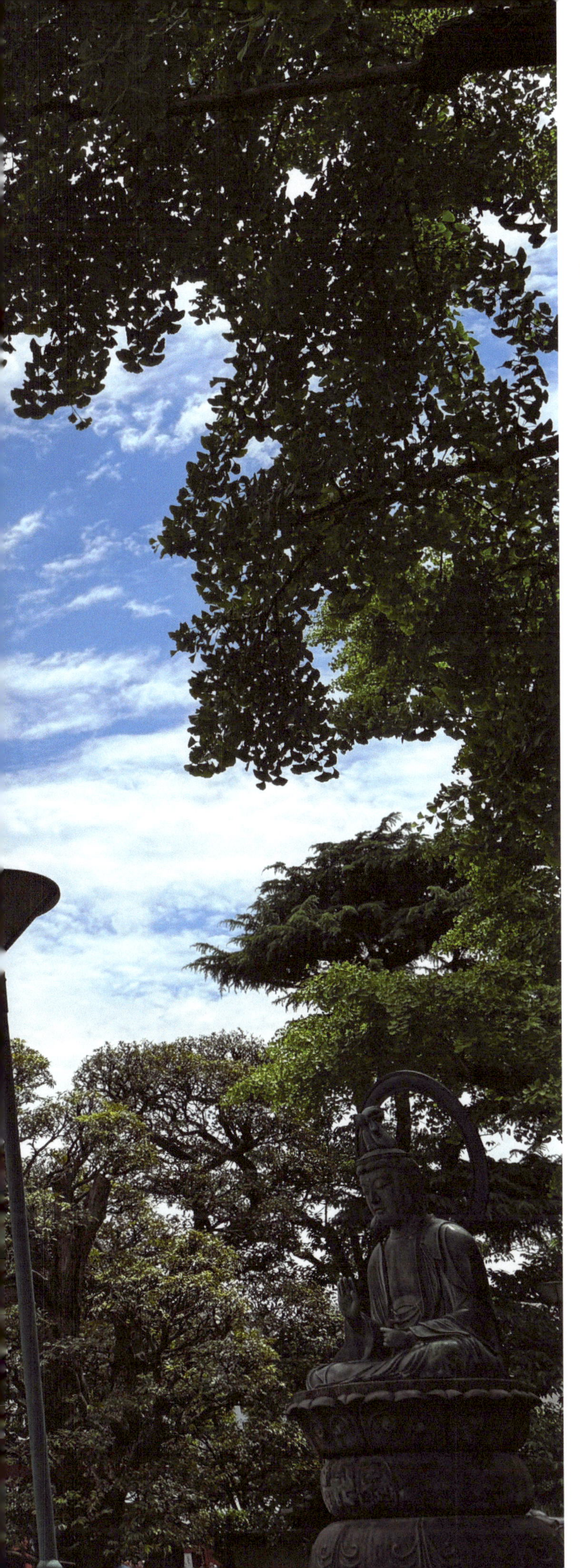

Modern Connections

EIGHT

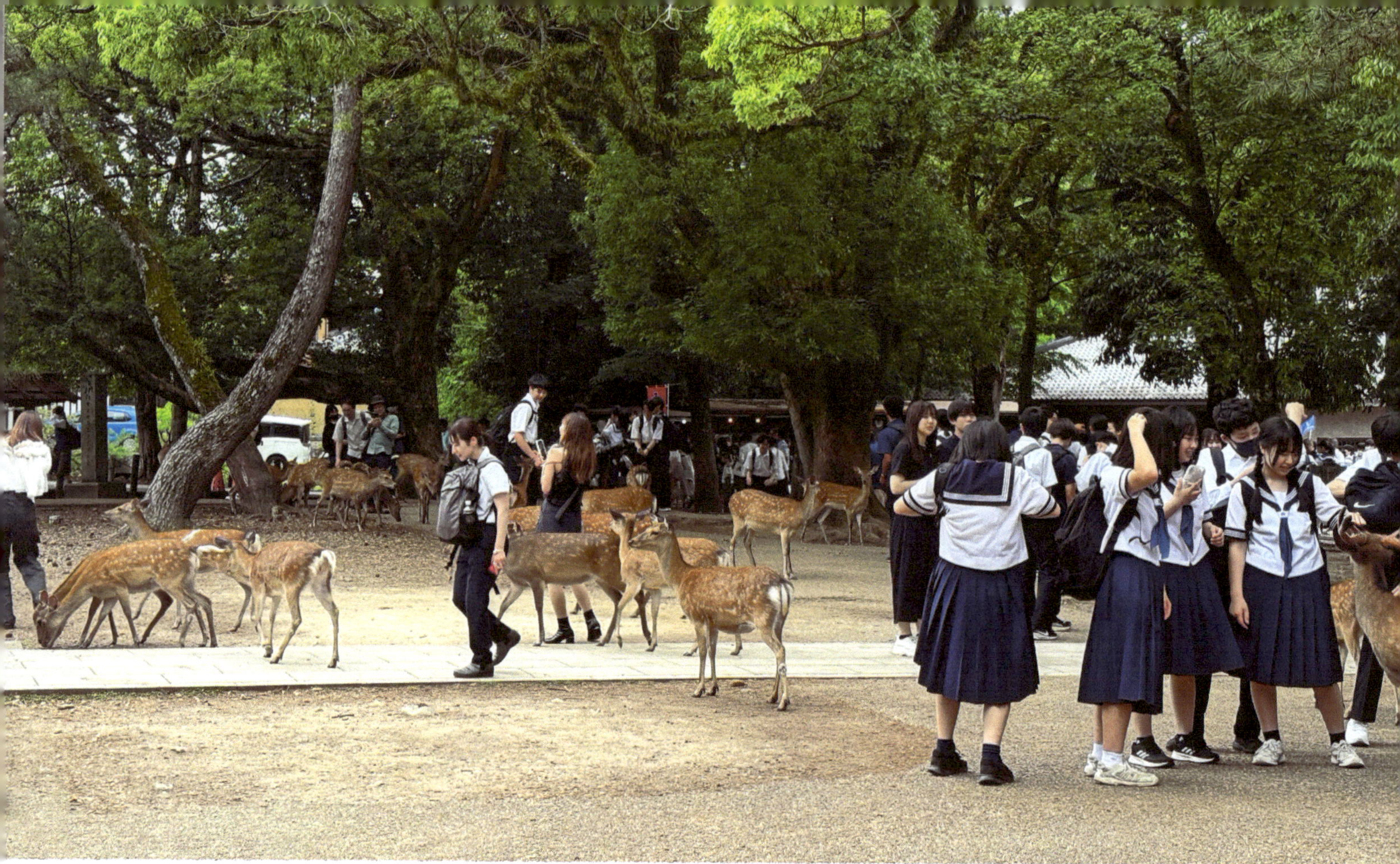

Opposite page (clockwise from top left).
Daruma Dolls – *Ginza, Tokyo; Benzaiten, Chikubushima; Enmaten, Kyoto; Nishiki Market, Kyoto*

Daruma dolls originated in the town of Takasaki. After the Usui River flooded in 1673, townspeople pulled up a fragrant log from the riverbed and placed it in a small Kannon temple. Shortly after, Bodhidharma appeared in a dream to the traveling monk Ichiryō Kōji and told him to carve his likeness from that same log enshrined at the Kannon temple.

After a volcanic eruption, the Tenmei famine struck the region in the 1780s. The temple's priest carved wooden molds and taught villagers to make papier-mâché daruma as a livelihood craft, and the doll's *okiagari* (self-righting form) helped it spread from local festival sales into a widely adopted good-luck charm across Japan by the mid-1800s.

What makes daruma endure is how clearly it turns perseverance into an object: Jp. *nanakorobi yaoki*, "fall seven times, stand up eight," is a proverb that the doll personifies. The rounded figure is also linked to the belief that his arms fell away during intense meditation, and the heavy-lidded eyes reflect that same meditative focus. The iconic red wrapping echoes his red monk's robes. A common practice is to paint the first eye when you commit to a goal and the second when you achieve it.

Today, daruma dolls are among Japan's most popular good-luck symbols and a national cultural icon. They are bought especially around New Year as fresh "goal-setters," but also venerated yearlong in shops, offices, and classrooms. In politics and business, oversized daruma are used to mark election campaigns and major targets by "opening" the eyes in stages, including at companies such as Toyota, Nissan, and Mitsubishi. Temples and markets also sell local, deity-linked versions, including daruma tied to deities such as Benzaiten or Enmaten.

Opposite page.
Deer Park – *Tōdai-ji, Nara*

Nara's Deer Park is based on Sarnath's Deer Park in India, the place where the Buddha gave his first sermon. The deer are also sacred in Shintoism, where they are regarded as messengers for the deity of sumo wrestling. It is interesting that the deer lower their heads in a "bow" when approaching people, perhaps having learned this from the pilgrims who have been visiting this site for over a thousand years.

Tōdai-ji draws students from all over Japan, as it is not only a spiritual site but also an important part of Japanese culture. Temples across Japan are popular for field trips and tourism for the same reason because they are spiritually and culturally significant.

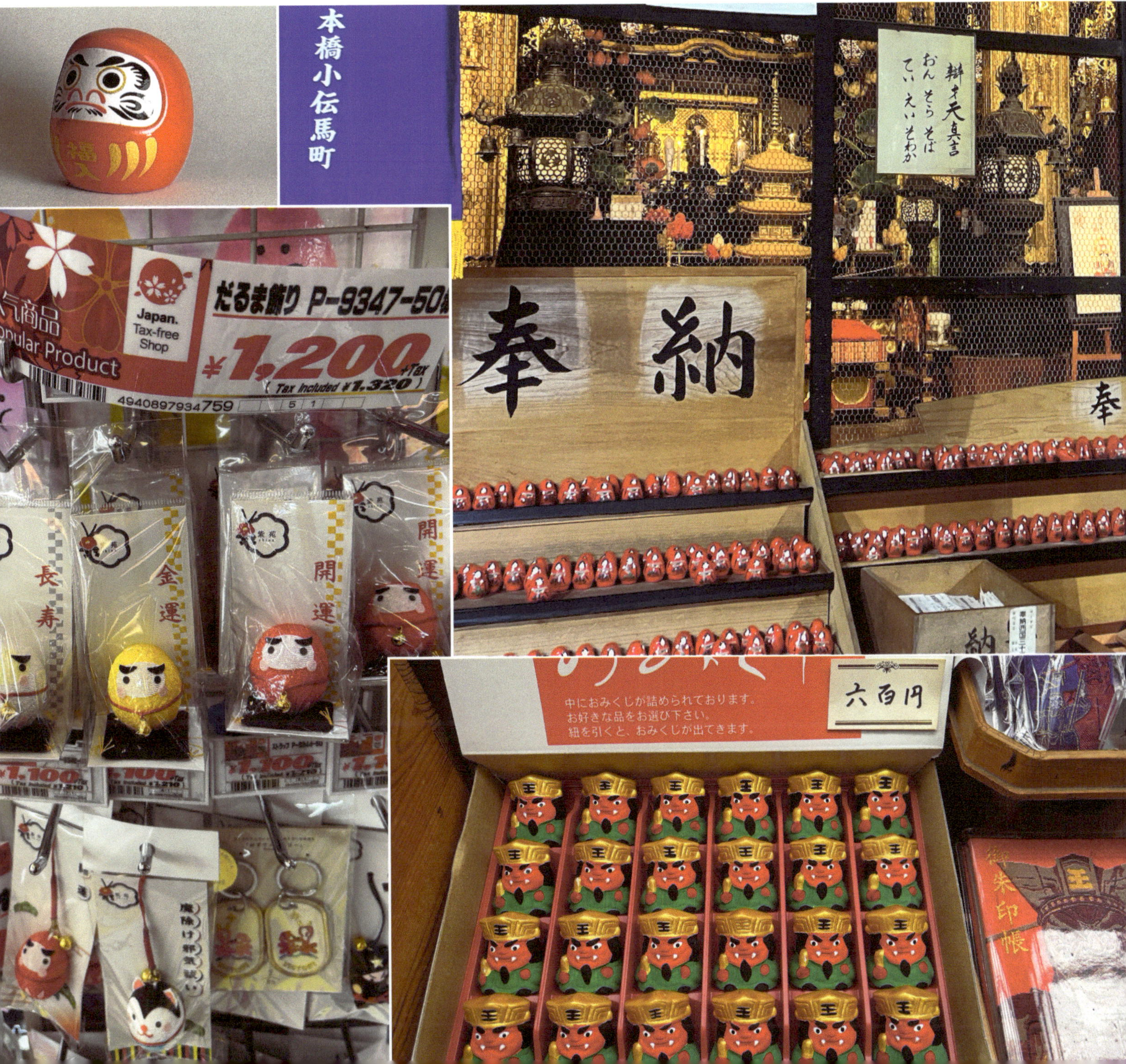

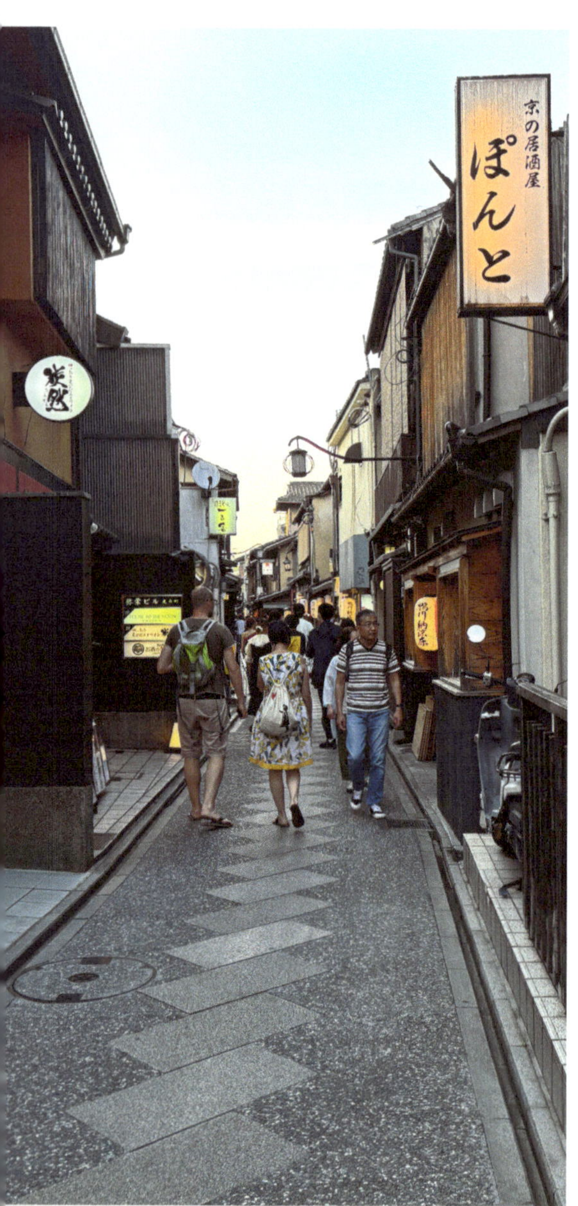

Opposite page (clockwise from top left).
Buddhism in Everyday Transit – *Tawaramachi Station, Tokyo; Shinbashi, Tokyo; Okayama Station; Tennōji Station, Osaka; Shinagawa Station, Tokyo*

Metro stations regularly feature advertisements for Buddhist altars for home worship (Jp. *reihai*, Skt. *pūjā*). Shinto purification rites are often performed to mark the inaugural run of shinkansen. Even in major stations such as Okayama, temple tour advertisements are prominent. Locale names derived from temples are also common across Japan: Tennōji takes its name from the nearby temple associated with the Four Heavenly Kings (Skt. *Lokapālas*), while the nearby locale Teradachō literally means "the temple on the rice field." Advertisements at busy stations like Shinagawa further promote special rites (Jp. *kitō*; and Skt. *rakṣā-pūjā*) for family well-being and traffic safety, at places like Kawasaki Daishi Temple.

This page (left and below).
Gion – *Kashiwayachō and Kameya Kiyonaga (sweet shop), Kyoto*

Gion takes its name from Skt. *Jetavana* (Jeta's Grove) in what is now Uttar Pradesh, India, one of early Buddhism's best-known monastery sites, where the Buddha is traditionally said to have spent 19 rainy-season retreats teaching. Kyoto's Gion centers on Yasaka Shrine, dedicated to Gozu Tennō (often syncretized with the Shinto deity Susanoo), an adaptation of *Jetavana*'s patron deity, Skt. *Gośīrṣa Devarāja*. Japan's largest festival, the Gion Matsuri, began as a way to thank him for averting plagues. Elsewhere in Tokyo, the Hachiōji ("Eight Princes") area is named for a legend in which the monk Myōkō encountered Gozu Tennō and his eight sons on a local mountain. Kyoto's Gion began as a resting area for pilgrims to nearby temples and shrines, then became the center for Gion Matsuri, *ochaya* (teahouses), and the *geiko* tradition.

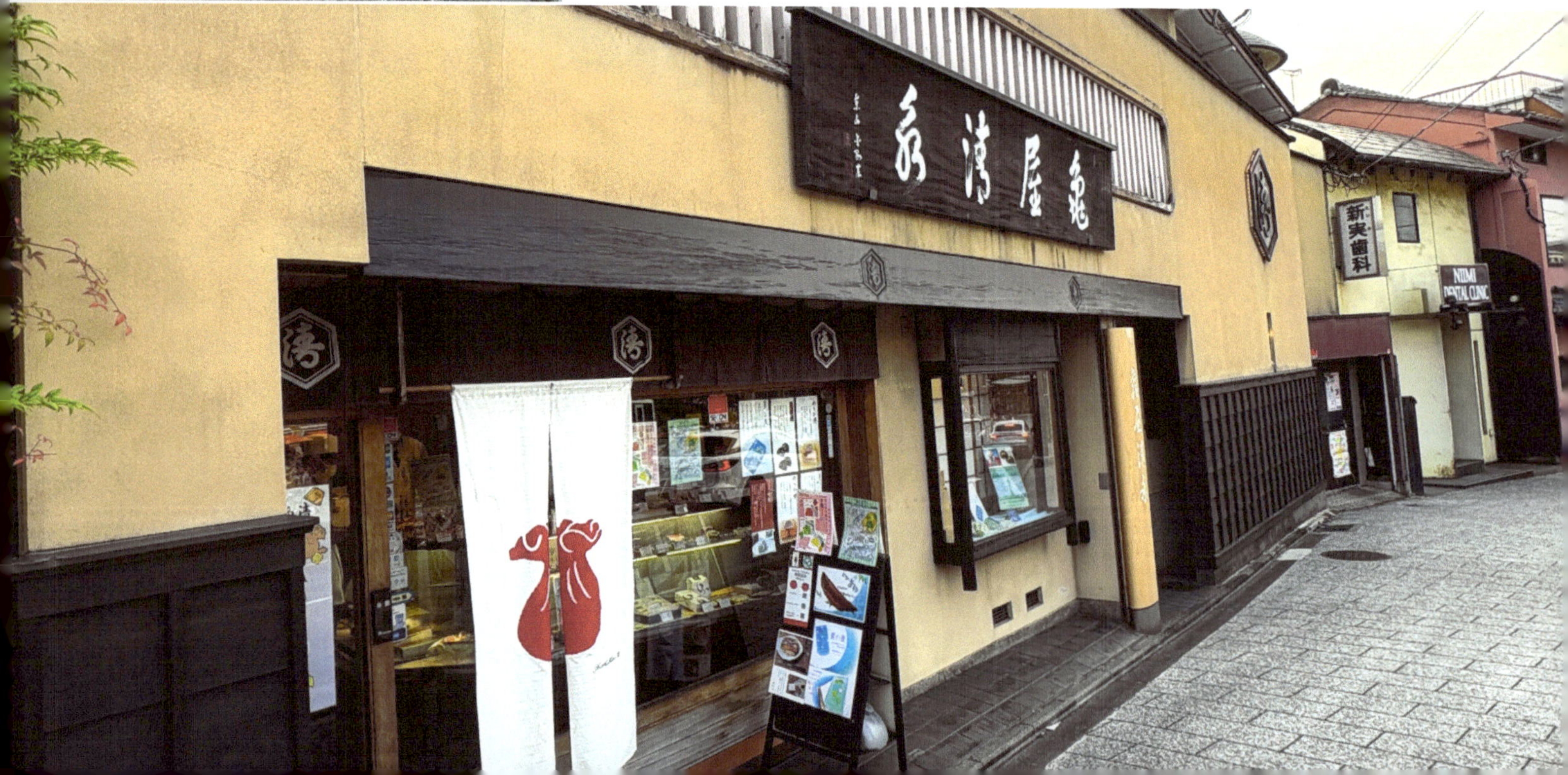

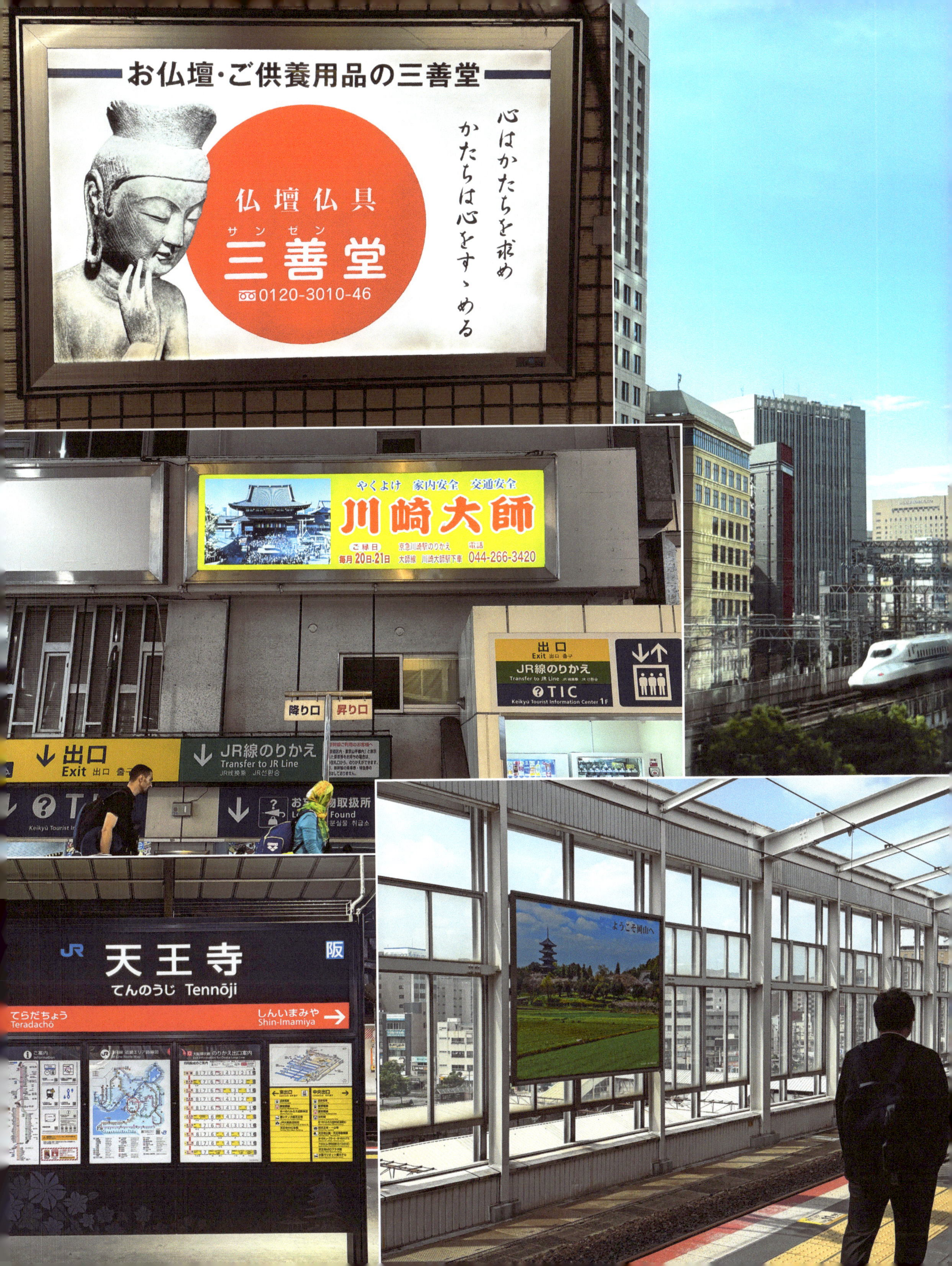
お仏壇・ご供養用品の三善堂
仏壇仏具
サンゼン
三善堂
0120-3010-46
心はかたちを求め
かたちは心をすゝめる
やくよけ 家内安全 交通安全
川崎大師
ご縁日
毎月20日・21日
京急川崎駅のりかえ
大師線 川崎大師駅下車
電話
044-266-3420
出口
Exit
JR線のりかえ
Transfer to JR Line
TIC
Keikyū Tourist Information Center 1F
降り口
昇り口
出口
Exit
JR線のりかえ
Transfer to JR Line
JR
天王寺
阪
てんのうじ Tennōji
てらだちょう
Teradachō
しんいまみや
Shin-Imamiya
ようこそ岡山へ

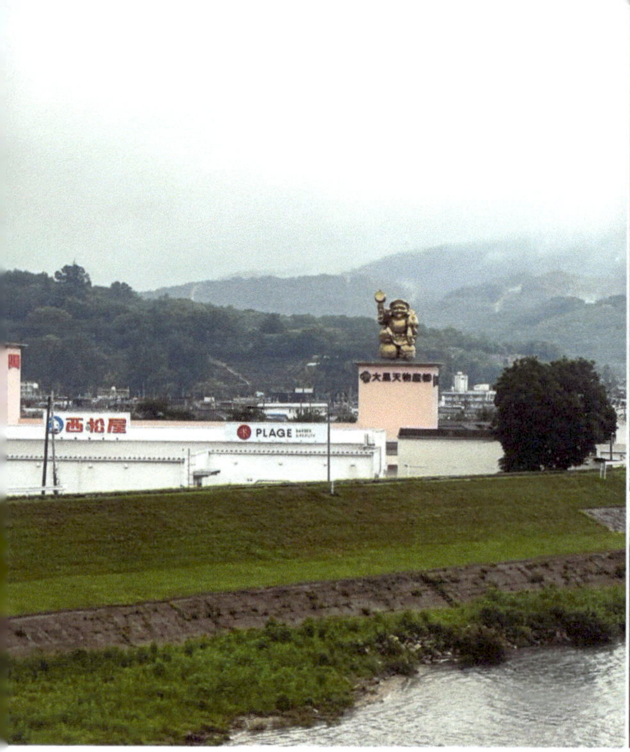

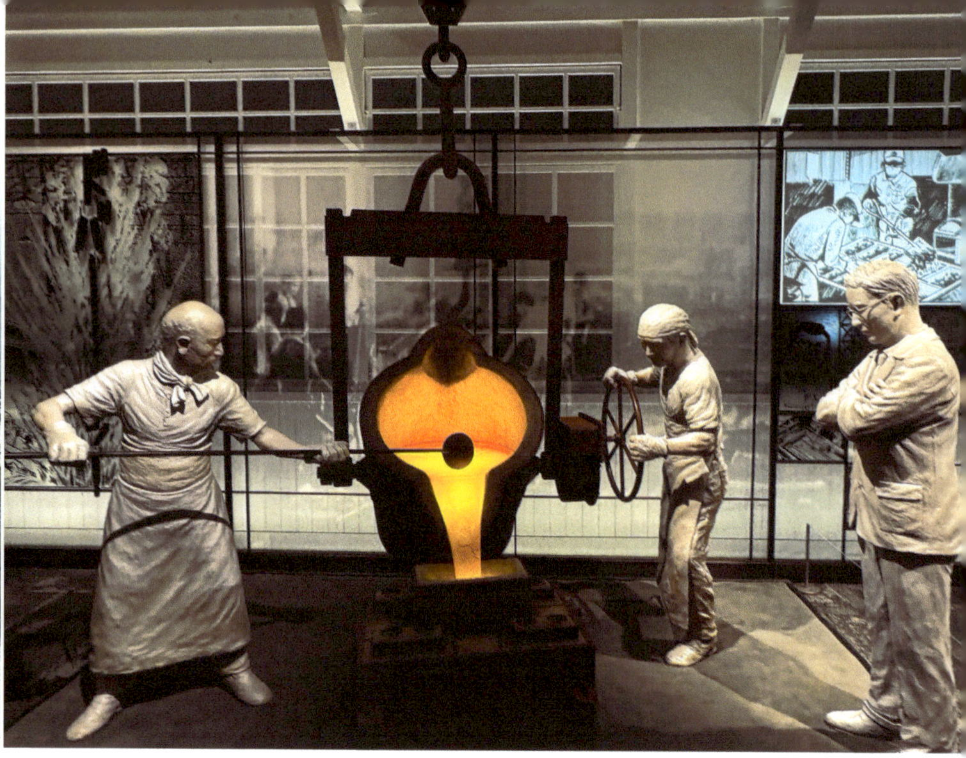

This and opposite page (clockwise from above left).

LAMU supermarket chain with Daikokuten (Skt. *Mahākāla*) logo – *Okayama*
Toyota Commemorative Museum of Industry and Technology – *Nagoya*
Canon camera branding origins
Panasonic corporate memorial plot, Okunoin Cemetery – *Kōyasan*

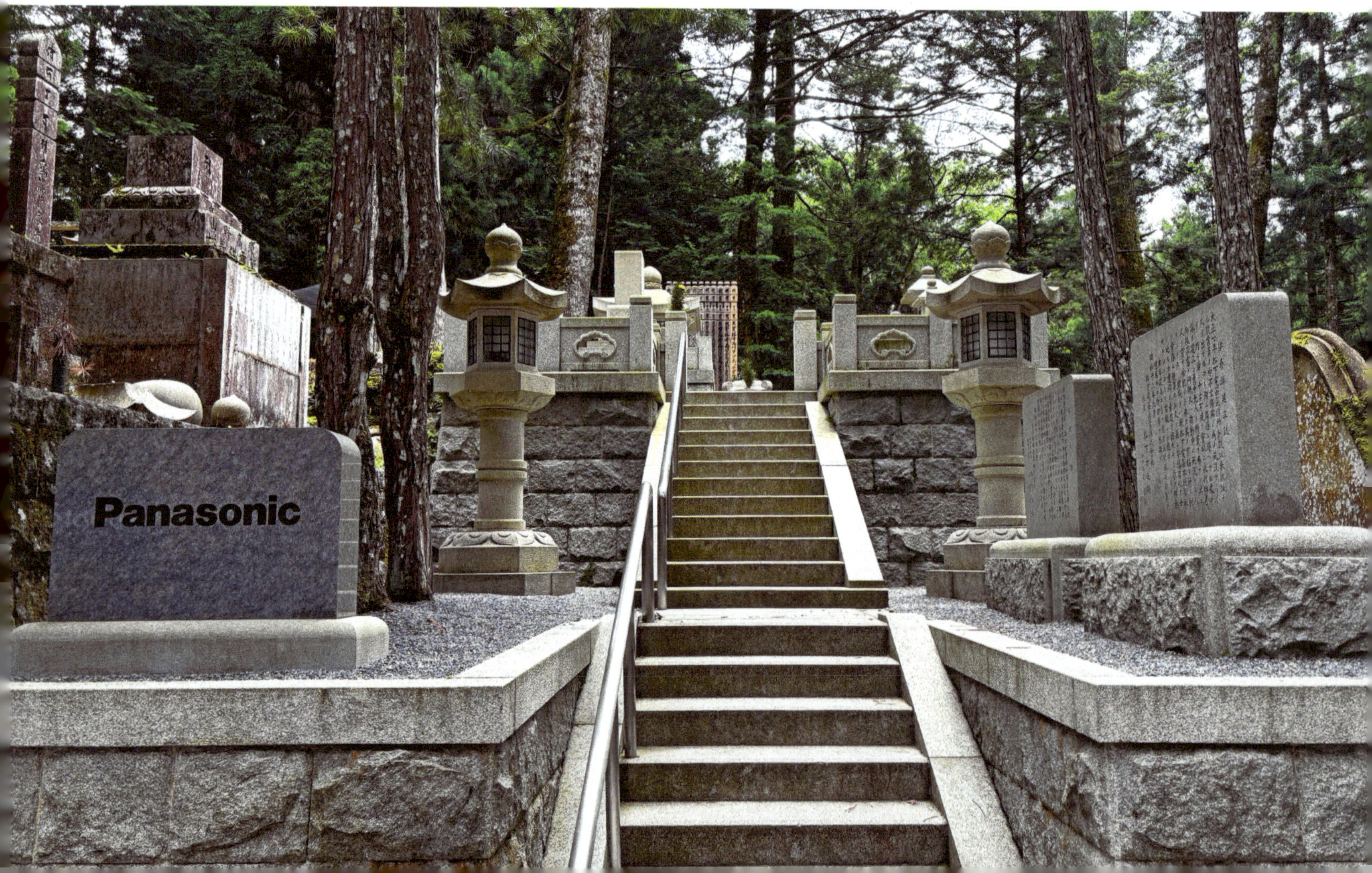

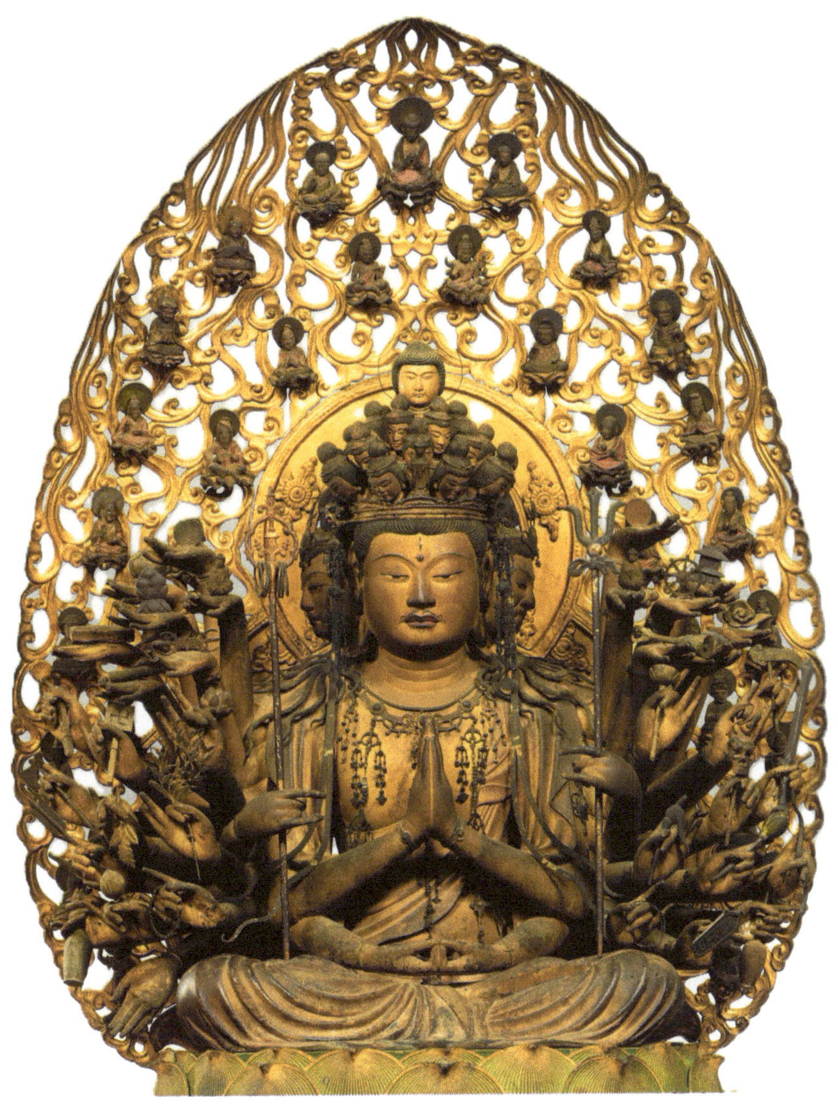

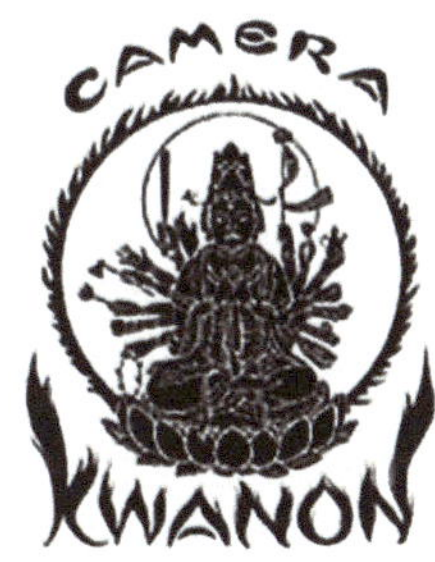

Some connections to Buddhism are direct. The supermarket chain, LAMU, has Daikokuten as a store logo, a prosperity figure in Japanese Buddhism historically linked to Skt. *mahākāla*.

At the Toyota Commemorative Museum, the company's founding principles refer to honoring the Buddhas (*butsu*). Toyota also built Shōkō-ji, a Buddhist temple in Nagano dedicated to traffic safety, and Kiichirō Toyoda, the founder, is remembered for practicing *zazen* (seated meditation; Skt. *dhyāna*) before major decisions, including after factories were destroyed in World War II. Toyota is only one example of pervasive Buddhist ideas in business. Many Japanese companies hold Buddhist ceremonies at key moments in the corporate year, including when employee bonuses are distributed, and it is not unusual for senior leaders to treat meditation and ritual observance as part of responsible decision-making.

Canon's early story begins with Kwanon, named for Kannon Bosatsu (Skt. *Avalokiteśvara*), and early branding drew on the thousand-armed form (Skt. *Sahasrabhuja*).

At Okunoin in Kōyasan, many people hope to have their ashes placed near Kūkai (Kōbō Daishi), and companies have also placed memorials for their own employees, such as the Panasonic plot seen here. In a nation where lifelong employment has long been the norm, firms often take responsibility for employees even into death.

This page (right and below).
Peace Stupa and Peace Flame at the A-Bomb Hypocenter – *Hiroshima*

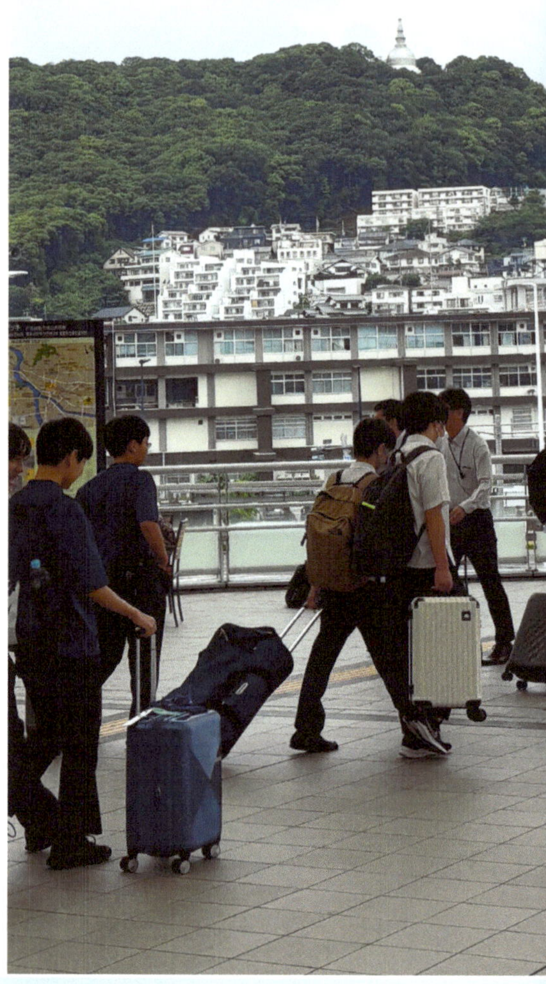

The Hiroshima Peace Stupa uses the Buddhist stūpa form as a memorial, built in 1966 by the Nichiren monks of the Nipponzan Myōhōji-Daisanga order for peace and for those lost in the atomic bombing. It explicitly enshrines Buddha relics, including gifts of the Buddha's ashes from India and Mongolia.

The Peace Flame is a continuous fire of remembrance and resolve, lit in 1964 and meant to burn until nuclear weapons are abolished. Its flame was kindled using the "Eternal Fire" (Jp. *kiezu no hi*; Skt. *akhaṇḍa jyoti*) from Mt. Misen's Reikadō, a Shingon sacred fire credited to Kūkai, associated with Fudō Myōō, and described as burning for over 1,200 years, connecting Shingon practice to Hiroshima's modern peace memorial.

The practice of eternal flames has its origins in Hindu practices, in the form of Skt. *akhaṇḍa jyoti*, an oil or ghee lamp kept burning continuously as an act of devotion. One example, among many in India, is the *akhaṇḍa jyoti* at Jyotīreśvara ("Lord of the flame") Śiva Temple in Jyotirmath in the Himalayas, established by Ādi Śaṅkara, where temple tradition describes the flame as burning continuously for over 2,500 years.

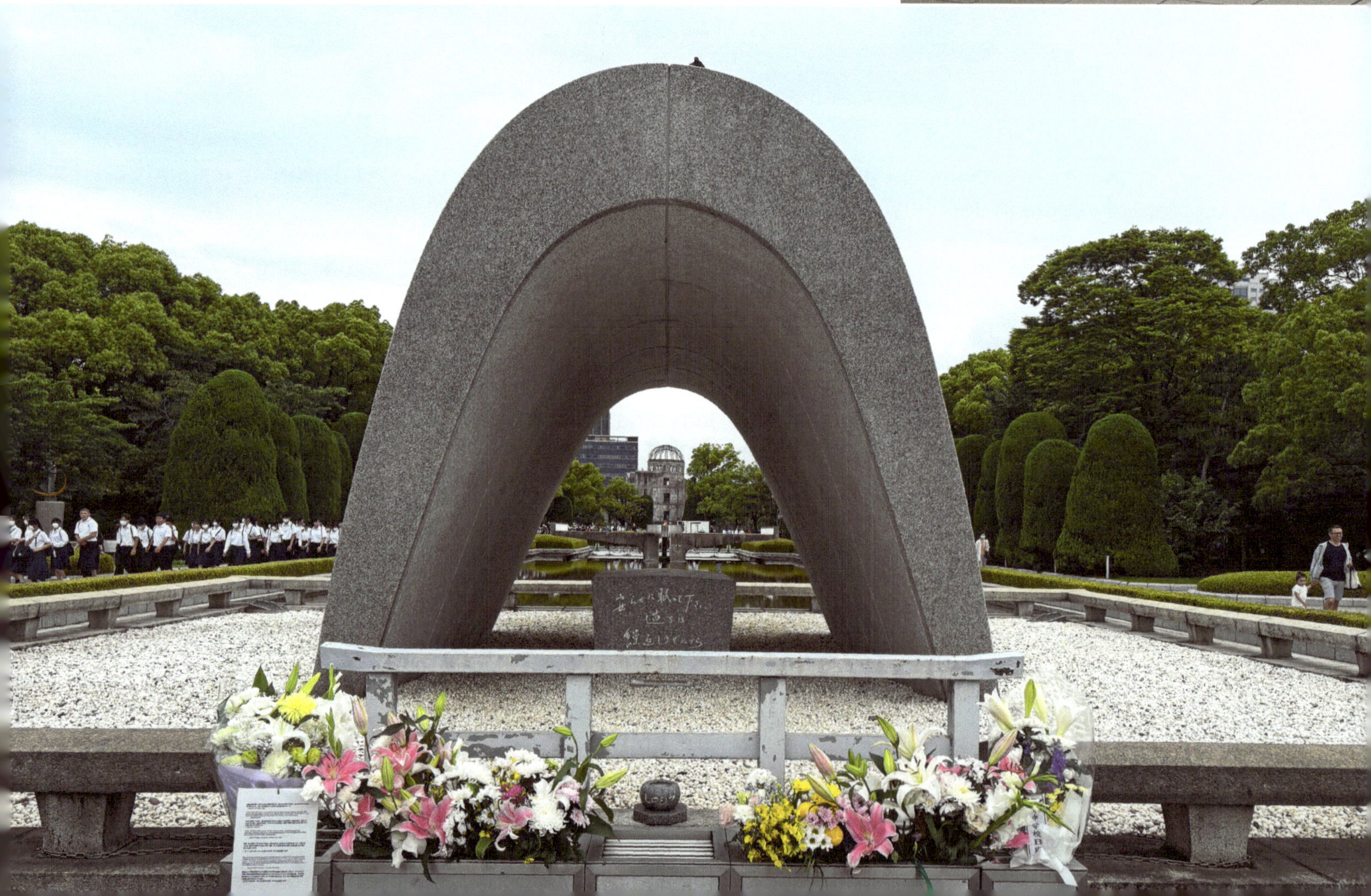

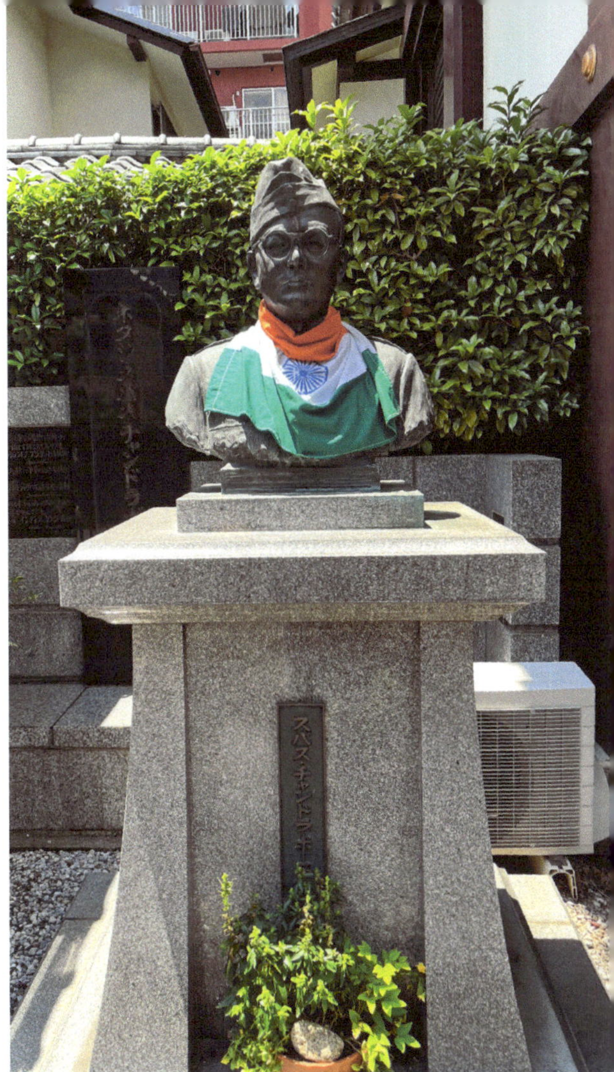

This page (right and below).
Subhas Chandra Bose Memorial – *Renkō-ji, Tokyo*

Born in India, Bose was raised in a wealthy family, went to England, topped the Indian Civil Service exam, but opted out and returned to India, citing Indian nationalism as his higher calling; after becoming president of Gandhi's Congress Party, he resigned over disagreements about nonviolence and was placed under British house arrest. During World War II, he escaped to Germany seeking support for an armed independence struggle, but when Germany could not help, Japan did, driven by pan-Asian nationalism and realpolitik aims to weaken Britain and gain an ally in Asia; with this backing he formed the Indian National Army (INA), initially from British-Indian POWs (prisoners of war) captured by the Japanese, later expanded it into a formidable force, captured frontier towns, and led the first hoisting of the Indian flag on Indian territory before the atomic bombing of Japan forced withdrawal. Just before Japan's surrender, Bose died in a plane crash in then-Japanese Taiwan en route to the mainland as a Japanese general's guest, was cremated in Taipei, and his ashes were brought by an officer to Renkō-ji where they remain; his campaign is credited with galvanizing the naval mutinies that accelerated India's indepdendence in 1947, and the temple pamphlet says it is honored to hold the ashes of the man who "brought freedom to the land of the Buddha."

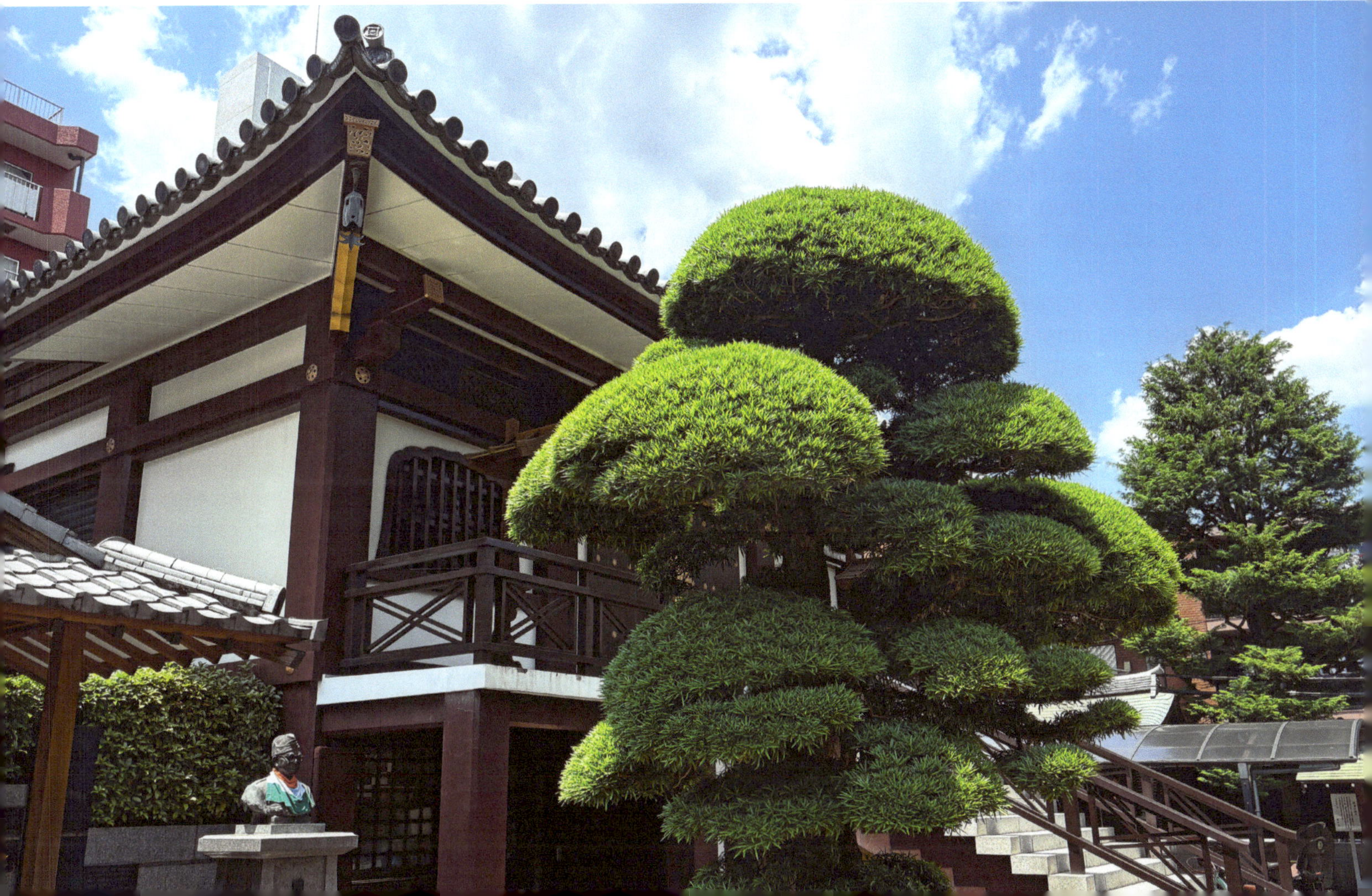

Reflections

Among the developed nations of the world, Japan is an anomaly. Every single other major developed nation besides Japan is white and Christian. Their cultural heritage draws from Greece and Rome, and they use the Latin script. Japan is extremely different. It is Asian and Shinto-Buddhist. Its cultural heritage draws from India and China, and it uses a Sanskrit- and Tang-based character system. At the same time, its society is as developed, perhaps more in some ways, than almost any Western nation. I think this plays a large role in Western cultural fascination with Japan: it is a highly developed society with a very different cultural heritage. For us Hindu-Buddhist people, this aforementioned "different" cultural heritage to Westerners is very similar to our cultures.

Unfortunately, most of the Hindu-Buddhist countries were colonized and looted by Western powers. I have extensively traveled through India, and I will speak of my experience there. Due to nearly a thousand years of foreign invasion, India was stripped of its great wealth and has few resources to maintain or upkeep its ancient sites. As such, many ancient temples with some of the finest craftsmanship man has ever produced are crumbling or not kept up well. Additionally, due to colonization by Western powers, there is a perception of inferiority when Indians view their own traditional Indian culture, and anything Western is perceived to be superior. This leads to a great imbalance: some sections of society, such as priests, remain deeply traditional but engage little with the technologies of the modern world and often lack financial means, while others who work in advanced technological fields and have financial means and access to technology are often Westernized and tend to look down upon traditional Indian culture. This imbalance may help explain why many ancient temples struggle to receive the care they deserve.

Japan is one of the few countries that did not get colonized by Western powers and, as such, has preserved most of its culture through all sections of society while adopting the best of Western technology and perfecting it. Other factors that contributed to Japan's cultural preservation include a continued political order, with Japan's Yamato dynasty being the oldest continuous dynasty (about 1,400 years old) in the world. Additionally, unlike its East Asian neighbors, it never destroyed all of its traditional culture for "modernity," and was ironically able to modernize far before, and far better than, any East Asian nation. As a result, Japan has very ancient traditions preserved for the modern era.

A perfect example of what I mean is the world's oldest company, Kongō Gumi from Osaka (kongō = vajra and gumi = group). An interesting side note: kongō has been a traditional Japanese symbol of strength, with the largest class of Japanese battleships during World War II called the Kongō kyūsenkan (vajra-class battleships). Kongō Gumi was founded in 578 CE and has been run by the same family since that time. They specialized in temple construction in ancient times, constructing ancient, well-known temples such as Shitennō-ji, Hōryū-ji, and the temples of Kōyasan. In modern times, they specialize in the upkeep and maintenance of temples in the traditional manner, often for temples they themselves constructed over a thousand years ago. For example, they originally constructed Shitennō-ji in 593 and reconstructed it in the 1950s after the Americans bombed it during World War II. Kongō Gumi also began using CAD to create comprehensive digital models of major temples and shrines in case a natural disaster strikes.

Other thousand-year-plus Japanese companies, which are among the oldest in the world, include Tanaka-Iga Butsugu (founded in 885), which specializes in creating *butsudan* (Buddhist home altars).

It pioneered the use of CAD for customers to custom-design their own butsudan from their homes before having it handcrafted by artisans of the Manju-ji Temple in Kyoto, named after Manju Bosatsu (Skt. *Mañjuśrī Bodhisattva*). Another is Shūmiya Shinbutsuguten (founded in 1024), which specializes in creating *kesa* (Skt. *kāṣāya*), the robes of monks and priests.

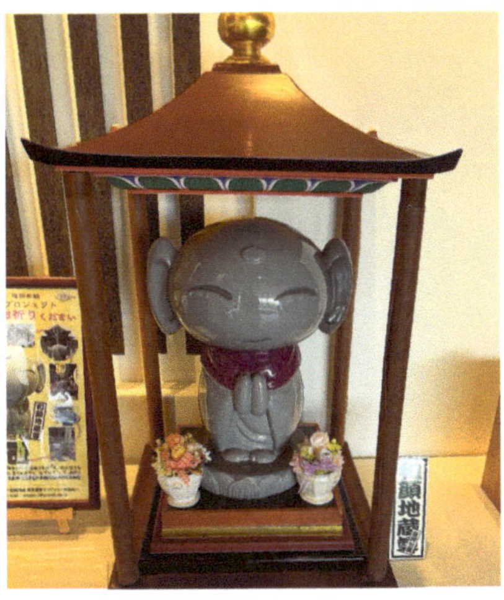

Enma-ō's "honorable dog" (Skt. Yama), spotted in an ordinary Kyoto shopping street

A very personal example of Japan's combination of the old and the new was my experience in the town of Ikoma, where Hōzan-ji is located. Ikoma is a bedroom community of Osaka and, as such, has a vast train station for commuters and visitors from the city. In the heart of the station were a few expertly handcrafted dioramas of local attractions, with the Hōzan-ji temple taking a prominent place. Behind all these dioramas was a humanoid robot pointing out the attractions, their histories, and visiting information in Japanese. Whenever it said Kangiten (my name in Japanese) while giving information about Hōzan-ji, it would give a small bow.

Such examples bring me back to my point about two worlds. In addition to being interested in learning about history and cultures, especially those of the Hindu-Buddhist world, I am very interested in technology, and I have a few scientific publications and patents. Until I went to Japan and experienced the culture firsthand, I thought these two interests of mine were mutually exclusive. But after seeing, with my own eyes, a cutting-edge humanoid robot talking about temples connected to my own name, I realized that these two interests of mine need not be mutually exclusive.

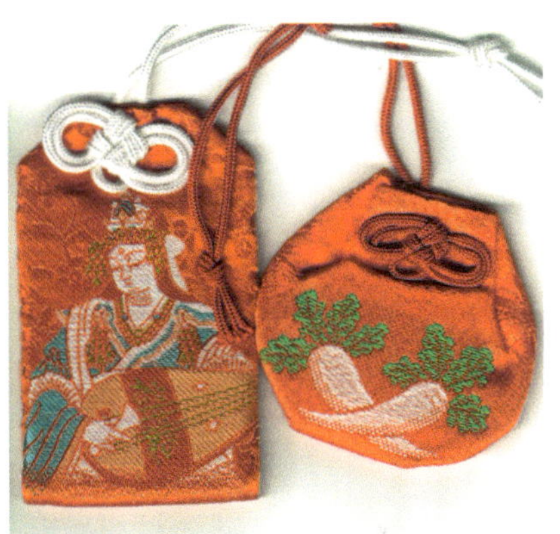

Omamori (blessed amulet) for Kangiten (Skt. Gaṇapati) and Benzaiten (Skt. Sarasvatī), often seen on student backpacks

Upon further research, I learned that this fusion of technology with ancient heritage was not a new concept in Japan, and that, in addition to his spiritual contributions, Kūkai himself was an ardent engineer. When he was traveling through Shikoku, locals requested him to help them create a reservoir. That reservoir became the Mannō reservoir, which is still Japan's largest reservoir.

The most obvious and jarring example of Japan preserving its culture is the sheer prevalence of the Japanese language. I love languages, and I tend to notice the use of languages wherever I travel. Something that makes me immensely sad is how little Telugu, my mother tongue, is used in the Telugu-speaking regions of India. English is seen as the global language, and families often do their best to give their kids an English education. Law, higher education, medicine, software, and all other "modern" communication is almost always conducted in English, even when only Telugu-speaking people are present. It is a great misfortune that, when driving through a city in the Telugu-speaking world, one is bound to see more English signage than Telugu signage.

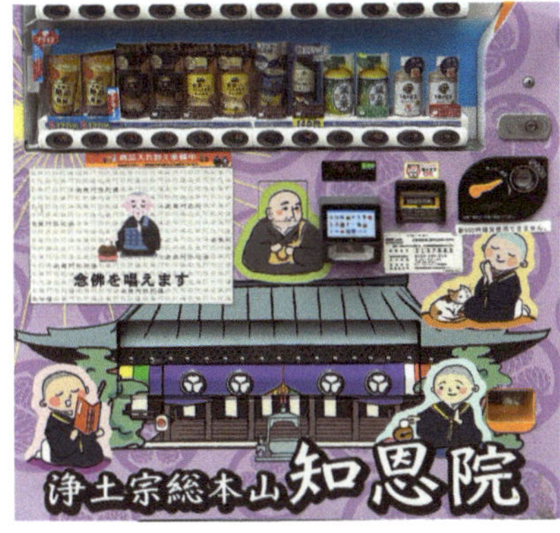

Jidōhanbaiki (vending machine) with cartoon bōzu (Buddhist monk)

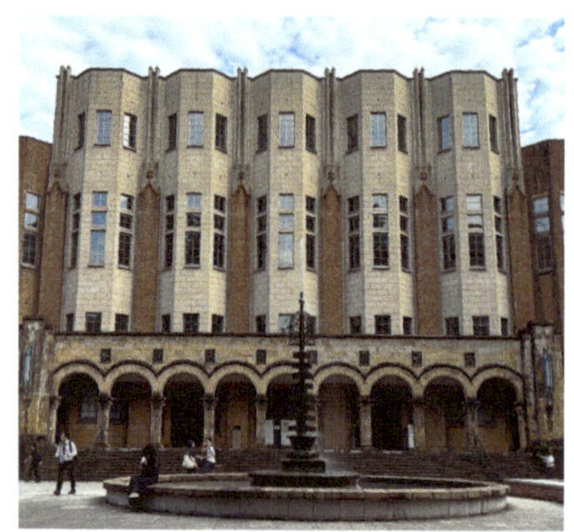

Eight-tier fountain signifying Buddhist hasshōdō (Noble Eightfold Path), University of Tokyo

Japan was a complete contrast. Everyone spoke Japanese for everything, from business executives in the skyscrapers of Tokyo running some of the world's most famous companies to terrace farmers in the mountains of Wakayama working on their paddies. Many Japanese have little interest in learning English, seeing it as unnecessary unless one wants to travel extensively out of Japan. Signage was the same with nearly everything, from bullet train stations to deity names in temples, being written in Japanese.

When seeing all the ancient temples of Japan, it is easy to think that all these cultural connections are of a bygone era and no longer relevant to most modern people. I had a very interesting experience that shattered that notion near Hōzan-ji. As I was exploring the temple, I had a few questions and asked an old lady lighting incense, who answered them before returning to her prayers. As I came down from the cave in the mountains near Hōzan-ji, where Kūkai is said to have trained, the same old lady asked me if I was Indian. My heart slipped a beat. I had been in Japan for a little over a week at that point and had not yet experienced any racism, and I thought this streak would be broken. I hesitantly said yes.

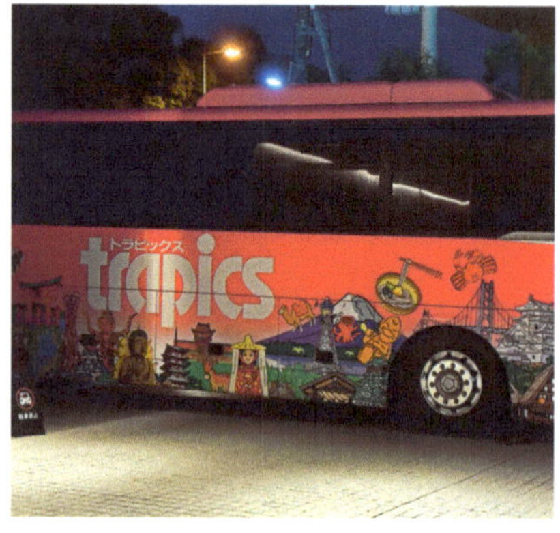

Bonten (Skt. Brahmā) on a tour bus, Osaka

What happened next was something I could have never expected. She asked me if I knew about Sai Baba, and I said yes. She smiled and said she was a devotee of Sai Baba, and that her parents had gone to Puttaparthi in the 1960s to live with Sai Baba for a few months. She said that Sai Baba appeared in the dream of a man from a small village in Ehime in the 1950s after curing him of a disease doctors thought was incurable, and word about this miracle guru spread rapidly across Japan, impacting many people, from her parents to the parents of the famous Japanese musician Fujii Kaze, who himself is a Sai Baba devotee and named his first album after Sai Baba's famous catchphrase, "Help Ever Hurt Never."

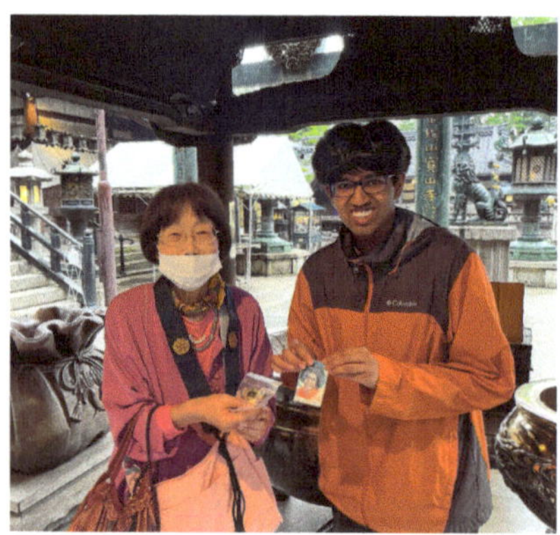

Author with a devotee of Satya Sai Baba, Hōzan-ji

She also said she was the head of the Sai Baba devotees' Kansai chapter with hundreds of members, and that they often sing bhajans in Japanese and do community service throughout the Kansai area. She expressed admiration for my vegetarian lifestyle and said that she is trying her best to be vegetarian while strictly avoiding beef. She showed me her amulet of Sai Baba that she always keeps in her bag.

It was such a unique experience to meet her and realize that the cultural connections are still enduring in the present. She doesn't speak English or any Indian languages and has never left Japan, but she has still been so profoundly influenced by Sai Baba. At the end of our conversation, she told me to travel carefully and said that she had to return because her kids and grandkids would be waiting for her.

I asked her if this type of multigenerational household was still common in Japan, and she replied, *"mochiron,"* of course. This was especially interesting and touching, because I grew up with my grandma living in my home, something uncommon and very foreign to most Americans. Additionally, my mother, although highly educated with a double master's degree from Duke, chose not to work so she could properly raise me and my sister with cultural values and healthy food. Some people in America and Westernizing India have looked down on this and found it strange despite being significantly less educated themselves. I was pleasantly surprised when I learned that not only is this common in Japan, but it is also seen as a cultural ideal for a highly educated woman to use her knowledge to properly raise her children.

Tourism is also centered around temples, with temples often topping the charts of the most visited sites of Japan. Throughout Japan, I saw groups of students from across the country visiting temples on field trips. In Osaka, I saw a tour bus with motifs of Buddhist deities, including Bonten.

It is impossible to overstate the prevalence of Buddhism in Japanese life. The moment I landed at Tokyo's Narita Airport, I saw mesmerizing pictures of temples and five-story pagodas on the walls as I walked to customs from the jet bridge. In fact, I challenge you to go on Google Maps and zoom into any inhabited location in Japan, and I guarantee that within seconds you will see the *manji* (Skt. *svastika*) logo for a temple. It is important to remember that the *svastika* was originally a symbol of auspiciousness in a Hindu-Buddhist context, composed of the Sanskrit words *su* ("well") + *asti* ("being") + *ka* ("object"), before the Nazis usurped it for their twisted agenda.

Even things that may not look Buddhist at first sight often are linked to Buddhism. Outside the library at the University of Tokyo stood a traditional Japanese fountain with eight layers. I wondered if that number meant anything, and it turned out the eight was supposed to signify the Noble Eightfold Path of Buddhism. This is one of the reasons I named this book the way I did: so many things like this are hidden in plain sight.

Buddhism is so integrated into Japanese life that it even shows up in dialogue about Japan outside of the country. Recently, I was in a bookstore in the U.S. and I was checking out a Japanese language textbook that contained a story about the Buddha with a translation at the end. There was a translator's note stressing how difficult it is to translate the sheer amount of respect built into the language around the Buddha.

Anime is one of Japan's greatest and most recognizable cultural exports, and there are hundreds of excellent anime series that touch Buddhism explicitly. What's striking is that even the most universally known anime often carry Buddhist themes and symbolism in the background.

For example, *Dragon Ball* extensively uses Buddhist symbolism. Son Goku is based on Sun Wukong, the hero of the Chinese tale *Journey to the West*, in which a Buddhist monk (inspired by Xuanzang) travels to India to retrieve Buddhist scriptures. Sun Wukong, in turn, was directly inspired by the Hindu deity Hanumān. Additionally, the Dragon Ball resembles wish-fulfilling Skt. *cintāmaṇi* jewels.

Naruto also has significant Buddhist and broader dharmic themes. Characters frequently form Skt. *mudras* inspired by Shingon Buddhism. The story also leans into explicitly dharmic frames through ideas like the “Six Paths” and through names and symbols that borrow from Buddhist iconography. For instance, the Senju clan is named after *Senju Kannon* (Thousand-Armed Kannon), and the clan emblem is vajra-like in shape.

An example of an explicitly Dharmic production is the Ramayana Anime by Yūgō Sakō (an orphan and trained to be a Buddhist priest), who developed an interest in Indian philosophy and filmmaking. In 1983, while working on *The Ramayana Relics*, a documentary film about excavations in India, he came to know the story of the *Rāmāyaṇa*. He liked it so much that he researched more deeply and went on to read 10 versions of the *Rāmāyaṇa* in Japanese. After reading it, he wanted to adapt it into animation because he didn’t think a live-action movie could capture its true essence: “Because Ram is God, I felt it was best to depict him in animation, rather than by an actor.” He raised money from the Indian and Japanese public and created a masterpiece anime depicting the *Rāmāyaṇa*, flying out experts from India and working with top Japanese animators including from Studio Ghibli.

Besides the cultural parallels, Japan, unlike both America and India, is spotless and extremely safe. Flying back to the U.S., I immediately noticed an overall lower level of refinement in the airport itself. Wires hung out. Information screens posted delays. Carts were left next to cars in the parking garage. In Japan, I did not encounter a single panhandler or homeless person throughout my travels where I have come across hundreds of thousands of people, and it looked as if nearly everyone was quite well off. In fact, many taxi drivers I talked with had gone to exotic destinations such as Bali, Hawaii, and even Finland. This type of widespread prosperity translates to protection of cultural heritage like temples or shrines. Oftentimes, I would see multinational companies, especially Hitachi, supporting temples.

Lastly, on the contemporary state of Buddhism in Japan: some consider Japan to not be a religious country. This is partially true. Japan is not religious in the exclusivist, norm-heavy Abrahamic sense, and many Japanese people despise religious extremism in the U.S. and the Middle East. On the other hand, Japan is very spiritual in the Dharmic sense, as the Dharmic religions aren’t quite religions but ways of life. Hinduism, Buddhism, and Shinto are not prescriptive but experiential. These religions can be seen as a complex set of philosophical and almost scientific beliefs that delve into the nature of being, one’s greater purpose in life, and one’s place in the world. They also have rituals that ancient sages and monks have found helpful to answer these questions and offer reverence to the natural elements that help us live.

Japan deeply follows these rituals, with temple visits, festivals, *jōya no kane*, and *butsudan* deeply integrated into Japanese culture to the level that some do not view it as religion, but simply as part of being Japanese. However, unlike Abrahamic religions, these religions (or ways of life) do not prescribe a single savior or a path but invite dialogue and inquiry. One can chart one’s own path to answer the fundamental questions of human life without strictly following the path of previous religious leaders. As such, these faiths have survived for thousands of years, perhaps because they are syncretic, with Buddhism in Japan incorporating local Shinto deities under the *shinbutsu-shugo* system and Hinduism in India incorporating Skt. *grāma devatā* (village deities). I think herein lies the beauty of these religions in their fundamental nature to be adaptable while retaining the core structure.

Japan showed me that modernity does not require cultural amnesia. If Japan could preserve, refine, and elevate many dharmic ideals while mastering modern technology, then I hope India can reclaim confidence in its own civilizational roots, modernize on its own terms, and continue offering something distinct to the world. It can do so by treating preservation as a national priority, strengthening Indian languages in public life, and fusing traditional ways of life with modern science and engineering. I hope to play a role in bridging this gap through this book and the future endeavors I take up.

As I write this on the last day of the year, I reflect upon this life-transforming journey. It has taken nearly a year of research, planning, travel, and work to complete this book. I hope you have learned just as much as I have about this great nation and its unique culture, and that you find a deep resonance the way I did. In conclusion, the parallels between my Hinduism and the Buddhism of Japan are as great as *gōgasha-sū*, “as many as the sands of the Ganga”, a poetic way of saying that something is truly innumerable. Thank you for reading my book. *Arigatō gozaimasu!*

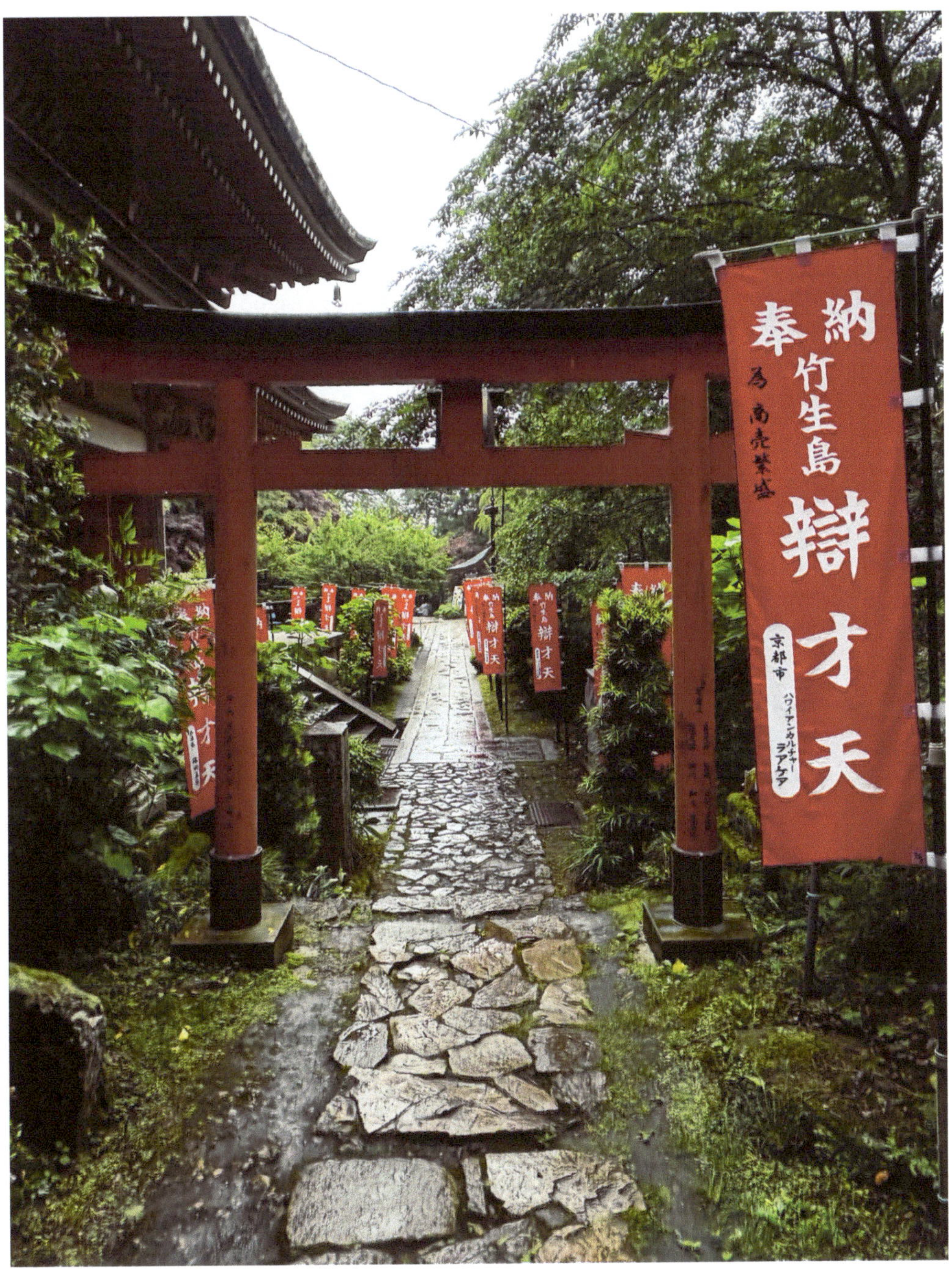

Appendix: Indian Visual Parallels

These pages offer a visual index of Indian temples that illustrate several of the parallels noted in this book. A complete, one-to-one visual parallel for every theme is beyond the scope of this book. Photographs are taken at places I visited and grouped by theme, with Sanskrit (Skt.) and Japanese (Jp.) terms listed side by side to serve as a quick translation reference.

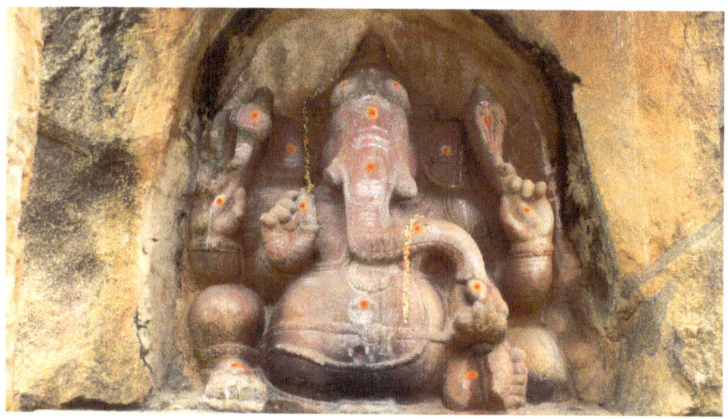

Skt. Gaṇapati / Jp. Kangiten with modaka (Jp. kangidan) – *Veerabhadra Temple, Andhra Pradesh*

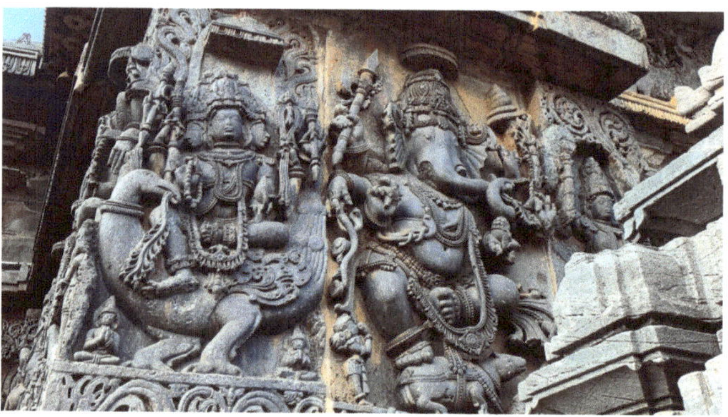

Skt. Kārttikeya / Jp. Idaten; peacock mount (Kujaku Myōō) – *Hoysaleśwara, Karnataka*

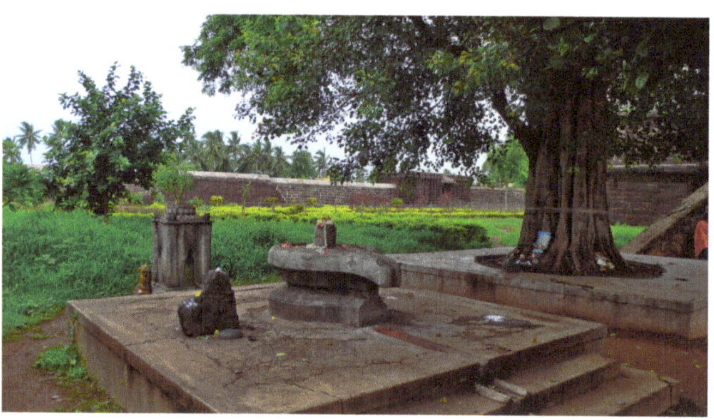

Skt. Śiva-liṅga; Skt. abhiṣeka / Jp. Konjō – *Kumārarāmam, Andhra Pradesh*

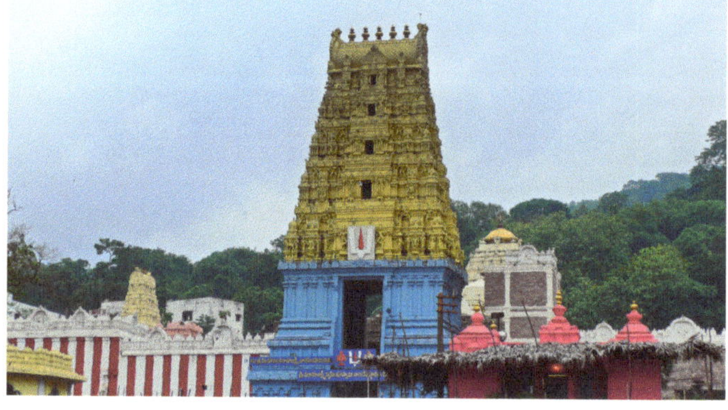

Skt. Varāhalakṣmī Narasiṃha (nijarūpa darśanam); Jp. hibutsu – *Simhāchalam, Andhra Pradesh*

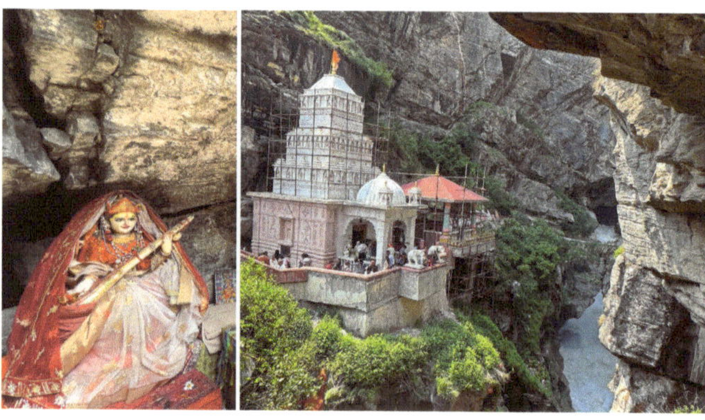

Skt. Sarasvatī / Jp. Benzaiten with vīṇā/biwa near Sarasvatī River source in Himalayas – *Uttarakhand*

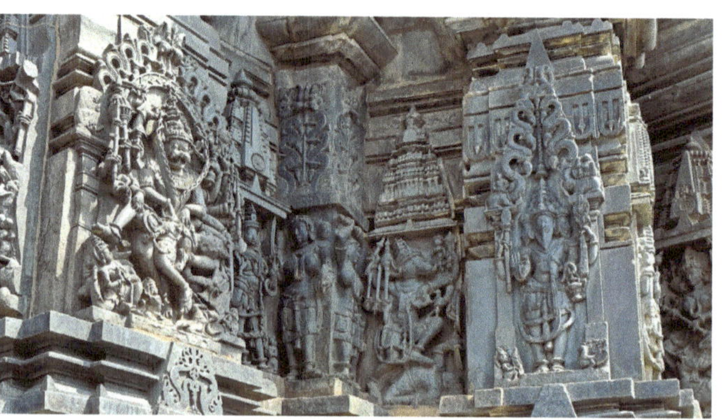

Skt. Brahmā / Jp. Bonten (rightmost, bearded) – *Chennakeśava, Belur, Karnataka*

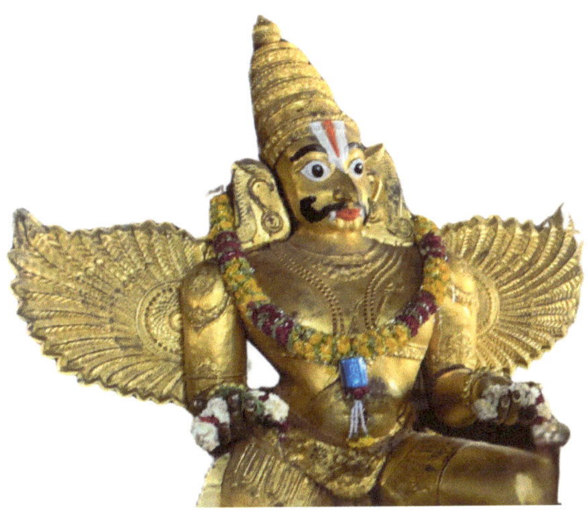

Skt. Garuḍa (eagle mount) / Jp. Karura – *Srirangapatna, Karnataka*

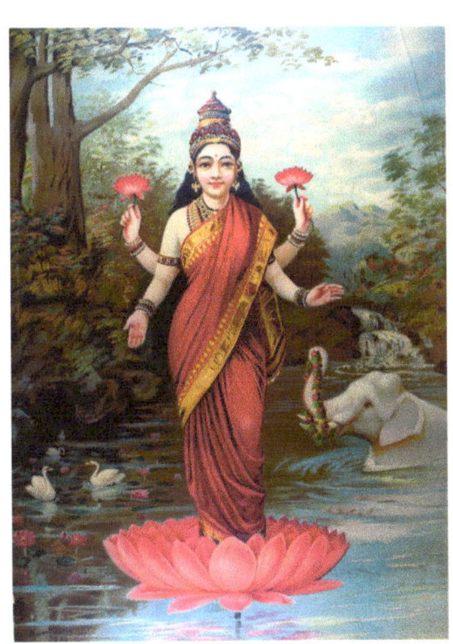

Skt. Lakṣmī: varada-mudrā (boon-giving), holding lotuses / Jp. Kichijōten

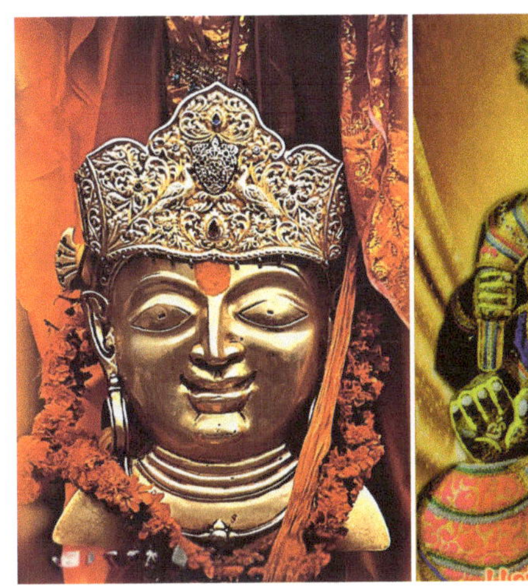

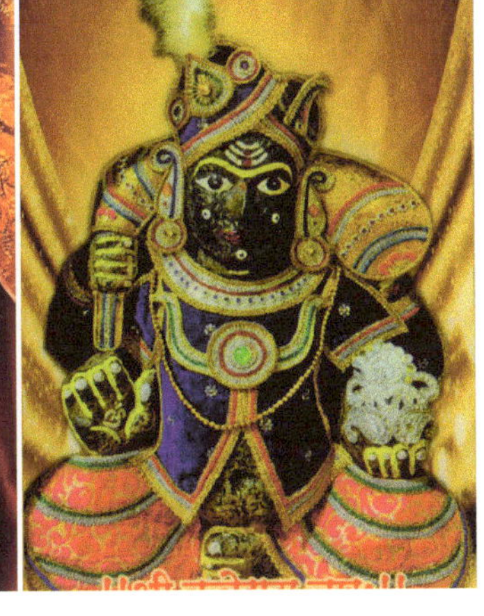

Skt. Kubera (Vaiśravaṇa) / Jp. Bishamonten – *Badrinath, Uttarakhand; Ujjain, Madhya Pradesh*

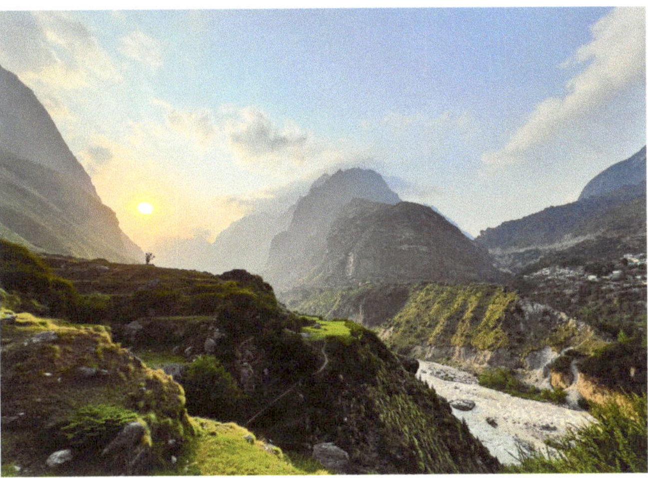

Skt. Kubera's abode, Alakāpurī beyond these peaks – *Alkapuri Glacier, Uttarakhand*

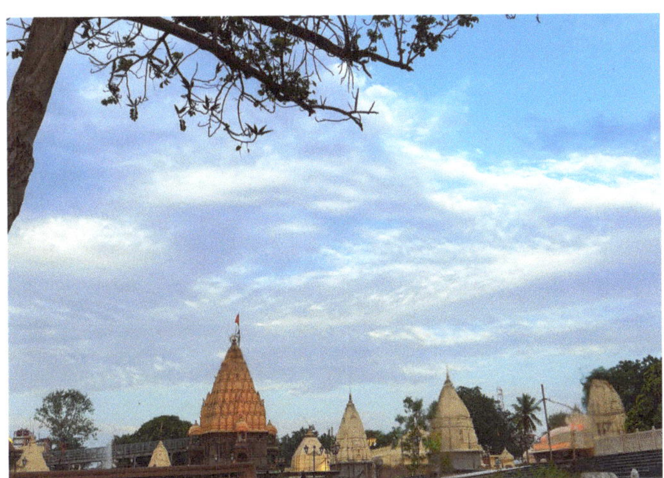

Skt. Mahākāla / Jp. Daikokuten – *Ujjain Mahākāleśvar, Madhya Pradesh*

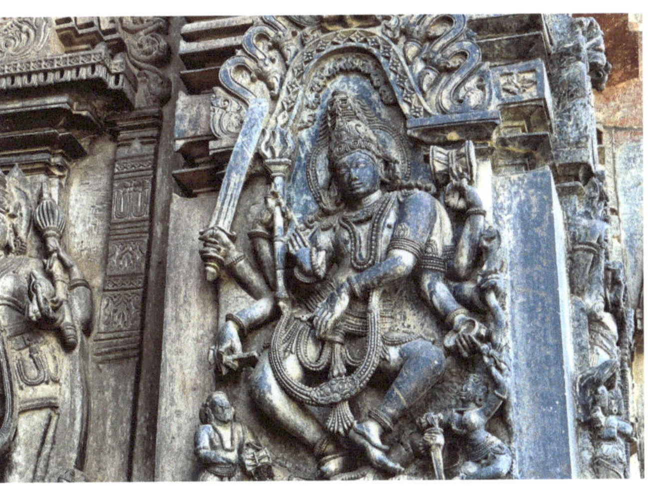

Skt. Śiva with khaḍga / Jp. Fudō Myōō (Skt. Acala) – *Chennakeśava, Belur, Karnataka*

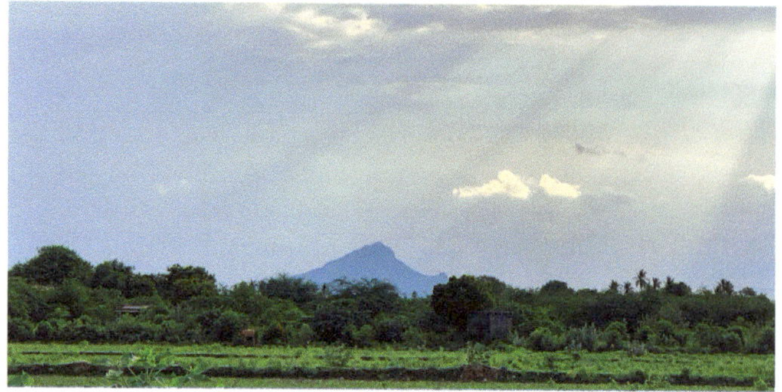

Skt. Arunācala (Śiva as mountain) / Jp. Fuji-san (deified mountain) – *Tiruvannamalai, Tamil Nadu*

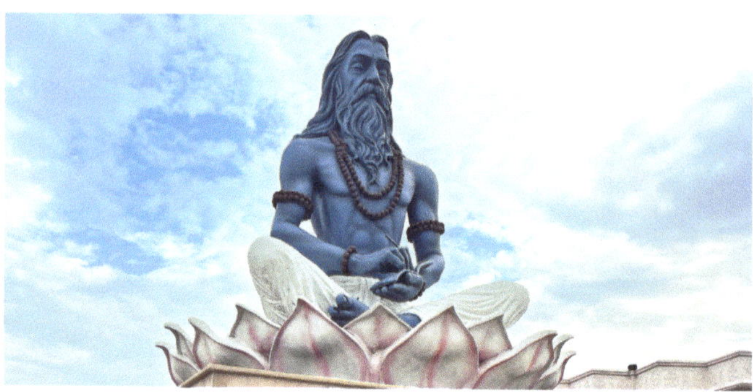

Vedic ṛṣi Bhāradvāja: lineage of Pindola Bhāradvāja (Binzuru) and Bodhisena

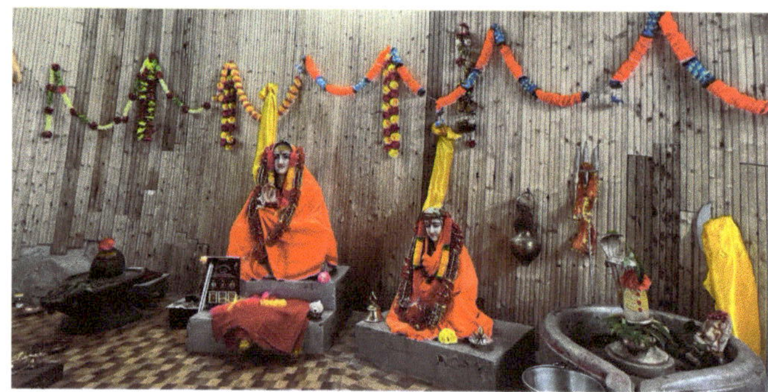

Ādi Śaṅkara in saffron robes / Daruma doll dress – *Totāka Cave, Jyotirmath, Uttarakhand*

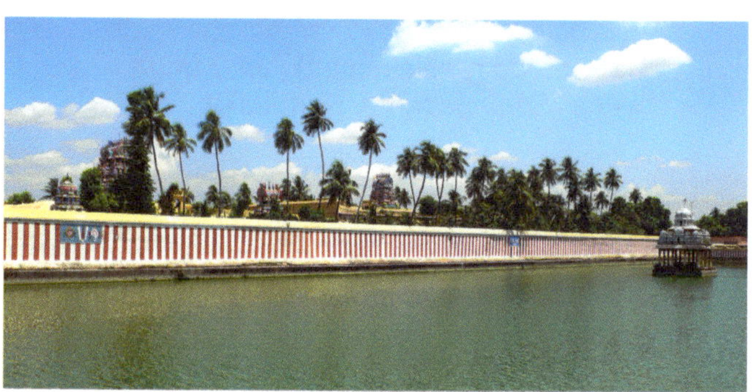

Red-white temple wall stripes – *Kumbhakonam, Tamil Nadu*

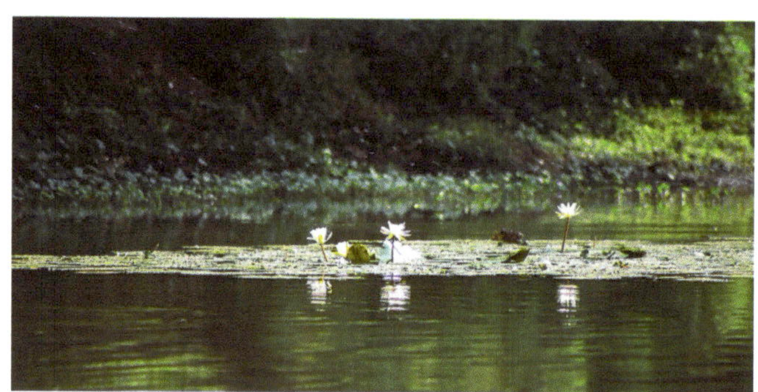

Skt. padma (lotus) – *Bhīmeśvara, Drākṣārāmam, Andhra Pradesh*

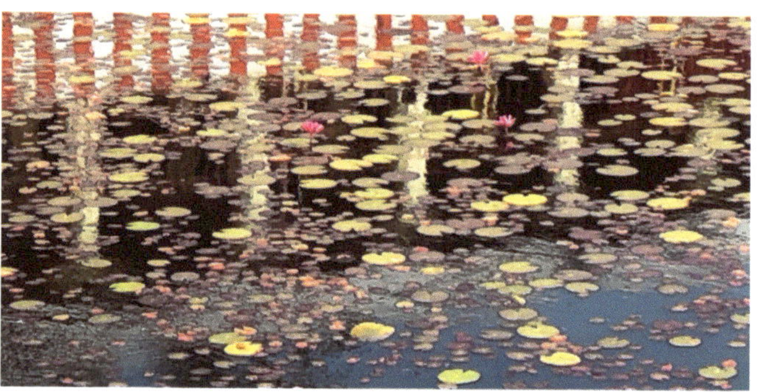

Skt. padma (lotus) – *Rāmanāthaswamy, Rāmeśvaram, Tamil Nadu*

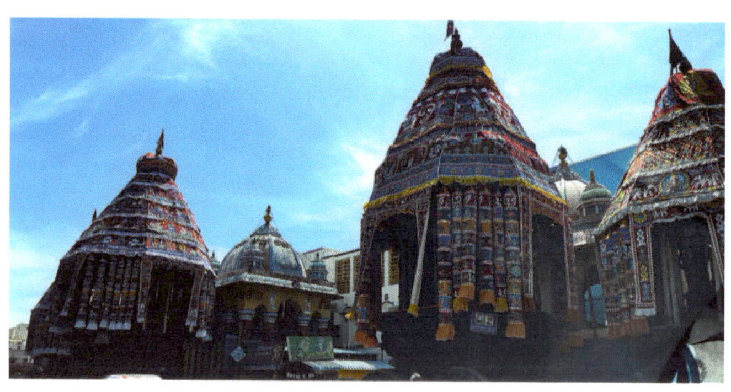

Skt. ratha / Jp. dashi – *Chidambaram, Tamil Nadu*

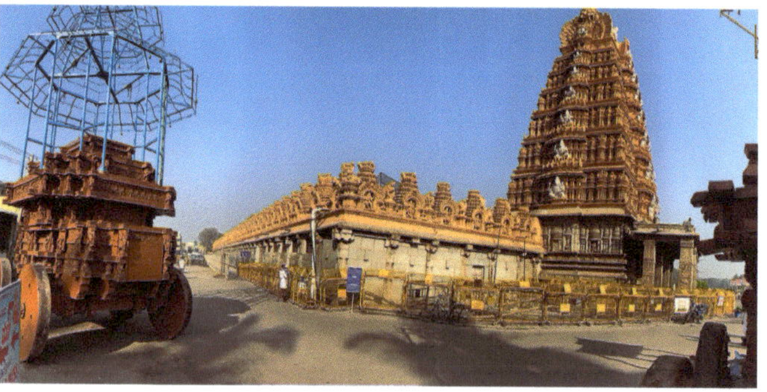

Skt. ratha (undecorated) – *Nanjundeshwara, Karnataka*

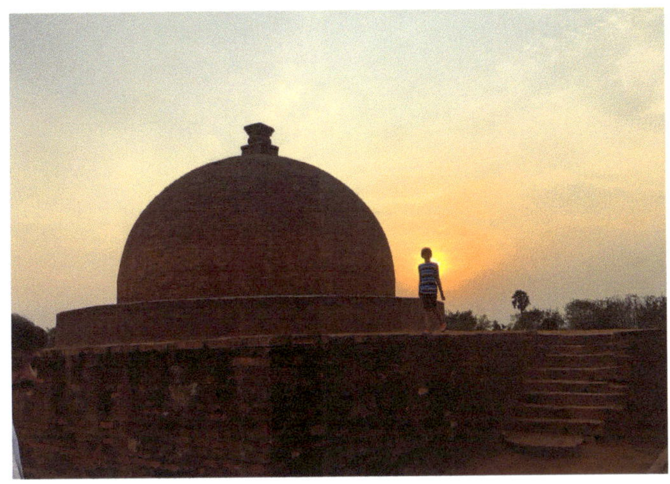

Skt. stūpa / Jp. sutūpa – *Thotlakonda, Andhra Pradesh* (3rd c. BCE; maternal uncle's hometown)

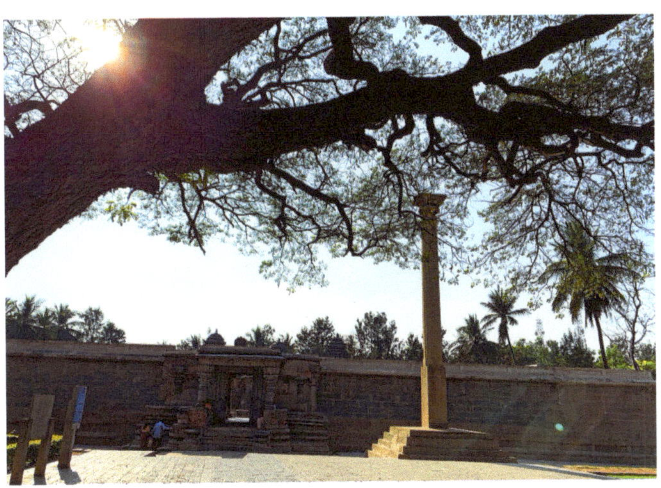

Skt. stambha (inscribed pillar) – *Keśava, Somanathapura, Karnataka*

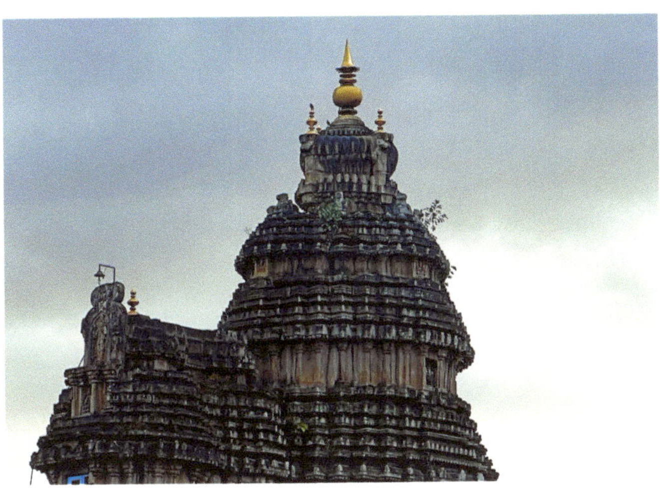

Skt. kalaśa / Jp. hōju – *Vidyāśaṅkara, Śṛṅgeri, Karnataka*

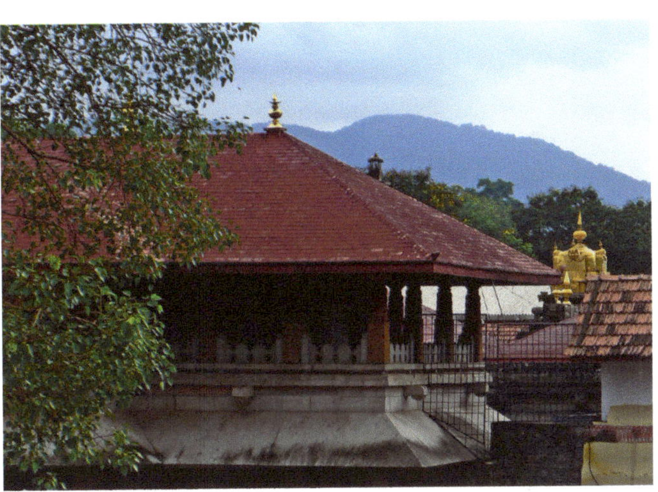

Skt. kalaśa / Jp. hōju – *Mookāmbikā, Kollur, Karnataka*

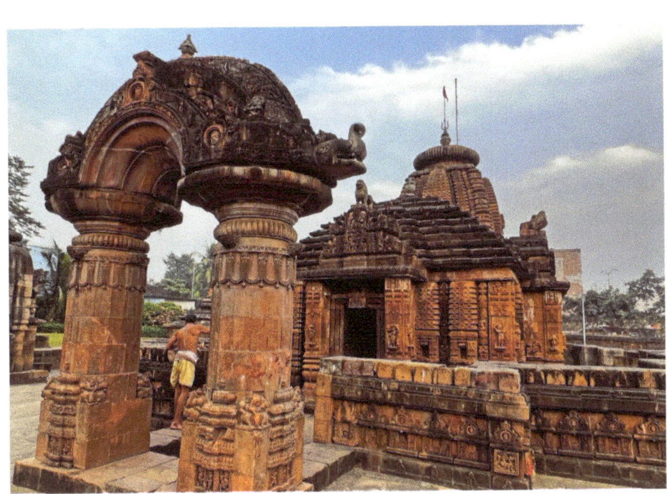

Skt. toraṇa / Jp. torii – *Mukteśvara Deula, Odisha*

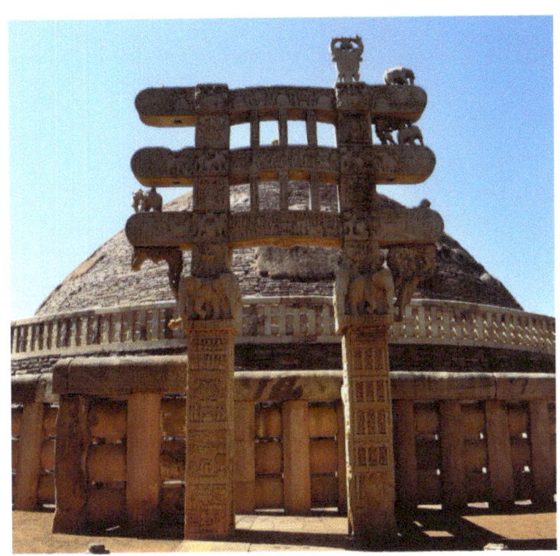

Skt. toraṇa / Jp. torii – *Sanchi Stupa, Madhya Pradesh* (3rd c. BCE)

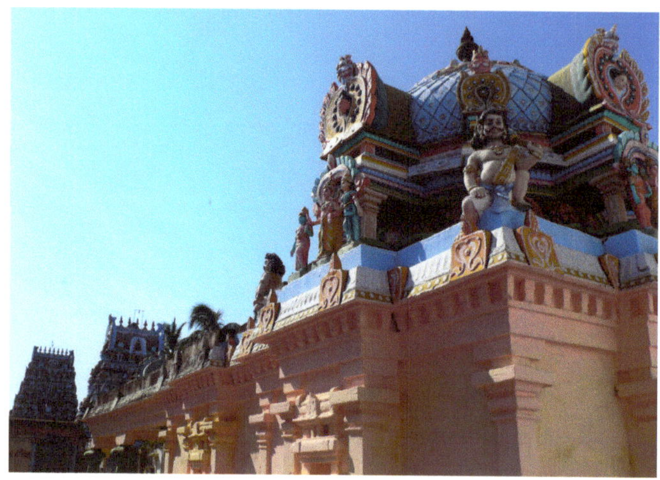

Skt. gaṇa on gopuram corner (temple imp-guardian) – *Kumbhakonam, Tamil Nadu*

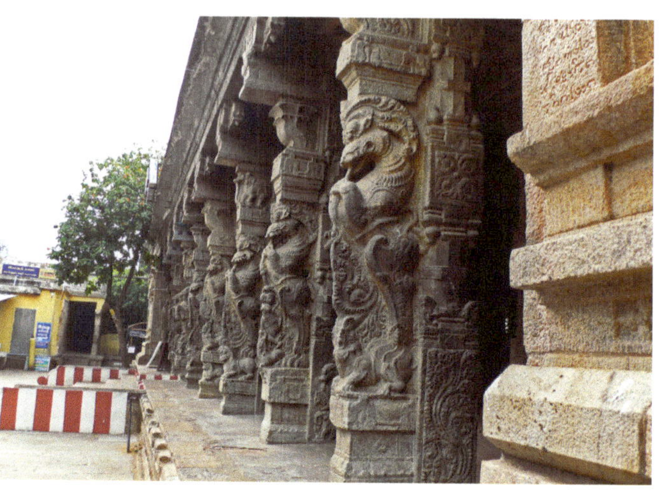

Skt. yāḷi row on pillars – *Tirunāgeśvaram, Tamil Nadu*

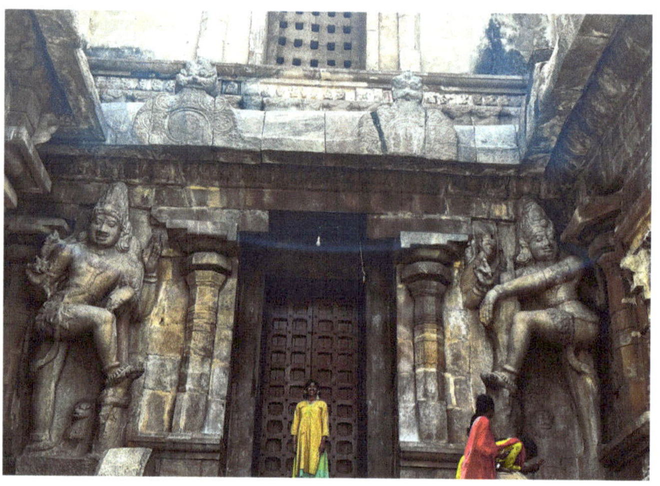

Skt. dvārapālaka / Jp. Niō – *Gangaikonda Cholapuram, Tamil Nadu*

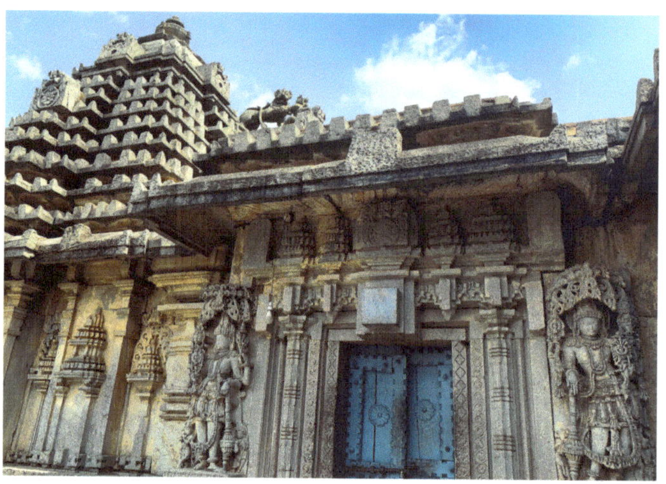

Skt. dvārapālaka – *Lakṣmī Devī, Doddagaddavalli, Karnataka*

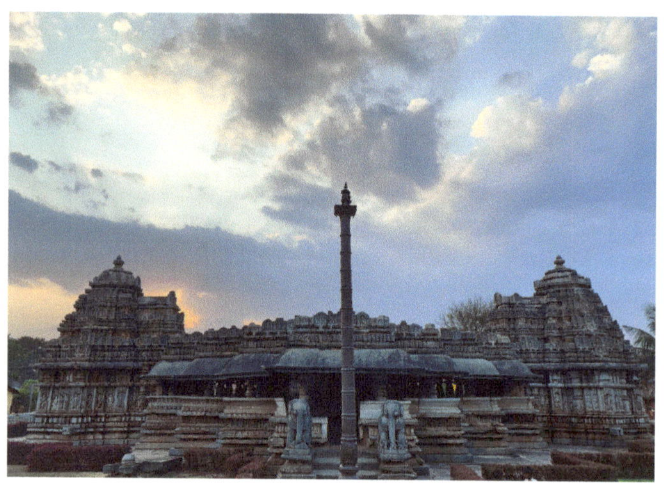

Elephant dvārapāla / Jp. komainu – *Vīra Nārāyaṇa, Belavadi, Karnataka*

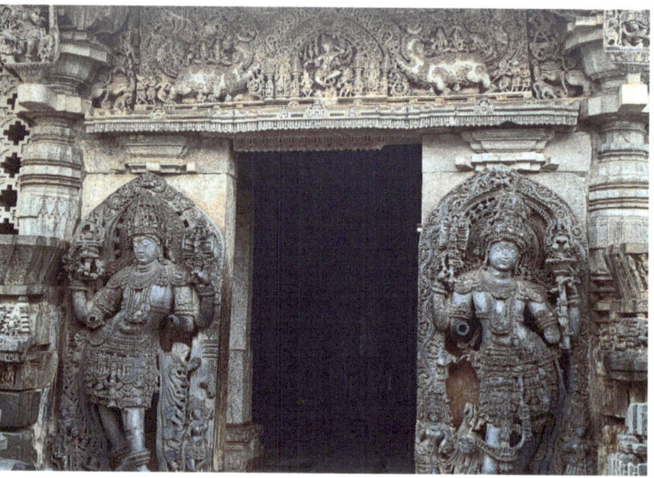

Skt. dvārapālaka – *Hoysaleśwara, Halebidu, Karnataka*

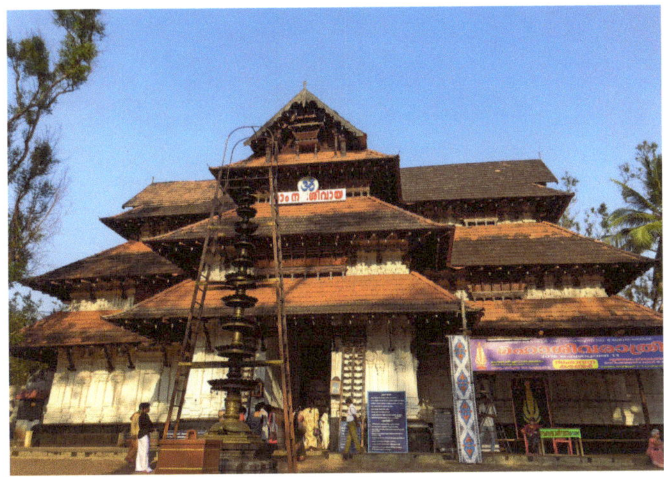

Skt. dīpa-stambha (temple lamp post) – *Vadakkunnathan, Thrissur, Kerala*

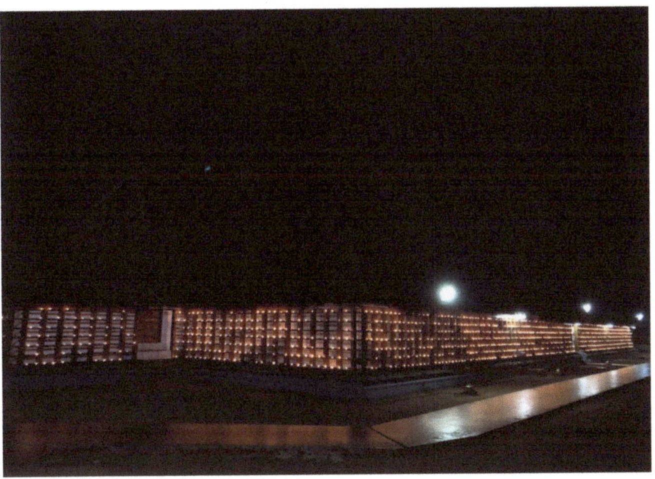

Skt. dīpa, oil lamps around temple – *Thrikkakara Vāmanamoorthy, Kerala*

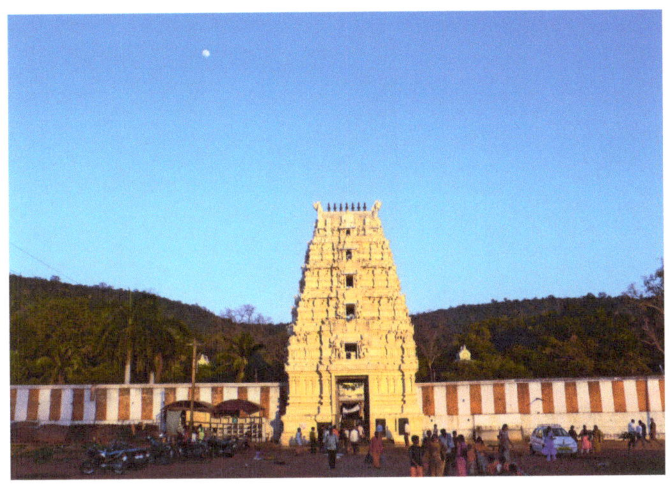

Red-white temple wall stripes – *Mahānandi, Andhra Pradesh*

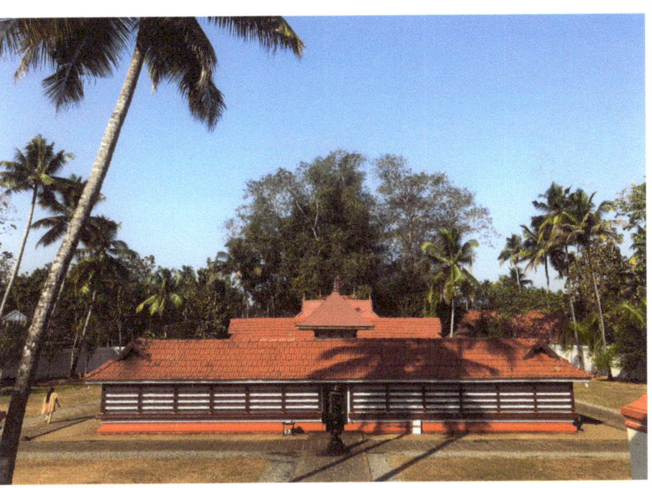

Red-white temple color scheme – *Karppillikkavu, (near Ādi Śaṅkara birthplace) Kerala*

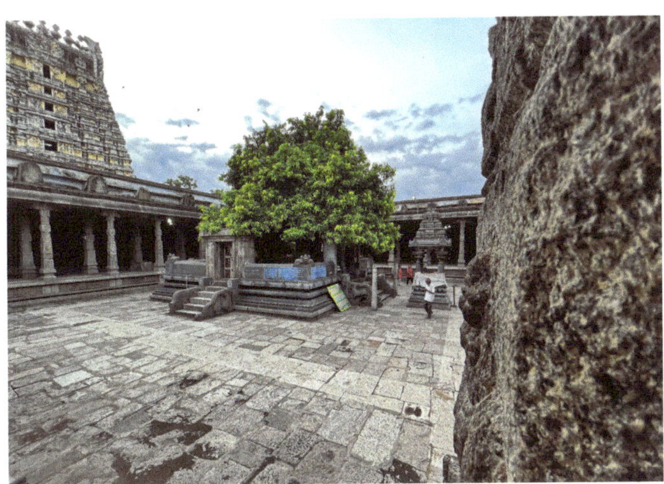

Sacred mango tree – *Kanchipuram (Bodhidharma birthplace); Jp. Daruma, Tamil Nadu*

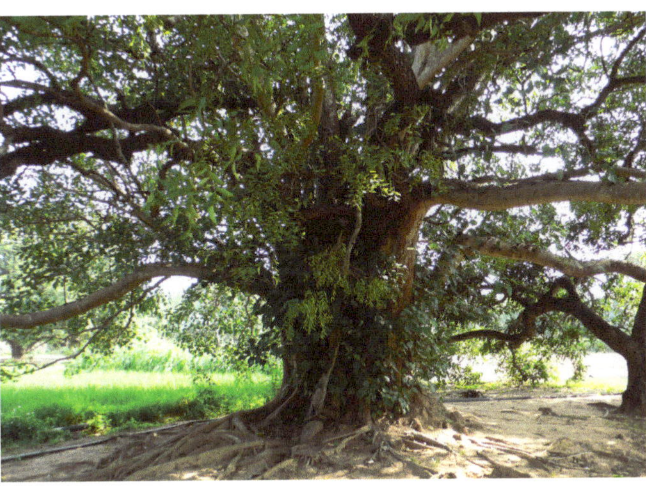

Nīm–Aśvattha (Buddha's Bodhi tree) sacred tree-pair – *Pamulavāripalem (my ancestral village), Andhra Pradesh*

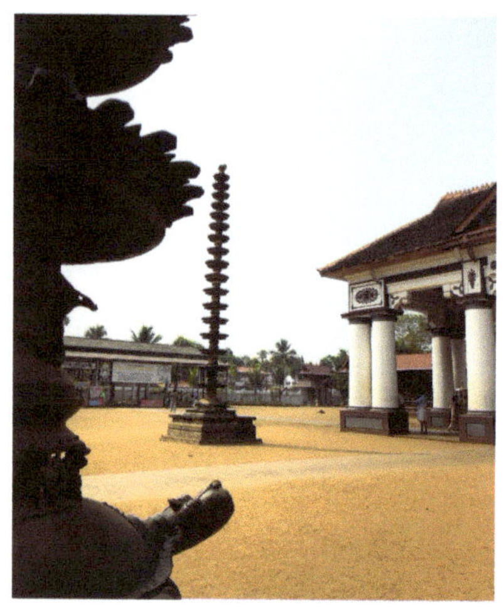

Temple lamp post – *Vaikom, Kerala*

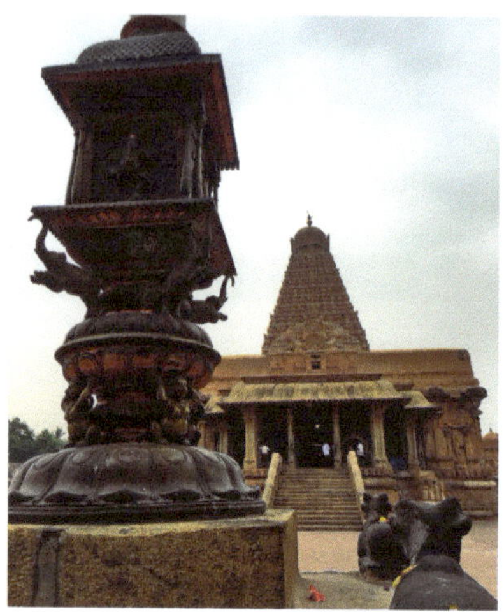

Lotus pedestal temple lamp post – *Bṛhadīśvara, Tamil Nadu*

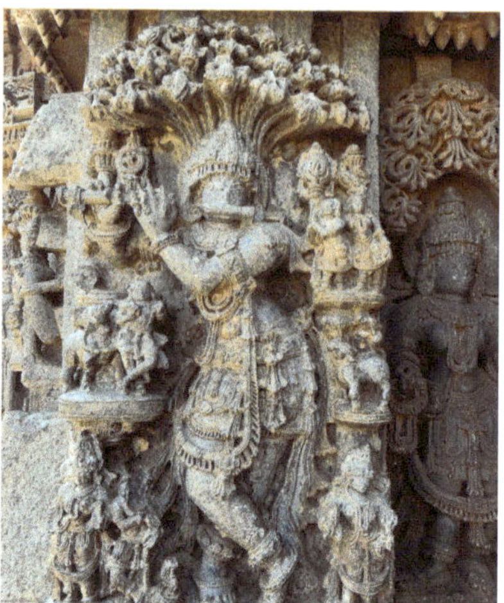

Skt. tribhaṅga, flute-playing Śrī Kṛṣṇa – *Keśava Temple, Somanathapura, Karnataka*

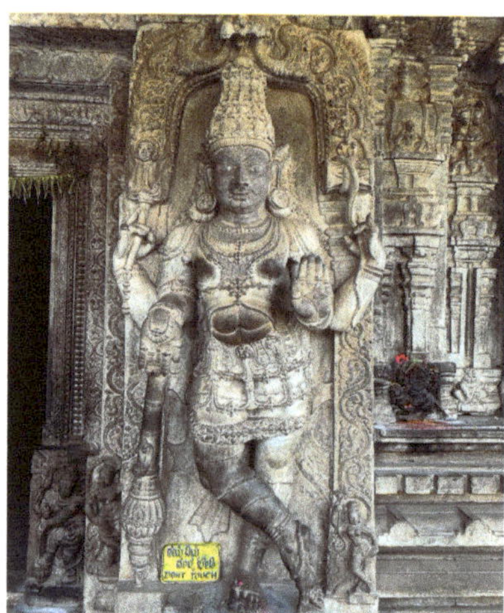

Skt. dvārapālaka with mace / Jp. Niō – *Vaidyanātheśvara, Talakad, Karnataka*

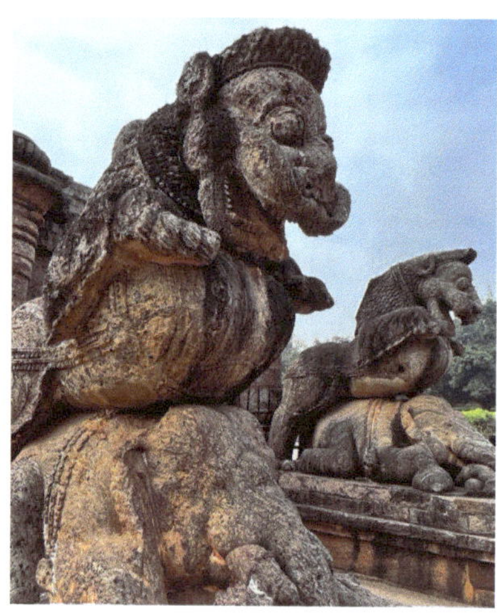

Skt. dvārapālaka threshold guardians: lion over elephant / Jp. komainu – *Konark, Odisha*

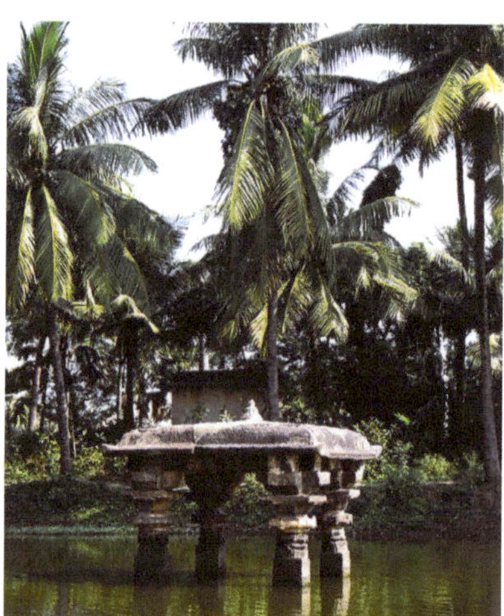

Skt. puṣkariṇī (temple pond) – *Drākṣārāmam, Andhra Pradesh*

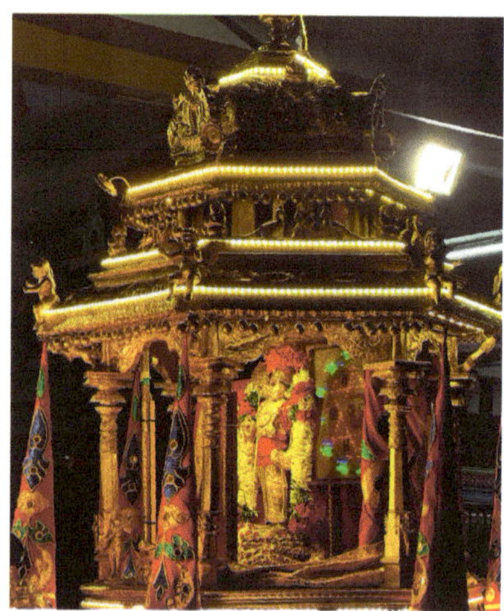

Skt. utsava procession / Jp. mikoshi – *Palani, Tamil Nadu*

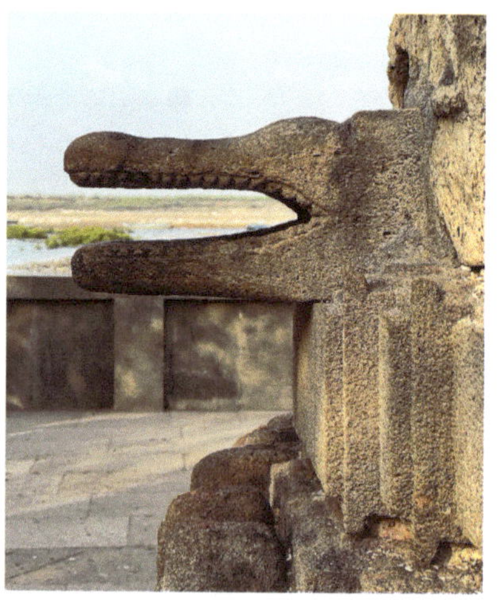

Skt. makara water-spout – *Rukmini Mandir, Dwarka, Gujarat*

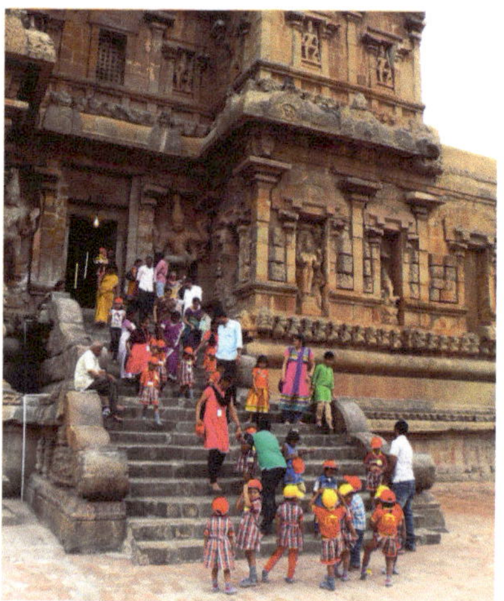

School field trip at *Bṛhadīśvara, Thanjavur, Tamil Nadu*

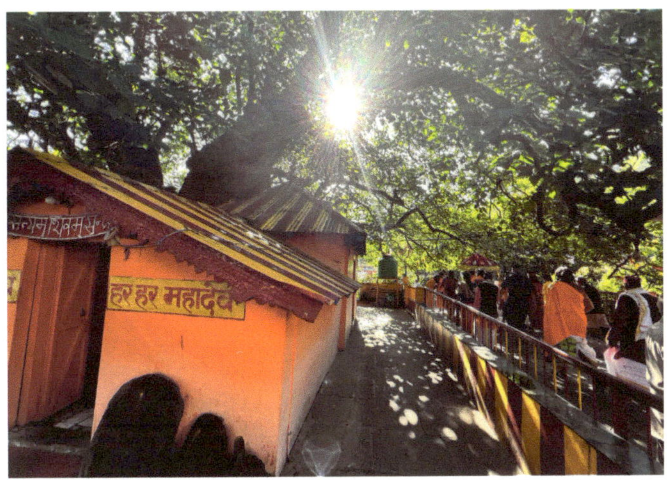

Skt. akhaṇḍa jyoti / Jp. kierazu no hi – *Jyotireśvar, Jyotirmath, Uttarakhand*

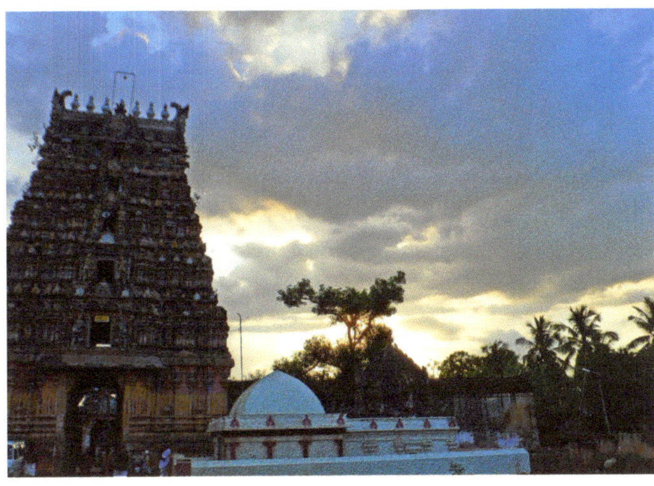

Skt. makara, kīrtimukha (face of glory) motif on rooftop / Jp. shachihoko – *Tamil Nadu*

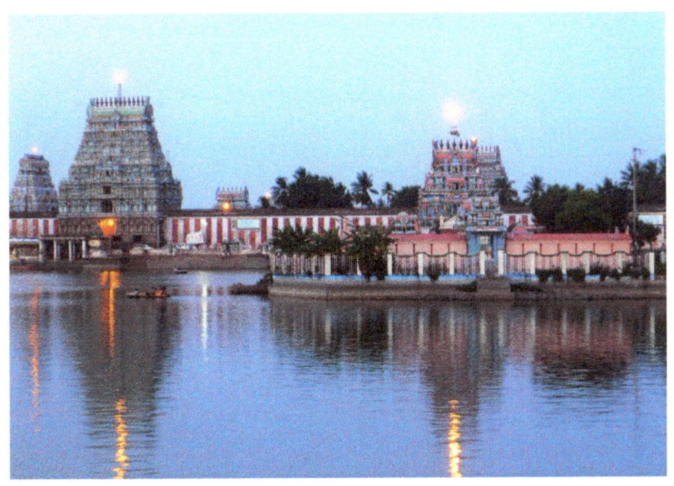

Skt. puṣkariṇī (temple tank) – *Thiruvarur, Tamil Nadu*

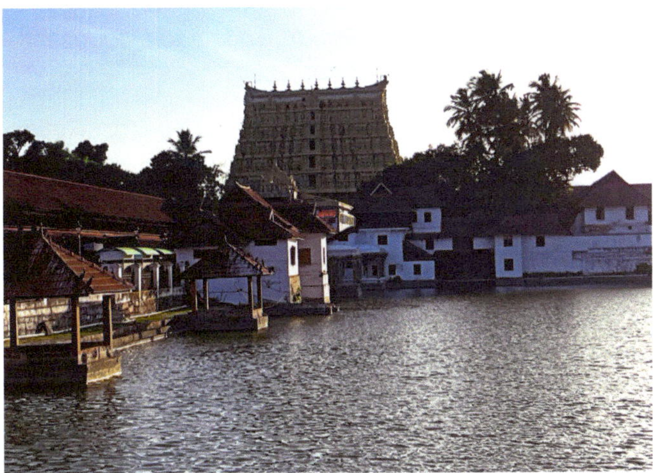

Temple tank – *Ananta Padmanābhaswamy, Thiruvananthapuram, Kerala*

References

Note on Sources: In addition to published sources, I relied on primary, on-site materials including temple and museum pamphlets, exhibit labels, and publicly posted information boards. Interpretive context was further informed by informal conversations with monks, guides, and local residents during visits. For how citations are handled in this book, see the Preface.

Behl, Benoy K. *Hindu Deities Worshipped in Japan*. The Hindu Group Publishing Private Limited, 2019.

Biswas, Sampa. *Indian Influence on the Art of Japan*. Northern Book Centre, 2010.

Chandra, Lokesh. *Cultural Interflow Between India and Japan*. Aditya Prakashan, 2014.

Chaudhuri, Saroj Kumar. *Hindu Gods and Goddesses in Japan*. Vedams eBooks (P) Ltd, 2003.

Fukahori, Yasukata. *India and Japan: Two Most Religiously Mature Nations: Forgotten History and Future Synergy Direction*. Indus Source Books, 2024.

Kaburagi, Yoshihiro. *Ancient Indian Influence on Japanese Culture: A Comparative Study of Civilizations*. Munshiram Manoharlal Publishers, 2012.

Medhasananda, Swami. *The Story of India–Japan Relationship*. Advaita Ashrama, 2021.

Mukhopadhyaya, Ranjana, and Togawa Masahiko, eds. *Buddhist Exchanges Between India and Japan: Japanese Buddhists Encountering India and Modern Buddhist Studies*. Routledge, 2025.

Nakamura, Hajime. *Japan and Indian Asia: Their Cultural Relations in the Past and Present*. K. L. Mukhopadhyay, 1961.

Nakamura, Hajime. "*Hinduism Influence on Japanese Culture.*" Reprinted by Ilankai Tamil Sangam. Accessed December 20, 2025.

Sasaki, Kosuke. *Kaikei Works Collection*. Tokyo Bijutsu, 2023.

Tō-ji Treasure Museum. *Tō-ji Temple's Heavenly Being Statues*. Tō-ji Treasure Museum, n.d.

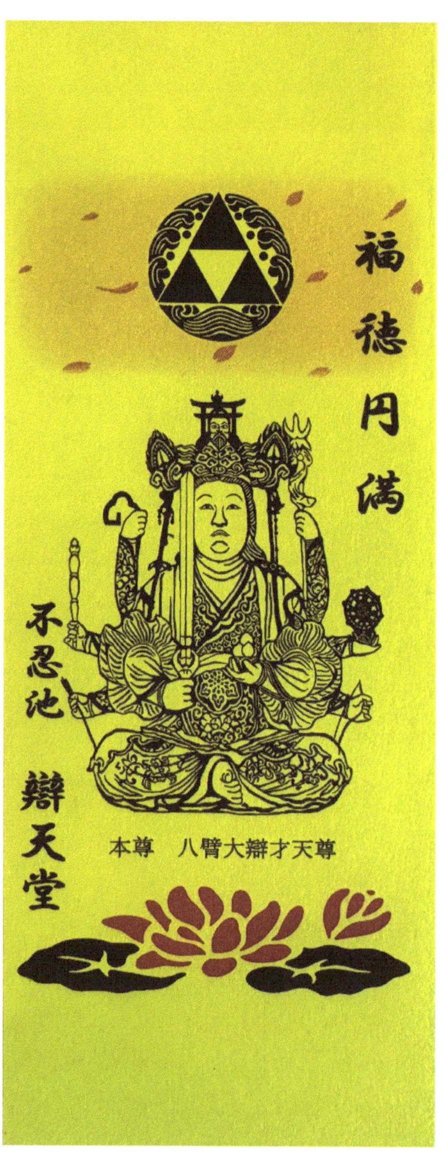

Swami Vivekananda on Japan *(1890s)*

"There, in Japan, you find a fine assimilation of knowledge, and not its indigestion, as we have here. They have taken everything from the Europeans, but they remain Japanese all the same."

"Especially to the Japanese, India is still the dreamland of everything high and good."

"I would wish that every one of our young men could visit Japan once at least in his lifetime."

"Japan to me is a dream – so beautiful that it haunts one all his life."

Instagram:
@ganapathi_108

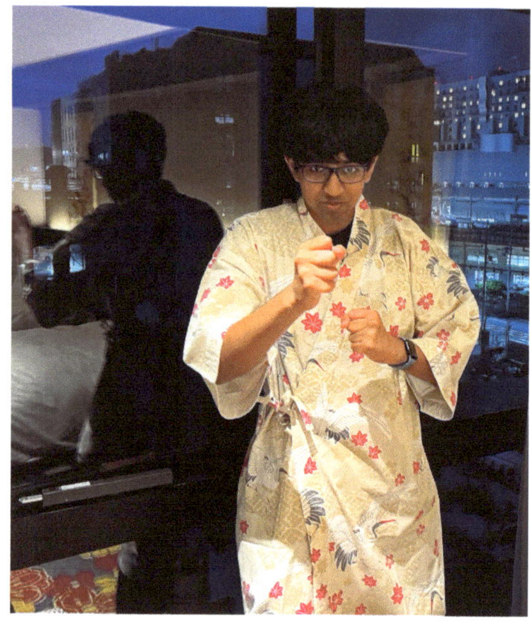

Email:
ganapathi.pamula@gmail.com

Ganapathi Pamula

The author is in 11th-grade at Durham Academy in Durham, North Carolina, USA. This book grew out of a long-standing fascination with Japan and a curiosity about the ways Indian religious, linguistic, and ritual traditions have shaped Japanese culture over time.

A Hindu American who has visited hundreds of temples across India, the author brings a lived, comparative lens to Japan's sacred spaces and the traces of Hindu culture woven through them. With a background in Sanskrit and a love of new languages, the author picked up conversational Japanese and basic reading within weeks. Traveling across Japan mainly by public transport, the author's outlook was shaped by everyday conversations in Japanese with ordinary people across Japan, and discussions with monks, priests, guides, scholars, and pilgrims, to complement academic sources.

This book blends visual storytelling with accessible scholarship because the author wanted something more engaging than an academic text, but more grounded than a photo book. This book is written for readers who want a bridge between scholarship and a photo-essay.

The author's other interests span science, technology, and storytelling. He has published two peer-reviewed research papers, holds two issued patents, and has won many innovation awards. He has also published a science fiction novel set in Japan, reflecting an ongoing interest in shaping the future with advanced technologies alongside studying the past.